NEOLIBERALISM
A Critical Reader

Edited by
Alfredo Saad-Filho and Deborah Johnston

Pluto Press
LONDON

First published 2005 by Pluto Press
345 Archway Road, London N6 5AA

www.plutobooks.com

Copyright © Alfredo Saad-Filho and Deborah Johnston 2005
The right of the individual contributors to be identified as the author of this work has been
asserted by them in accordance with the Copyright, Designs and Patents Act 1988.

British Library Cataloguing in Publication Data
A catalogue record for this book is available from the British Library

ISBN 978 0 7453 2298 8 paperback

Library of Congress Cataloging in Publication Data applied for

10 9 8 7 6 5 4 3 2 1

Designed and produced for Pluto Press by
Chase Publishing Services, Fortescue, Sidmouth, EX10 9QG, England
Typeset from disk by Newgen Imaging Systems (P) Ltd, India
Printed and bound in Great Britain by
Marston Book Services Limited, Didcot

Neoliberalism

For John Weeks

Contents

Acknowledgements

We are grateful to Elizabeth Wilson, who asked the question that inspired this book. Special thanks go to Anne Beech of Pluto Press and Costas Lapavitsas for all their support and encouragement in this project.

Introduction[1]

Alfredo Saad-Filho and Deborah Johnston

We live in the age of neoliberalism. It strongly influences the lives of billions of people in every continent in such diverse areas as economics, politics, international relations, ideology, culture and so on. In less than one generation, neoliberalism has become so widespread and influential, and so deeply intermingled with critically important aspects of life, that it can be difficult to assess its nature and historical importance. Yet such an assessment is essential for both intellectual and political reasons.

This reader includes 30 chapters critically reviewing neoliberalism from widely different angles and outlining a research agenda for concerned activists, students and social scientists. These essays are divided into three groups, including theoretical, applied and historical chapters. The essays included in this reader share several important features. First, they examine the origins, nature and implications of neoliberalism from the perspective of radical political economy. Second, although they come from distinct traditions, including the Marxian, post-Keynesian and Kaleckian schools of thought, the essays are closely related to one another both in content and approach. These commonalities illustrate the vitality of contemporary political economy, the extent and depth of the dialogue taking place between its schools of thought, and the potential for cross-fertilisation between them. Third, these essays offer a radical critique of neoliberalism, that is, a critique going to the root of the matter. They show that neoliberalism is part of a hegemonic project concentrating power and wealth in elite groups around the world, benefiting especially the financial interests within each country, and US capital internationally. Therefore, globalisation and imperialism cannot be analysed separately from neoliberalism. These claims are explained briefly below.

APPROACHES TO NEOLIBERALISM

It is impossible to define neoliberalism purely theoretically, for several reasons. First, methodologically, although neoliberal experiences share important commonalities (explained in what follows), neoliberalism is not a mode of production. Consequently, these experiences do not necessarily include a clearly defined set of invariant features, as may be expected in studies of 'feudalism' or 'capitalism', for example. Neoliberalism straddles a wide range of social, political and economic phenomena at different levels of complexity. Some of these are highly abstract, for example the growing power of finance or the debasement of democracy, while

1

others are relatively concrete, such as privatisation or the relationship between foreign states and local non-governmental organisations (NGOs). Nevertheless, it is not difficult to recognise the beast when it trespasses into new territories, tramples upon the poor, undermines rights and entitlements, and defeats resistance, through a combination of domestic political, economic, legal, ideological and media pressures, backed up by international blackmail and military force if necessary.

Second, as is argued in Chapters 7 and 9, neoliberalism is inseparable from imperialism and globalisation. In the conventional (or mainstream) discourse, imperialism is either absent or, more recently, proudly presented as the 'American Burden': to civilise the world and bring to all the benediction of the Holy Trinity, the green-faced Lord Dollar and its deputies and occasional rivals, Holy Euro and Saint Yen. New converts win a refurbished international airport, one brand-new branch of McDonald's, two luxury hotels, 3,000 NGOs and one US military base. This offer cannot be refused – or else.[2] In turn, globalisation is generally presented as an inescapable, inexorable and benevolent process leading to greater competition, welfare improvements and the spread of democracy around the world. In reality, however, the so-called process of globalisation – to the extent that it actually exists (see Saad-Filho 2003) – is merely the international face of neoliberalism: a worldwide strategy of accumulation and social discipline that doubles up as an imperialist project, spearheaded by the alliance between the US ruling class and locally dominant capitalist coalitions. This ambitious power project centred on neoliberalism at home and imperial globalism abroad is implemented by diverse social and economic political alliances in each country, but the interests of local finance and the US ruling class, itself dominated by finance, are normally hegemonic.

Third, historical analysis of neoliberalism requires a multi-level approach. The roots of neoliberalism are long and varied, and its emergence cannot be dated precisely. As Chapters 3 to 6 show, neoliberalism amalgamates insights from a range of sources, including Adam Smith, neoclassical economics, the Austrian critique of Keynesianism and Soviet-style socialism, monetarism and its new classical and 'supply-side' offspring. Their influence increased by leaps and bounds with the breakdown of the postwar order: the end of the 'golden age' of rapid worldwide growth in the late 1960s, the collapse of the Bretton Woods system in the early 1970s, the erosion of the so-called 'Keynesian compromise' in the rich countries in the mid 1970s, the meltdown of the Soviet bloc in the 1980s and the implosion of developmental alternatives in the poor countries, especially after balance of payments crises in the 1980s and 1990s. Chapters 1 and 2 show that the collapse of the alternatives provided space for the synthesis between conservative views and the interests of the US elite and their minions. The cauldron was provided by the aggressive populist conservatism of Ronald Reagan and Margaret Thatcher, and the broth was tendered by finance – that had become hegemonic worldwide after the 'coup' led by the chairman of the US Federal Reserve System, Paul Volcker, in 1979.[3] By persuasion and by force, neoliberalism spread everywhere.

It is, however, important to avoid excessively linear accounts of the rise of neoliberalism. For example, in the United Kingdom, key elements of Thatcher's monetarist economic platform had been imposed by the previous Labour government; she only expanded them and gave them a compelling rationale. There was also an irresolvable tension between the puritanical *claims* made by milk-snatching Thatcher, Reagan's ventriloquists, and the intellectual harlots peddling their wares around the US Imperial Court, and the political *practice* of these neoliberal administrations. For example, Reagan's 'voodoo economics' (in the words of his deputy, George Bush *père*) would have been unacceptable to the guardians of the scriptures. History shows that it is easier to impose pristine economic and political models in the dominions, because at home the strength of conflicting interests and the messy realities of limited power do not allow history to start anew on demand. This is best illustrated in Chapter 14's discussion of the asymmetric application of agrarian liberalism. It is relatively easy to parachute well-paid advisers into distant and unimportant countries, where Lord Dollar can easily bend the natives' will. This purifying ritual will make them almost civilised. However, should the ignorant masses and their brutal leaders reject dollar diplomacy and be reluctant to play by the (new) rules, weapons of mass destruction are available and they can be deployed increasingly effectively from great distances.

Although every country is different, and historical analysis can reveal remarkably rich details, the overall picture is clear. The most basic feature of neoliberalism is the systematic use of state power to impose (financial) market imperatives, in a domestic process that is replicated internationally by 'globalisation'. As Chapters 22, 23 and 30 argue in the cases of the United States, the United Kingdom and east and south-east Asia respectively, neoliberalism is a particular organisation of capitalism, which has evolved to protect capital(ism) and to reduce the power of labour. This is achieved by means of social, economic and political transformations imposed by internal forces as well as external pressure. The internal forces include the coalition between financial interests, leading industrialists, traders and exporters, media barons, big landowners, local political chieftains, the top echelons of the civil service and the military, and their intellectual and political proxies. These groups are closely connected with 'global' ideologies emanating from the centre, and they tend to adapt swiftly to the demands beamed from the metropolis. Their efforts have led to a significant worldwide shift in power relations away from the majority. Corporate power has increased, while finance has acquired unrivalled influence, and the political spectrum has shifted towards the right. Left parties and mass organisations have imploded, while trade unions have been muzzled or disabled by unemployment. Forms of external pressure have included the diffusion of Western culture and ideology, foreign support for state and civil society institutions peddling neoliberal values, the shameless use of foreign aid, debt relief and balance of payments support to promote the neoliberal programme, and diplomatic pressure, political unrest and military intervention when necessary. For example, Chapter 24 shows how the ruling economic and political forces in the European Union have instrumentalised the process of integration to ensure the hegemony of neoliberalism. This account is complemented by Chapter 25's analysis of the segmentation of Eastern Europe into countries that are being drawn into a Western European-style neoliberalism and others that are following Russia's business oligarchy model. In sum, neoliberalism is everywhere both the *outcome* and the *arena* of social conflicts. It sets the political and economic agenda, limits the possible outcomes, biases expectations, and imposes urgent tasks on those challenging its assumptions, methods and consequences.

In the meantime, neoliberal theory has not remained static. In order to deal with the most powerful criticisms levelled against neoliberalism, that it has increased poverty and social dislocation around the world, neoliberal theory has attempted to present the ogre in a more favourable light. In spite of the substantial resources invested in this ideologically inspired make-over, these amendments have remained unconvincing, not least because the heart of the neoliberal project has remained unchanged. This is discussed in Chapter 15 for poverty and distribution, while Chapter 21 unpicks the agenda of the 'Third Way', viewed by many as 'neoliberalism with a human face'.

A MULTI-PRONGED POWER PROJECT

Neoliberalism offered a finance-friendly solution to the problems of capital accumulation at the end of a relatively long cycle of prosperity. Chapters 1, 22 and 30 show that neoliberalism imposed discipline upon a restless working class through contractionary fiscal and monetary policies and wide-ranging initiatives to curtail social rights, under the guise of anti-inflation and productivity-enhancing measures. Neoliberalism also rationalised the transfer of state capacity to allocate resources inter-temporally (the balance between investment and consumption) and inter-sectorally (the distribution of investment, employment and output) towards an increasingly internationally integrated (and US-led) financial sector. In doing so, neoliberalism facilitated a gigantic transfer of resources to the local rich and the United States, as is shown by Chapters 11 and 15.

Neoliberal globalism is not at all a model of 'economic deregulation', and it does not promote 'private initiative' in general. Under the ideological veil of non-intervention, neoliberalism involves extensive and invasive interventions in every area of social life. It imposes a specific form of social and economic regulation based on the prominence of finance, international elite integration, subordination of the poor in every country and universal compliance with US interests. Finally, neoliberalism does not foster rapid accumulation. Although it enhances the power and the living standards of the global elite and its appendages, it is destructive for the vast majority. Domestically, the expansion of 'market relations' tramples upon rights of access to food, water, education, work, land, housing, medical care, transportation and public amenities as well as on gender relations, as is shown by Chapters 16 to 18. Laws are changed to discipline the majority, restrict their rights of association and make it difficult to protest against the consequences of neoliberalism and to develop alternatives. The police, the courts and the armed forces are available to quash protests in the 'new democracies' such as Bolivia, Ecuador, Nigeria, South Africa, South Korea and Zambia, as well as in 'old democracies' such as France, India, Italy, Sweden, the United Kingdom and the United States. Chapter 20 shows that democracy is everywhere limited by the rights of global capital to seize the land and exploit its people, while Chapter 8 reviews the systematic seizure of assets which has gone hand in hand with neoliberalism in many countries. Finally, an increasing share of global profits is being pumped into the rich countries, especially the United States. These transfers increase the pressure on the periphery, where rates of exploitation must increase sharply in order to support extraordinary levels of elite consumption domestically as well as in the United States. In other words, neoliberalism is a hegemonic system of enhanced exploitation of the majority. Chapter 12 shows that the neoliberal promise of rising living standards for poor countries has not been fulfilled, and Chapter 13 discusses the manner in which foreign aid has served this process of exploitation. These and other chapters in this volume argue that neoliberalism prevents the implementation of those very policies that would most likely contribute to economic growth and poverty reduction: as Chapter 28 argues for South Asia, neoliberalism has fatally narrowed the policy discourse.

This exploitative agenda is primarily but not exclusively the outcome of a shift in the power relations within (and between) countries. It is also the outcome of technological changes, especially cheaper international transportation, communications and computing power, the internet, the emergence of 'flexible' production, greater international integration between production chains and in the financial markets, and so on. These material changes responded to existing social changes at least as much as they induced them.

TRANSCENDING NEOLIBERALISM

In spite of its power, the transformations that it has wrought on the world economy, and the achievement of ever rising living standards for the minority, neoliberalism does not offer an efficient platform for capital accumulation. Under neoliberalism, economic growth rates have declined, unemployment and underemployment have become widespread, inequalities within and between countries have become sharper, the living and working conditions of the majority have deteriorated almost everywhere, and the periphery has suffered greatly from economic instability. In other words, neoliberalism is a global system of minority power, plunder of nations and despoilment of the environment. This system breeds economic, political and social changes, creating the material basis for its own perpetuation and crushing the resistances against its reproduction. Chapters 26 to 30 discuss the continuing crisis in Latin America, sub-Saharan Africa, South Asia, Japan and East and South-East Asia. They argue that neoliberal policies have enhanced instability everywhere, while Chapter 10 shows that the theoretical and empirical evidence cannot support neoliberalism's central hypothesis that trade openness is good for growth.

However, neoliberalism also destroys its own conditions of existence. Its persistent failure to deliver sustained economic growth and rising living standards exhausts the tolerance of the majority and lays bare the web of spin in which neoliberalism clouds the debate and legitimates its destructive outcomes. The endless mantra of 'reforms' which systematically fail to deliver their promised 'efficiency gains' delegitimises the neoliberal states, their discourse and their mouthpieces. The explosion of consumer credit that has supported the improvement of living standards in the centre, given the growing fiscal constrains upon the state, limits the scope for interest-rate manipulation – the most important neoliberal economic policy tool. Most importantly, popular movements have emerged and successfully challenged the neoliberal hegemony. Whatever their limitations, as Chapter 19 argues, the recent social explosions in Argentina, Bolivia, Ecuador, as well as more limited social movements elsewhere, show that neoliberalism is not invulnerable. This book details and substantiates these claims, and points toward an agenda of reflection, critique and struggle.

NOTES

1. We are grateful to Daniel Ayliffe, Francesca Campagnoli, Ana Maria Miranda, Walter Schmidt and Maria Laura Tinelli for their efficient research assistance.
2. For an outstanding review of different aspects of contemporary imperialism, see Panitch and Leys (2004).
3. M.J. Horgan, vice-president of Citibank, claimed that 'the world had changed' since the Fed's policy shift, while the future chairman of the US Federal Reserve System, Alan Greenspan, remarked that Volcker's policy shift was 'the most important monetary policy change since World War II' (*Business Week* 5 November 1979, p. 91 and 22 October 1979, p. 67).

REFERENCES

Panitch, L. and Leys, C. (eds) (2004) *The New Imperial Challenge: Socialist Register 2004*. London: Merlin.
Saad-Filho, A. (2003) 'Introduction', in *Anti-Capitalism: A Marxist Introduction*. London: Pluto Press.

Part I
Theoretical Perspectives

1

The Neoliberal (Counter-)Revolution

Gérard Duménil and Dominique Lévy

There is a dramatic contrast between the last 20 years of the twentieth century and the previous decades since the Second World War. It is common to describe the last 20 years of capitalism as 'neoliberalism'. Indeed, during the transition between the 1970s and 1980s, the functioning of capitalism was deeply transformed, both within countries of the centre and in the periphery. The earlier capitalist configuration is often referred to as the 'Keynesian compromise'. Without simplifying too much, those years could be characterised, in the centre countries – the United States (and Canada), Europe and Japan – by large growth rates, sustained technological change, an increase in purchasing power and the development of a welfare system (concerning, in particular, health and retirement) and low unemployment rates. The situation deteriorated during the 1970s, as the world economy, in the wake of the decline of the profit rate, entered a 'structural crisis'. Its main aspects were diminished growth rates, a wave of unemployment and cumulative inflation. This is when the new social order, neoliberalism, emerged, first within the countries of the centre – beginning with the United Kingdom and the United States – and then gradually exported to the periphery (see Chapters 2, 22 and 23).

We explore below the nature of neoliberalism and its balance sheet after nearly a quarter of a century. Neoliberalism is often described as the ideology of the market and private interests as opposed to state intervention. Although it is true that neoliberalism conveys an ideology and a propaganda of its own, it is fundamentally a *new social order* in which the power and income of the upper fractions of the ruling classes – the wealthiest persons – was re-established in the wake of a setback. We denote as 'finance' this upper capitalist class and the financial institutions through which its power is enforced. Although the conditions which accounted for the structural crisis were gradually superseded, most of the world economy remained plagued by slow growth and unemployment, and inequality increased tremendously. This was the cost of a successful restoration of the income and wealth of the wealthiest.[1]

A NEW SOCIAL ORDER

The misery of the contemporary world is too easily attributed to globalisation. One must be very careful in this respect. It is true that the two categories of phenomena, globalisation and neoliberalism, are related; but they refer to two distinct sets of mechanisms.

Globalisation, or the internationalisation of the world economy, is an old process, one that Marx identified in the middle of the nineteenth century, in the *Communist Manifesto*, as an inner tendency of capitalism (the establishment of a world market). The growth of international trade, the flows of capitals, and the global (at the scale of the entire globe) economy are, in no way, neoliberal innovations (see Chapter 7). The contemporary stage can, however, be characterised by growing foreign exchange transactions, the international mobility of capital, the expansion of transnational corporations, and the new role of international financial institutions such as the International Monetary Fund (IMF) and the World Bank. Though the dominance of the United States is not new, neoliberalism contributed to the US hegemony within the group of other imperialist countries, in a unipolar world after the fall of the Soviet Union.

The internationalisation of capitalism has always been marked by exploitation and direct violence. This is central to imperialism (see Chapters 8 and 9). It has been at the origin of numerous wars, and destroyed lives and cultures. It drove a fraction of humanity into slavery, and generated the most extreme forms of misery throughout the planet. The world of the Keynesian compromise coexisted with colonialism and the Vietnam war. Indeed, the call for a new internationalism (the 'other possible world' of the anti-globalisation movement) does not express a nostalgia for the past.

In contrast, neoliberalism refers to new rules of functioning of capitalism, which affect the centre, the periphery, and the relationship between the two. Its main characteristics include: a new discipline of labour and management to the benefit of lenders and shareholders; the diminished intervention of the state concerning development and welfare; the dramatic growth of financial institutions; the implementation of new relationships between the financial and non-financial sectors, to the benefit of the former; a new legal stand in favour of mergers and acquisitions; the strengthening of central banks and the targeting of their activity toward price stability, and the new determination to drain the resources of the periphery toward the centre. Moreover, new aspects of globalisation emerged with neoliberalism, for example the unsustainable weight of the debt of the periphery and the devastations caused by the free international mobility of capitals. The major feature of the contemporary phase of neoliberalism is, however, its gradual extension to the rest of the planet, that is *its own* globalisation.

THE RISE OF NEOLIBERALISM: CAPITAL RESURGENCE

As is always the case when dealing with events of this nature, it is difficult to identify precisely the first emergence of neoliberalism. The same will be true of its demise or supersession. A whole set of transformations had already taken place during the 1970s, in particular internationally. 'Monetarism' expressed the new theoretical and policy trends. But the emblematic year is certainly 1979, when the Federal Reserve decided to suddenly increase interest rates. This is what we call the *1979 coup*.

The 1970s stand out as a transition decade. In the late 1960s, the first lasting deficits in the balance of trade since the Second World War appeared in the United States. This was obviously related to the ongoing catching-up by European countries and Japan. Surpluses of dollars were accumulating in the rest of the world and, thus, the threat of conversion into gold was increasing. The dollar had to be devalued with respect to gold and other major currencies. The United States put an end to the convertibility of the dollar in 1971, introducing floating exchange rates.

In spite of the diminished comparative power of the United States in this context, the floating of currencies represented a new tool in the hands of the United States, a first component of what became, in the subsequent years, the neoliberal framework. New components were rapidly added, such as the liberalisation of capital flows, which the United States established in 1974 after the limitations of the 1960s. The United Kingdom joined the movement in 1979, and was followed by other European countries. The dynamics of neoliberalism were under way, while Keynesian policies were already under criticism.[2]

In the last years of his mandate, Jimmy Carter attempted to stimulate the US economy, calling in vain for international co-operation; in particular, Germany showed a growing concern with inflation and the remodelling of the international monetary system (the rising role conferred to the mark). The decision to curb inflation led to the nomination of Paul Volcker to the head of the Federal Reserve, and the ensuing surge in interest rates, up to real (corrected for inflation) rates of 6 to 8 per cent. Besides inflation, a rising wave of unemployment, in Europe and in the United States, created the conditions for a new discipline of labour, imposed by Reagan and Thatcher.

It is probably difficult to find a data series that informs more about the roots of neoliberalism than the data shown in Figure 1.1. The variable is the share of the

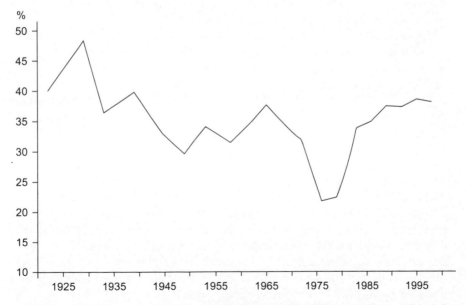

Figure 1.1 Share of total wealth held by the wealthiest 1 per cent of US households (wealth includes housing, securities and cash, and durable consumption goods).

Source: Wolff (1996)

total wealth of households in the United States, held by the richest 1 per cent. As can be seen, this 1 per cent used to hold approximately 35 per cent of total wealth prior to the 1970s. This percentage then fell to slightly more than 20 per cent in the 1970s, before rising again during the following decade (see also Piketty and Saez 2003).

Both the causes and consequences of this movement must be addressed. The profitability of capital plunged during the 1960s and 1970s; corporations distributed dividends sparingly, and real interest rates were low, or even negative, during the 1970s. The stock market (also corrected for inflation) had collapsed during the mid 1970s, and was stagnating. It is easy to understand that, under such conditions, the income and wealth of the ruling classes was strongly affected. Seen from this angle, this could be read as a dramatic decline in inequality. Neoliberalism can be interpreted as an attempt by the wealthiest fraction of the population to stem this comparative decline.

The structural crisis of the 1970s was also a period of alleged or real decline in the domination of the United States (in the wake of the defeat in Vietnam). Japan and Germany were seen as rising stars. The risk of the assertion of a global order, organised around three centres (the triad of the United States, Europe, and Japan), was growing. This threat played a significant role in the convergence in the United States among various business and financial interests that strongly influence political parties and elections in that country (Ferguson 1995). This risk stimulated the populist component in the campaigning for the presidential election, in which national pride was invoked. Such circumstances were crucial to the election of Reagan in 1979, at the very moment finance was instigating Volcker's action. (For finance, the rise of interest rates had three advantages: fighting inflation, raising the income and wealth of creditors,[3] and using the growing indebtedness of the state as an argument to launch an attack against the welfare state.)

These events cannot be assessed independently of the failure of Keynesian policies to stimulate the economy. Keynesianism could not solve the structural crisis of the 1970s. But the neoliberal offensive against alternative models in which state intervention was strong, as in Europe and Japan and many countries of the periphery, was already under way. European 'socialism' rapidly conformed to the rules of neoliberalism; these included the framework of international capital mobility and the accompanying macro-policies; the privatisation of public firms and the diminished involvement in the provision of public services; and the favourable attitude towards mergers and acquisitions. However, in Europe, popular resistance conserved much of the framework of social protection. Thus emerged a hybrid social configuration, that of 'social neoliberalism' (see Chapters 16, 24, 25 and 29).

Although neoliberalism defines a specific power configuration, it does not preclude the continuation of long-term trends in the transformation of capitalism. The dramatic rise of financial institutions and the parallel centralisation of capital since the late nineteenth century has reached new heights since the 1980s. These financial activities and the corresponding power are concentrated within gigantic financial holdings (for example, Citigroup comprises more than 3,000 corporations located in many countries, and its total assets amounted to 400 billion dollars in 2000). They combine the traditional banking and insurance activities with new functions, for example asset management, at an unprecedented scale. In the

United States, securities are gathered within a whole range of institutions, such as mutual and pension funds. All traditional 'capitalist' tasks are delegated to large staffs of managerial and clerical personnel. In all fields, financial or non-financial, a revolution of management is under way.

Concerning macro-policies, it is important to stress that, during the 1980s, finance did not oppose the strength of the central banks but, instead, took control of them. Monetary policy became a crucial instrument in the hands of finance, for enforcing policies favourable to its own interests. The Keynesian objective of full employment was replaced by the preservation of the income and wealth of the owners of capital, by the strict control of the general level of prices. A whole set of rules and policies is required to this end, within advanced capitalist economies. Therefore the institutions of Keynesianism were not at issue, but their objectives.

COSTS AND BENEFITS

Neoliberalism was beneficial to a few and detrimental to many. This property reveals its class foundations. This section describes some of the main features of this contrasted balance sheet, moving from the United States to Europe, to Japan and gradually toward the periphery.

WHOSE BENEFIT, WHOSE COST? A CLASS ANALYSIS

The rise of interest rates in 1979 was breathtaking and put an end to the inflationary wave. In spite of the gradual decline of nominal interest rates, high real interest rates were maintained throughout the 1980s and 1990s. This can be seen in Figure 1.2, which shows long-term interest rates in the United States and in France. Obviously, such high rates are favourable to creditors, whether individual or institutional. Moreover, high rates of dividends were also paid to shareholders. In the 1960s, the share of profits (after paying taxes and interest) distributed as dividends was approximately 30 per cent. This gradually rose to nearly 100 per cent by the end of the twentieth century. Stock-market indexes followed up, reaching their maximum in 2000.

Simultaneously, one fraction of households increased its position as creditors. In the 1960s and 1970s, in the United States, the financial assets of households amounted to approximately 100 per cent of their disposable income (that is their income after paying taxes); this reached 150 per cent during the neoliberal decades. Symmetrically, households (partly another fraction) increased their debt, from 60 per cent of their disposable income to more than 100 per cent by the end of the twentieth century. The state was also affected. Large real interest rates sharply increased budget deficits in the United States. In France, these were directly the origin of the deficits. (Neoliberal propaganda seeks to reverse the direction of causation, pinning large interest rates on deficits.)

This new course of capitalism made financial investment, and financial activities in general, more attractive. The term 'financialisation' has been coined to account for these new trends toward financial investment (see Chapter 11). The size of the financial sector (financial corporations) increased considerably in

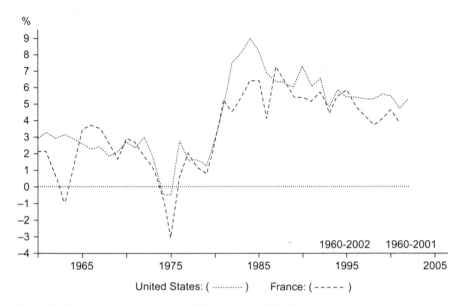

Figure 1.2   Long-term real interest rates: France and the United States.
Source: OECD, *Statistical Compendium 2001*

relation to its rising profitability. In the 1960s, still in the United States, the own funds (total assets minus debt) of financial corporations amounted to 25 per cent of that of non-financial corporations; during the structural crisis of the 1970s, this fell to 18 per cent; by 2000, it had reached nearly 30 per cent. The gradual involvement of non-financial corporations in financial activities, either directly or through affiliates, was also dramatic. Moreover, the ownership of securities was being more and more concentrated within financial institutions, such as mutual or pension funds.

One of the primary effects of neoliberalism was the restoration of the income and wealth of the upper fractions of the owners of capital, whose property is expressed in the holding of securities, such as shares, bonds or bills. This confers a financial character to their ownership. Broader segments of the population hold such securities and receive the corresponding income, in particular within their pension funds, as in the United States. Obviously—according to national and, above all, international standards – these intermediary classes enjoy a comparatively favourable situation. This is the neoliberal method of providing retirement benefits. These social groups are led to believe that they are richer, and are now part of the capitalist class. This impression was strengthened by the increase in the value of their portfolios during the second half of the 1990s, which was ephemeral. The rising wealth of those groups was an objective of neoliberalism only to the extent that it gained their support. The concentration of their assets within large funds provided a very powerful tool in the hands of finance.[4] The new situation that they must, however, confront in the early twenty-first century is the threat to their ability to retire to a decent life after work.[5]

SLOW GROWTH, STAGNATION AND CRISIS

Neoliberalism was not responsible for the crisis of the 1970s, but the drain on incomes by finance, beginning when the structural crisis was still raging, prolonged the effects of the crisis – in particular slow growth and unemployment.

After the decline of the profit rate—within the main capitalist countries from the late 1960s to the early 1980s—which caused the structural crisis of the 1970s, new upward profitability trends occurred. The benefits of this restoration within non-financial corporations, however, accrued to rich households and financial institutions. Thus no restoration of profitability is apparent in a measure of the profit rate of non-financial corporations, where profits are measured after paying interest and dividends. Such a measure went on declining to the end of the twentieth century. There would be no problem with such 'generous' distributions, provided that the issuance of new shares or borrowings allow for the return of a decent fraction of these sums to the non-financial sector to finance real investment, the condition for growth. It appears, however, that this was not so, and was still not the case in the early twenty-first century. The pattern of capital accumulation (the growth of the stock of fixed capital resulting from investment) followed exactly these profit rates after paying interest and dividends. Thus the neoliberal bias in favour of financial interests had devastating effects on growth and employment.

To different degrees, the growth of the economies of the centre, after the Second World War, was highly dependent on development models favourable to the non-financial economy, sometimes labelled 'mixed economy.' This is because of the strong intervention of the state. Profits remained within non-financial corporations, due to low interest rates and dividends flows, and were invested in fixed capital.

Consider the example of the French economy. During the 1960s, the growth rate of the stock of fixed capital (after depreciation) in France amounted to 8 per cent. It declined gradually to about 2 per cent at the end of the century! These mechanisms are part of a more general transformation. Since the 1990s, French corporations have attempted to reduce their debt. (The rate of self-financing of investment remained above 100 per cent for a number of years.) They are also involved in a process of streamlining and concentration. These adjustments are detrimental to the building of new capacity: *more profitable rather than larger, or merging rather than growing.* As shown in Table 1.1, the cost in terms of growth and employment was large.

Even in the United States, neoliberalism cannot be considered a model of growth and accumulation. Growth rates fluctuated in the United States during the 1980s and 1990s, at levels inferior to those reached during the previous decades (see Table 1.1). The picture is less dramatic than in France, but no neoliberal miracle is evident. The records of the US economy in terms of growth are very dependent on the 'long boom' which occurred between 1993 and 2000, before the recession. This boom was, to a large extent, a consequence of exceptional flows of capital from the rest of the world (Duménil and Lévy 2003).

Thanks to its pattern of financing prior to neoliberalism, Japan escaped from the effects of the rise of interest rates in the early 1980s. Interest rates on capital

Table 1.1   Average annual growth rates

Period	1950–59	1960–69	1970–79	1980–89	1990–99
United States	4.11	4.41	3.24	2.98	3.00
France	4.54	5.71	4.10	2.37	1.72

Sources: National Accounting Frameworks (BEA, INSEE)

markets in Japan increased as anywhere else during the decade, but corporations were borrowing from banks at more favourable rates. The transformation of Japanese financial institutions was, however, under way, and the opening to international finance was gradual. The major change, which can be described as a *second* neoliberal shock, occurred between 1985 and 1990. Corporations progressively resorted more to the sources of financing available on capital markets. Borrowing became more costly, and corporations were drawn into the dynamics of stock markets and the corresponding governance. This opening provoked, within a few years, a financial bubble, promptly followed by speculation in real estate. The burden of a costly financing rapidly proved unsustainable for non-financial corporations. Financial institutions were gradually transformed according to the new rules of international finance. Plunged into the speculative euphoria of stock markets, the financial sector was deeply hurt by the bursting of the bubble in 1990. Japan entered a lasting crisis. As in other countries, this crisis, actually resulting from the neoliberal transformation of the Japanese economy, was used as an argument in favour of an even more thorough adjustment.

Though in a distinct configuration, that of a country at the frontier of the periphery, Korea also provides a convincing example of the damage caused by neoliberalism. During the last decades of the twentieth century, up to the crisis in 1997, Korea registered record growth rates, even larger than in Japan during the heyday of the Japanese model. Then Korea entered a period of partial opening to neoliberalism, under forms similar to those implemented in Japan (see Chapters 29 and 30). The cost of the financing of corporations rose during the second half of the 1990s, exhausting profits. Foreign capital, whose objectives in terms of returns had been adjusted to neoliberal requirements, had gradually entered the country, bringing an increasing bias toward liquid assets. They suddenly moved out of the country when the first symptoms of a financial disruption became apparent in the East Asian countries. The shock therapy of the IMF added to the dramatic consequences of the ensuing crisis. It is still too early to tell what will be the effect of the entry of Korea into the realm of global neoliberal capitalism. Will it thoroughly destroy the huge growth potential of the earlier model? Will growth rates be diminished? Will a new macroeconomic instability be established? We don't know yet.

The mechanisms described above can be summarised as follows. International finance (that is, to a large extent, that of the United States), developed a strategy in two steps: (1) obtaining financial deregulation, allowing for its entry into particular countries (with the complicity of national agents); (2) transforming the relationship between the non-financial sector and financial institutions, to the advantage of the latter, and in particular of itself (US finance).

THE EXPLOITATION AND DEVASTATION OF
THE COUNTRIES OF THE PERIPHERY

The further a country was from the centre, the more damaging was its transition toward neoliberalism. The first manifestation of neoliberalism within countries of the periphery was the so-called 'Third World debt crisis'. To a large extent, the decision to lend to these countries, during the 1960s and 1970s, was in response to a major political goal: the fight against communism. But political conditions were different at the interstices of the 1970s and 1980s. The main cause of the crisis was the rise in real interest rates in 1979. This was aggravated by the structural crisis of the main capitalist countries, which had a negative impact on the exports of the countries of the periphery. The decline of the prices of raw materials and energy also contributed to the deterioration of the situation in these countries, as the variations in the price of oil affected the economy of Mexico. The crisis started in August 1982, when Mexico announced that it was unable to ensure its earlier commitments. A chain reaction was initiated, and one year later, 27 countries had rescheduled their payments. Four countries in Latin America (Mexico, Brazil, Venezuela, and Argentina) held 74 per cent of the international debt.

The real interest rate (using the GNP deflator in the United States) on the debt of the so-called 'developing countries' (in the definition of the World Bank), jumped from negative rates to rates of approximately 2 per cent. In 2000, the debt of the countries of the periphery was four times larger than in 1980. The other side of the coin was obviously the large flows of interest, transferred from these countries to the banks of the centre, notably in the United States. When the output of these developing countries is deflated by the GNP deflator in the United States, the volume of this output had not, in 1996, reached its levels of 1979.

Independently of the negative impact of the debt, the countries of the periphery have been injured by the imposition of neoliberalism, due to the rejection of autonomous development strategies. The idea that capital exports are conducive to development is a myth. No less dangerous is the view that the stability of the exchange rate with respect to the dollar can stimulate foreign investment. Indeed, such stability may encourage financial investment in the short term, but it proves incompatible with sustained development. The combination of a high cost of financing, exchange rate stability, and free international mobility of capitals defines the basic neoliberal cocktail, a recipe for stagnation and crisis.

Figure 1.3 shows the profile of output (GNP), since 1960 or 1971, in Brazil, Mexico and Argentina. With small differences, the decades of neoliberalism mark a break in growth rates. For Mexico or Brazil, growth rates were divided by two or three. It is also obvious that recessions occurred. Slow growth and recession – this is the bottom line of the new neoliberal course for its astute observers in the periphery. The case of Argentina is slightly more complex since, after a phase of lasting stagnation in the 1980s, the turn to neoliberalism in 1990, at first, stimulated a new growth dynamic during the first half of the 1990s. As is well known,

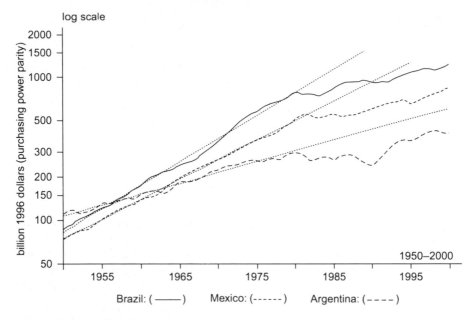

Figure 1.3   Output: Brazil, Mexico, and Argentina.
Source: PennWorld Tables 2003.

the episode ended in crisis, misery, and social dislocation at the end of the decade
(see Chapter 26).

The benefits for the economies of the centre have often been described. At issue
are: the appropriation of natural resources (agriculture, mining, energy) at low and
declining prices; the exploitation by transnational corporations of segments of the
cheap labour force of these countries, who are subjected to often extreme working conditions; and the draining of the flows of interest resulting from the cumulative debt of these countries. To this, one must add the gradual appropriation of
the major, potentially more profitable, segments of the economy, including the
opportunities opened up by the privatisation of public companies, which allows
transnational corporations to buy entire industries, for example telecommunications, at low prices.

In 2000, US financial investments (treasury bills, bonds, commercial paper,
stock shares, direct investment, etc.) in the rest of the world amounted to 3,488
billion dollars. The corresponding income was 381 billion dollars, that is, a return
of nearly 11 per cent. It is interesting to note that this income was approximately
equal to the total after-tax profits of all corporations in the United States, excluding
such flows from abroad—that is a ratio of 100 per cent.[6]

These mechanisms confirm that neoliberalism is a predatory system. In different contexts and to distinct degrees, the strengthening of the power of the upper
fractions of the ruling classes has been detrimental to growth everywhere, whether
in their own countries or in the periphery. Indeed, assessed by its own objectives,

it has been very successful in restoring the income and wealth of these classes, as well as consolidating the pre-eminence of the US economy. But to the rest of the US population and the world, the cost of this pre-eminence has been enormous.

NOTES

1. The analysis in the following sections borrows from Duménil and Lévy (2004).
2. The role of states in the rise of neoliberalism is analysed by Helleiner (1994).
3. The fight against inflation was a component of this second objective.
4. Besides the profits derived from the management of pension funds, a very profitable business, finance uses its capability to assign capital to one corporation or another, to one country or another, to discipline private management and public policies. In addition, the illusion by intermediary classes of participating in the actual ownership of the means of production is politically crucial in the maintenance of the neoliberal order.
5. In the United States, the lower half of the labour force does not have a retirement plan.
6. In 1950, this ratio was only 10 per cent. It rose suddenly at the beginning of the 1980s, with the imposition of neoliberalism, mostly in relation to the rise of interest rates.

REFERENCES

Duménil, G. and Lévy, D. (2004) *Capital Resurgent: Roots of the Neoliberal Revolution*. Cambridge, MA: Harvard University Press.

Duménil, G. and Lévy, D. (2003) *Neoliberal Dynamics – Imperial Dynamics*. Paris: Cepremap, Modem <http://www.cepremap.ens.fr/levy/>.

Ferguson, T. (1995) *Golden Rule: The Investment Theory of Party Competition and the Logic of Money-Driven Political Systems*. Chicago: University of Chicago Press.

Helleiner, E. (1994) *States and the Reemergence of Global Finance: From Bretton Woods to the Nineties*. Ithaca, N.Y.: Cornell University Press.

Piketty, T. and Saez, E. (2003) 'Income Inequality in the United States, 1913–1998', *Quartely Journal of Economics* 118 (1), pp. 1–39.

Wolff, E. (1996) *Top Heavy*. New York: The New Press.

2
From Keynesianism to Neoliberalism: Shifting Paradigms in Economics

Thomas I. Palley

For the last 25 years, economic policy and the public's thinking have been dominated by a conservative economic philosophy known as neoliberalism. The reference to 'liberalism' reflects an intellectual lineage that connects with nineteenth-century economic liberalism associated with Manchester, England. The Manchester system was predicated upon laissez-faire economics, and was closely associated with free trade and the repeal of England's Corn Laws, which restricted importation of wheat. Contemporary neoliberalism, which emphasises the efficiency of market competition, the role of individuals in determining economic outcomes, and distortions associated with government intervention and regulation of markets, is principally associated with the Chicago School of Economics.[1]

Two critical tenets of neoliberalism are its theories of (1) income distribution, and (2) aggregate employment determination. With regard to income distribution, neoliberalism asserts that factors of production (labour and capital) get paid what they are worth. This is accomplished through the supply and demand process, whereby payment depends on a factor's relative scarcity (supply) and its productivity (which affects demand). With regard to aggregate employment determination, neoliberalism asserts that free markets will not let valuable factors of production (including labour) go to waste. Instead, prices will adjust to ensure that demand is forthcoming and all factors are employed. This assertion is the foundation of Chicago School monetarism, which claims that economies automatically self-adjust to full employment, so that use of monetary and fiscal policy to permanently raise employment merely generates inflation.[2]

These two theories have been extraordinarily influential, and they contrast with the thinking that held sway in the period between 1945 and 1980. During this earlier era, the dominant theory of employment determination was Keynesianism, which maintains that the level of economic activity is determined by the level of aggregate demand (AD).[3] Additionally, Keynesians maintain that capitalist economies are subject to periodic weakness in the AD generation process, resulting in unemployment. Occasionally, this weakness can be severe and produce economic depressions – as exemplified by the Great Depression. In such a world, monetary and fiscal policy can stabilise the demand-generation process.

With regard to income distribution, Keynesians have always been divided, and this created a fatal division that facilitated the triumph of neoliberalism. American Keynesians (known as neo-Keynesians) tend to accept the neoliberal 'paid what

20

you are worth' theory of income distribution, while European Keynesians (widely associated with Cambridge and known as post-Keynesians) reject it. Instead, post-Keynesians argue that income distribution depends significantly on institutional factors. Thus, not only do a factor's relative scarcity and productivity matter, but so too does its bargaining power, which is impacted by institutional arrangements. This explains the significance of trade unions, laws governing minimum wages, employee rights at work, and systems of social protection such as unemployment insurance. Finally, public understandings of the economy also matter, since a public that views the economy through a bargaining power lens will have greater political sympathies for trade unions and institutions of social protection.

THE GREAT REVERSAL: THE DECLINE OF KEYNESIANISM AND THE REVIVAL OF NEOLIBERALISM

For the 25 years after the Second World War (1945–70), Keynesianism constituted the dominant paradigm for understanding the determination of economic activity. This was the era in which the modern tools of monetary policy (control of interest rates) and fiscal policy (control of government spending and taxes) were developed. It was also a period in which union coverage rose to historical highs, and 'New Deal'-style institutions of social protection and regulation were expanded.

In the mid 1970s the Keynesian impulse went into reverse, to be replaced by a revived neoliberalism. This revival piggybacked on the social and economic dislocations associated with the Vietnam War era and the OPEC oil price shocks that marked the 1970s. However, these dislocations only provided an entry point. The ultimate cause of the neoliberal revival is to be found in the intellectual divisions of Keynesianism and its failure to develop public understandings of the economy which could compete with the neoliberal rhetoric of 'free markets'.

Throughout the period of Keynesian dominance, there remained deep conservative opposition within the United States that provided a base from which to launch a neoliberal revival. This opposition had been present in the period of the New Deal, as manifested in conservative opposition to the creation of the Social Security retirement income system. And it continued after the Second World War, as illustrated by the conservative sponsored Taft–Hartley Act (1947), which sowed the seeds that have ended up eviscerating the rights of American workers to form unions, by undermining union power and ability to organise (see Chapter 22).

The revival of neoliberalism was also aided by economic and cultural factors. At the economic level, the success of New Deal Keynesianism may have contributed to its own undoing. Thus rising prosperity, built upon Keynesian policies and the postwar social contract between business and labour, may have contributed to beliefs that the core economic problems of income distribution and mass unemployment had finally been solved. As a result, the public may gradually have come to view the policies and institutions – such as unions – which had brought about this condition as no longer needed.

At the cultural level, America has always celebrated radical individualism, as epitomised in the image of the frontiersman. This radical individualism was further promoted by the ideological conflict embedded in the cold war, which fostered antipathy to notions of collective economic action and denial of the limitations of market capitalism. In particular, collective economic action was tarred by identification with the communist approach to economic management. The cold war therefore provided fertile ground for popularising an economic rhetoric which spoke of 'natural' free markets that exist without government, and in which government regulation reduces well-being (see Palley 1998a, pp. 31–8).

Political and cultural factors are undoubtedly important in explaining the revival of neoliberalism. But Keynesianism also suffered from internal intellectual divisions that made for weakness. One source of division was the theory of income distribution. Keynes was a believer in the marginal product theory of income distribution, whereby workers get paid what they are worth to the firm. This gives little justification for trade unions and other forms of labour-market intervention, all of which can be painted as market distortions rather than corrections of market failure associated with unequal bargaining power. In effect, whereas Keynes and the Keynesians contributed greatly to understanding the determinants of AD and its role in determining employment outcomes, there was no matching analysis of production conditions and how they interact with and impact AD.[4]

A second Keynesian weakness was the belief that downward price and (especially) nominal wage rigidity were responsible for unemployment. This position emerged in the 1940s, the decade after the publication of Keynes's (1936) *General Theory*. The argument was that lower nominal wages would lower prices, thereby increasing the real value of money holdings, which in turn would stimulate consumption spending and AD. In addition, lower prices would increase the real money supply, thereby lowering interest rates and stimulating investment spending. In this fashion, lower nominal wages and prices could solve the problem of unemployment.

This neo-Keynesian view of price and wage flexibility was adopted especially strongly by American economists. In effect, it states that price and wage rigidities are responsible for unemployment, and these rigidities include such factors as trade unions and minimum wage laws. In a sense, the American neo-Keynesian position was implicitly a forerunner of today's neoliberal labour-market flexibility agenda. This neo-Keynesian analysis contrasts sharply with the post-Keynesian analysis, which has unemployment resulting from demand shortages caused by uncertainty about the future and weak business confidence. In a monetary economy, spending can dry up if people decide to hold onto money, and price flexibility can make the demand problem worse owing to debt. Thus, lower prices and nominal wages increase the interest payment burden of debtors, causing them to cut back on spending and possibly to default.[5] The post-Keynesian bottom line is that money-based contracting yields great economic efficiency by lowering transacting costs, but it also makes economic adjustment through price and nominal wage flexibility highly problematic.

These twin differences, regarding the determination of income distribution and the role of downward nominal wage rigidity in creating unemployment, created deep internal divisions among Keynesians. At the policy level, the differences opened the way for neoliberals to characterise the labour-market innovations of the New Deal as market distortions rather than corrections of market failure. As such, these innovations lacked an economic efficiency rationale, and could at best only be justified for reasons of equity.

Furthermore, these divisions opened the way for an attack on Keynesian full employment monetary and fiscal policies. American neo-Keynesians supported such policies on the pragmatic grounds that prices and wages were downwardly rigid in practice, and for this reason government policy interventions were needed. Thus it was not the theoretical benefits of flexibility that neo-Keynesians contested, but rather the empirical possibility of price and nominal wage flexibility. Intellectually, this was a bastardisation of Keynes's message, and it provided a public policy opening for neoliberal economists to argue that economic policy should abandon targeting full employment and instead focus on making wage flexibility a reality.

NEOLIBERAL POLICY IN PRACTICE

As noted above, neoliberalism can be understood in terms of its theories of income distribution and employment determination. According to the former, the market ensures that factors of production are paid what they are worth, thereby removing the need for institutions of social protection and trade unions. Indeed, institutions of social protection can lower social well-being and cause unemployment, by interfering with the market process. According to the latter, price adjustment ensures an automatic tendency to full employment. Within this framework, policy interventions to increase employment either cause inflation or raise unemployment, by destabilising the market process. This was Milton Friedman's claim regarding the Great Depression, which he argued was caused by mistaken monetary tightening by the Federal Reserve. The policy implication is that macroeconomic policy makers should discard Keynesian policies of activist demand management aimed at full employment. Instead, they should adopt transparent policy rules that take the discretion out of policy decisions, thereby avoiding policy mistakes and letting market forces solve the problem.[6]

In practice, the application of neoliberal policy in the United States has often seen a slip between the cup and the lip – that is, pragmatism has forced neoliberal policy makers to depart from theory. Regarding income distribution, neoliberal policy has consistently sought to promote the cause of labour market deregulation. This has taken the form of allowing the real value of the minimum wage to fall, undermining unions, and generally creating a labour market climate of employment insecurity. In this, neoliberal policy has been true to its theory, which maintains that employment protections and wage rigidities are not needed. The result has been widening wage and income inequality (Mishel et al. 2001; Palley 1998a). For neoliberals, this is because the market is now paying people what they are worth. For post-Keynesians, it is because the balance of power in labour markets has tilted in favour of business.

With regard to macroeconomic policy, neoliberalism has been applied inconsistently and opportunistically, and has departed from its theoretical rhetoric. In the early 1980s, neoliberal policy makers sought to apply Chicago School monetarist prescriptions that abandoned Keynesian interest rate fine tuning in favour of money supply targeting. The result was a massive increase in OECD unemployment that pushed unemployment rates to the highest level since the Great Depression, a sharp rise in global real interest rates, and the emergence of significant financial market volatility. This forced abandonment of the monetarist experiment, and a return to interest-rate-based policy.

However, while there was a return to the use of interest rate targeting and activist Keynesian stabilisation policy, the goal of policy was changed. In particular, the concept of full employment was abandoned, and replaced with the notion of a 'natural rate of unemployment' (also known as the non-accelerating inflation rate of unemployment, NAIRU, which is supposed to be that rate of unemployment at which inflation shows no tendency to accelerate or decelerate; see Chapter 21). This natural rate is unobservable, and is supposedly determined by the forces of demand and supply in labour markets. The adoption of natural-rate rhetoric has served two purposes. First, it has provided political cover for higher average rates of unemployment, which have undermined the bargaining position of workers. Second, it has provided cover for keeping real interest rates at a higher level, thereby benefiting the wealthy and the financial sector. Thus, even though interest rates have been adjusted counter-cyclically to mitigate the business cycle, their average level has been higher. Likewise, fiscal policy has also been adjusted counter-cyclically to combat the business cycle, but it too has been used to favour the wealthy and special political interests. This is most clearly evident in tax policy, where tax cuts have been targeted towards upper income groups.

The neoliberal co-option of stabilisation policy raises two issues. First, whereas stabilisation policy is the right policy response, neoliberal policy makers have employed it in a suboptimal manner. This is illustrated by recent US tax policy. Thus the Bush administration used the 2001 recession opportunistically to cut taxes, but these tax cuts were (1) directed predominantly toward the wealthy, thereby yielding less economic bang per buck, and (2) structured to be permanent, when fighting recession called only for temporary tax cuts. Second, the need for recourse to stabilisation policy speaks to the inadequacy of the neoliberal theoretical account of the economy. After all, according to the neoliberal model, market economies are supposed to automatically and rapidly self-adjust to full employment.

Putting the pieces together, the challenge confronting post-Keynesians is to move the debate at two levels. First, there is the need to challenge the particulars of neoliberal stabilisation policy, which has been suboptimal. Second, there is the need to challenge the underlying neoliberal conceptual framework. This twin task is difficult, since engaging in a debate on policy particulars risks having the debate perceived as a matter of differences of degree rather than of fundamental differences in economic conception.

THE ECONOMIC RECORD UNDER NEOLIBERALISM

The elections of Mrs Thatcher in 1979 and Ronald Reagan in 1980 can be viewed as inaugurating the formal period of neoliberal economic policy dominance (see Chapters 22 and 23). The 25 years since have seen an expanding application of neoliberal policy ideas within the economies of both industrialised and developing countries. Compared to the 1945–80 era, this has been a period of substantially slower economic growth and widening income inequality, both within and between countries (Mishel et al. 2001; Weisbrot et al. 2002).

Within industrialised countries, the economic conversation has been dominated by policies associated with the 'US model'. These include deregulation of financial markets, privatisation, weakening of institutions of social protection, weakening of labour unions and labour market protections, shrinking of government, cutting of top tax rates, opening up of international goods and capital markets, and abandonment of full employment under the guise of the natural rate. International economic policy has been dominated by the 'Washington consensus', which advocates privatisation, free trade, export-led growth, financial capital mobility, deregulated labour markets, and policies of macroeconomic austerity.

The failure of the Washington consensus to deliver faster growth in developing countries – it has actually delivered slower growth – has contributed to a backlash that has significantly discredited it. There is now widespread recognition that: international financial markets can be prone to instability; export-led growth is not sufficient for domestic development and can promote global deflation and the race to the bottom; democracy and institutions promoting social inclusiveness are needed for development; and labour market protections are needed to prevent exploitation. However, though much progress has been made in countering the Washington consensus, little progress has been made in combating the 'US model', which is the ultimate source of neoliberal policy, including the Washington consensus (see Chapter 12).

Within public debate, the United States is presented as a model economy and contrasted with European economies which are labelled as sclerotic and inflexible. However, the facts are more complex, and speak to both models having strengths and weaknesses. The strengths of the US neoliberal model are a lower average rate of unemployment, a higher employment-to-population ratio, and faster output growth (in part driven by population growth caused by legal and illegal immigration). Its weaknesses relative to the European model are higher and worsened income inequality (exemplified by the explosion of CEO pay in the United States), higher poverty rates, lower productivity growth (until the mid 1990s), longer working hours, and wage stagnation for those in the bottom half of the wage distribution. Research (Blanchflower and Oswald 2002) into the economics of happiness shows that happiness in the United States has shown a downward trend, while happiness in the United Kingdom has remained level. These two economies have pursued the neoliberal path most aggressively, but it has not translated into more happiness for their citizens (see Chapters 16 and 24).

The differences in US and European economic outcomes can be understood using Figure 2.1.[7] Macroeconomic policy determines the overall rate of unemployment, while microeconomic policies concerning labour-market and social-protection institutions determine patterns of income inequality. Expansionary macro-policy lowers unemployment, while contractionary macro-policy increases unemployment. Eroding institutions of social protection increases income inequality, while maintaining protections holds income inequality constant. A pure neoliberal

		Macro-policy options	
		Contraction	*Expansion*
Micro-policy options	*Erode protections*	Pure neoliberalism	United States
	Maintain protections	Europe	Post-Keynesianism

Figure 2.1 Differences in economic policy between neoliberalism and post-Keynesianism, and between the United States and Europe

policy configuration would aim at eroding protections, as these are a form of market distortion, and it would also abandon full-employment counter-cyclical policy as unnecessary.

In practice, policy has not been applied as pure neoliberal theory would suggest. The United States has pursued a policy of expansionary macro-policy built on large budget deficits and counter-cyclical interest rates, combined with policies eroding social protections. The result has been relatively full employment and worsening income distribution. Contrastingly, Europe has pursued contractionary macro-policies centred on high interest rates and fiscal austerity, while maintaining its institutions of social protection. The result has been high unemployment, and only a modest deterioration in income inequality.

Finally, Figure 2.1 can also be used to understand the policy configuration recommended by a post-Keynesian perspective. At the microeconomic level, there is need for institutions of social and labour-market protection to ensure an appropriate distribution of income. At the macroeconomic level, policy should have an expansionary tilt to ensure full employment. This policy configuration fits with the underlying theoretical framework, which has income distribution significantly impacted by social and institutional forces, while full employment requires management of the level of aggregate demand. The challenge is to ensure that institutions of social protection are designed such that markets retain the appropriate incentives for the provision of labour effort and entrepreneurship, while firms have an adequate level of flexibility. Side by side with this, macroeconomic policy must provide adequate aggregate demand, but not so much that it generates unacceptably high inflation.

The above analysis in terms of macro- and micro-policy is also revealing of some important political lessons. Both the US and European models are flawed in important ways. Yet politically, the US model – with its lower rate of unemployment – has been hard to dent. At the same time, the European model has been under pressure to weaken its institutions of labour market and social protection. This suggests that low unemployment trumps income distribution and fairness concerns amongst electorates. Such a conclusion is supported by the research on the economics of happiness, which reports that unemployment carries a very high happiness cost. People are concerned with fairness, but not enough to be politically decisive. This means that a successful economic model must address the problem of unemployment, and it shows how the European social model is being sabotaged by the continent's macroeconomic policies.

REINVENTING GOVERNMENT IN ECONOMIC DISCOURSE

In addition to reshaping public understandings of what constitutes the best mix of macro- and micro-policies, there is also a need to reconfigure public understandings of the economic role of government. The traditional liberal explanation for government economic involvement has focused on 'market failure' related to problems of monopoly, natural monopoly, public goods, and externalities.[8] The basic idea is that market failure leads to suboptimal provision (there may be too little or too much production), calling for government intervention – through regulation, taxes and subsidies, or outright government control of production – to remedy the problem.

The concept of market failure has proved extremely powerful, but it has in turn generated a neoliberal counter-argument framed in terms of 'government failure'. The claim is that though markets may fail, having government remedy that failure may be worse, owing to bureaucratic inefficiencies and lack of market-styled incentives.

The government failure argument has had great resonance in the United States, with its culture of radical individualism. However, the role of government in a market economy runs far deeper, and this contribution is inadequately understood. Not only does government have a role to play in remedying market failure, but it is also a provider of essential services related to education and health. In addition, government plays a critical role in stabilising the business cycle through fiscal and monetary policy. Deeper yet, government is integral to the workings of private markets, through its provision of a legal system that supports the use of contracts. Without the ability to contract, the benefits of a market economy would be enormously diminished.

Particularly poorly understood is the role of government in preventing 'destructive competition'. Such competition is associated with conditions characterised by the prisoner's dilemma. This corresponds to a situation in which market incentives induce agents to engage in actions that generate a suboptimal equilibrium, and the market cannot generate incentives that can support the socially optimal equilibrium. This type of situation is illustrated by the bribery problem. Bribery is economically destructive because it allocates business on the basis of bribe paying rather than of economic efficiency. For this reason, societies should aim to avoid bribery. However, unregulated markets tend to produce bribery. If one agent bribes while others do not, that agent is made better off while others suffer. As a result, all agents have an incentive to bribe. Left to itself, the market therefore generates a 'bad' equilibrium in which all agents pay bribes. The 'good' equilibrium in which none pay bribes can only be supported by laws imposing penalties that deter bribery. This illustrates how government action may be needed to support optimally efficient outcomes. The real world is regularly afflicted by situations generating destructive competition – examples include bribery, excessive advertising expenditures, tax competition between jurisdictions to attract business investment, and the global race to the bottom which has countries ratcheting down labour standards to attract business. All of these situations require government intervention to remedy them.

POST-KEYNESIANISM VERSUS THE THIRD WAY:
SIMILARITIES AND DIFFERENCES

In closing, it is worth comparing the above post-Keynesian construction with the 'Third Way' approach of UK prime minister, Tony Blair.[9] The Third Way is an alternative attempt to topple neoliberal domination of public policy (see Chapter 21). It seeks to articulate a humane path between the first way of laissez-faire capitalism and the second way of centrally planned state economies. In this, it has some resonance with the mixed economy of the 1960s, which argued for a combination of privately owned and nationalised industries.

However, though the Third Way seeks to humanise the market, it is fundamentally different from a post-Keynesian perspective because it basically accepts the major theoretical tenets of neoliberalism regarding income distribution and the stability of capitalist economies. Viewed in this light, the Third Way represents an updating of the earlier market failure approach that also aims to counter the neoliberal government failure argument. Thus, the Third Way emphasises how market failure can result from imperfect information. This imperfect information argument is an additional source of market failure that has gained theoretical recognition over the last 20 years. Additionally, rather than have government take over production through nationalised industries and risk government failure, the Third Way instead emphasises taxation and regulation as the preferred means of changing private-sector behaviour. Similarly, when it comes to production of essential services such as health and education – which markets under-provide – the Third Way is comfortable having government contract for these services, and then have the private sector produce them.

While these Third Way innovations are in principle consistent with the post-Keynesian approach, it is still the case that post-Keynesianism differs fundamentally from the Third Way because of its rejection of the neoliberal approach to income distribution and claims of an automatic tendency to full employment. Labour is not automatically paid what it is worth by an anonymous neutral market process. Rather, the pattern of income distribution is impacted by labour-market institutions, and institutional interventions are needed because markets have a tendency to favour capital over labour. Furthermore, capitalist economies are subject to fluctuations of AD that give rise to unnecessary unemployment. Downward price and wage flexibility cannot resolve this problem, and actually aggravate it. Consequently, there is need for monetary and fiscal policy interventions to correct the problem of deficient demand, and institutions that prevent generalised declines in prices and nominal wages are highly desirable to avoid destructive debt deflations. These analytical differences fundamentally differentiate post-Keynesianism from the Third Way, and they explain the policy disagreements that mark 'old' and 'new' Labour in the United Kingdom, and 'old' and 'new' Democrats in the United States.

NOTES

1. Key figures in the Chicago School are Milton Friedman, George Stigler, Ronald Coase, and Gary Becker – all of whom have been awarded the Nobel Prize in economics.
2. Monetary policy is conducted by central banks, who manage interest rates to affect the level of economic activity. Fiscal policy refers to government management of spending and taxation to affect economic activity.
3. Aggregate demand is the total level of demand for goods and services in an economy. Keynesians believe that firms produce on the basis of their expectations of the level of aggregate demand, so that the level of aggregate demand therefore determines the overall level of economic activity.
4. This theme is developed in Palley (1998a).
5. For a formal analysis of the destabilising possibilities of price and nominal wage reduction see Palley (1996, ch. 4; 1999).
6. In addition, Friedman's rules-based policy argument has been supplemented by a second-generation Chicago School political economy argument to the effect that politicians are motivated by self-interest, and actively engage in deceiving the public and working against its interests. According to second-generation Chicago School economists, this calls for independent policy institutions that are free of political control. The problem with this claim is that removing political accountability does not remove the self-interest of those who remain in control (Palley 1997).
7. The analysis here is drawn from Palley (1998b).
8. Monopoly may result from private actions or from the nature of technology. In both cases it precludes the benefits of competition. Public goods refer to such activities as provision of defence and street lighting. Markets under-provide public goods because private producers cannot prevent agents from freely consuming the good. Externalities refer to actions of one agent that impact the well-being of others. The costs and benefits of this impact are not taken into account by individuals when deciding on the action, resulting in a sub-optimal outcome.
9. Arestis and Sawyer (2001) provide a survey of the economics of the Third Way, as applied around the world by governments that have adhered to the Third Way.

REFERENCES

Arestis, P., and Sawyer, M. (eds) (2001) *The Economics of the Third Way: Experiences From Around the World*. Cheltenham: Edward Elgar.

Blanchflower, D.G. and Oswald, A.J. (2002) 'Well-being over Time in Britain and the USA', unpublished manuscript.

Keynes, J.M. (1936) *The General Theory of Employment, Interest and Money*. London: Macmillan.

Mishel, L., Bernstein, J. and Schmitt, J. (2001) *The State of Working America 2000–2001*. Ithaca, N.Y.: Cornell University Press.

Palley, T.I. (1999) 'General Disequilibrium Analysis with Inside Debt', *Journal of Macroeconomics* 21, pp. 785–804.

Palley, T.I. (1998a) *Plenty of Nothing: The Downsizing of the American Dream and the Case for Structural Keynesianism*. Princeton: Princeton University Press.

Palley, T.I. (1998b) 'Restoring Prosperity: Why the US Model is not the Right Answer for the US or Europe', *Journal of Post-Keynesian Economics* 20, pp. 337–54.

Palley, T.I. (1997) 'The Institutionalisation of Deflationary Policy Bias', in H. Hagerman and A. Cohen (eds) *Advances in Monetary Theory*. Dordrecht: Kluwer Academic Publishers.

Palley, T.I. (1996) *Post-Keynesian Economics: Debt, Distribution, and the Macro-Economy*. London: Macmillan.

Weisbrot, M., Baker, D., Kraev, E. and Chen, J. (2002) 'The Scorecard on Globalisation 1980–2000: Twenty Years of Diminished Progress', Briefing Paper, Centre for Economic Policy Research, Washington, D.C.

3
Mainstream Economics in the Neoliberal Era

Costas Lapavitsas

The neoliberal ascendancy in economic theory and policy commenced during the second half of the 1970s. Its prevalent characteristic is the conviction that free markets provide the optimal organising mechanism for capitalist economies. This is at bottom an economic belief, though it also has political, ideological, institutional and social implications. Neoliberal belief in the efficacy of free markets has characterised mainstream economic theory during the last three decades, especially within leading universities, international organisations, such as the International Monetary Fund and the World Bank, and economic ministries.

The intellectual origins of neoliberalism are closely associated with Friedrich von Hayek, one of the most prominent exponents of Austrian neoclassical economics (see Chapter 6). But the direct influence of Hayek on mainstream economics during the neoliberal era has been small. Moreover, in the 1990s, mainstream economic theory started to retreat from the worst excesses of neoliberalism, especially within the international organisations. A new interventionism has gradually emerged within the mainstream, seeking to regulate markets, but without challenging the notion that they comprise the optimal organising mechanism for capitalist economies.

This chapter accordingly focuses on two related developments within mainstream economics during the neoliberal period. The first is the decline of postwar Keynesian macroeconomics, which advocated control over markets as well as state intervention in the economy, in contrast to neoliberalism (see Chapter 2). It is important however to note that, despite the decline of official Keynesianism, the fiscal and monetary techniques used by governments throughout the neoliberal era have retained a Keynesian character. The prevalence of such techniques has often led activists and journalists to imagine that official postwar Keynesianism has returned. This misconception has been especially pronounced during the last few years as neoliberalism has frayed at the edges and a new interventionism has gradually appeared within mainstream economics. It is shown below that this new interventionism is not as radical as traditional Keynesianism, and it does not represent a decisive break with neoliberalism.

The new interventionism draws on the second major development within mainstream economics, namely the gradual incorporation of information, institutions and social customs into microeconomic analysis. This has offered fresh scope for economic analysis of the occasional, or even systematic, failure of free markets to deliver optimal results. Mainstream economics now increasingly accepts that free markets might malfunction due to a number of reasons, including asymmetry of information among market participants, poorly performing social institutions, or even lack of trust across society. The importance of this development should not be underestimated, since is offers legitimacy to state intervention in the economy, provided that government policies improve information flows, create or mend institutions, or promote social customs that allow markets to perform better. Nevertheless, the new economic interventionism does not challenge the core of neoliberalism.

In this light, the next section considers briefly the decline of post-war Keynesianism. With hindsight, this development amounts to little more than the re-emergence of the old belief that the capitalist economy is essentially crisis-free. The following section turns to the new economics of information, institutions and customs, showing that it does not provide an effective theoretical critique of capitalism. The final section briefly concludes.

THE DECLINE OF KEYNESIANISM

The Second World War rescued international capitalism from the Great Slump of the 1930s. The war restored production levels, employment, productivity and profitability in the USA, the heartland of the international capitalist economy. The Marshall Plan and associated political attacks on the organised socialist movement in Europe created appropriate conditions for capitalist production also to revive in the ravaged continent. Abundant labour supplies, continuous technological progress and gradual emergence of mass consumption sustained a long economic boom unprecedented in the history of capitalism. The boom rested on US hegemony operating through international institutions, such as the Bretton Woods Agreement, which fixed exchange rates, the International Monetary Fund and the World Bank. Extensive poverty and inequality, as well as oppression and injustice, did not disappear in the developed capitalist world. But the majority of working people in the USA and Western Europe in the 1950s and 1960s could expect stable employment and rising real wages.

At the time, much of the credit for this miracle was laid at the feet of John Maynard Keynes, the most influential economist of the twentieth century. In his *General Theory*, written in the midst of the Great Slump of the 1930s, Keynes attacked the prevailing economic orthodoxy, which he associated with the 'classical' economists, from Adam Smith to his own teacher, the neoclassical Alfred Marshall. The assault was especially poignant because, first, the Great Slump appeared to confirm the tendency of capitalist economies toward crisis and, second, Keynes was a leading figure of mainstream economics, moving comfortably in government circles. Keynes's book had three radical aspects that deeply upset the economic mainstream.

First, Keynes (1936, pp. 18–21) rejected Say's Law, one of the fundamental tenets of economic orthodoxy. Say's Law claims that effective demand and supply in a capitalist economy tend to be equal. The significance of this claim becomes clear in the context of capitalist crises. Such crises are periods during which commodities cannot be sold and workers become unemployed, that is, they are periods during which aggregate supply exceeds aggregate demand. Thus Say's Law essentially claims that long-lasting, spontaneous capitalist crises are impossible. In contrast, Keynes argued that aggregate demand systematically falls short of aggregate supply in capitalist economies. For Keynes, the systemic deficiency of aggregate demand means that free markets fail to clear, thus producing mass unemployment.

Second, and closely related to the first, Keynes rejected the Quantity Theory of Money. This theory, which has been in existence since the eighteenth century, claims that the level of prices is ultimately determined by the quantity of money. Thus the proximate cause of systematic price increases during any period of time is an expansion of the money supply. It is not surprising that Keynes dismissed the Quantity Theory of Money, given that he had already rejected Say's Law. If it is possible for masses of unsold commodities and unemployed workers to emerge in a capitalist economy, as is implied by rejection of Say's Law, it follows that some capitalists must have sold commodities without subsequently spending the money proceeds on other commodities. These capitalists are hoarding money, thus locking up purchasing power and preventing effective demand from reaching the level required to eliminate stocks of unsold commodities and unemployed workers. To capture this phenomenon, Keynes (1936, ch. 15) developed the theory of liquidity preference, i.e. of money hoarding by capitalists and others.

Third, for Keynes, economic activity takes place in irreversible historical time, and therefore economic agents are obliged to form expectations about the future. But the formation of expectations is never entirely rational, and always involves purely psychological impulses. Moreover, economic agents must also form expectations about what others expect, and what others expect still others to expect. There is an irreducible psychological component to economic decision making, which is crucial to Keynes's rejection of orthodox economic thinking.

Keynes's assault on orthodoxy placed him in the camp of economic 'heretics' and 'radicals'. His aim was to build a new macroeconomics that would stand comparison with classical political economy. By postulating that capitalist economies are characterised by systemic deficiency of aggregate demand, Keynes accorded legitimacy to regular government economic intervention. Government measures that boost public expenditure, cut taxes and lower interest rates, with a view to strengthening aggregate demand and reducing unemployment, suddenly became theoretically justified. It is important to note, however, that Keynes's macroeconomics does not rely on a theory of value that differs from that of neoclassical orthodoxy. Equally problematic is Keynes's failure to reconsider in sufficient depth the economic interaction between capitalists and workers. His macroeconomics rests on subjective value theory, while largely accepting the microeconomic fundamentals of neoclassicism. This is a major weakness of Keynes's assault on economic orthodoxy, which allowed neoclassical theory eventually to win the day and remove the radical content of Keynes's macroeconomics.[1]

During the long boom that followed the Second World War, the state played an increasingly direct role in developed capitalist economies (see Chapter 16). The share of government spending in gross domestic product increased steadily and much productive capacity (especially in public utilities) came under public ownership. Moreover, extensive systems of welfare provision were constructed, dealing with health, unemployment benefits, education and housing. It was possible to believe that state economic intervention, theoretically legitimised by Keynes, had finally dealt with the capitalist tendency to generate economic crisis and social dislocation. Apparently, state intervention limited the excesses of private capitalism, eliminated unemployment and provided welfare support for all. Keynesianism became an ideological term that captured the self-satisfied outlook of the 'mixed economy' of the immediate postwar decades.

This ideology found academic support in the macroeconomics of the 'neoclassical synthesis', a theoretical construct that emerged gradually in the 1950s and 1960s in the economics departments of leading US and UK universities. Academic economists watered down the more radical elements of Keynes's macroeconomics until they were unrecognisable. For the 'neoclassical synthesis', mass unemployment would occur only if wages were inflexible downwards, in which case the government had to intervene and shore up aggregate demand. The epitome of this thinking was the Phillips Curve, a shallow concept postulating an inverse relationship between unemployment and inflation, and purporting to offer governments a menu of choice between the two. With hindsight, it is incredible that in the 1960s entire academic libraries were filled with scholarly work focusing on the finer points of the 'neoclassical synthesis'. Contemporary mainstream economics treats the bulk of this theoretical work with indifference and even contempt. Yet it is salutary to remember that the high priests of postwar official Keynesianism were as arrogant and as confident in the validity of their economics as the current crop of academic theorists.

Official Keynesianism was destroyed by the crisis that followed the first oil shock of 1973–74. The persistent combination of high unemployment and high inflation proved impervious to the 'scientific' economic interventions of the major capitalist states. Even worse, increases in public expenditure led to persistent government deficits and appeared to exacerbate the phenomena of global crisis. Profitability collapsed in the mid 1970s, and the price system across several developed countries was severely disrupted, especially through rapid and persistent inflation. The institutions that sustained the postwar boom faced intolerable pressure, none more so than the Bretton Woods Agreement, which was put in abeyance in 1971 and finally collapsed in 1973.

Neoliberalism arose as government reaction to the economic disasters of the second half of the 1970s. In terms of economic policy, its fundamental and longer-lasting component was the abandonment of interventionism that aimed at full employment. Unemployment came to be seen as a necessary price for the restabilisation of capitalist economies. The inevitable accompaniment of this shift was wholesale attacks on labour organisations, especially prominent in Britain under the Thatcher government. Labour market flexibility (in other words, imposing real wage reductions, creating mass unemployment, and favouring the expansion of casual labour) gradually became the mark of healthy capitalist economies. Welfare provision also came under increasing strain, and the state began to retreat from ownership of productive capacity, most notably by privatising public utilities. In the years that followed, official economic ideology increasingly proclaimed the virtues of freely operating markets, and associated state intervention with misallocation of economic resources.

In mainstream economic theory, the charge against Keynesianism was led by Milton Friedman's monetarism, which is a resurrected version of the Quantity Theory of Money.[2] Inflation, the key economic problem of the 1970s, was treated by Friedman as a purely monetary phenomenon resulting from too much money chasing after too few goods. For Friedman, it is not possible for governments to choose among combinations of inflation and unemployment. He argued that capitalist economies have a 'natural rate' of unemployment, and any attempt to bring the actual rate of unemployment below the 'natural' would merely lead to inflation. If governments wished to avoid inflation, they had to rely on the ancient prescriptions of the Quantity Theory, that is, they had to restrain the growth of the money supply. This message was adopted with alacrity by the Thatcher government in Britain and the Reagan administration in the USA in the 1980s, aiming to restrain the rapid inflation that marked the late 1970s.

It did not take long for the essential vacuity of the Quantity Theory of Money to be shown up in practice. During the first half of the 1980s, the empirical relationship between money supply and price inflation became very unstable across the developed capitalist world, giving the lie to the monetarist notion that the quantity of money affects prices in a predictable way. To make things worse, both the British and the US governments actually failed to restrain growth of the money supply. But monetarist policies exacerbated the economic crisis and tremendously increased the numbers of the unemployed. Inflation eventually fell, but only due to the crushing weight of economic recession on consumption and investment.

As Friedman's monetarism fell by the wayside during the 1980s, mainstream macroeconomics gradually came to be dominated by 'new classical economics', associated primarily with Robert Lucas (see Lucas 1972, 1973). The influence of Lucas on macroeconomics during the neoliberal period has been broad and persistent, above all, because it stresses the inherent market-clearing properties of the capitalist economy. In effect, Lucas has resurrected Say's Law, claiming that long-lasting excess supply is not possible. If there is unemployment, that is the result of government policy itself, i.e. of wrong-headed attempts to force aggregate output above levels warranted by the free economic choices of those who participate in the capitalist economy. The implications for government policy are profound: since the economy is essentially self-equilibrating, the state ought to abstain from intervening in its operations. The message of Lucas is stark and has left a strong mark on mainstream macroeconomic policy during the neoliberal era: government macroeconomic intervention is worse than useless – it is actually counterproductive.

Nevertheless, developed capitalist countries have not abandoned the practice of macroeconomic intervention, despite the ideological arguments produced by mainstream economics. On the contrary, whenever economic crises have appeared (a regular phenomenon of the 1980s and 1990s), governments have typically attempted to ameliorate their effects by using combinations of fiscal and monetary policy, that is, through tax cuts, increased public expenditure and lower interest rates. The persistence of macroeconomic intervention, using essentially Keynesian tools and despite official adherence to neoliberalism, has been most apparent in

Japan. During the 1990s, a series of expansionary macroeconomic policies were introduced in an attempt to confront persistent slump. Even in the USA, the original home of neoliberal ideology, expansionary fiscal and monetary policies have often been adopted to confront the spectre of recession, notably after the stock market bubble of 1998–2000.

Thus the practice of macroeconomic intervention has remained very much alive throughout the neoliberal era. Moreover, state expenditure as a proportion of gross domestic product has remained substantial in all developed capitalist countries. The torrents of neoliberal ideological attacks on state economic intervention during the 1980s and 1990s should not obscure the simple fact that the state retains a commanding presence in the operations of contemporary capitalist economies. But what has vanished irretrievably is the notion – characteristic of postwar Keynesianism – that economic intervention should aim at achieving full employment and securing social welfare.

The continuing importance of macroeconomic intervention throughout the 1980s and 1990s has meant that governments have remained constantly in need of economic advice on how to structure their interventions. In this respect, the theoretical attacks on Keynesian macroeconomics during the neoliberal era have done the capitalist state a disservice, since they have offered little to replace postwar Keynesianism as a guide to government action. In recent years, mainstream economics has begun to fill this gap, by relying on theories that analyse information dissemination and the role of institutions in the capitalist economy. But there has been no fundamental break with the underlying neoliberal belief in the beneficial properties of free markets.

ECONOMICS OF INFORMATION, INSTITUTIONS AND SOCIAL NORMS

Contemporary mainstream microeconomics rests on the framework of General Equilibrium developed by Kenneth Arrow and Gerard Debreu after the Second World War (see Arrow and Hahn 1971). General Equilibrium analysis pivots on the 'rational individual', a fantastic creature that aims exclusively at private gain, has no altruism and strictly calculates the necessary means to achieve desired ends, but deploys neither power nor violence to achieve them (see Chapter 5). The natural terrain of economic activity is assumed to be the market, to which the individual brings commodities to be exchanged for those of others. By making further (extremely unrealistic) assumptions, such as full information available to all, a complete range of markets, generalised price taking, and no 'externalities' (i.e. no unintended side effects of market decisions) General Equilibrium analysis can show that free-market exchange achieves economic efficiency.

During the years of neoliberal ascendancy, however, important theoretical developments have taken place within neoclassical microeconomics. The spur for these developments has been provided by the existence of widespread economic phenomena and institutions in a capitalist economy that could not be easily accounted for through the approach of General Equilibrium. One notorious example is the very existence of money. Since money is an asset that is neither directly consumed nor used productively, it appears illogical for 'rational individuals' permanently to keep a part of their wealth as barren money instead of commodities. The observation that money is used as means of exchange cannot provide an answer since, if 'rational individuals' are fully informed price-takers who operate in a complete range of markets, as General Equilibrium assumes them to be, there is no reason for them to use a means of exchange. They could instead plan a series of direct commodity exchanges in advance, avoiding the need to hold money that confers no benefits of consumption or production. In short, for pure General Equilibrium, money has neither a logical place nor a role in a capitalist economy. Modern neoclassical microeconomics finds itself in the bizarre position of treating capitalism – the most heavily monetised society ever - as a society of direct exchange, or barter.

Since the early 1970s, neoclassical microeconomics has devoted much effort to confronting awkward theoretical puzzles, such as those posed by money, but also by banks, various labour practices and market irregularities. The favourite approach has been to relax the assumption of full information among those who are economically active. Instead, economists typically assume that capitalist markets are characterised by the asymmetric spread of information among participants. The capitalist economy is still taken to comprise rational and egoistic individuals, but they are assumed to possess different amounts of information regarding the uses of commodities, the productivity of labour, the quality of investment plans, and so on. The point is that, if two asymmetrically informed individuals entered into economic give and take, the better informed could take advantage of the other, thereby obtaining a disproportionately large share of the benefits. It is intuitive, and can be shown formally, that under such conditions the putative efficiency of free markets would disappear. Information asymmetry implies that free-market trading is inefficient, a result that could be used theoretically to account for a variety of economic phenomena.[3]

The burgeoning of information-theoretic analysis within mainstream economics has been accompanied by increasing theoretical emphasis on the institutions and norms that pervade the capitalist economy. Douglass North, one of the pillars of this approach, has stressed that economic institutions are social conventions that shape the choices of 'rational individuals' (see North 1981, 1990, 1999). For North, economic transactions in open markets always carry costs for the participants. These vary from the costs attached to reaching an agreement (designing a contract) to those implied in enforcing it. The institutions that surround markets determine the magnitude of these costs. Consequently, the performance of institutions influences the decision making of economic agents and therefore the efficiency of the capitalist economy. Naturally, the institution that ultimately exercises the greatest influence on economic activity is the state, which always operates within a cultural and historical context. Along similar lines, Oliver Williamson has also focused on the transactions costs of commodity exchange, and stressed the role of institutions in lessening these costs and therefore improving market efficiency. For Williamson, economic institutions are characterised by hierarchy and direct command over others; these features of institutions improve the allocation of resources and reduce transactions costs (see Williamson 1975, 1985).

The stress on institutions and transactions costs within mainstream microeconomics has accompanied a broader shift toward incorporating social norms and customs into economic analysis. Microeconomics has traditionally recognised only economic motivations and impulses for the 'rational individual' (the dry calculus of cost and benefit). However, in the 1980s and 1990s mainstream economists have begun to acknowledge that market participants may also act under the influence of social norms. These are practices and stimuli resulting from social influences that extend beyond the narrowly economic, such as social etiquette, or sexual behaviour. The social norm of 'working', for instance, the prevalent notion among workers that work is 'good', while unemployment is 'bad', could exercise a significant influence on the labour market behaviour of young workers. In a similar spirit, economists could claim that there is tension between, on the one hand, the norm of 'working' and, on the other, the 'laziness' generated by welfare handouts, which could affect individual decisions to enter the labour market.[4]

The gradual transformation of microeconomics since the early 1970s has contributed to the emergence of a 'new political economy' that has often been critical of the neoliberal belief in free markets. Information asymmetries, for instance, could lead to inefficient performance, or even collapse, of markets. It follows that appropriate institutions are required to support markets and forestall their collapse. A favourable light is once again shone on state economic intervention, provided that such intervention is 'friendly' to markets and aims at removing their imperfections.

The labour market could provide an example of such intervention, since its imperfections could be thought to cause unemployment. Hence state intervention might be necessary to improve information flows as well as the design and enforcement of employment contracts, thus presumably securing higher levels of employment. Another example is given by financial markets, which could malfunction grossly in the face of asymmetric information (lack of transparency). Hence the state would be justified in intervening in the sphere of finance, as long as its interventions improved information and removed imperfections. More broadly, the social norms underpinning capitalist economic activity, such as honesty and trustworthiness, could be manipulated or strengthened through social policy in order to improve economic efficiency. Gradually and imperceptibly, a new interventionism has emerged within mainstream economics, focusing on the microeconomic aspects of the capitalist economy and advocating market-friendly government action to ameliorate market imperfections.

The leading figure in the new interventionist current has been Joseph Stiglitz, Nobel prizewinner and adviser to US presidents and international institutions. Stiglitz's influence became marked in the 1990s, especially in connection with developing countries. In the realm of development economics, theoretical thinking until the early 1970s was dominated by the desirability of state intervention and the need consciously to manage the development process. After the early 1970s, and as neoliberalism rose in the developed world, the so-called Washington consensus came to dominate development thinking, especially within the IMF, the World Bank and other international organisations (see Chapter 12 and Fine et al. 2001). The Washington consensus is a set of neoliberal ideas, demanding of developing countries that they should achieve macroeconomic stability (typically by cutting government spending, including subsidies to the poor), deregulate their domestic markets, privatise state enterprises, and open their economies to foreign trade and finance. Not surprisingly, the results of such policies have been deeply disappointing in terms of growth and income per capita throughout the 1980s and 1990s. Meanwhile, financial crises have become a regular occurrence in the developing world. Since the early 1990s, Stiglitz has led a sustained attack on the Washington consensus, drawing on information-theoretic analysis and advocating state intervention with some limited controls on markets.

Stiglitz's attack on the Washington consensus has been naturally attractive to those engaged in confronting neoliberalism, especially in the developing world. Consequently, it is important to recognise that Stiglitz's radicalism is far less profound than that of Keynes. Despite his criticisms of free markets, Stiglitz has no fundamental theoretical quarrel with contemporary mainstream neoclassicism. Much less does he seek to show that the capitalist economy is inherently unstable, tending to generate unemployment and crisis. On the contrary, for Stiglitz, if markets could operate as stipulated by pure economic theory, capitalism would indeed be the most efficient system possible. Unfortunately, however, markets have imperfections due to informational reasons, which prevent them from operating perfectly. Consequently, Stiglitz's essential message is that state intervention should deal with market imperfections in order precisely to improve the performance of markets.

Both the neoliberal Washington consensus and Stiglitz's alternative approach take it for granted that markets are superior to all other social mechanisms for allocating resources and organising the economy. The common ground between the two is evident in so far as arguments from the new microeconomics have already become incorporated in the policy prescriptions and analyses of international economic organisations. The pronouncements of the IMF and the World Bank since the early 1990s have been typically replete with references to the need to improve information flows, increase transparency, reduce corruption, and generally create a social environment within which markets can perform better. Meanwhile, the neoliberal core of the economic policies of the international organisations has remained unaltered.

INSTEAD OF A CONCLUSION: THE CONTINUING RELEVANCE OF MARXIST POLITICAL ECONOMY

The years of neoliberal ascendancy have not been kind to Marxist political economy. Gradually but inexorably, Marxist economics has lost prestige and influence, including within the academe. It is not easy to explain this marginalisation, especially since it has occurred during a period of repeated international capitalist crises, but the loss of influence of the workers' movement and the collapse of the Soviet Union have undoubtedly contributed to it. Despite the loss of influence, Marxist political economy remains the main alternative to mainstream economics, and is as relevant as ever to those opposed to capitalist exploitation and oppression. Marxist economics demonstrates the inherent instability of capitalist economies and the inefficiency of free markets. It has little difficulty confronting the more thoughtless defences of free markets and the ideological rants of free-market warriors. It has even less difficulty showing that the adoption of neoliberal policies across the world, particularly in developing countries, has brought disastrous results for the poor and the weak.

It has been shown in this chapter that the peak of the theoretical influence of neoliberalism has passed. Even from within mainstream economics, critical currents of thought focusing on information, institutions and social norms have shaken the simple ideological belief in the optimality of capitalist markets. The rise of a new interventionism within mainstream economic theory poses complex challenges for Marxist political economy. Marxism gives pride of place to the social framework within which the capitalist economy operates, and treats institutions, information and social norms as vitally important for the performance of the capitalist economy. But Marxist economics also demonstrates the exploitative and oppressive character of the capitalist economy. Capitalist institutions and social norms are deeply influenced by the class divisions at the heart of capitalist society. The performance of the capitalist economy cannot be separated from exploitation, oppression and conflict among classes in capitalist society (see Chapter 5). This also holds for the economic interventions of the capitalist state, which are never innocent of class interests and conflicts.

Mainstream economic critics of neoliberalism have successfully refocused attention on the weaknesses of capitalist markets, while taking cognisance of the social aspects of the capitalist economy. But even the most radical among the critics typically avoid recognising the implications of capitalist class divisions and power. Indeed, they recoil at the mere mention of social class in theoretical analysis. Consequently, they are incapable of providing effective support to those engaged in opposing capitalist exploitation and oppression. This task continues to fall to Marxist political economy.

NOTES

1. In this respect, there is a sharp contrast between Keynes and Marx, who also rejected Say's Law and the Quantity Theory of Money. Marx based his economic analysis on the labour theory of value and the exploitative nature of capitalist–worker relations. His theoretical challenge to economic orthodoxy has proved longer lasting than that of Keynes (Itoh and Lapavitsas, 1999, ch. 2, p. 6).
2. Friedman's extensive work, despite enjoying enormous influence in the 1970s and 1980s, is very little read today. Key texts for the summary given here are Friedman (1956, 1970).
3. See, for instance, Akerlof (1970), Spence (1973), Stiglitz (1974), Grossman and Stiglitz (1980) and Stiglitz (1994).
4. For examples of the significance of social norms on the performance of various markets see Akerlof (1984).

REFERENCES

Akerlof, G. (1970) 'The Market for "Lemons": Quality Uncertainty and the Market Mechanism', *Quarterly Journal of Economics* 84, pp. 488–500.
Akerlof, G. (1984) *An Economic Theorist's Book of Tales*. Cambridge: Cambridge University Press.

Arrow, K. and Hahn, F. (1971) *General Competitive Analysis*. Amsterdam: North Holland.

Fine, B. Lapavitsas, C. and Pincus, J. (eds) (2001) *Development Policy in the Twenty-First Century*. London: Routledge.

Friedman, M. (1956) 'The Quantity Theory of Money: A Restatement', in *Studies in the Quantity Theory of Money*. Chicago: University of Chicago Press.

Friedman, M. (1970) *The Counter-Revolution in Monetary Theory*. IEA Occasional Paper 33, Institute of Economic Affairs: London.

Grossman, S. and Stiglitz, J. (1980) 'On the Impossibility of Informationally Efficient Markets', *American Economic Review* 70, pp. 393–408.

Itoh M. and Lapavitsas C. (1999) *Political Economy of Money and Finance*. London: Macmillan.

Keynes, J.M. 1936 (1973) *The General Theory of Employment, Interest, and Money*. London: Macmillan.

Lucas, R. (1972) 'Expectations and the Neutrality of Money', *Journal of Economic Theory* 4, pp. 103–24.

Lucas, R. (1973) 'Some International Evidence on Output-Inflation Tradeoffs', *American Economic Review* 63(3), pp. 326–34.

North, D.C. (1981) *Structure and Change in Economic History*. New York: W.W. Norton.

North, D.C. (1990) *Institutions, Institutional Change and Economic Performance*. Cambridge: Cambridge University Press.

North, D.C. (1999) *Understanding the Process of Economic Change*. London: Institute of Economic Affairs.

Spence, M. (1973) 'Job Market Signalling', *Quarterly Journal of Economics* 87, pp. 355–74.

Stiglitz, J. (1974) 'Incentives and Risk Sharing in Sharecropping', *Review of Economic Studies* 41, pp.219–55.

Stiglitz, J. (1994) 'The Role of the State in Financial Markets', *Proceedings of the World Bank Annual Conference on Development Economics 1993*, pp.19–52.

Williamson, O. (1975) *Markets and Hierarchies*. New York: Free Press.

Williamson, O. (1985) *The Economic Institutions of Capitalism*. New York: Free Press.

4

The Economic Mythology of Neoliberalism

Anwar Shaikh

We live in a world characterised by enormous wealth and widespread poverty. The richest countries have an annual GDP per capita greater than US$30,000, while the poorest countries have one less than US$1,000. And even that appalling lower level is misleadingly high, because great inequality within countries means that the poor live on far less than the average. More than 1.2 billion people, one in every five people on this earth, are forced to live on less than US$1 a day. Except in China, the past decade of rapid globalisation has been associated with increased poverty and hunger. More than 13 million children died from diarrhoeal disease over this period. At present, over half a million women die each year in pregnancy and childbirth, one for each minute of the day. More than 800 million suffer from malnutrition (see Chapter 15 and UNDP 2003, pp. 5–8, 40). Yet we have long had the means, on a world scale, to provide decent food, medical care, and shelter for the earth's whole population.

What is the best way, for the world as a whole, to tackle such problems? The prevalent answer is surprising in its simplicity: through unrestricted global trade. This is the essence of the doctrine called neoliberalism.

THE THEORY AND PRACTICE OF NEOLIBERALISM

Neoliberalism dominates modern globalisation. Its practice is justified by a set of theoretical claims rooted in standard economic theory. Markets are represented as optimal and self-regulating social structures. It is claimed that if markets were allowed to function without restraint, they would optimally serve all economic needs, efficiently utilise all economic resources and automatically generate full employment for all persons who truly wish to work. By extension, the globalisation of markets would be the best way to extend these benefits to the whole world. To quote Mike Moore, former Director General of the World Trade Organisation, 'the surest way to do more to help the [world's] poor is to continue to open markets' (cited in Agosin and Tussie 1993, p. 9). This is the first axiom of neoliberalism.

From this point of view, the reason that we have poverty, unemployment and periodic economic crises in the modern world is because markets have been constrained by labour unions, the state, and a host of social practices rooted in culture and history. This reading of history is meant to apply not only to conditions in the poor countries of the world, but also to those in the rich ones. It follows that successful globalisation requires the creation of 'market-friendly' social structures throughout the world: by curtailing union strength so that employers can hire and fire whom they choose; by privatising state enterprises so that their workers will fall under the purview of domestic capital; and by opening up domestic markets to foreign capital and foreign goods. This is the second axiom of neoliberalism.

The theory and practice of neoliberalism has generated substantial opposition from activists, policy makers and academics. Nonetheless, this conception still has enormous authority. It continues to be a major influence in the social sciences, in popular understanding, and most of all, in policy circles. As a practical matter, the powerful nations and institutions supporting this agenda have succeeded in greatly extending the rule of markets. And as an equally practical matter, enormous poverty and deep inequality continue to exist, and crises continue to erupt, all around the globe.

FREE TRADE THEORY AS THE ECONOMIC RATIONALE FOR NEOLIBERALISM

The rationale for neoliberalism rests on the orthodox theory of free trade, whose central claim is that competitive free trade will automatically benefit all nations (see Chapter 10). As Paul Krugman has noted, this is a 'sacred tenet' of (standard) economic theory (Krugman 1987, p. 131). To appreciate its significance, consider the following dialogue. Critics point out that the world today is very far from the competitive conditions assumed in standard free trade theory. They remind us that although the rich countries now preach free trade, when they were themselves climbing the ladder of development they relied heavily on trade protectionism and state intervention. They point out that even now, rich countries often do not follow their own preaching (Agosin and Tussie 1993, p. 25; Rodrik 2001, p. 11; Chang 2002; Stiglitz 2002).

The defenders of neoliberalism have a ready response to this charge. Truly competitive conditions did not hold in the past, they say, so the past is not a useful guide. However, with the help of international institutions, competition can be spread throughout the globe. And when it is, free trade will work as promised. It is therefore essential to eliminate restrictions on markets, particularly in the developing world (Bhagwati 2002, lecture 1). This is the central conclusion of neoliberalism.

Posed this way, the debate centres on how closely, and at what social cost, actual markets can be made sufficiently competitive. To the critics of neoliberalism, markets will never work in the textbook manner because power rules the modern world: monopoly power, class power, state power and the power of the centre over the periphery (McCartney 2004). Attempting to force-fit a competitive model onto actual society would be unsuccessful, and would lead to widespread 'collateral damage'. To the defenders, the putative long-term benefits of the market justify the short-term transition costs. All the more so if the cost happens to be borne by others. In its extreme form, which used to be called 'shock therapy' by its proponents, it is claimed that the best way to proceed would be through an all-out assault on the offending institutions and practices.

What is striking about this debate is that both sides accept a fundamental premise of neoliberalism. Namely, that given sufficiently competitive conditions, free trade *would* work as promised. This chapter argues that this claim is wrong, even on its own grounds. It is not the absence of competition that produces development alongside underdevelopment, wealth alongside poverty, employment alongside unemployment. *It is competition itself.*

Free trade between nations operates in much the same manner as competition within a nation: it favours the (competitively) strong over the weak. From this point of view, collateral damage from globalisation is to be expected. This also tells us that the developed countries were quite right to recognise, when they were on the way up, that unrestricted international competition was a threat to their own plans for development. What they so strenuously deny now, they knew to be true then. Namely, that the great power of the market is best utilised when it is harnessed to a broader social agenda.

THE LOGIC OF STANDARD FREE TRADE THEORY

Textbook introductions to free trade theory begin with a deliberate misrepresentation. We are asked to treat two nations as *individuals* engaged in freely undertaken barter. Such individuals, we are told, would only give over something in return for something else if they each thought they were going to gain in the process. And if their expectations were correct, each would indeed gain. Hence free trade would benefit all those who engage in it. All the rest is detail.

But like any magic trick, this incorporates a central misdirection. In a capitalist world, it is *businesses* that engage in foreign trade. Domestic exporters sell to foreign importers who in turn sell to their residents, while domestic importers buy from foreign exporters and sell to us. At each step in the chain, it is profit that motivates the business decision. The theory of international trade is actually a subset of the theory of competition. In order to make standard free-trade theory come out right, it is therefore necessary to show that international competition is always beneficial. This is the real thrust of standard free-trade theory, and the real foundation of neoliberalism. If it is addressed at all, it is only in advanced textbooks.[1] Doubts might creep in, otherwise.

Several things are necessary to make the story come out right. First, if trade between any two nations leads to imbalances between exports and imports, it is necessary that these provoke compensating relative price changes. Suppose a nation is running a trade deficit. This means that the value of the goods sold abroad by its exporters is less than the value of the goods sold domestically by its importers. For this imbalance to be automatically corrected, it is necessary that exports become cheaper to foreigners, who would then presumably buy more; and that imports become more expensive to domestic buyers, who would then presumably buy less. Second, these relative price changes must be effective in reducing the trade deficit. This means that they must raise the money value of exports relative to that of imports. The opposite is perfectly possible. For instance, suppose that export prices fall by (say) 10 per cent, and foreigners buy 5 per cent more of these goods. Then the total money value of exports will have *fallen* rather than risen, because the decline in price was greater than the rise in quantity. Thus the standard theory also needs to assume that quantities sold are sufficiently responsive to prices.[2] In the language of international trade theory, the first requirement is that a country's terms of trade (export prices relative to import prices, in common currency) automatically fall when it experiences a trade deficit, while the second requirement is that this fall be sufficient to eliminate the trade deficit. Taken together, these two assumptions would ensure that trade deficits, and trade surpluses also, would be self-negating. Then, regardless of differences in levels of development, in resources, in labour costs, or in anything else, each nation would be able to hold its own in the world market. In other words, free trade would then ensure that each nation ends up being competitive in the world market (Arndt and Richardson 1987, p. 12).

While the preceding assumptions are necessary to make the story work, they are not sufficient. We also need to consider the implications for employment. Countries exposed to trade may lose jobs in some sectors and gain them in others. Some firms may prosper, while others may go out of existence. None of this excludes the possibility of overall job losses in the countries involved. So we need something more. Standard theory solves this problem by assuming that competitive markets automatically provide jobs for all who desire them. When this is carried over to trade theory, it ensures that the international adjustments will not lead to any overall job losses, because those who lose one job are presumed to find another. This is the third pillar of the conventional theory of international trade.

To summarise. Standard trade theory relies on three claims. First, that any deficit in a nation's trade would provoke a fall in its export prices relative to its import prices, i.e. a fall in its terms of trade. Second, that such a fall would increase the money value of exports relative to that of imports, i.e. would improve the trade balance. This requires the relative physical ratio of exports to imports to rise more than the fall in relative price of exports to imports, i.e. that the 'elasticities' be propitious. And third, that once the dust has settled, no nation would suffer overall job losses from international trade. These three propositions constitute *the neoclassical theory of comparative cost advantage*. They collectively imply that nations will always gain from international trade.

It is important to distinguish between the theory of comparative *cost* advantage and the theory of comparative *factor* advantage. The two are often confused, although they are conceptually distinct. The theory of comparative cost advantage implies that international trade between nations will settle at balanced trade with no departure from full employment in both nations. Even if one of the nations had absolutely lower costs when trade opened, and was therefore able to run an initial trade *surplus*, the theory of comparative costs says that free trade would automatically eliminate this initial superiority. To understand what this implies, suppose that when trade opened we were to rank all industries in the surplus nation according to their degree of absolute cost advantage over their foreign competitors. Then, for free trade automatically to erode the trade surplus, the industries with the *least* initial absolute advantage would be the first to lose their cost advantage (we will shortly return to the mechanism proposed by the theory). This would have to be repeated on the survivors, until the tide of red ink had proceeded sufficiently far up the chain to make the initial trade surplus disappear altogether. The final survivors would then be from those industries at the top of the chain, i.e. from those with the greatest initial 'comparative' cost advantage. Obviously, the reverse would hold for the country whose initial absolute inferiority in trade led it to begin with a trade deficit. Here, the most favoured would be the industries with the least initial comparative cost *dis*advantage.

Comparative factor advantage theory assumes that the theory of comparative cost advantage regulates trade, and seeks instead to explain which particular industries in a given country would be at the top of the comparative cost advantage chain. The basic answer is that it would be those industries whose production benefits the most from the cheap local input. And the locally cheap input would in turn be explained by the relative abundance of the corresponding 'factor of production' (land, labour, capital). Thus if land was relatively abundant in some country, then according to factor advantage theory, land-intensive industries such as agriculture would be the most likely to have a comparative cost advantage in international trade.[3]

TROUBLE IN PARADISE

We have seen that standard trade theory concludes that market forces would automatically eliminate trade imbalances, while maintaining full employment throughout. Thus international trade provides access to cheaper, and/or more desirable, commodities without harming anyone. All would be best in the best of all possible worlds, if nations only allowed the market to work its magic.

The first difficulty with this story is that the empirical evidence does not support it at all. Trade imbalances have not been automatically eliminated, not in the developing world, not even in the developed world, not in the past, not in the present, not under fixed exchange rates, not under flexible exchange rates (Harvey 1996). On the contrary, persistent imbalances are absolutely common. For instance, the United States has been running a trade deficit for almost 30 years and Japan has been enjoying a trade surplus for almost 40. A similar problem arises for the claim that full employment is a natural consequence of competitive markets. Just in the last decade, even developed countries have suffered unemployment rates ranging from 3 per cent to 25 per cent. Matters are much worse, of course, in the *developing* world, where there are 1.3 billion unemployed or underemployed people at the current time (ILO 2001), many of whom have no prospects of reasonable employment in their lifetime. A significant number of economists argue that capitalism produces no automatic tendency towards full employment, even in the advanced world. This has long been the foundation of Keynesian and Kaleckian analysis (see Chapters 2 and 3).

The second difficulty is that standard international trade theory requires one to perform an extraordinary theoretical about-face in the treatment of competition. When economists discuss competition *within a nation*, they are clear that it rewards the strong over the weak. If two sets of firms are competing in the same market, those with lower costs will tend to beat out those with higher costs. The former will expand their reach, while the latter will contract. Economists celebrate this outcome as a virtue of competition, since it winnows out weaker firms. The same reasoning applies to any two *regions* within a nation. A region with low-cost producers will tend to be able to sell many of its products in the high-cost region, without buying much from it. Thus the low-cost region will enjoy a regional trade surplus, while the high-cost region will suffer a regional trade deficit. Orthodox economists do not find this problematic, because they assume that those who lose jobs in the weaker region will find new jobs in the stronger one.

Yet when these same economists discuss competition *between nations*, i.e. international trade, they abandon their previous theory and substitute a different one. Whereas competition within a country is said to punish the weak and reward the strong, competition between countries is said to fortify the weak and debilitate the strong. While this may be appealing as a biblical vision, it is somewhat lacking in descriptive value. Where, then, is the catch?

REAL COMPETITION ON AN INTERNATIONAL SCALE

International trade theory stops being mysterious as soon as one recognises that real international competition works in the same way as national competition: it favours the competitively strong over the competitively weak (Shaikh 1980, 1996; Milberg 1993, 1994).

Let us return for a moment to the case of competition within a nation, between two of its regions. We saw that all schools agree on the outcome in this instance: the region with low-cost producers will tend to enjoy a regional trade surplus, while the high-cost region will tend to suffer a regional trade deficit. In the case of competition between two nations, all schools also agree that a similar outcome obtains *at first*, when international trade is opened up. The country with the initially lower costs of production will tend to enjoy a national trade surplus, and the other a trade deficit. Moreover, all sides agree that the country with the trade surplus will be a net recipient of international funds, since it will be selling more abroad than it is buying. The trade deficit country will in turn suffer an outflow of funds.

It is at this point that a critical divergence arises between standard trade theory and the theory of real competition. Standard trade theory says that in the country with a trade surplus, if the authorities maintained the exchange rate at a fixed level, the resulting inflow of funds would raise the country's general price level. This means that export prices would be raised also. Conversely, if the authorities allowed the exchange rate to respond to market pressures, standard theory says that the inflow of funds would raise the exchange rate, which would make exports more expensive to foreigners. The opposite movement would take place in the trade deficit country. Thus the surplus country would find its export prices rising in foreign markets, and its import prices falling in domestic markets, due to automatic movements in the real exchange rate (the nominal exchange rate adjusted for the price level).[4] In other words, the terms of trade of the surplus country would automatically rise, while that of the deficit country would automatically fall. This is the foundational premise of the theory of comparative costs.

It is a necessary implication of comparative cost theory that once nations engage in international trade, relative prices of commodities are *no longer* regulated by their relative costs of production. At the opening of trade, competition in each nation would have produced relative prices regulated by relative costs. Hence the terms of trade, which are merely international relative prices, would initially also be regulated by the relative costs of exports and imports. But comparative cost theory requires that the terms of trade subsequently move in such a way as to balance trade. It follows that they can no longer be regulated by relative costs. They cannot serve two masters (Shaikh 1980, 1996).

The theory of real competition comes to the very opposite conclusion. Competition forces prices, and hence terms of trade, to be regulated by relative real costs at all times. In a country that enjoys an initial trade surplus, the resulting inflow of funds would enhance the availability of credit, which would lower interest rates. Conversely, in the country with the initial trade deficit, the fund outflow would tighten the credit market and raise interest rates. With interest rates lower in the surplus country and higher in the deficit country, profit-seeking capital would flow from the former to the latter. Thus the surplus country would become a net lender on the world market, and the deficit country a net borrower. Instead of eliminating the trade imbalances, this would end up offsetting them with capital flows. Trade imbalances would be *persistent* and deficit countries in particular would become international debtors. This is an exceedingly familiar historical picture.

The theory of real competition therefore implies that international trade will favour those countries able to produce at the lowest real costs. Real costs are in turn dependent on three factors: real wages, the level of technological development and the availability of natural resources. High real wages raise costs, but high levels of technology and easily available natural resources lower costs.

Rich countries have high levels of technology, often have abundant natural resources, but have high real wages. Poor countries generally have low levels of technology, sometimes have abundant natural resources, and have low real wages. International competition, i.e. free trade, would bring these two different constellations into collision. In each country, internationally competitive sectors would gain, while those at a disadvantage would suffer. Jobs would be created in expanding sectors, and lost in contracting ones.

Given the situation, the poor countries would tend to be forced into those sectors in which their low wages more than compensated for their less developed technologies, and those in which their natural resources, if any, gave them a sufficient cost advantage. Conversely, rich countries would tend to have an advantage in high technology sectors and in certain natural resources.

But this is not a viable international division of labour. First of all, nothing in real competition guarantees that trade will be balanced in any country. Indeed, it is entirely possible that individual countries might have very few sectors that would be competitive on the world market, and hence might have very limited exports. Countries with persistent trade deficits (exports less than imports) would be forced to run down their reserves and to depend on foreign borrowing (foreign capital inflows) to cover such deficits. Currency crises and economic crashes often result in such circumstances. Secondly, nothing guarantees that job gains would cancel out job losses. So it is entirely possible that some countries would be worse off than before in terms of employment. Thirdly, even the low-wage advantage of poor countries would be eroded unless their technologies advanced *more rapidly,* and/or their real wages advanced *less rapidly* than in the rich countries. The crucial variable in this dynamic is the differential in technological progress: if the rich countries are advancing at a faster pace, then the poor countries have to widen the real-wage gap even to maintain what cost advantages they have. This would be the very antithesis of development. Yet there is nothing in free trade that would ensure that poor countries would develop at a sufficiently rapid technological pace. Finally, it is possible that cheap labour in poor countries could become a powerful attractant for foreign capital, whose advanced technologies would allow them to take full advantage of the low wages. They might move operations, so that workers in the rich countries might lose some jobs; or they might create new operations. But in either case, they would drive out local labour-intensive production and displace many workers. Foreign capitals would certainly profit in the process, but it does not follow that they would create more jobs than they would destroy. This is certainly not their goal, at any rate.

DEVELOPMENT AS AN END IN ITSELF

Neoliberalism claims that free trade is the best way to foster economic development. But its doctrine is premised on the faulty notion that international competition levels the mighty and raises up the weak. Real competition operates quite differently: it rewards the strong and punishes the weak. From this perspective, the neoliberal push for unfettered free trade can be viewed as a strategy that is most beneficial to the advanced firms of the rich countries.

This also explains why the Western countries themselves, and subsequently Japan, South Korea and the Asian Tigers, resisted free-trade theories and policies so strenuously when they were themselves moving up the ladder. Equally importantly, it allows us to make sense of the actual policies that they followed in their rise to success: using international access to markets, knowledge and resources as part of a greater social agenda. The object should not be to level the playing field, but to bring up the levels of the disadvantaged players. In this regard, practising neoliberalism on the poor of the world is a particularly cruel sport.

NOTES

1. Intermediate textbooks sometimes cover the gap between the fictional story of nations-as-individuals and the required elaboration of the real laws of international competition by substituting a normative proposition in between the two. 'Nations', it is said, *should* engage in trade according to the principles of comparative advantage, because then each will benefit from trade. This is like saying that nations should not engage in imperialism, wars or looting. It may be gratifying as a hope; it comes up a bit short on explaining actual outcomes (Magee 1980, pp. xiv, 19).

2. This last requirement is known as the 'elasticities conditions'. The trade balance can be expressed as the ratio of the value of exports to the value of imports. If this is less than one, the nation has a trade deficit. If export prices fell and this induced a rise in the quantity of exports sold, this does not guarantee that the *value* of exports would rise. Similarly, a rise in import prices might lower the quantity of imports sold but does not guarantee that the value of imports would fall. Thus the balance of trade need not improve even if terms of trade behave in the manner assumed, unless quantities are sufficiently responsive (elastic). The elasticities conditions are a set of restrictions needed to make the story come out right.

3. The neoclassical version of this argument is formalised in the standard Heckscher–Ohlin–Samuelson (HOS) model. This model advances the further proposition that international trade in commodities alone, without any need for direct flows of labour and capital, will tend to equalise real wages and profit rates across countries. This is known as the 'factor price equalisation theorem' of the HOS model (Magee, 1980, ch. 2).

4. Consider the following example. Japan opens international trade with a trade surplus, an average export price of 1,000 yen per unit and an average import price of 2,000 yen per unit ($20 per imported unit at an exchange rate of 0.01 $/yen). The initial terms of trade is therefore 1,000/2,000 = 1/2. According to standard theory, if the exchange rate were fixed, the Japanese trade surplus would cause inflation in Japan, and the US trade deficit would cause deflation in the United States. Thus Japanese export prices would rise to say 1,200 yen per unit, while US export prices, which are Japanese import prices, would fall to say $16 per unit (1,600 yen per unit at the fixed exchange rate). Alternately, if the exchange rate were flexible, it might rise to say 0.015 $/yen. This would not affect domestic prices of Japanese exports (1,000 yen), but would raise the price of imports from the US to 1,333 yen ($20/0.015). In either case, the Japanese terms of trade would have risen from 1/2, to 1,200/1,600 = 1,000/1,333 = 3/4. Japan's initial competitive advantage would therefore have been automatically eroded, as would the initial competitive *dis*advantage of the United States.

REFERENCES

Agosin, M.R. and Tussie, D. (1993) 'Trade and Growth: New Dilemmas in Trade Policy – An Overview', in *Trade and Growth: New Dilemmas in Trade Policy*. London: Macmillan.

Arndt, S.W. and Richardson, J.D. (eds) (1987) *Real-Financial Linkages among Open Economies*. Cambridge, Mass.: MIT Press.

Bhagwati, J. (2002) *Free Trade Today*. Princeton: Princeton University Press.

Chang, H.-J. (2002) *Kicking Away the Ladder: Development Strategy in Historical Perspective*. London: Anthem Press.

Harvey J.T. (1996) 'Orthodox approaches to exchange rate determination: a survey', *Journal of Post-Keynesian Economics* 18 (4), pp. 567–83.

ILO (International Labour Organisation) (2001) *World Employment Report*. Geneva: ILO.

Krugman, P. (1987) 'Is Free Trade Passé?', *Journal of Economic Perspectives* 1 (2), pp. 131–46.

Magee, S.P. (1980) *International Trade*. Reading, Mass.: Addison-Wesley.

McCartney, M. (2004) 'Liberalisation and Social Structure: The Case of Labour Intensive Export Growth in South Asia', *Post-Autistic Economics Review* 23 (5) <http://www.btinternet.com/~pae_news/review/issue23.htm>.

Milberg, W. (1993) 'The Rejection of Comparative Advantage in Keynes and Marx', mimeo, Department of Economics, New School for Social Research.

Milberg, W. (1994) 'Is Absolute Advantage Passé? Towards a Keynesian/Marxian Theory of International Trade', in M. Glick (ed.) *Competition,Technology and Money: Classical and Post-Keynesian Perspectives*. Aldershot: Edward Elgar.

Rodrik, D. (2001) *The Global Governance of Trade: As if Trade Really Mattered*, United Nations Development Programme (UNDP).

Shaikh, A. (1980) 'The Law of International Exchange', in E.J. Nell (ed.) *Growth, Profits and Property*. Cambridge: Cambridge University Press.

Shaikh, A. (1996) 'Free Trade, Unemployment and Economic Policy', in John Eatwell (ed.) *Global Unemployment: Loss of Jobs in the 90s*. Armonk, N.Y.: M.E. Sharpe.

Stiglitz, J.E. (2002) *Globalisation and its Discontents*. New York: W.W. Norton.

UNDP (United Nations Development Programme) (2003) *Human Development Report*. Geneva: UNDP.

5

The Neoliberal Theory of Society

Simon Clarke

Neoliberalism presents itself as a doctrine based on the inexorable truths of modern economics. However, modern economics is not a scientific discipline but the systematic elaboration of a very specific social theory. The foundations of neoliberalism go back to Adam Smith's *Wealth of Nations*. Over the past two centuries, Smith's arguments have been formalised and developed with greater analytical rigour, but the fundamental assumptions underpinning neoliberalism remain those proposed by Adam Smith (see Chapter 3).

Smith laid the foundations of neoliberalism with his attack on the parasitic mercantilist state that derived its revenues from the restriction of trade. Smith argued that free exchange was a transaction from which both parties necessarily benefited, since nobody would voluntarily engage in an exchange from which they would emerge worse off. As Milton Friedman put it, neoliberalism rests on the 'elementary proposition that both parties to an economic transaction benefit from it, provided the transaction is bilaterally voluntary and informed' (1962, p. 55). Consequently, any restriction on the freedom of trade will reduce well-being by denying individuals the opportunity to improve their situation. Moreover, Smith argued, the expansion of the market permitted increasing specialisation and so the development of the division of labour. The advantages gained through exchange were not advantages gained by one party at the expense of another. Exchange was the means by which the advantages gained through the increased division of labour were shared between the two parties to the exchange. The immediate implication of Smith's argument is that any barriers to the freedom of exchange limit the development of the division of labour and so the growth of the wealth of the nation and the prosperity of each and every one of its citizens.

Adam Smith did not expect his scientific arguments to have much impact, because of the political weight of the vested interests associated with the mercantilist state; but by the beginning of the nineteenth century, Smith's doctrines had been transformed from a subversive attack on a parasitic state to become the ideological orthodoxy of a liberalising state (Clarke 1988, ch. 1). The role of the state was no longer to restrict and to tax trade, but to use all its powers to extend the freedom of trade within and beyond its national boundaries.

THE ROMANTIC AND SOCIALIST CRITIQUES OF LIBERALISM

The liberal doctrines propounded by Adam Smith came under attack from two directions. On the one hand, Smith's ideal society was one of isolated individuals, each pursuing his own self-interest (while women and children remained dependants within the family) – as Margaret Thatcher notoriously proclaimed: 'There is no such thing as society. There are individual men and women, and there are families' (*Woman's Own*, 3 October 1987; see Chapter 17). Smith's 'romantic' critics argued that this model ignores the most distinctive characteristics of human society – morality, religion, art and culture – which provide higher values than the individual and elevate humanity above the animal condition of seeking immediate gratification. On the other hand, experience soon showed that the benefits of free trade flowed overwhelmingly to the more economically advanced and/or politically powerful party (see Chapter 4). While free trade brought prosperity to the most advanced producers, it imposed destitution on those who were unable to compete, provoking periodic crises in which less advanced producers were bankrupted, masses of people were thrown out of work and the trade of whole nations came to a standstill. This experience gave rise to demands for state protection for small producers and for the national industry of the productively less advanced countries. Small producers saw the source of their difficulties in the power of the bankers, who denied them access to the credit they needed to sustain themselves, while capitalists of less advanced countries sought tariff protection for their national industries. For the liberal political economists, of course, periodic crises and bankruptcy were part of the healthy operation of the market, the stick that accompanied the carrots offered to the more enterprising producers. The market was not just an economic, but also a moral force, penalising the idle and incompetent and rewarding the enterprising and hard-working.

The conservative critics of liberalism sought to negate the evils of capitalism by turning the clock back to an idealised form of medieval society in which individualism was subordinated to the values and institutions of community, nation and religion. However, the dramatic increases in prosperity that capitalism offered to those who were able to benefit from its dynamism meant that such a reactionary response was politically unrealistic in the capitalist heartlands, where the dominant critiques of liberalism have been not reactionary but reformist, seeking to retain the benefits of capitalism while introducing reforms that would eliminate its negative consequences. In the nineteenth century, reformism focused on the regulation of the monetary system, since distress always appeared as a shortage of money imposed by bankers seeking to exploit their control of credit to their own advantage. In the twentieth century, reformism came to focus more on the direct intervention of the state in the regulation of markets, protecting the vulnerable from the full force of competition. The central thrust of reformism, however, is always the same: to keep the 'good' parts of capitalism while eliminating the 'bad'. The liberal response to reformism has also always been the same: the good and the bad are two sides of the same coin; penalties for failure are inseparable from rewards for success. The 'evils' associated with capitalism cannot be ascribed to capitalism, but represent the failures of those who are unwilling or unable to live up to its standards. Liberalism, therefore, is not so much the science of capitalism as its theology. God cannot be blamed if sinners find themselves in hell; the way to avoid hell is to live a virtuous life.

Socialist critics of capitalism, since the early nineteenth century, have developed a more radical critique of capitalism and its legitimising ideologies, based on the critique of its silent presupposition, private property. Adam Smith's economic agents are not just isolated individuals, they are property owners, and it is because they are the owners of property that some have the power, embodied in legal right, to profit from the labour of others. Socialist critiques saw the inequalities which capitalism creates not as the result of the failure of markets, but as an expression of the unequal distribution of property, and 'market socialists' called for the equalisation and/or the socialisation of private property and the organisation of production on the basis of common ownership, sustained by the free availability of credit.

THE MARXIST CRITIQUE OF LIBERALISM: THE SOCIAL DETERMINATION OF PRIVATE INTERESTS

The most radical critique of liberalism was developed by Karl Marx and Friedrich Engels, whose starting point was the socialist critique of private property. Marx took this one step further by pointing out that the evils of capitalism did not derive from the unequal distribution of property, but from the institution of private property itself. Capitalist private property is based on the private ownership of the products of labour, which are sold as commodities. Private property is therefore not some natural institution, inscribed in human nature and sanctioned by God, but is only the expression of a particular form of social production, in which the activity of producers is mediated through and regulated by the market. Moreover, capitalist private property is not so much the ownership of things as the ownership of values, expressed as sums of money. The magnitude of these values is not given, but is determined through the social processes of exchange and can be inflated or destroyed overnight by the rise and fall of market prices.

In a capitalist society, in which the production of commodities is generalised, it is not only the products of labour that are exchanged as commodities, but the capacity to labour itself. The great mass of the population do not have the means to engage in independent production, but are compelled to sell their capacity to labour to a small minority of capitalists who have sufficient money to buy the labour power and means of production required to engage in production on a large scale. As the owners of all of the means of production, the capitalists are the owners of the whole product, which they sell in the market. The profit that is appropriated by the capitalists depends on their ability to induce or compel those they have employed to produce commodities that can be sold for a greater sum of money than that originally laid out for their production. In this sense, the source of profit is the surplus labour, over and above that required to cover the subsistence of their employees, that the capitalists are able to extract from their labour force. This is the insight that is captured in Marx's labour theories of value and surplus value (Clarke 1991, ch. 4).

Capitalist private property is quite different from personal property such as household goods. It is social property, the means and products of social production, which have been privately appropriated. Moreover, it is his or her ownership, or lack of ownership, of property that determines the participation of the individual in society. The members of a capitalist society are not private individuals and their families, they are individuals who are already defined as members of particular social classes, on the basis of the character and scale of the property that they own, which is only an expression of the mode of their participation in social production and access to their essential means of subsistence. In this sense Marx inverts Margaret Thatcher's dictum:

> private interest is itself already a socially determined interest, which can be achieved only within the conditions laid down by society and with the means provided by society; hence it is bound to the reproduction of these conditions and means. It is the interest of private persons; but its *content* as well as the *form* and means of its realisation, is given by social conditions independently of all (Marx 1973, p. 156, my emphasis).

In a critique of the 'market socialists', Marx argued that even if society started with an equalisation of property, market processes would necessarily give rise to inequality and a polarisation of wealth and poverty, as money accumulated in the hands of a minority, while the majority lost the means to earn their own living and were forced to labour for others. Thenceforward, the minority would further accumulate their capital on the basis of their appropriation of the unpaid labour of the majority, so that the polarisation of wealth and poverty would be cumulative. The unequal distribution of property is not a distortion of the formal equality of the market, but is its necessary presupposition and its inevitable consequence. The great mass of the population at best earn only enough to secure their own subsistence, with no prospect of accumulating enough wealth to survive as independent producers, and so are condemned to a life of wage labour. The mass of capitalists, meanwhile, regularly augment their capital from the profits obtained from realising the products of the surplus labour of their employees, and the more surplus labour they are able to extract, the greater will be that profit. The inevitable result of generalised commodity production is therefore the polarisation of wealth and poverty, the reproduction of inequality and the exploitation of the mass of the population on an increasing scale.

Of course, class identity is not the only determinant of the life experience and life prospects of the members of society, although it is inevitably the most fundamental determinant. The fate of those condemned to work for a wage is determined by their competition in the labour market. Those with scarce skills may be able to earn significantly more and enjoy more favourable working conditions than those with skills that are not in short supply, although such privileges are always provisional, constantly threatened by changes in production and labour market conditions. Those who are unable to meet the demands of capital, by reason of age or infirmity or the lack of appropriate skills, will be condemned to unemployment and dependence for their subsistence on others. Not all capitalists prosper. Small capitalists may be able to earn only enough to meet their own subsistence needs and so be unable to accumulate capital. Smaller and less successful capitalists may fall by the wayside and join the ranks of the working class. The working class and the capitalist class are, therefore, differentiated, but such differentiation does not in any way undermine the fundamental class character of capitalist society (see Chapter 3).

Similarly, individual capitalists and workers may not identify themselves subjectively as members of one or the other class. Although their social identity is defined objectively by their class membership, they participate in society and relate to one another as individuals with a whole range of social characteristics. The worker depends for his or her wages and for the security of his or her employment on his or her particular skills and on the continued prosperity of his or her employer. The worker may, therefore, identify his or her interests not with other workers, or the working class as a whole, but with his or her trade, employer, branch of production or the interest of 'the nation' in competition with other nations. The capitalist depends on his ability to compete with other capitalists and may secure advantages in such competition through the exercise of monopoly powers or through fiscal privileges and state regulations. The capitalist may, therefore, identify his interests, not with those of the capitalist class as a whole, but with the competitive interests of his own enterprise, his industry or his nation-state. The capitalist similarly depends on his ability to harness the initiative and commitment of his employees, which may best be secured by providing relatively favourable wages and working conditions, which helps to foster the identification of employee and employer. Finally, however much social identity might be under-pinned by the perception of economic interests, it may be overlain and even dominated by other, cultural and political, sources of identification. But, whatever may be the basis of the subjective identification of capitalists and workers, this does not in any way undermine the fundamental objective character of their opposing class interests and the objective determination of their life experience and prospects by their class position.

THE DYNAMICS OF THE CAPITALIST SYSTEM OF PRODUCTION

Adam Smith had presumed that 'consumption is the sole end and purpose of all production', a maxim that he claimed 'is so self-evident that it would be absurd to attempt to prove it' (1910, vol. 2, p. 155), and this has always been a pillar of the liberal defence of capitalism. But even the most superficial understanding of capitalism suffices to show that, however self-evident such a maxim might be as a characterisation of rational human endeavour, its absurdity in a capitalist society is self-evident testimony to the irrationality of capitalism. Marx and Engels showed that the sole purpose of capitalist production is not the production of things to meet human need, but the constant thirst for profits to maintain the accumulation of capital. Of course, the capitalist has to find a market for his products, but far from being the purpose of production, the need to sell the product is for the capitalist only a barrier to the further accumulation of capital.

The thirst for profit is not a matter of the free choice of capitalists, but is imposed on them as a condition of their survival. In order to secure their profits, and so to maintain their status as capitalists, capitalists have constantly to innovate and invest, in order to reduce their production costs. The capitalist who can produce more cheaply than his competitors can earn a higher rate of profit and drive his competitors from the market, so every capitalist has to run ahead in order to stand still.

Competition not only forces capitalists to innovate and invest in order to increase the productivity of labour and develop new products, it also compels capitalists to seek constantly to force down wages, intensify labour and reduce the number employed. The less technologically advanced capitalist, in the face of competition from the more advanced, can only maintain his profits by extending the working day, reducing wages and intensifying the labour of his employees, laying off those who are thus made surplus to requirements. The more advanced capitalist may have the capacity to provide more favourable working conditions, but he is intent on making the best of his advantage before his competitors can catch up, so even he will intensify labour and reduce employment to the greatest degree possible, even if he compensates his remaining employees with higher wages. The inherent tendency of capitalist accumulation, imposed on every capitalist by the pressure of competition, is therefore to the intensification of labour, the extension of the working day and the redundancy of labour. The result for the working class is an increasing insecurity of employment in response to the ever changing demands of capital. The intensification of the demands of capital throws more and more people into the ranks of the unemployable. The accumulation of capital necessarily leads to the polarisation of overwork and unemployment, prosperity and destitution. This Marx characterised as the 'absolute general law of capitalist accumulation' (1976, ch. 25).

The transformation of methods of production to increase the productivity of labour, the intensification of labour and the extension of the working day are all imposed on capitalists by the pressure of competition. These means of overcoming competitive pressure lead to a constant increase in the quantity of commodities produced, the overproduction of which in turn intensifies the competitive pressure, which is merely the form in which overproduction confronts each individual capitalist. The market is, therefore, by no means the beneficent sphere in which social production is subordinated to social need as consumers exercise their freedom of choice; it is the arena in which capitalists desperately seek to dispose of their surplus product at a profit. Capitalist competition is not a deus ex machina, but the expression of the constant tendency to overproduction which presents itself as a barrier to the further accumulation of capital, a barrier which is only overcome through the creation of new needs, the intensification of labour, the destruction of productive capacity and the redundancy of labour on a global scale (Clarke 1994). Far from responding to the needs of consumers, capitalism thrives on the constant creation of unsatisfied needs; far from generalising prosperity, capitalism generalises want; far from relieving the burden of labour, capitalism constantly intensifies labour, to the extent that a growing proportion of the population – the young, the old, the infirm, those with inadequate skills – are unable to meet the demands of capital and are condemned to destitution. The market is an instrument of 'natural selection' that judges not on the basis of an individual's ability to contribute to society, but on the basis of the individual's ability to contribute to the production of surplus value and the accumulation of capital. This is the moral law that is expressed in the platitudes of neoliberalism.

Neoliberals contest Marx's analysis of the 'absolute general law of capitalist accumulation' on the grounds that the living standards of the employed population have steadily risen on the basis of capitalist accumulation, thereby undermining the 'pauperisation thesis' that is often falsely attributed to Marx. However, the validity of the law at the global level is 'so self-evident that it would be absurd to attempt to prove it'. The accumulation of capital has been concentrated in the metropolitan centres of accumulation, where the living standards of the employed have certainly increased, but the inherent tendency to overproduction has led capitalism from its inception to spread its tentacles worldwide, developing the world market in the attempt to dispose of its surplus product. Indigenous producers in the peripheral regions have confronted global capitalist competition in the form of falling prices for their products, which has led to falling incomes of petty producers and the mass destruction of indigenous capitalists, while those capitalists who remain have only been able to survive by forcing down wages and intensifying labour. The accumulation of capital in the metropolitan centres has only been sustained by the pauperisation of the rest of the world, leading to a polarisation of wealth and poverty, overwork and unemployment, on a global scale.

Even in the metropolitan centres of accumulation the inherent tendencies of capitalist accumulation are undeniable. While real wages may have risen, the creation of new needs by capital has meant that the socially determined subsistence needs of the population have risen more rapidly, forcing an ever growing proportion of the population to seek work to augment the household income in the attempt to meet those needs. At the same time, a growing proportion of the population is unable to meet the ever increasing employment demands of capital, while those in employment face the ever growing threat of losing their jobs. Those who are not able to meet their subsistence needs through waged employment are forced into dependence on others, either other members of their families or households or collective provision from charitable or state institutions. State provision of pension and benefit incomes to those unable to work has provided some security for the victims of capitalist accumulation, but this has not been through the beneficence of capital, it has been won through the trade union and political struggles of the working class. Moreover, the mounting cost of collective provision to counter the tendencies of capitalist accumulation has given force to the neoliberal attempt to replace collective provision with private provision through insurance-based systems, which provides yet another channel through which capital can intensify the exploitation of the mass of the working population by intensifying and profiting from their fear of misfortune (see Chapter 16).

For Marx and Engels capitalism was not entirely evil. It has undoubtedly developed the productive capacity of society to a hitherto undreamed of degree. But it has done so at enormous human (and, we can add today, environmental) cost. To this extent Marx and Engels agreed with the liberals in their critique of reformism: the costs of capitalism are inseparable from its benefits. Unreconstructed liberals believe that every individual has the freedom to choose the fate that will befall him or her, so the judgement of the market is a moral judgement. Hard work, foresight, initiative and enterprise will be rewarded, while the idle and lethargic will suffer their just punishment. Those liberals who recognise that the judgement of the market may not display such justice nevertheless believe that the benefits of capitalism outweigh its costs, and that the costs can be ameliorated through compensatory mechanisms – a 'social safety net', through which the beneficiaries can compensate the victims. Such moderate liberals do not believe that capitalism is perfect, but they do believe that it is the best of all possible worlds. Again in the words of Margaret Thatcher, 'There is no alternative'.

Marx and Engels believed that the alternative was a completely different kind of society in which social production is under the self-conscious democratic control of the freely associated producers, in which production is organised on the principle 'from each according to his [her] ability, to each according to his [her] needs' (Marx 1962, p. 24). They believed that capitalism was creating the social and material conditions for such a society by socialising production and by developing the productive forces to the extent that all human needs could be satisfied within a democratically organised society, although they certainly underestimated the extent to which capitalism constantly creates new unsatisfied needs and so demands a further development of the productive forces to meet them. The plausibility of such an alternative has been severely dented by the experience of the regimes which have proclaimed themselves Marxist, such as the Soviet Union and China; but these regimes have offered only a parody of the Marxist vision, building a communist society on the basis of undeveloped forces of production, and with social production under the bureaucratic control of a militarised authoritarian state.

The question of whether or not the Marxist vision can be realised is not one that is settled by the experience of the Soviet Union and China, nor is it one that can be resolved theoretically. It is not a theoretical but a practical question, and it is not a question that is posed by Marx and Engels, but a question that is posed to humanity by capitalism. Social development has been dominated by the accumulation of capital for less than 200 years of human history, although accumulation has been regularly interrupted by periodic crises and massively destructive armed conflicts. The destruction of the depression of the 1930s and the Second World War prepared the way for a renewal of capitalist accumulation that has been sustained for more than 50 years, sometimes fitfully, by the expansion of capitalism on a world scale. It is only in the last decade that capitalist domination has reached its geographical limits, extending to every corner of the globe, so that in order to overcome the barriers to capitalist accumulation, capital now has to turn in upon itself. The fact that capitalism has not yet destroyed humanity or the environment does not mean that it will not do so in the not-too-distant future, nor that its expansion will continue to proceed unchecked by the renewed massive destruction of capital through global crisis or war. The unbridled expansion of capitalism is the future for humanity that neoliberalism celebrates. The Marxist critique echoes the response of millions, even billions, of people across the world: 'There must be an alternative'.

THE NEOLIBERAL PROJECT

Neoliberalism represents a reassertion of the fundamental beliefs of the liberal political economy that was the dominant political ideology of the nineteenth century, above all in Britain and the United States. The arguments of political economy were based on intuition and assertion rather than on rigorous analysis, but their strength rested on their ideological appeal rather than on their analytical rigour. The ideological appeal of liberalism waned towards the end of the nineteenth century, with the growing demands for 'social reform' precipitated by the rise of the organised working class and a growing awareness of the 'social problems' that the development of capitalism had thrown up in its wake. The dominant strands of economics no longer rejected demands for social reform on the basis of the primacy of the market, but sought instead to identify and delimit the scope of reform by identifying the 'market imperfections' that led the reality of the market economy to fall short of the liberal ideal. The liberal model of society remained the ideal, but it was recognised that this ideal could not be attained by the power of the market alone, which would have to be supplemented by the guiding hand of the state. Piecemeal social reform through the first half of the twentieth century was replaced after the war by the more systematic reformism of the 'Keynesian welfare state', which was based on the systematic application of fiscal policy as a means of redistribution, and macroeconomic regulation to remedy the deficiencies of the market.

Neoliberalism emerged as an ideological response to the crisis of the 'Keynesian welfare state', which was precipitated by the generalised capitalist crisis associated with the end of the postwar reconstruction boom and was brought to a head by the escalating cost of the US war against Vietnam at the beginning of the 1970s (Clarke 1988, chs 10–11). The crisis manifested itself in a slowing of the pace of global capitalist accumulation alongside escalating inflation and a growing difficulty of financing government budget deficits, which forced governments to impose restrictive monetary policies and cut state expenditure plans. What was seen as a mark of the abject failure of Keynesianism was acclaimed as a positive virtue by neoliberals, who, amid the recession of the early 1980s, reasserted the traditional liberal dogma of the purgative powers of the market, a reassertion that appeared to be justified by the subsequently resumed expansion of global capital on the basis of the further liberalisation of the world market.

Neoliberalism owes its strength to its ideological appeal, but neoliberalism is not merely an ideology, it purports to rest on the scientific foundations of modern liberal economics. Modern neoliberal economics is no less dogmatic than its nineteenth-century predecessor in resting on a set of simplistic assertions about the character of the market and the behaviour of market actors. The economist critics of neoliberalism have repeatedly exposed how restrictive and unrealistic are the assumptions on which the neoliberal model is based. However, to argue that the neoliberal model is unrealistic is somewhat to miss the point, since the neoliberal model does not purport so much to describe the world as it is, but the world as it should be. The point for neoliberalism is not to make a model that is more adequate to the real world, but to make the real world more adequate to its model. This is not merely an intellectual fantasy, it is a very real political project. Neoliberalism has conquered the commanding heights of global intellectual, political and economic power, all of which are mobilised to realise the neoliberal project of subjecting the whole world's population to the judgement and morality of capital.

REFERENCES

Clarke, S. (1988) *Keynesianism, Monetarism and the Crisis of the State*. Cheltenham: Edward Elgar.

Clarke, S. (1991) *Marx, Marginalism and Modern Sociology*. London: Macmillan.

Clarke, S. (1994) *Marx's Theory of Crisis*. London: Macmillan.

Friedman, M. (1962) *Capitalism and Freedom*. Chicago: University of Chicago Press.

Marx, K. (1962) 'Critique of the Gotha Programme', in K. Marx and F. Engels *Selected Works*, vol. 2. Moscow: FLPH, pp. 13–37.

Marx, K. (1973) *Grundrisse*. Harmondsworth: Penguin.

Marx, K. (1976) *Capital*, vol. 1. Harmondsworth, Penguin.

Smith, A. (1910) *The Wealth of Nations*, 2 vols. London: Dent.

6
Neoliberalism and Politics, and the Politics of Neoliberalism

Ronaldo Munck

Neoliberalism dominates the political horizon at the moment both for the powers that be and for the movements that challenge them. It has established a new socio-political matrix that frames the conditions for political transformation across the globe. This chapter examines the political impact of neoliberalism, but also the politics of neoliberalism itself, something less often focused on. It begins with an examination of the political *making* of the free-market system, contrary to what we might call the 'naturalist' views of the neoliberal ideologues. It continues with a critical review of the ways in which the capitalist state has been *restructured* by neoliberalism, again contrary to the neoliberal orthodoxy that stresses only the driving back of the state by the market. This section closes with a review of the new political *matrix* created by neoliberalism and the impact that it has had on all aspects of political life. A second section turns to the politics of the neoliberal project itself and the possibilities for moving beyond it through a transformative political project. The way democracy has become 'devalued' as a political currency is perhaps the most damaging effect of the neoliberal hegemony over the last quarter of a century. Yet in the last few years this hegemony has been contested and the cosy confidence that 'there is no alternative' (TINA) to neoliberalism has been partially dissipated. This has, arguably, created space for political movement 'beyond' neoliberalism, the various permutations of which are considered in the last section.

We must distinguish at the outset between neoliberalism as a system of thought and actually existing neoliberalism. While the first can be traced back to the ideas developed in the writings of Frederick Hayek during the Second World War and their popularisation in the 1970s by Milton Friedman (1962), the latter is a more practical vision centred on a programme of macroeconomic stabilisation, liberal-isation of trade and privatisation (or destatisation) of the economy (see Chapter 3). Neoliberalism in practice means the Washington consensus as a practical devel-opment strategy whose advocates can, with some justification, distance them-selves from the particular neoliberal theories developed by the so-called Austrian school launched by Hayek. Thus John Williamson, who actually coined the term 'Washington consensus', has argued that he never intended the term 'to imply policies like capital account liberalisation . . . monetarism, supply-side econom-ics, or a minimal state . . . which I think of as the quintessentially neoliberal ideas' (Williamson 2002, p. 2). These notions in fact never commanded a consensus in Washington or elsewhere other than in small right-wing pressure groups. This is an important distinction to stress, as it is one often conflated in critical accounts of neoliberalism (see Chapters 3 and 12).

NEOLIBERALISM AND POLITICS: THE MAKING OF THE MARKET

For neoliberalism, the market symbolises rationality in terms of an efficient distribution of resources. Government intervention, on the other hand, is deemed undesirable because it transgresses that rationality and conspires against both efficiency and liberty. The market-based society will, according to Hayek, nurture individual freedom. But, as Barry Smart (2002, p. 95) comments: 'This society achieves its coherence not through design but through the market and its processes of exchange, through supplying goods and services for others and seeking, in turn, goods and services for others.' The overall order created by the market is deemed superior in terms of efficiency and equity compared to any deliberate or engineered form of societal organisation. As Polanyi (2001, p. 60) puts it, this system means that '[i]nstead of economy being embedded in social relations, social relations are embedded in the economic system' or, even more starkly, 'a market economy can function only in a market society'. The market continuously seeks to make a society in its own image.

If we take a historical rather than a theological view of the making of markets we can see, contrary to the neoliberal vision, that this has always been a contested political process and not a natural event. Karl Polanyi, who wrote during the Second World War of the first 'great transformation' of the nineteenth-century Industrial Revolution, showed clearly that 'the emergence of national markets was in no way the result of the gradual and spontaneous emancipation of the economic sphere from governmental control' (Polanyi 2001, p. 258). Market society and market rules did not evolve naturally or through some process of self-generation. That is why, in the strongest possible sense, we refer here to the *making* of markets. On the contrary, as Polanyi argued, 'the market has been the outcome of a conscious and often violent intervention on the part of government which imposed the market organisation on society for non-economic ends' (2001, p. 258). So politics is always 'in command' and there is no such thing as a purely economic process if we look beneath the surface of political rhetoric. As Marx argued with regard to the 'primitive accumulation' that was necessary for the building of capitalism, the making of the market and a market society was often a violent affair with very clear winners and losers.

The notion of a self-regulating market was at the core of classical liberalism and is still today reflected in the discourse of global neoliberalism. Indeed, as Polanyi once put it: 'The true implications of economic liberalism can now be taken in at a glance. Nothing less than a self-regulating market on a world scale could ensure the functioning of this stupendous mechanism' (2001, p. 145). Liberalism is thus only realised in the current phase of world history through the complex cluster of economic, political, social and cultural processes we know as globalisation. To carry through this project, the transnational capitalist class made a concerted bid during the 1970s and 1980s to create a 'disembedded liberalism', which led to the triumph of neoliberal globalisation as discourse and practice in the 1990s. Capital mobility was facilitated, free trade was sanctified, labour was made more 'flexible' and macroeconomic management became fully market compliant. Of course, the question then arises as to whether markets can be 'disembedded' from social relations and the political order without engendering social disintegration and political disorder.

We find today that actually existing neoliberalism does not really believe in a straightforward 'roll back' of the state (see next section), and understands the need for a constant making and remaking of the market and the rules that govern it. The international trade regime – first GATT (General Agreement on Tariffs and Trade) and now the WTO (World Trade Organisation) – is the main mechanism through which the global market is effectively regulated and disputes are resolved through a formalised system. It was precisely the qualitative leap in the volume of world trade that necessitated the move from the GATT to the more formal and 'judicialised' system of rules that the WTO seeks to enforce, notwithstanding the political obstacles in terms of global power to obtain consensus for them. A whole set of international rules was established to regulate the vastly increased volume of international trade in terms of contract law, patents and arbitration procedures. This set of international rules is negotiated by the powerful states of the world that dominate the multilateral economic organisations; they are not generated spontaneously as neoliberalism would pretend (see Chapter 10).

RECONFIGURING THE STATE

We have seen how government intervention was crucial to the making of markets, yet neoliberalism has as a central tenet the seemingly contradictory mission of 'driving back' state intervention. Indeed, following Unger, we can say that the main source of ideological unity in actually existing (or, as he calls it, 'operative') neoliberalism, and one of its central *political* tenets, is 'the negative unity of the disempowerment of government: it disables the state from interfering with the established order of society' (Unger 1999, p. 58). That in practical terms represents a key task for the neoliberal politician. For the liberal theorists such as Hayek, the target was always what was seen as an 'excessive' or 'bloated' state sector, its intrusion into and attempts at regulation of the 'free' market and, ultimately, the erosion of freedom this represented for the individual. The state's intervention in the economy would lead to an unbridled 'collectivism' (the thin end of the wedge of communism according to the neoliberal political creed) and, as in the title of Hayek's most influential treatise 'The Road to Serfdom'. In practice, however, actually existing neoliberalism has not simply acted to 'roll back' the state or to remove the market from the realm of regulation.

The first phase of global neoliberalism began with the Pinochet military coup in Chile in 1973 and the 'Chicago Boys' (a group of Chilean economists trained at the University of Chicago under a broadly 'Friedmanite' programme) project that followed. It took on its more established form with the economic policies followed by Margaret Thatcher in the United Kingdom after 1979 and by Ronald Reagan in the United States after 1981. Taking their cue from Hayek and Friedman, Pinochet, Thatcher and Reagan used a strong state to 'roll back' state interference and consolidate free market mechanisms. This was the first stage of the neoliberal revolution, based on forcing a retreat from the Keynesian and developmental state political matrix. The labour market was to be 'deregulated' and labour made more 'flexible'. Management's 'right to manage' was to be restored in all its splendour and the market would not be allowed to suffer from 'political' constraints. While the paths towards neoliberalism were diverse – being shaped by historical context and political process – by the end of the 1980s it had become remarkably hegemonic, with previous welfare and development state models seeming archaic. This was when TINA had an awful truthfulness about it.

The second phase of global neoliberalism began in the 1990s, committed to a 'roll out' of new policies rather than just a 'roll back' of the state. As Peck and Tickell (2002, pp. 388–9) argue, once the natural limits of the negative phase of neoliberalism had been reached, a more 'positive' or proactive policy was called for; thus 'the outcome was not implosion but reconstitution, as the neoliberal project itself gradually metamorphosised into more socially interventionist and ameliorative forms by the Third Way contortions of the Clinton and Blair administrations'. One could add the Fernando Henrique Cardoso administration in Brazil (1995–2002) to show that this was not only a North Atlantic shift in the modalities of neoliberalism. Simply extending the logic of the market through liberalisation and commodification was no longer sufficient and the neoliberal project had to be extended to the social domain with issues such as welfare reform, penal policy, urban regeneration and asylum seekers coming to the fore. It was no longer sufficient to drive back the state; now recalcitrant members of society such as migrants, single-parent families, prisoners and 'deviants' or socially 'excluded' members of society needed to be brought under control and regulated in the interests of the neoliberal *political* agenda. This was the social regulation aspect of neoliberalism being implemented.

So in terms of reconfiguring the state we can say that neoliberalism has transformed the state rather than driven it back as Hayek would have liked. The much-vaunted policies of 'deregulation' (removal of state regulatory systems) have, in fact, been creating new forms of regulation with new market-oriented rules and policies to facilitate the development of the 'new' capitalism. Society is transformed in the image of the market and the state itself is now 'marketised', or as Philip Cerny puts it in developing his model of the 'competition state', this turn towards 'commodification of the state' is 'aimed at making economic activities located within the national territory, or which otherwise contribute to national wealth, more competitive in international development terms' (Cerny 2000, p. 30). This competition state model is no longer geared towards national economic development but, rather, towards the promotion of neoliberalism on a global level. The political arena of the nation-state is thus restructured and the old divide between 'inside' the nation-state and 'outside' is eroded. As the function of the state become reorganised to fit with the new global order, so the state begins to act even more clearly as a market 'player' itself and not a 'referee' as in the old national order of states. Regulation is seen as something carried out not on behalf of the common good but, rather, on behalf of the globalisation project itself.

MATRIX RENEWAL

It is often said that the triumph of neoliberalism depended on the perceived failure of the Keynesian model in the West and the development model in the South. Each of these politico-economic paradigms can be conceived of as a socio-political matrix that set the parameters of social, political and economic development for a whole era. For Garretón and co-authors, who deploy the concept to study Latin America, a socio-political matrix (or SPM)

> refers to relationships among the state, a structure for representation or a party political system (to aggregate global demands and involve subjects politically), and a socio-economic base of social actors with cultural orientations and rela- tions (including the participation and diversity of civil society outside formal state structures) – all mediated institutionally by the political regime. (Garretón et al. 2003, p. 2)

For our purposes we shall seek to examine to what extent neoliberalism represents a new socio-political matrix for capitalist development on a global scale, recon- figuring the public–private domains and the nature of economy–politics–society relationships.

The international system of the nineteenth century rested according to Polanyi on the balance-of-power system between the Great Powers, the international gold standard, the self-regulating market and the liberal state but, he adds, 'the fount and matrix of the system was the self-regulating market' (Polanyi 2001, p. 3). The international system that developed in the last quarter of the twentieth century has variously been called 'globalisation', the 'information society', and the 'network society', but its fount and matrix has undoubtedly been the global market. The emphasis on 'competitiveness' at all levels of society and at the various scales of human activity, from the household to the world economy, prevails utterly. The development model shifts from the state as matrix of the development process to the 'private sector' as main vector of development, with only minimal regulation. The very model of modernity and civilisation shifts under the influence of this new political matrix. The individualist and rationalist market-based model of the West is deemed the one true path and all others are discounted or devalued. The horizon of political possibilities has dramatically closed in.

Much of the analysis of the political effects of neoliberalism has been focused on the advanced industrial societies of the West. Neoliberalism has fundamentally recast the traditional relationship between the private and public domains in society and has 'depoliticised' politics to put it that way. However, the neoliberal revolu- tion has had a much more devastating effect on the countries of the East that were once state socialist or bureaucratic socialist regimes, but where the state firmly regulated the impact of market forces. Even the World Bank has had to admit the disastrous social and political consequences of the 'market transition' in the East. Yet it is in the poor, or 'developing', nations of the South where the effects of the turn to neoliberalism have been most devastating. Classical and radical develop- ment theory alike was cast aside and replaced by a 'one size fits all' neoliberal set of remedies (see Colcough and Manor eds 1993). The 'Washington consensus' codified the actual implementation of neoliberalism across the South and set the terms of the new development debates. All development debates would have to be within the parameters of this so-called consensus.

A political matrix is only as effective as the discourse that supports and expresses it, and here neoliberalism has been spectacularly successful until quite recently. The struggle for hegemony waged by the neoliberal project was, at least in part, a struggle over meaning. Thus the term 'reform' ceased to be associated with land distribution or income distribution, to become synonymous in the neoliberal discourse with opening up of the economy and the 'freeing' of the market from political controls or regulation. Neoliberalism successfully articulated neoclassical economic theories with a liberal individualist conception of political freedom. Thus a theory such as neoliberalism, which should never really have existed outside the pages of a textbook, became singularly effective at '*making itself true* and empirically verifiable', as Bourdieu (1999, p. 2) argues in analysing neoliberalism as a 'strong discourse'. It is that discursive power that neoliberalism brings to bear as a political project, as we shall explore in the next section.

POLITICS OF NEOLIBERALISM: DEMOCRACY DEVALUED

For neoliberalism, the market is not only the most efficient way to allocate resources but also the optimum context to achieve human freedom (see Friedman 1962). It is government intervention in economic life that threatens freedom, according to the neoliberal theorists. Competitive capitalism is seen as the necessary base for capitalist democracy against all 'totalitarianisms' of the left. Of course, in practice the neoliberal gurus saw no contradiction in supporting General Pinochet's bloody imposition of neoliberalism in Chile after 1973. Restrictions on party-political life and repression of trade unions were seen as necessary to restore the market-friendly version of democracy they espoused. What is remarkable, though, is the way in which this fundamentally conservative political vision of the neoliberals was successfully presented as progressive, even 'revolutionary'. Basic social conquests related to labour rights, for example, and fundamental political freedoms were presented as backward-looking anachronisms. The future belonged to neoliberalism, the new 'common sense' for the new post-socialist era (see Chapter 20).

Neoliberalism Sought to Convert the Citizen into a Consumer: 'I Shop Therefore I Am.'

The complex and empowering vision of citizenship in its classic democratic presentation was reduced, in the era of neoliberalism, to the power of the credit card and the pleasures of the shopping mall, realisable or not according to one's position in a sharply hierarchised class structure between and within nation-states. Even the 'political' notion of citizenship became banalised, in practice reduced to infrequent and token visits to the polling booth – in any case a dubious indicator of democratic participation, given the dramatic decline in electoral turnout in many countries, not least the USA. Citizenship was equated with government and the bad old ways before the neoliberal revolution. The individual could express his or her identity much better through consumption, went the unsaid argument. While production, under the old industrial capitalism, had served as a marker of identity and class divisions, now consumption came to the fore. Clearly consumption in the new global market serves a vital economic need, but it also makes for a cultural restructuring of society. The whole consumer process – from conception to sale, through advertising, marketing and fashion building – has fragmented identities and made them more fluid as consumption is continuously revolutionised. The public space of politics is seen as more static and as not fulfilling the needs of the citizen-become-consumer.

As Unger puts it, 'The form of politics preferred by . . . neoliberalism is relative democracy: democracy but not too much' (Unger 1999, p. 68). The new democracy is thin and anaemic, it is restricted and delegative at best. Personal freedoms hitherto submerged by the weight of the state were highlighted by neoliberalism's ideologies, but democracy as a system of political representation was devalorised. The rules of the market would apply also in politics. Behind the hostility expressed towards bureaucracy and the desire to deprofessionalise politics there was a profoundly anti-democratic intent. Money became the key to political influence as never before, and politics became packaged and marketed like any other commodity. Not surprisingly, many citizens lost interest in politics and a general mood of disenchantment if not alienation in regard to the whole political process became common. Political choice became far more restricted insofar as the neoliberal economic agenda became the shared underpinning of most political parties and political differences were flattened.

Neoliberalism also managed to subvert traditional democratic concepts such as 'civil society' and introduce new conservative concepts such as 'social capital' into the democratic lexicon. Under the authoritarian regimes of the South and the East during the 1970s, it was in the domain of civil society (a terrain between the state and the economy, following Gramsci) where citizens organised and mobilised for democracy. Since then, 'civil society' has been mobilised by the neoliberal project in its crusade against 'big government'. All non-state actors are encouraged to supplant or rein in the state, from NGOs (non-governmental organisations) to the trade unions. The World Bank in particular has become a champion of a depoliticised 'civil society', for reasons other than a support for democracy. The concept of 'social capital' was then also taken up by the World Bank to codify in neoliberal economic terms what was once known as community organisation. This process of co-option of democratic discourses was a key element in the legitimisation of neoliberalism in the 1990s.

NO ALTERNATIVE?

TINA seemed to be a plausible discourse up to the 1990s, when the hegemony of neoliberalism seemed undisputed. In particular, the architects of the transition to capitalism in the East became fervent supporters of the neoliberal credo, as did many political leaders in the South, even if due to *faute de mieux*. In France, neoliberalism as a creed was called the *pensée unique*, one system of thinking, one way to see the world, that all parties from right to left agreed on, at least in terms of essentials. Yet in the mid 1990s the World Bank was openly debating how to move 'beyond' the Washington consensus. Beyond the bland new slogan that 'institutions matter', the World Bank seemed to be recognising that the neoliberal revolution was storing up major social problems in terms of the stability of capitalist governance in the long term. Was Polanyi's famous 'counter-movement' coming into play, with society effectively protecting itself from the depredations of an unregulated free market?

First of all, against any 'necessitarian' political theory we need to understand that there are always political alternatives. There is much in Roberto Mangabeira Unger's wide-ranging political philosophy that could help us to develop a more nuanced perspective on economic liberalism than the rather 'necessitarian' approach that currently prevails. Against what he calls the 'mythical history' of democracy, for example, Unger asks us to recognise how many of the economic and political institutional arrangements of democracy are accidental or at least socially constructed. Against the 'deep structure' theorists who find hidden causes for all political phenomena, he shows the limitations of a 'structure fetishism' that denies us the ability to change our formative contexts. Against all kinds of necessitarian assumptions lying behind much social and political analysis, Unger aims: 'to break loose from a style of social understanding that allows us to explain ourselves and our societies only to the extent we imagine ourselves helpless puppets of the social worlds we build and inhabit or the law-like forces that have supposedly brought these worlds into being' (Unger 1999, p. 7). But history can be surprising and social (re)invention can occur even in the most unlikely of circumstances.

Even within the logic of the global neoliberal project, there is what might be called a 'high road' and a 'low road'. Just as there are many varieties of capitalism, so there are different paths to neoliberalism or even through it. Basic consensus around the efficiency of market mechanisms should not mask the considerable debates now ongoing in the corridors of economic and political power on the appropriate mix of market and state regulation. Against a 'low road' based on a low wages/low skill approach, there is a 'high road' based on economic 'growth with equity' as promoted by the neo-structuralist development theorists effectively contesting neoliberal hegemony, especially after the disastrous economic collapse of Argentina in 2002. That event or process was probably as significant for neoliberalism as the collapse of the Soviet Union was for the socialist project. The dominant discourse is not now about how the market can regulate itself, society and politics but is much more focused on how 'governance' needs to be improved, if only to save neoliberalism from itself.

We need always to bear in mind, following Wendy Larner's helpful typology (2000), that neoliberalism is a policy (or set of policies), it is an ideology (or discourse) but it is also fundamentally about 'governmentality'. While neoliberalism may be about promoting less government it does not mean that governance is any less important; on the contrary, perhaps. Governance is often seen as a 'post-political' steering of the political process towards less directive, more networked, modalities than in the past. Governmentality, developed from Foucault's last writings, is about the institutionalisation of knowledge and the way political programmes are aligned with the neoliberal individual. To envisage an alternative to neoliberalism it is essential to understand it in all its complexity. Neoliberalism is not just a set of economic policies, or even an ideology, as focused on by its critics, but much more a strategy for governance of the complex global world we now live in. Any alternative needs to answer the complex problem of global governance in the twenty-first century.

BEYOND NEOLIBERALISM?

According to Alain Touraine (2001, p. 24), 'The triumph of capitalism has been so costly and intolerable that everyone, on all sides, is trying to find a way out of the "neoliberal transition".' Maybe this statement underestimates the resilience and mutability of neoliberalism and overestimates the crisis it is in, but certainly the political debate is now under way on life 'after', 'beyond' or 'post' neoliberalism. The augmented or revamped Washington consensus now being pursued by the World Bank and others is a tacit recognition that actually existing neoliberalism has to some extent failed. The 'good governance' measures now being extolled are not, however, the same as democratic development, still singularly undeveloped in the majority of the world. While recognising that markets are not self-regulating or self-legitimising, the new neoliberal agenda is still only building institutions to regulate the market (to deal with externalities, for example) and to legitimise the market (social partnerships and social protection, for example).

To develop a progressive and more democratic alternative to neoliberalism we need to go beyond the now accepted truism that 'markets don't take care of everything'. The meaning of democracy itself is at stake in these debates. The problem is that while many are clamouring for an alternative to neoliberalism, the proposals at present are either lukewarm adaptations of the market or piecemeal measures of resistance to it. The main issue facing those seeking to articulate a progressive political alternative to neoliberalism is the construction of a global democratic project. That would need to avoid equally the rather vacuous Western-centred notions of 'cosmopolitan democracy' and the temptation of localist or 'fundamentalist' alternatives that simply reject global neoliberalism. Nor can any alternative political economy ignore the heartfelt need across society for macroeconomic stability and for no return to the days of hyperinflation that caused such social devastation and political instability in the past.

Before this process of debate and renewal, however, it is necessary to consider how it is possible to reverse neoliberalism's deliberate policy of depoliticisation. Only by restoring politics to its proper place in representing people's interests and debating political futures will that be possible. There are some signs of a reactivated public realm, especially at an international level, in, for example, the anti-war mobilisations of 2003. The neoliberal rhetoric of 'participation' and 'self-determination' can be subverted and made to work for a renewed notion and practice of the active citizen. Neither classical social democracy nor neoliberalism seems able to offer solutions to the vastly increased levels of inequality created within and between nations by neoliberal globalisation. From within civil society – from what might be described as a 'social' left – practical alternatives are now emerging in many spheres, from participatory budgets and local democracy campaigns to global social movement unionism.

In the transition from a narrowly defined 'political' public sphere to a repoliticised civil society, alternatives to neoliberalism will emerge (see Chapter 19). The World Bank certainly understands the importance of civil society in achieving social support for neoliberal globalisation and giving it a 'social' face. What is at stake now is the concept of 'freedom', itself reduced by neoliberalism to the 'free' market. Karl Polanyi argued in his time that '[t]he discarding of the market utopia brings us face-to-face with the reality of society' (Polanyi 2001, p. 267). The dividing line then is seen to be political – the nature of freedom or democracy – and not the relative technical merits of diverse economic theories. The (re)discovery of society marks the potential rebirth of freedom. Freedom in a complex society can only come, following Polanyi, through (political) regulation towards a diametrically opposed political philosophy to 'the market view of society which equates economics with contractual relationships, and contractual relationships with freedom' (2001, p. 266).

REFERENCES

Bourdieu, P. (1999) *Acts of Resistance Against the Tyranny of the Market*. Cambridge: Polity Press.

Cerny, P. (2000) 'Structuring the political arena: public goods, states and governance in a globalising world', in R. Palan (ed.) *Global Political Economy: Contemporary Theories*. London: Routledge.

Colcough, C. and Manor, J. (eds) (1993) *States or Markets? Neoliberalism and the Development Policy Debate*. Oxford: Clarendon Press.

Friedman, M. (1962) *Capitalism and Freedom*. Chicago: University of Chicago Press.

Garretón, M.A., Cavarozzi, M., Cleaves, P., Gereffi, G. and Hartlyn, J. (2003) *Latin America in the Twenty-First Century: Towards a New Sociopolitical Matrix*. Florida: North–South Centre Press.

Hayek, F. (1976) *Law, Legislation and Liberty*, vol. 2: *The Mirage of Social Justice*. London: Routledge & Kegan Paul.

Larner, W. (2000) 'Theorising neoliberalism: policy, ideology and governmentality', *Studies in Political Economy* 63, pp. 5–26.

Peck, J. and Tickell, A. (2002) 'Neoliberalizing Space', *Antipode* 34 (3), pp. 380–404.

Polanyi, K. (2001) *The Great Transformation: The Political and Economic Origins of Our Times*. Boston: Beacon Press.

Smart, B. (2002) *Economy, Culture and Society*. Cambridge: Polity Press.

Touraine, A. (2001) *Beyond Neoliberalism*. Cambridge: Polity Press.

Unger, R.M. (1999) *Democracy Realised: The Progressive Alternative*. London: Verso.

Williamson, J. (2002). 'Did the Washington Consensus Fail?', Institute for International Economics <www.iie.com/publications/papers/williamosn1102.htm>.

7

Neoliberalism, Globalisation and International Relations

Alejandro Colás

One of the signal triumphs of neoliberalism as a contemporary ideology has been the appropriation of 'globalisation' as a process denoting the universal, boundless and irreversible spread of market imperatives in the reproduction of states and societies across the world. Neoliberalism involves both a set of theoretical principles and a collection of socio-political practices, all of which are directed toward extending and deepening capitalist market relations in most spheres of our social lives (see Chapters 5 and 6). Much of this neoliberal onslaught on conceptions of 'the public' and its accompanying institutions has been justified with recourse to the notion of globalisation. This process is generally presented as being inevitable, and indeed as the necessary panacea against poverty, inequality and economic backwardness. Neoliberal policies ranging from fiscal austerity to anti-labour legislation are thus naturalised through the mantra of globalisation as 'the only game in town'. Such policies are also conveniently externalised in ways that place responsibility for their adoption on the seemingly alien and elusive forces of the 'global market'.

This chapter challenges most of these neoliberal claims about the inevitability of globalisation. The last three decades or so have plainly seen a restructuring of the global political economy and the reconstitution of the international order. But these changes are not necessarily explicable through the concept of 'globalisation', and certainly not through the neoliberal deployment of this category. Globalisation is a descriptive term which encompasses various distinct processes, some of which must be explained with reference not only to the socio-economic dynamics of the global economy but also to the political authority exercised by ruling classes and capitalist states. The first section of this chapter therefore considers the various meanings of globalisation and distinguishes between the different phenomena it refers to. It will hopefully become apparent there that neoliberal usages of the term evade the central paradox of this process, namely that globalisation is heavily mediated, when not actually *authored*, by states. The second section of the chapter expands on this last claim, suggesting that neoliberal globalisation – both as concept and policy – is in fact aimed at restructuring the relationship between states and markets on a global scale. On this reading, neoliberalism emerges as a thoroughly *political* project which not only privileges the private, economic power of markets over the public, political authority of states, but does so, paradoxically, through the state-led, multilateral *re-regulation* of markets in favour of dominant classes. A third section offers some empirical instances of such neoliberal re-regulation from an international perspective. Here, the focus will be on the role of transnational classes, the collapse of communism, and the international multilateral agencies – such as the Bretton Woods institutions or the World Trade Organisation (WTO) – in reproducing neoliberal globalisation. Whilst recognising the power of such institutions in imposing neoliberal policies upon subordinated states and economies, the local sources of such authority will also be underlined. For in the end, neoliberal globalisation is – like all social phenomena – not some disembodied and mysteriously unfathomable external power, but a process aided and abetted by named institutions and social groups: in this account, capitalist states and their ruling classes.

THE MEANINGS OF GLOBALISATION

The English word 'globalisation' became popular in the 1990s in describing the intensification of socio-economic and political interconnections across national borders. One authoritative rendition speaks of globalisation as the 'compression of time and space' in social relations, whilst others emphasise the growing power of political rule above and beyond the national state (e.g. through the devolution of political authority to multilateral agencies, or the 'pooling' of sovereignty in the European Union). The prevailing view one way or another has been that globalisation involved the relative decline of the national state and the attendant expansion of transnational flows, whether in narcotics, money, human beings, ideas, musical rhythms or toxic pollutants. Some have added a qualitative dimension to this quantitative definition of globalisation, by suggesting that the inhabitants of the planet increasingly share common socio-political norms such as universal human rights or cultural forms such as television 'soap opera'. For many, this makes 'globality' the defining feature of the contemporary human condition. Such claims, however, need to be contextualised, qualified and in some cases, dismissed outright, if we are to retain a useful definition of globalisation.

We should firstly reject the notion that globalisation involves either a process of homogenisation or convergence of worldwide social relations, as some of the more extreme neoliberal advocates of this phenomenon suggest. Globalisation is in fact a very uneven process which tends to reproduce both new and pre-existing socio-economic and political hierarchies. Foreign direct investment (FDI) is, for instance, often cited as an indicator of the growing globalisation of the economy. It is indeed the case that FDI flows have increased substantially over the last 30 years, but they are overwhelmingly concentrated in the core capitalist economies of Europe, East Asia and North America.

If we take globalisation as a political process, the universalisation of institutions, norms and values fares no better. Consider the example of democratisation. Once again, the 1980s and 1990s witnessed the collapse of numerous dictatorial regimes across Latin America, Asia and eastern and central Europe. Yet this burst of (electoral) democratisation was neither irreversible nor unlimited. A significant proportion of the world's population continues to be governed by regimes which are not freely elected, and many of those states which were rid of dictatorial authority have reverted to authoritarian rule – particularly in Africa and the former

Soviet Union. The much-lauded 'third wave' of democratisation has therefore hit upon the implacable barriers of state authority. Regimes like that of the People's Republic of China or those of the Middle East remain impervious to the forces of political globalisation, as their ruling classes are able to combine economic liberalisation with socio-political repression.

Finally, much has been made of the 'hybridisation' of culture facilitated by globalisation. Cultural referents ranging from Michael Jackson to Manchester United, rap music to *The Lord of the Rings* have, according to some observers, become so universally recognisable that we can today speak of a shared 'global culture'. Others have argued in a similar vein that new cultural forms are emerging *as a result* of globalisation. The worldwide transit of ideas, language, images, musical forms or culinary styles, so it has been argued, has generated *sui generis* global, or at least transnational cultural products such as 'world music', 'fusion cooking' or the 'post-colonial novel' which cannot be placed within the bounds of a specific culture. It would be churlish to deny the 'hybridisation' of cultural forms across and within national boundaries, facilitated among other things by the prodigious advances in communications technology and the concentration of diverse cultures in so-called global cities such as Tokyo, Sydney, New York or London. But once more, it is important to emphasise the unevenness of such hybridisation and its hierarchical dimensions. As a result of the structural obstacles of poverty, illiteracy and lack of social or geographical mobility, most of the world's population is unable to share in the delights of fusion cooking or the post-colonial novel.

It is clear, then, that globalisation in its socio-economic, political and cultural expressions is neither unlimited nor irreversible. Yet these qualifications do not in themselves negate the existence of a series of interactions which, by extending their reach across national boundaries, can be usefully analysed under the rubric of 'globalisation' or, better still, 'transnationalisation'. The number and scope of multinational corporations has increased substantially, international NGOs and the transactions they encompass have grown exponentially and the range and power of international multilateral organisations has also expanded. Empirically, therefore, it is hard to deny that transnational relations have intensified over the past 30 years. Equally, however, because of its inherently uneven and hierarchical nature, capitalist globalisation must be understood as an unfolding *tendency*, rather than an accomplished *condition*. Such an approach also allows a further general qualification to the prevailing view of globalisation, namely that this is not a historically unprecedented tendency. Much of the literature on globalisation is premised on the existence of a radical break sometime after the Second World War (usually 1973) in the socio-economic and geopolitical organisation of the world. This 'era of globalisation' is often contrasted to previous historical periods, during which economics, politics, culture and society are said to have been organised principally around the authority of the national state and geared towards the requirements of territorially bounded communities. One of the features of globalisation, so the argument runs, is the 'overflow' of such socio-economic, cultural and political activities beyond the purview of the nation-state over the past three decades.

This is not the place to engage in the intense historical debates over the novelty or otherwise of globalisation (for a useful summary, see Held et al. 1999). Plainly, most of the transnational flows (finance, telecommunications, migration) and supranational institutions (international organisations, international advocacy groups, pan-nationalist or regionalist movements) associated with globalisation pre-date the Second World War. As for cultural 'hybridisation', it is as old as humanity itself. It may therefore suffice to note that once globalisation is understood as a tendential process and not an accomplished condition, there is greater scope for accepting the previous existence of similar moments of intense socio-economic and political interdependence and interpenetration in the past, particularly during the late-nineteenth-century 'Age of Empire' (1875–1914). Thus, on this view, globalisation is not so much new as renewed; it is not so much marked by qualitative transformation as by quantitative acceleration. It refers, in short, to a specific historical period when the universalising tendencies of capital accumulation, so powerfully captured by Marx and Engels in their 1848 *Communist Manifesto*, have been unleashed with greater intensity, mainly through the mediation of the capitalist state.

NEOLIBERALISM, THE STATE AND GLOBALISATION

Both neoliberals and their critics agree that globalisation is a process which is fuelled by the boundless dynamics of capitalism. For neoliberal theorists and policy makers, this universalising dynamic of the capitalist market is precisely its great attraction. Globalisation is thus seen by most neoliberals as a natural outcome of an untrammelled capitalist market; as a positive process which unfolds smoothly once artificial distortions created by the state, political interests or archaic customs are removed from the path of free and equal exchange. The guiding assumption in such neoliberal (or neoclassical) renditions of the capitalist market is that the world is made up of rational, utility-maximising units (generally firms) which, by pursuing profit through free and unencumbered exchange, eventually generate a market equilibrium. This point of equilibrium marks the most efficient way of generating wealth and allocating limited resources (whether human, natural or manufactured), thereby demonstrating the virtues of the 'free market' and 'comparative advantage'. Writ large, it is this understanding of the capitalist market which has governed neoliberal conceptions of globalisation as the process which undermines the artificial political constraints imposed by states and other 'special interest' groups, and secures global wealth creation and distribution through competitive resource allocation on a world scale. The global capitalist market is here understood as a non-political, purely 'economic' sphere.

Critics of neoliberalism see the capitalist market in a very different way. Taking their cue from an eclectic range of social theorists, including Marx, Gramsci and Polanyi, they conceive of the capitalist market as a realm not of opportunity, but of necessity. Thus Marxists in particular emphasise how the capitalist market has, since its emergence in the seventeenth century, expanded through force and coercion, compelling vast swathes of the world's population to reproduce themselves through market imperatives (see Chapter 8). Contrary to neoclassical conceptions, this understanding of the capitalist market denaturalises commodity exchange and instead underlines how historically unique our contemporary forms of social reproduction are – how peculiar it is to rely on the market for such basic needs as food, shelter, education or care. More importantly, for our purposes, Marxist and other critical approaches emphasise the crucial role of politics and the state in the reproduction of the global capitalist market. They see capitalism not just in 'economic' terms, but as a set of *social relations* which encompass the 'political' authority of states, as well as other 'cultural' or 'ideological' aspects of our social lives. This political economy of global capitalism can be understood in at least two senses.

First, critics of neoliberal theories of globalisation point out that the global capitalist market relies on the authority of the state – its legal, coercive and ideological powers – to secure the reproduction of 'free and equal' exchange. Far from being a natural, organic process free from mechanisms of 'social engineering', capitalist market exchange requires the kind of social infrastructure, institutional regulation and legal enforcement which only the modern state can provide. In more abstract terms, although the logic of capitalist valorisation is premised on the appropriation of time (both labour time and future returns on capital), it also requires accumulation within a particular place. On this reading, capitalist globalisation cannot be understood without reference to its 'spatial fixes' (see Harvey 2000); that is, the various sites of regulation, control and surveillance – from factory walls to a border crossings – which, with the legitimation of the state, sustain the reproduction of the capitalist market. The more sophisticated neoliberals recognise this need for a 'nightwatchman state' and even the requirement for the state to generate some basic 'human capital' in the form of education and training. However, they typically see this role as being politically neutral; as an institutional adjunct which simply enables the much more efficient dynamics of the market. In other words, they see the state as a force which is entirely autonomous from the market.

Critics of neoliberal globalisation on the other hand highlight the role of politics in a second sense, by constantly focusing on the antagonistic social relations which underpin the reproduction of the global capitalist market. As opposed to the disembodied, utility-maximising rational actors of neoclassical analysis, critical approaches to globalisation and neoliberalism emphasise the inescapably *social* character of any market exchange, and consequently, its contested, exploitative and often oppressive nature. Marxists in particular interpret capitalist globalisation as the product of class struggles, both within and across states, so that, for instance, the transfer to the EU via the recent European 'stability pact' of political authority over, say, budgetary deficits can be read as a strategy for deflecting domestic class antagonisms onto an international and therefore more politically neutral and distant plane (see Chapter 24). Similarly, as we shall see in a moment, historical materialist analyses consider social classes themselves as vehicles of globalisation, organising on a transnational level and articulating their own policies and programmes on a self-consciously global scale. Either way, what these critical approaches point to is the fact that neoliberal globalisation is a process actually co-ordinated by identifiable institutions and social groups, and generally driven by socio-economic and political antagonisms between (and often within) social classes.

We have seen, then, that neoliberals and their critics differ not only in terms of their policy prescriptions, but also with regard to their basic assumptions about how to analyse our social world. Whereas the former view the state and other political authorities as 'rent-seeking' institutions which hinder and distort the natural progress of the market towards competitive efficiency, prosperity and equality of opportunity, the latter understand the capitalist state and its political institutions as social mediators of class interests, in existence mainly to secure the reproduction of the capitalist market. Seen from a global perspective, these marked theoretical differences deliver radically opposing views on the nature of globalisation. Neoliberals interpret the process as the outcome of unbridled markets finally pursuing their natural and healthy appetite for international trade, global economic integration and competitive growth. Their critics, on the other hand, understand globalisation as a process facilitated and actively engineered through political decisions aimed at making greater areas of our social lives dependent on the global capitalist market. Both camps agree that capitalism is at the heart of globalisation, but they differ fundamentally on whether capitalism is simply the outcome of 'human nature' or quite the opposite, the naturalisation of very inhuman market dependence. The following section will focus more narrowly on the recent history of neoliberal globalisation, with the aim of illustrating how neoliberal policies and principles relate to capitalist globalisation as a process.

HOW AND WHY DID THE WORLD BECOME NEOLIBERAL?

Neoliberalism did not cause capitalist globalisation, but it certainly accompanied and facilitated this process. In fact, neoliberalism – as both theory and policy – can be explained as the response to the crisis in the world capitalist system after 1973, which in turn deepened and accelerated the transnational tendencies of capitalist globalisation. The crisis was both political and economic. It questioned the legitimacy of states (capitalist and revolutionary alike), and plunged advanced capitalist economies into an extended period of inflation, recession and mass unemployment. It also subordinated weaker capitalist economies to neoliberal restructuring through the discipline of international debt. Out of this crisis there emerged a set of policy prescriptions supported by a new configuration of social forces which, through recourse to the neoclassical principles outlined above and elsewhere in this book, encouraged the kinds of interdependence and multilateral regulation we today know as globalisation. Like capitalist globalisation, the spread of neoliberalism was an uneven and protracted process, subject to all kinds of socio-political contestation and contingencies. Some core capitalist states, such as Germany or Japan, adopted a fairly diluted form of neoliberalism, whilst larger developing economies, such as India or the People's Republic of China, have implemented these policies at their own pace, marked by domestic, rather than international, political and economic determinants. It is therefore important to identify different moments in the global spread of neoliberal programmes, and to distinguish between the various ways in which these policies were implemented by states with very different capabilities and locations in the hierarchy of the international system.

The 1980s marked the heyday of neoliberal globalisation, but already in the 1970s Pinochet's Chile demonstrated the possibilities of combining a free economy with a repressive state. By opening its economy to foreign capital, reorienting domestic production toward the export market, privatising state-owned companies, rolling back social expenditure and employment rights, abolishing taxes on wealth and capital gains, and embarking upon the systematic repression of the labour movement, Chile served as a source of inspiration for later neoliberal 'counter-revolutions' which also emerged out of deep socio-economic and political crises (see Taylor 2002). Thatcher's election as British prime minister in 1979 and Ronald Reagan's victory in the US presidential contest of 1980 signalled the rise of the 'New Right' as the alternative to crisis-ridden welfare capitalism and the heightened class antagonism in the capitalist heartlands. Other chapters in this book consider the nature and consequences of this rightward turn in politics at greater length, so it may be sufficient here to highlight three international dimensions of this phenomenon.

The first of these might more properly be called the 'transnational' dimension of neoliberalism. This refers to the emergence on both sides of the North Atlantic during the 1970s and 1980s of an elite of opinion formers and practitioners who have self-consciously advocated the so-called 'Washington consensus' on economic policy involving fiscal discipline, financial and trade liberalisation, privatisation and opening up to FDI (see Chapter 12).[1] Using the concept of 'class fraction', Marxist scholars inspired by the work of Gramsci argue that sectors of the bourgeoisie across the advanced capitalist world have organised transnationally through private and public institutions ranging from the Trilateral Commission to the Group of Seven (now Eight) industrialised economies, in order to formulate, promote and co-ordinate worldwide neoliberal policies.[2] On this account, neoliberalism and globalisation reinforce each other as the liberal–cosmopolitan fractions of capital endorse the globalisation of the economy and thereby affirm their own centrality vis-à-vis the more domestically oriented fractions of capital in the management of such a globalised economy. Some 'transnational historical materialists' have even argued that neoliberalism is premised on the rise of a new transnational state and ruling class, 'comprised of the owners of the leading worldwide means of production as embodied principally in the transnational corporations and private financial institutions' (Robinson 2001, p. 215). Irrespective of whether one accepts such claims wholeheartedly, either empirically or conceptually, it is difficult to ignore the transnationalisation of benchmarking, management, auditing, regulation or quality assurance as socialising mechanisms of capitalist globalisation. Neoliberalism in this respect can properly be called an ideology of globalisation, insofar as it standardises and universalises codes of conduct, 'good practices' and communication formats through business schools, chambers of commerce or software packages. It also reproduces these values through audio-visual media which, more often than not, export stereotypical renditions of the 'American way of life'.

A second international aspect to the globalisation of neoliberalism resides in the political decline of the Left in the North and the crisis of non-capitalist forms of development in the South, particularly those inspired and supported by the

Soviet bloc. For the globalisation of neoliberalism was not just the result of 'New Right' victories, but also the consequence of left-wing defeats. By the 1980s, the Left in the capitalist core either abandoned any pretence at socialist transformation or faced electoral decline. Even the communist and the more radicalised socialist parties of southern Europe opted for reform rather than rupture in the course of their respective transitions to liberal democracy. When faced with the prospect of substantive political departures, as in France under the 1981 Socialist–Communist government, or in Spain with the 1986 referendum over NATO membership, the Left buckled under domestic and international political and economic pressure. In the United Kingdom, successive electoral defeats and Thatcher's crushing of the miners' strike in 1984–85 left the labour movement demoralised and in disarray. By the late 1980s, all social–democratic parties, and most communist parties in the advanced capitalist world had undergone ideological and organisational transformations which placed them firmly within the moderate, left-of-centre end of the political spectrum. This rightwards shift was consecrated with the 'Third Way' ascent into office, led by Clinton, Blair and Schröder and closely followed by Mbeki and Cardoso (see Chapter 21).

In the periphery, the sudden collapse of 'actually existing socialism' in 1989–91 simply marked the end of a secular decline in the legitimacy of post-colonial revolutionary states. For all their advances in the extension of basic needs and the promotion of socio-economic and political equality – both domestically and internationally – Third World revolutionary states were, long before the collapse of communism, failing to match the socio-economic and political expectations of the generations born after independence. The liberation of lusophone Africa in the 1970s, coupled with the revolutionary victories of 1979 in Nicaragua and Iran, served as temporary morale boosters for the global Left and arguably caused sufficient concern among the international Right for it to regroup as the 'New Right'. But the weakening of these new revolutionary states through the counter-revolutionary wars of attrition in Africa and central America, coupled with the consolidation of fundamentalist rule in post-revolutionary Iran, soon dampened the prospect of a rekindled socialist internationalism. As the dictatorships in Asia, southern Africa and the Americas collapsed in the 1980s and early 1990s, they gave way not to socialist, but to liberal democracies. The prospect of a non-capitalist route to democratic development became even more elusive. Indeed, in several African states the veneer of communism had worn so thin that it took only months after the fall of the Berlin Wall for erstwhile 'states of socialist orientation' to refashion themselves as fully-fledged 'neoliberal emerging markets'. In this international climate of ideological defeat for the Left, it was just short of inevitable for the neoliberal counter-revolution to sweep the political board.

For the weaker states and economies in the international system, neoliberalism arrived as an even more ostensibly external force, principally in the shape of international financial institutions (IFIs). This third international dimension to the spread of neoliberalism has mainly played itself out through the mechanism of Structural Adjustment Programmes (SAPs) in the 1980s (known today as Poverty Reduction Strategy Papers), which were implemented as a condition for receiving loans from IFIs. The history of SAPs is a complex and variegated one, but, in essence, they emerged as a result of the Third World debt crisis of the 1980s.[3] Successive defaults in the early 1980s led to the design by the International Monetary Fund (IMF) of programmes aimed at 'restabilising' and 'adjusting' the 'macroeconomic fundamentals' of debtor countries in order to secure repayment. Cutbacks in public spending, currency devaluation, export promotion, opening up of both trade and capital accounts, privatisation and tax reductions were amongst the core components of such SAPs. Unsurprisingly, they were vigorously endorsed by the lending institutions – both national and multilateral – run by, or on behalf of, neoliberal governments, and by the 1990s no major IFI would extend credit to countries unwilling to undertake structural adjustment.

There is no question therefore that IFIs and other related multilateral institutions such as the WTO or the OECD have acted as vehicles of neoliberal globalisation. But it is also important to note that domestic social forces have been instrumental in steering this process. Some of the more powerful developing economies, such as Mexico, Brazil and India, have undergone neoliberal adjustment, not simply because economists in Washington, D.C. tell them to, but because their ruling classes (or fractions thereof) have decided, often on the back of electoral mandates, that it is in their collective interest to do so. Other countries (e.g. Zimbabwe) have carried out structural adjustment without the IMF, whilst many states constantly renegotiate, interrupt or simply disregard agreements with the IFIs. In other words, developing countries are not simply hapless victims or passive objects of global neoliberalism: they are, like other states, populated by classes and social forces with their own interests and strategies, many of which are consonant with the ruling ideology of neoliberalism.

BEYOND NEOLIBERAL GLOBALISATION?

In 1848 Marx and Engels (perhaps thinking of the forcible opening of Chinese ports to international trade by the British Navy five years earlier) said of the revolutionary power of the bourgeoisie that '[t]he cheap prices of its commodities are the heavy artillery with which it batters down all Chinese walls . . . It compels all nations, on pain of extinction, to adopt the bourgeois mode of production.' It has taken over a century and a half, but with the accession of the People's Republic of China to the WTO in 2001, the process of turning the world into the image of capitalism increasingly appears close to becoming a reality (albeit with the price of Chinese commodities this time battering other 'Wal-Marts'!).

Some have argued that we no longer live in a neoliberal world and that a 'post-Washington consensus', which recognises the role of the state in correcting 'market failures', now dominates the global centres of power. It is certainly the case that neoliberalism is no longer as stridently confident and all-conquering as it was in the 1980s and 1990s. But we should not be fooled by appearances, for a decline in prominence also speaks of a silent victory: the neoliberal counter-revolution has in fact been so successful in transforming our societies that it no longer needs to justify its conceptual claims or defend its policies in the open. Neoliberal assumptions, such as the inevitability of structural unemployment, monetarist economics and the need for labour flexibility, which seemed so politically unpalatable 20 years ago, have become today's political common sense. Neoliberal policies involving low income tax, the privatisation of public utilities or the opening up of trade and capital accounts are now the mainstay of any left-of-centre party worth its salt. And underpinning much of this 'radical centre' is of course the discourse of globalisation as an inevitable and unstoppable feature of our times.

Yet, since neoliberal globalisation was crafted politically through the victories of the 'New Right', it can also be politically undone by the mobilisation of democratic forces against capitalism. In the end, it is not neoliberalism per se, and even less is it 'globalisation', which are the driving forces behind the deep inequalities, gross injustices and wanton destruction which characterise our world. It is rather the passion for profits of the capitalist class and their supporters which naturalises this condition. Neoliberalism is not an inescapable system of social reproduction, but a set of reversible policies. Similarly, few critics of capitalist globalisation would want to do away with the increased social, economic and cultural interconnections and co-operation between and across states. The point instead is to democratise and equalise these positive aspects of globalisation. The greatest challenge to neoliberal globalisation is therefore the challenge of a global democratic alternative to capitalism.

NOTES

1. The term 'Washington Consensus' was coined by Williamson (1993).
2. The classic statement of this position can be found in van der Pijl (1984, 1998). See also Gill (1990).
3. A good overview can be found in Mohan et al. (2000).

REFERENCES

Harvey, D. (2000) *Spaces of Hope*. Edinburgh: University of Edinburgh Press.
Held, D., McGrew, A., Goldblatt, D. and Perraton, J. (1999) *Global Transformations*. Cambridge: Polity Press.
Gill, S. (1990) *American Hegemony and the Trilateral Commission*. Cambridge: Cambridge University Press.
Mohan, G., Brown, E., Milward, B. and Zack-Williams, A.B. (2000) *Structural Adjustment: Theory, Practice and Impacts*. London: Routledge.
Pijl, K. van der (1984) *The Making of An Atlantic Ruling Class*. London: Verso.
Pijl, K. van der (1998) *Transnational Classes and International Relations*. London: Routledge.
Robinson, W.I. (2001) 'Capitalist Globalisation and the Transnationalisation of the State', in M. Rupert and H. Smith (eds) *Historical Materialism and Globalisation*. London: Routledge.
Taylor, M. (2002) 'Success for Whom? A Historical-Materialist Critique of Neoliberalism in Chile', *Historical Materialism* 10 (2), pp. 45–75.
Williamson, J. (1993) 'Democracy and the "Washington Consensus"', *World Development* 21 (8), pp. 1329–36.

Part II
Surveying the Landscape

8

Neoliberalism and Primitive Accumulation in Less Developed Countries

Terence J. Byres

This chapter is concerned with processes of primitive accumulation and their significance in the era of neoliberalism in contemporary less developed countries (LDCs). In order to analyse these adequately – and, indeed, to grasp the notion of primitive accumulation – we need to place them in historical context: that of the now advanced capitalist economies, of colonialism, and of the 'developmentalist state'. That we do in the first three sections.

The now advanced capitalist economies experienced, in the past, capitalist transformation, in which capitalist industrialisation was central. Accumulation of capital is one of capitalism's defining characteristics. This, at its simplest, we may identify as accumulation of the means of production (buildings, machinery, raw materials, implements).

Driven by competition, the urge to accumulate is capitalism's central dynamic; and capital accumulation is the form taken by economic growth under capitalism. When this has become a structural feature of an economy dominated by capitalist relations of production we may refer to capitalist accumulation. Such accumulation is regular and has a powerful tendency to proceed on an expanded basis. It is not, however, without contradictions (as it proceeds, it may embody tendencies that slow it down: for example, a declining rate of profit); and it may be subject to crises of overaccumulation (in which more is produced – both capital and consumer goods – than can be absorbed by consumers: referred to by Marxists as a realisation crisis), lasting for prolonged periods.

All of this is obviously so for advanced capitalist economies, and their analysis requires treatment of the complex mechanisms integral to capitalist accumulation. For it to have become so, however, and for capitalist industrialisation to have transformed economically backward economies, certain conditions are necessary and have had to be created historically, via prolonged and turbulent processes.

Those processes are captured in the notion of primitive accumulation. That is to be distinguished from capitalist accumulation, and is an idea first developed by Marx in the first volume of *Capital* (1976, pp. 714, 775, 873–940) with respect to the transition from feudalism to capitalism in Europe. It was held to be necessary for two reasons: first, as a means of making surplus available to finance early form of accumulation, in circumstances in which capitalist profit was exiguous; and second, as a way of creating the home market for capitalist commodities.

We may define primitive accumulation as the transfer of assets, most notably land, by non-market means, from non-capitalist to potentially capitalist classes, and usually with state compliance or mediation: by *force majeure*, whether via theft, eviction, or purchase at a nominal price. The classic example in England was enclosures (whereby open fields and common land were appropriated by landlords and let out in compact blocks to large, capitalist tenants).

The central feature of primitive accumulation was the separation of peasants from their land and other means of production: transferring assets to potential capitalists. A labour force for capitalist industry and for capitalist agriculture was thereby created, and with that labour force – a proletariat – torn from the means of subsistence, a home market for capitalist commodities was made.

COLONIAL PRIMITIVE ACCUMULATION

Marx further argued that before capitalist accumulation was fully secured in western European countries, accumulation was enabled by processes of primitive accumulation initiated outwith their national borders, in a colonial periphery. Marx saw this as of considerable significance. We may identify it as colonial primitive accumulation and distinguish it from domestic primitive accumulation.

From the late fifteenth century, colonial primitive accumulation spread, through force and violence, to the Americas, to Asia and to Africa. This involved plunder, land appropriation from indigenous populations and its vesting with colonial settlers, slavery and slave plantations, and unequal exchange (manifested, for example, in colonial countries running large unrequited export surpluses with the metropolis). In the colonial era, the costs of primitive accumulation were imposed savagely upon native populations, to the clear economic advantage of the colonial state and colonial and metropolitan dominant classes. Broadly, we may say that between its beginnings in the late fifteenth century and its demise after 1945, colonialism extended domestic primitive accumulation in two ways: first, colonial profits, remitted to the metropolis, by augmenting domestic agricultural and industrial profits and, second, colonial markets, by adding significantly to the metropolitan home market, contributed critically to capitalist industrialisation, together making possible far higher rates of domestic capital formation than would otherwise have prevailed (for an excellent treatment of slavery in this respect see Blackburn 1997, pp. 509–80).

Colonial primitive accumulation experienced resistance and struggle, just as primitive accumulation in Europe did. But, as in Europe, it was not halted in its relentless path by such struggle. The profound difference, however, was that those who, stripped of land and the means of production, became a proletariat, could find little employment in either agriculture or industry. They would, for the most part, remain trapped as surplus labour in the countryside.

Colonial primitive accumulation had been far less complete in its separation of the producers from the means of production than domestic primitive accumulation was in western Europe. Although it had created a large reservoir of surplus labour, it had also left a large stratum of poor peasants in possession of land (largely as tenants and often as sharecroppers). With independence, there was much scope for further primitive accumulation, and indeed, such primitive accumulation in LDCs would be necessary if capitalist transformation were now to be secured. But if the

European experience offered any lesson, it was that such transformation would come neither painlessly nor quickly.

DOMESTIC PRIMITIVE ACCUMULATION IN LDCs IN THE POST-1945 DEVELOPMENTALIST ERA

We abstract from any discussion of attempted socialist transformation: as in the Soviet Union after the October Revolution, in eastern European countries after 1945, and in China, North Korea, North Vietnam and Cuba. But in those countries, too, analogous processes of domestic primitive accumulation were unleashed. It was in the Soviet Union in the 1920s, before collectivisation, and as efforts to expand the industrial base were being made, that Preobrazhensky coined the phrase 'primitive socialist accumulation' to describe these processes (Preobrazhensky 1965, pp. 77–146): the use of extra-economic power by the Soviet state to appropriate surplus from the pre-socialist parts of the economy. They were at work, too, in other attempts at socialist transformation.

In non-socialist LDCs, independence did not mean any halt in processes of primitive accumulation. Primitive accumulation was now, however, in the era of the 'developmentalist state', set in an altogether different context. It did now offer the *possibility* that it might be part of a domestic capitalist transformation, with capitalist industrialisation at its core. For so long as the conditions for capitalist accumulation had not been established, domestic primitive accumulation would be necessary.

Whereas the now advanced capitalist countries were able to augment significantly domestic primitive accumulation via colonial primitive accumulation, contemporary LDCs had no such source to draw upon. Flows of aid and private capital via multinationals might ease the burden, but, on the best possible reading, to nothing like the degree that colonial primitive accumulation had done historically. A critical difference, apart from the divergence of scale, is that while colonial primitive accumulation was wholly within the coercive power of the colonial state, contemporary LDCs are subject to superior economic power.

In the post-1945 developmentalist era, which lasted from the 1940s to the early 1970s, domestic primitive accumulation was in clear evidence. Under the aegis of developmentalist states, there were widespread attempts at land reform, which took two broad forms: tenurial reform and redistributive reform. To the extent that land reform is an attempted transfer of resources (i.e. land) by non-market means, in circumstances in which there has been limited capitalist transformation, it is an archetypal form of primitive accumulation. Of its two main forms, redistributive land reform is more obviously a mechanism of primitive accumulation, since it seeks to redistribute land from those with large holdings to those with small holdings or with no land at all. Tenurial reform is less obviously so, but, to the extent that it might encourage dispossession, by motivating rich peasants to acquire more land by non-market means, it may be seen in such terms.

Redistributive reform was largely unsuccessful, with two exceptions, both very unusual – South Korea and Taiwan. Here land was transferred by non-market means to proto-capitalist peasants, who secured a more productive agriculture: an instance of primitive accumulation successfully associated with capitalist transformation. In each case, the transformed agriculture contributed effectively to capitalist industrialisation.

Elsewhere, however, while redistributive land reform had little success in reaching its goals, it did have the effect of hastening dispossession of poor peasants: often, they would be ejected in anticipation of legislation (as, say, in India). Tenurial reform, which embodied a series of measures to improve the terms upon which land was held and worked (getting rid of sharecropping, controlling rents, eliminating fragmentation of holdings, etc.) had some success with reference to rich and middle peasants, but benefited poor peasants hardly at all. On the contrary, it encouraged their dispossession.

This, with the exceptions noted, was nothing like sufficient to bring about capitalist transformation in the countryside or to facilitate capitalist industrialisation. Indeed, there seemed to be pervasive stagnation in agriculture in LDCs and a marked failure of programmes of industrialisation.

By the mid 1960s, a crisis was looming in LDCs: in essence, an accumulation crisis – a crisis not of over-accumulation but of under-accumulation (an insufficiency of the means of production). By the early 1970s, a response to that crisis had been made. The 'new technology' (a combination of new biochemical inputs, such as new high-yielding seeds, and new mechanical inputs, most notably tractors) was introduced in the countryside from the late 1960s onwards, with its massively 'betting-on-the-strong' bias. It was in full swing by the early 1970s, and brought with it a powerful intensification of processes of primitive accumulation in the countryside. It started in Asia (very powerfully in India) and spread to countries throughout Africa and Latin America. The 'developmentalist state' was dead, and the era of neoliberalism was ushered in.

DOMESTIC PRIMITIVE ACCUMULATION IN THE ERA OF NEOLIBERALISM

In the era of neoliberalism, such non-market transfers endure powerfully, and are often the subject of class struggle in the countryside. Indeed, with the demise of the 'developmentalist state' they intensified. But they are now different in nature, as we shift to a qualitatively different set of conditions.

We need to distinguish the Chinese case. If, indeed, primitive capitalist accumulation is currently at work there, it is different in kind and in its significance from that operating elsewhere. It is discussed in the next section.

In the neoliberal era, in some ways, direct state-mediated primitive accumulation diminished. Thus, land reform disappeared from the policy agenda. Primitive accumulation proceeded in other ways. Some of those did derive from direct state legislation. Others did not. With the withdrawal of the state – one of the major policy prescriptions of neoliberalism – cruder, often illegal, forms of primitive accumulation manifested themselves. That is not to say that they did not receive tacit state support. The neoliberal state, manifestly, has not intervened to stop them; and is likely, indeed, to have been complicit in their pursuit. They are various in nature and widespread in their manifestation.

In Latin America, by the late 1980s, 'the peasantry ha[d] been unable to protect its access to land and average farm size has been declining forcing peasant households to seek sources of income outside the farm, most particularly on the agricultural labour market' (de Janvry et al. 1989, p. 396). At one level, the state has withdrawn and neoliberalism has produced a liberal economy that has driven down prices of staples and increased indebtedness, especially of small producers. At another, it is not that the state has withdrawn, but that it now intervenes in different ways: 'Neoliberal land policies abandoned the previous focus on expropriation, emphasising instead privatisation, decollectivisation, land registration and land titling' (Kay 2000, p. 129). One form of primitive accumulation gave way to another, as legislation was introduced that helped break up indigenous communities and encouraged the sale of their land. Such communities are dispossessed by extra-economic means and there is clear proletarianisation. There have been powerful movements from below – land invasions and occupations – in response to this, in which the discourse of dispossession, a discourse generated by primitive accumulation, is prominent. These have not, however, been conspicuously successful.

Peters points to 'the pervasive competition and conflict over land' in contemporary Africa, which 'call into serious question the image of relatively open, negotiable, and adaptive customary systems of land-holding and land use and, instead, reveal processes of exclusion, deepening social divisions, and class formation' (2004, p. 269). That competition and conflict over land have increased in the neoliberal era is clear. This is the modus operandi of primitive accumulation. In African countries, in the neoliberal/structural adjustment era, 'as African government controls on land and labour markets have been lifted, the classic Marxist paradigm of primitive accumulation gains relevance' (Bryceson 2000, p. 55). But it had clear relevance before then, in both the colonial and immediately preceding post-colonial eras. Before the neoliberal era it proceeded under the obvious aegis of the state. Now, however, with the withdrawal of the state, quite clearly the access of poor peasants to land has weakened and they have been forced into wage labour or petty trading. African peasants are like their Latin American counterparts, in this respect at least. These poor peasants are the obvious casualties of primitive accumulation.

In Asia, we may illustrate the extremes of ongoing primitive accumulation in one case: that of Bangladesh. Thus: 'Even a casual glance at newspapers tells us that in countries like Bangladesh land grabbing and "non-market" transfers are common, and many individuals fail to retain their land in a context of great uncertainty about property rights' (Khan 2004, p. 98). In Bangladesh:

Non-market transfers of this type involve the powerful and the well-connected using the police, the courts, the land record offices and frequently private armies of thugs to fabricate documents, institute false cases, and directly use violence or the threat of violence to extort and wrench land from the politically weak. (ibid.)

Precisely the same may be said of, say, Bihar in contemporary India, of many African countries, and of parts of Latin America.

This is primitive accumulation in the crudest form. But does it feed into capitalist transformation? Does it serve to create a source for the financing of capital formation and the fuelling of capitalist industrialisation, and to augment the home market?

If we take this one instance, which may be seen to exemplify many others, 'in countries like Bangladesh it seems that primitive accumulation (like the market) only contributes to a permanent process of "churning" of small parcels of land between relatively small farms' (pp. 98–9). We have an ongoing and self-reproducing process of what has been termed 'change in changelessness' (p. 94). Where this is so, primitive accumulation is no more than a zero-sum game: in the classic definition, a game in which the amount of 'winnable goods' is fixed; whatever is gained by one actor is lost by the other; and there can be no net social or economic advance.

With a few exceptions, it is not obvious that capitalist transition is proceeding vigorously: the most notable exceptions being in 'non-socialist' East Asia – Taiwan and South Korea – and in China. We consider China in the next section. Primitive accumulation is a necessary condition for capitalist transformation. It is not, however, sufficient. Among other necessary conditions that do not exist among a large number of LDCs are: an accumulating urban bourgeoisie of sufficient size; a resolution of the agrarian question, in the sense of creating an agriculture capable of contributing to overall capitalist transformation; and a state capable of purposive intervention. Neoliberal policies stifle any tendencies towards capitalist transformation: most obviously, by preventing necessary state intervention, by denying protection to LDCs, and by frustrating the required agrarian change.

So it is that against the obvious casualties of primitive accumulation, in a large number of LDCs there is no compensating, clear capitalist transformation, no successful capitalist industrialisation that would ultimately generate employment opportunities. At best, in the great majority of cases, progress has been painfully slow. But that is what one would expect from the historical record.

CHINA AND PRIMITIVE ACCUMULATION

That there is a significant shift away from socialism in China is suggested by the following. Firstly, decollectivisation of agriculture (started in 1978 and complete by 1984) broke up the communes, privatised much of the agricultural sector, and, via long-term leases, restored family farming. Secondly, while the state sector in urban industry has been firmly retained, privatisation began in the 1990s, cautiously, but quite perceptibly; in addition, stock markets were established in 1991 and joint stock companies emerged following 1988 legislation. The new private units might be seen as at least proto-capitalist in nature. Thirdly, there has been, since 1978, an embracing of the market, which has now become substantial. In both agriculture and industry, a series of price reforms has been introduced. Already by 1988 only around 25 per cent of prices were set by the state. Thereafter, after a lull, significant price reforms continued.

There are, further, certain features that might indicate the operation of domestic primitive accumulation. The first is that in the countryside, from 1978 onwards, millions of Chinese were driven off the land, i.e. were effectively dispossessed and proletarianised. Bramall (2000, p. 175) suggests that 'a vast pool of surplus labour appears to have been created by the radical reorientation of the Chinese development strategy at the end of the eighties'. There emerged a 'floating population' of temporary migrants, of between 50 and 70 million by the late 1980s. Secondly, rural industrialisation was financed, in part, by funds from clearly non-capitalist sources. In the 1980s, the growth of the private non-farm sector in the countryside was dramatic. A key role was played by local government, which used expanding farm-sector profits to invest in rural industry (p. 397). The new enterprises were leased out to the private sector for management. Here were possibly future capitalist enterprises, financed by funds from a sector that was no longer socialist and was not yet capitalist. Thirdly, in the cities, aspiring capitalists gained access to capital, often through corruption, siphoning off state funds to set up private businesses (Holstrom and Smith 2000, p. 8); i.e. through gaining access to non-capitalist sources. So it is that the creation of a capitalist class has proceeded. Finally, large numbers of state workers have been forced out of state employment and on to the market; i.e. segments of a capitalist proletariat have been created. As part of this process, there have been steps taken to break the so-called 'iron rice bowls', i.e. 'guaranteed jobs, state-subsidised housing, free medical care' (ibid.).

Thus the funding of capital formation from non-capitalist sources (whether the state sector or the non-capitalist farm sector), the separation of rural workers from the means of production (especially land), and the detaching of workers from state enterprises are clear. These are recognisably forms of domestic primitive accumulation.

In all of this, China has been far more careful and far more successful than Russia, and has had far fewer casualties. Certainly, China is growing with extraordinary speed, and industrialisation is proceeding at a rate and on a scale that are impressive. The Chinese economy must, surely, be the most dynamic in the world today. Industrialisation has had considerable success. If we take one crude, but illuminating, measure, the structure of the labour force: the proportion in agriculture declined, dramatically, from 81 per cent in 1970, through 62 per cent in 1985, to 50 per cent in 1998; and that in industry rose, over the same dates, from 10 per cent, to 21 per cent, to 23 per cent. The base for this was laid before the present era. But it might plausibly be argued that a form of primitive capitalist accumulation is currently driving it forward.

CONCLUSION: THE IMPORTANCE OF THE STATE

Primitive accumulation has, historically, been central to the earliest stages of the transition to capitalism, and has involved immense suffering and social waste. Yet, while it has been a necessary condition for successful capitalist transition and its accompanying structural transformation, it has never been more than a preliminary to them. Such transition has required full-scale capitalist industrialisation and a transformed, productive agriculture; and this has entailed cumulative capitalist accumulation. These have necessitated certain kinds of class formation. All of the relevant processes have been mediated, in one way or another, by an emerging capitalist state. Critical have been the creation of accumulation-oriented capitalist classes and of a proletariat (both rural and urban) – the latter made possible by the separation of peasants from their land and other means of production.

Neoliberal policies have, surely, acted to hasten primitive accumulation among LDCs, by intensifying and quickening processes of dispossession. But, in the absence of appropriately strong states, these have not notably served to accelerate the pace of capitalist transformation.

The Chinese case is instructive. China has not adopted anything resembling a neoliberal policy package. Privatisation of industry, the embracing of the market and so on have proceeded relatively slowly and been pursued with due caution. Moreover, and critically, the Chinese state has not withdrawn. It has been an actively interventionist, growth-promoting state.

REFERENCES

Blackburn, R. (1997) *The Making of New World Slavery: From the Baroque to the Modern, 1492–1800*. London: Verso.

Bramall, C. (2000) *Sources of Chinese Economic Growth, 1978–1996*. Oxford: Oxford University Press.

Bryceson, D. (2000) 'African Peasants' Centrality and Marginality: Rural Labour Transformations', in D. Bryceson, C. Kay and J. Mooij (eds) *Disappearing Peasantries? Rural Labour in Africa, Asia and Latin America*. London: Intermediate Technology Publications.

Holstrom, N. and Smith, R. (2000) 'The Necessity of Gangster Capitalism: Primitive Accumulation in Russia and China', *Monthly Review* 51 (9).

Janvry, A. de, Sadoulet, E. and Young, L.W. (1989) 'Land and Labour in Latin American Agriculture from the Fifties to the Eighties', *Journal of Peasant Studies* 16 (3), pp. 396–424.

Kay, C. (2000) 'Latin America's Agrarian Transformation: Peasantisation and Proletarianisation', in D. Bryceson, C. Kay and J. Mooij (eds) *Disappearing Peasantries? Rural Labour in Africa, Asia and Latin America*. London: Intermediate Technology Publications.

Khan, M. (2004) 'Power, Property Rights and the Issue of Land Reform: A General Case Illustrated with Reference to Bangladesh', *Journal of Agrarian Change* 4 (1–2), pp. 73–106.

Marx, K. (1976) *Capital: A Critique of Political Economy*, vol. 1. Harmondsworth: Penguin.

Peters, P. (2004) 'Inequality and Social Conflict Over Land in Africa', *Journal of Agrarian Change*, 4(3), pp. 269–314.

Preobrazhensky, E. (1965) *The New Economics*. Oxford: Clarendon Press.

9

Neoliberal Globalisation: Imperialism without Empires?

Hugo Radice

This chapter looks at the changing nature of imperialism and its relation to the ideology and practices of neoliberalism. Straight away, there is an apparent contradiction. Neoliberalism is supposedly all about regulating economic life by means of free markets, with a minimal role for the state; imperialism is traditionally about the exercise of power by one state over other states, through political and military means. So how can the two be reconciled? Is it just that neoliberals are hypocritical or racist – freedom for the rich white North, oppression for the poor non-white South? And do we now have 'imperialism without empires', or what Negri and Hardt call simply 'Empire'?

A key problem in answering these questions is that imperialism has been defined in lots of different ways. Mainstream political scientists have analysed it largely as a form of political rule, whose fundamental elements do not change across different historical epochs. Marxists have related it directly to the nature of a given mode of production: in the case of capitalism, to its peculiar *political economy*. The changing nature of imperialism brings out very clearly one of the most important features of the political economy of capitalism: how the 'economics' of markets and the 'politics' of states play *complementary* roles in expanding and consolidating capitalism as a social order based on exploitation and oppression.

In what follows, this chapter looks at how capitalism and imperialism have changed since 1945. The first section looks at the apparent 'end of empire', the period of decolonisation and national development after 1945. The second section examines the transformation in the postwar order that took place in the 1970s, with the demise of national Keynesianism in the North and developmentalism in the South. The third section then looks at the new imperialism of the present period, a very different form of global political economy based on transnational capital and the subordinated sovereignty of Southern states.

DECOLONISATION – END OF LIBERALISM, END OF EMPIRE?

In modern times, the concept of imperialism has most often been associated with the period from the 1870s to 1945, in which the political economy of global capitalism centred on competition between the colonial empires established by the leading imperial powers. In Lenin's classic analysis, colonial imperialism was intimately connected to the rise of industrial monopolies and the fusion of industrial and banking capital into the new form of finance capital. Foreign investments were aimed at exploiting natural resources and gaining control over new markets in the colonial territories; they were safeguarded and extended by territorial conquest and direct political rule.

For Lenin and most twentieth-century Marxists, the natural consequence of this form of imperialism was war between the rival empires, which in turn would lead to rising worker discontent and the overthrow of capitalism in the imperial heartlands. While there were certainly wars aplenty, these did not, with the exception of Russia in 1917 and China in 1949, lead to socialist revolution. Rather, they led eventually to the construction of an international order to regulate relations between the powers, and to replacement of colonial empires by a 'Third World' of independent nation-states. These new developments could first be seen in the aftermath of the First World War, with the break-up of the remaining old-style European empires (Russian, Austro-Hungarian and Ottoman) into new nation-states, the establishment of the League of Nations, and the growth of anti-colonial independence movements in Asia, Africa and the Caribbean.

After the Second World War, the period from 1945 to 1979 seemed indeed to signal the end of colonial imperialism. The architecture of the United Nations system, like that of the League of Nations, was explicitly based on *universal* principles of sovereign statehood and non-interference – with the important addition of human rights and self-determination. The new international economic order, crafted by the USA and Britain, was based not only on the liberal principles of free trade, but also on collective, co-operative solutions to the international financial disorder of the inter-war years (see Chapter 11). The dismantling of the colonial empires, not only of the defeated Axis powers but also of the victorious Allies, transformed the politics of global capitalism from the late 1940s. In this new world order, *national reconstruction and development* became the central task of sovereign states, old and new.

At the same time, both liberal capitalism and its dominant ideology – neoclassical economics – had been thoroughly discredited by the economic, social and political disasters since 1914. As the Second World War drew to a close, the economic historian Karl Polanyi (2001), the economist Joseph Schumpeter (1975) and the welfare advocate William Beveridge (1960) all agreed that 'free-market' capitalism was doomed: what was required was a major dose of state regulation and social redistribution, if not out-and-out socialism. Most importantly, Keynes (1936) seemed poised to sweep away neoclassical economics altogether and provide a new economic ideology fitted to the new era of state capitalism. While none of these authors (apart from Schumpeter in much earlier work) was directly concerned at this time with imperialism, they certainly helped to inspire scholars, activists and politicians engaged in anti-imperialist struggles to develop policies and programmes for post-colonial economic development, to repair the economic ravages of imperial exploitation (see Chapters 3 and 6).

If the postwar order seemed to herald a new age of political self-determination and state-led development, it rapidly became clear that this did not put an end to international economic inequalities and underdevelopment. The postwar boom did not entirely pass by the newly-titled Third World, but the centre of gravity in both trade and foreign investment shifted from the colonial 'North–South' pattern to one of increasing economic relations among the industrialised countries. Furthermore, North–South trade and investment patterns barely shifted from those of the colonial past: the focus remained on the extraction and sale of the primary products required by accelerating industrial growth and consumption in the north. It was argued, notably by Raúl Prebisch of the UN Economic Commission for Latin America and the development economist Hans Singer, that the terms of trade enjoyed by primary producers – that is, the amount of their products that they needed to sell to be able to buy a given bundle of northern manufactures – had tended steadily to worsen between 1870 and 1939: although this was not necessarily inevitable, it provided a powerful reason for developed countries to seek effective strategies of industrialisation in order to reduce their dependence on traditional colonial-type exports.

Two other trends also became visible. First, it was exceedingly difficult in the Third World to establish new industries without a significant period of protection from the competition of established producers: this, the so-called 'infant industry' problem, was exactly what had fuelled protectionism by the late industrialisers of the nineteenth century, when faced with Britain's industrial supremacy. Secondly, although in the postwar order continuing controls on international finance ruled out the sort of 'financial imperialism' that had funded primary product development in the pre-1914 South, a new institution was emerging which could play a similar role in structuring North–South economic relations: the multinational corporation, which presented itself as the indispensable source of capital, technology and market access to aspiring developmental states.

From the critical analysis of these three features there emerged the theses of 'neo-imperialism' and 'neocolonialism', both among orthodox (communist) Marxists, and among the emerging New Left. The American scholar Paul Baran further identified a crucial *political* constraint on post-colonial transformation: the entrenched position of a local 'comprador bourgeoisie', whose wealth and power were tied to maintaining colonial patterns of trade and investment. In the 1960s, the critique evolved into what came to be called 'dependency theory', in which an economic imperialism was identified which perpetuated the exploitation of the South, but now without the direct political rule of colonialism. But quite apart from this, the supposedly harmonious new world order, based on self-determination and national sovereignty, turned out to be nothing of the sort. First of all, the existence of an alternative 'world-system', that of Soviet communism, meant an overarching 'East–West' superpower conflict that immediately 'internationalised' social conflicts within the Third World. In this context, the eschewing of direct political *rule* in no way ruled out direct *intervention*, both political and military, whenever powerful Western interests were threatened: in Brazil, Guatemala, the Dominican Republic, the Congo, Egypt, Iraq, Iran, Vietnam and Indonesia, to name but a few examples. Above all, the efforts of Third World leaders to join together in challenging Northern dominance and interference, in the Non-Aligned Movement that originated at the Bandung Conference of 1956, were systematically opposed by the North.

The imperialism of the period after 1945 thus took on new forms. The exploitation of the South by the North was undertaken first and foremost by 'economic' means. Primary producers could not generate sufficient revenues to fund economic development; while the multinationals exploited their control of money, knowledge and markets to garner the lion's share of the benefits of what little industrialisation took place. Political independence, meanwhile, was exercised on sufferance, subject to the constraints set by the new 'great powers'. But now the world turned again, and entered a new phase in which the structures of imperialism were once more transformed.

THE DEMISE OF KEYNESIANISM AND NATIONAL DEVELOPMENT

Three characteristics of the post-1945 order posed serious challenges to the attempt to restore the fortunes of capitalism under the auspices of the Keynesian/ developmental state models.

The first important feature was that in the industrial North there emerged a combination of high wages, high productivity and full employment, which successfully wooed Northern industrial labour away from socialist politics, but at the cost of removing the sanctions traditionally available for imposing capitalist discipline – pay cuts and unemployment. The Keynesian alternative of relying instead on manipulating fiscal and monetary policy depended on the existence of social consensus at home, and supportive economic institutions abroad – notably the export of capital from the USA and the timely assistance of the IMF in correcting balance-of-payments deficits. But as capitalism revived in western Europe and Japan, with the participation of US capital, so rising trade and investment flows led inexorably to their greater liberalisation, with falling tariffs and weakening controls on international capital movements. The heightened international competition of the 1960s not only undermined the Bretton Woods international monetary order – fixed exchange rates and the gold–dollar link – but also generated strong inflationary tendencies as workers sought to maintain and extend their postwar economic gains. Attempts to shore up the Keynesian compromise, centred on incomes policies and fiscal and monetary expansionism, served only to make matters worse, with inflation accelerating and being transmitted around the world through trade and currency speculation. The period from 1967 to 1972 saw domestic social and economic crises, centred on inflation and employment, in the United Kingdom, France, Italy and the USA, involving high inflation, currency adjustments, mass labour unrest and the end of full employment. The cure proposed by the monetarists, led by Milton Friedman and F.A. Hayek, demanded the restoration of the free market (especially for labour) and the strong state (centred first on fiscal and monetary discipline). The appointment of Paul Volcker (by Carter, not Reagan) as chairman of the US Federal Reserve Board in 1979, together with the imposition of budget cuts in 1976 in the United Kingdom, led to the application of these policies in the two most significant centres of globalising capital (see Chapters 1–3, 11 and 22).

The second feature of the postwar world was the rise of the Third World as a force in global politics. The 1970s in particular saw renewed efforts by developing countries to redress the international balance of wealth and power. Challenges to the global dominance of the North included the election of Allende in Chile, the

OPEC oil price rises, the defeat of the USA in Vietnam, the dissolution of the last remaining colonial empire (that of Portugal), the launching of the liberation war in Rhodesia, and the overthrow of the Shah of Iran. In this context, the Southern call for a New International Economic Order represented the culmination of post-war developmentalism, effectively proposing to reconstitute Keynesianism at a global level. However, within a few short years, these gains were dramatically reversed.

One important element in this was the rapid globalisation of finance. Led by the USA, overseas lending by banks had been steadily growing since the mid 1950s, and had led to the emergence of 'offshore' finance – especially the so-called Eurodollar markets, based on lending and borrowing of dollars held outside the USA. The sharp rise in oil prices imposed by the Organisation of Petroleum Exporting Countries in 1974 brought to those states huge windfall revenues, which they could not possibly spend at once; instead the revenues were deposited in private Northern banks, which in turn lent the funds to oil-consuming countries, and more generally to the cash-strapped Third World. For a time this boosted economic growth, but then developing countries were caught in the backwash of the new monetarist policies adopted, as we have seen, in the North. Interest rates rose sharply, increasing the cost of debt service, while cuts in both state and private spending led to a slump in demand for Third World exports, and therefore also in their prices. In August 1982, the government of Mexico announced that it could no longer service its debt, and ushered in the debt crisis that persists to this day. As the same time, there was a new aggressiveness in the foreign policies of Northern countries towards the South. In Africa, the Middle East and Indochina, the USA led the way in a global war of containment and attrition, supporting (covertly or openly) South African puppets against the radical new regimes in Angola and Mozambique; Ba'athist Iraq against Iran; and Pol Pot's Cambodia against Vietnam. In all of this, the common interests of the Northern great powers were increasingly maintained through the reconstitution of the IMF and the World Bank as debt collectors for the North; through the growth of public intergovernmental summitry (meetings of the G5/6/7 group), culminating in the 1985 Plaza Accords that resolved the trade tensions between the USA and Japan; through the burgeoning number and range of intergovernmental institutions and processes; and through the more shadowy efforts of the Trilateral Commission and the Bilderberg and Davos meetings.

The third cornerstone of the postwar system was its 'bipolar' nature, divided between capitalist West and communist East. In the 1970s, East–West relations underwent a dramatic zigzag. The course of the Vietnam war, Russia's unchallenged invasion of Czechoslovakia, and the new liberation struggles in Africa seemed to indicate that the 'first cold war' of nuclear confrontation had reached stalemate for the West. Hence the change to détente: Brandt's Ostpolitik of pursuing better economic and diplomatic relations with the USSR, Nixon's visit to China, and the Helsinki agreement on co-operation and security in Europe – even if this was belied by continued hostilities in the Third World. But even before the elections of Reagan and Thatcher, a new cold war was in the making: notably, the US government covertly supported the Islamic guerrilla groups fighting against the Soviet-backed regime in Afghanistan, with the clear aim of drawing the USSR into a costly and unwinnable conflict. Reagan's proclamation against the 'evil empire' signalled the start of a new offensive, through sharp increases in military spending, a reimposition of technological and economic embargoes, further support for proxy wars, and the ideological hijacking of dissident movements in the Soviet Union and eastern Europe. Whereas the 'first cold war' – the nuclear confrontation of the 1950s and 1960s – had ended in the stalemate of 'mutually assured destruction', by the 1970s the Soviet bloc had entered a long period of stagnation rooted in the lack of internal democracy and economic dynamism: the fall of the Berlin Wall in 1989 precipitated the collapse of communism throughout the bloc. Coupled with the pro-market reforms in China under Deng Xiaoping, this signalled a triumph for capitalism on a global scale.

NEOLIBERAL GLOBALISATION, THE HIGHEST STAGE OF CAPITALISM?

These three strands of the restructuring of the world order since the 1970s are of course closely intertwined, and neoliberalism has provided a common ideological framework. If we associate the term 'imperialism' not with formal colonial empires, but with a set of historically changing and contingent structures and processes that reproduce global inequalities of wealth and power, then what sort of imperialism do we now have? Thirty years ago, Marxists discussed the balance between three possible types: the Leninist conception of imperialism as a world of inevitable competition and conflict between rival powers; the Kautskyan vision of collective 'ultra-imperialism' jointly run by the powers; or the 'super-imperialism' of postwar US hegemony. However, from the 1970s this debate was rendered largely irrelevant by the simultaneous rise of globalisation and neoliberalism. Globalisation has centred on the rapid growth of trade, foreign investment and global finance, which have significantly increased the interdependence of national political economies: while the rise of neoliberalism is apparent in the routing of Keynesianism as the dominant ideology of postwar capitalism, and in the dramatic shift in economic policies towards the so-called 'Washington consensus' of monetary and fiscal stringency, privatisation and liberalisation.

The links between the two have commonly been regarded as centred on a *rolling back* or *weakening* of the state; yet this conceals a dramatic divergence in experience between the 'strong' states of the developed North/West and the 'weak' states of the South/East. It is emphatically not the case that states have become 'weaker' as a whole – which is the common belief of most analysts of globalisation, whether they are for or against it. What *is* the case is that globalisation is not just a matter of 'economics', to be encouraged or resisted by states; rather, states themselves have become globalised (see Chapters 6 and 7). The key to understanding this is to focus on capitalist politics as a means of manufacturing consent, in Noam Chomsky's phrase.

Within the overarching ideology of neoliberalism, the norms of government for capitalist nation-states have been reorganised around the ideology of international competition. The message for workers is that employment and security can only be guaranteed by winning world markets on the basis of low costs, and that since only the private sector is efficient in doing this, capitalists must be enticed to invest by the prospects of high profits and low taxes. This is the domestic politics of 'there is no alternative': in every country, the same arguments are used to cut welfare, to privatise and to deregulate labour markets. This is the new form taken for the central purpose of the capitalist state – to manage labour on behalf of capital.

At the same time, the imperialism of this period of globalisation reconstructs the world order around a new ideology of liberal internationalism – or internationalised liberalism. If workers everywhere are to accept multinationals as the ultimate source of their employment and the providers of their means of subsistence, then the competing ideology of national self-determination must be expunged. As the dependency theorists argued, global capital needs the consent and support of elites and 'middle classes' everywhere, and the complex apparatuses of economic, political, social and cultural control are refashioned for this purpose. Global media peddle the vacuous consumerism that grips these social classes the world over; poverty is everywhere rebadged as 'social exclusion' based on individual inadequacies; and politics are reduced to periodic elections in which near-identical teams of rentier–politicians compete for the right to make comfortable careers out of packaging the masses for exploitation. Once the ideology of liberal individualism takes root, the state's conformity to the new norms of government is ensured by a combination of internal and external pressures, both representing ultimately the exigencies of capital.

But of course not all national elites succeed in refashioning their domestic politics in this way: they meet resistance domestically, and they face the ever present possibility of losing out in the wider world of international competition. In the 1990s, this problem was reformulated by academics and international institutions as one of 'state failure'. In cases where state failure is connected to ethnic, religious or other 'vertical' social divisions, and affects the basic functioning of the state, the boundaries of sovereign states are no longer inviolate: they may be redrawn through subdivision or merger, or they may be transgressed by other states acting as regional or global enforcers of human rights. The same treatment is accorded to 'rogue' states such as Afghanistan and Iraq, which fail to give due obeisance to the new order.

On the other hand, where state failure is due rather to 'horizontal' social divisions, to *class* struggles – as in post-communist eastern Europe, or in Venezuela and Argentina most recently – the preferred option for elites is to enlist the support of foreign powers and their international institutions to secure their power. They may request a timely loan or a trade concession, and depict their domestic opponents as posing a threat to such largesse; and if that is not sufficient, the 'free trade' in arms supplies them with the means of physical repression. At the same time, elites do not hesitate to draw from the historical wellsprings of nationalism, including the shameless use of ethnic and religious differences, to urge on their citizens to compete economically with workers of other countries.

CONCLUSION

In broad historical terms, what this new form of imperialism amounts to is nothing less than the extensive 're-embedding' of capitalism across the world, as a social order that is at once global and national. The postwar order entailed major political concessions by capitalists: to restore the world economy while keeping communism at bay, they gave us the Keynesian welfare state in the North, and the developmental state in the South. But these concessions provided the foundation for further political challenges, from organised labour in the North and post-colonial regimes in the South, to the inequalities of wealth and power that imperialism sustains, both within and between nations. The new order of global capitalism, in contrast, seeks to fashion a new politics that, both nationally and globally, closes off these challenges. The role of neoliberalism is to provide the ideological justification for this closure. The response of those who are still opposed to capitalist exploitation and oppression will increasingly have to become global too, linking the internationalism that has been such an important feature of anti-capitalist struggles in the past with local and national political initiatives.

REFERENCES

Beveridge, W. (1960) *Full Employment in a Free Society: A Report*, 2nd edn. London: Allen and Unwin.

Keynes, J.M. (1936) *The General Theory of Employment, Interest and Money*. London: Macmillan.

Polanyi, K. (2001) *The Great Transformation: The Political and Economic Origins of Our Times*. Boston: Beacon Press.

Schumpeter, J.A. (1975) *Capitalism, Socialism and Democracy*. New York: Harper & Row.

10
Neoliberalism in International Trade: Sound Economics or a Question of Faith?

Sonali Deraniyagala

Since the 1980s, a neoliberal belief in free trade has come to represent the orthodoxy in international economics. This orthodoxy has been translated into policy advice, particularly for developing countries, for which trade liberalisation is a major focus of policy. Whilst the orthodoxy in development policy has undergone some revisions since the late 1990s, the conviction that free trade promotes growth and prosperity remains steadfast.

This chapter examines the theoretical and empirical basis of the neoliberal case for free trade. Our intention is to show that this case is based on shaky theoretical grounds and inconclusive empirical support. Ultimately, it appears that the neoliberal position on trade is rooted in a belief in the efficacy of free-market processes and in a faith which has little grounding in theory or empirics.

NEOLIBERALISM AND INTERNATIONAL TRADE: THE MAIN PROPOSITIONS

The neoliberal approach to international trade is based on the proposition that free trade promotes economic growth and global prosperity (see Chapter 4). The neoliberal resurgence in international economics since the early 1980s gave almost axiomatic status to the optimisation potential of free trade, a view which has now come to represent the conventional wisdom on trade policy. The belief in free trade was an essential part of the 'Washington consensus' propagated at the height of the neoliberal resurgence.

This neoliberal position on international trade and trade policy consisted of several propositions: free trade optimises global resource allocation; free trade maximises consumer welfare; free trade leads to increased productivity growth and promotes economic growth; government intervention in trade policy is generally distortionary, reducing welfare and growth; countries with liberal trade regimes grow faster than countries with 'closed' regimes; trade liberalisation by lowering tariffs and non-tariff barriers should be the focus of trade policy.

Although this neoliberal Washington consensus has undergone some revisions since the late 1990s (see Chapters 3 and 12), faith in the efficacy of free trade still remains largely unquestioned. The prevailing neoliberal view on trade policy augments the earlier propositions with a newer set of trade policy reforms. Trade policy reform is no longer confined to tariff reduction, but also includes extensive institutional, legal and political reform. This view is clearly reflected in the objectives of the international organisation which co-ordinates global trade policy, the World Trade Organisation (WTO). The WTO seeks to bring about the international harmonisation of institutional, regulatory and legal standards through a variety of agreements and standards. Trade policy, therefore, now extends to issues previously considered to be beyond the realm of international trade, such as domestic investment, intellectual property and legal reform. The central and defining feature of the revised neoliberal view, however, remains the belief that free trade and global integration is the best way to promote growth and development and to reduce poverty.

INTERNATIONAL TRADE, GROWTH AND POVERTY: THE NEOLIBERAL VIEW

Within trade theory, the conclusion that free trade is optimal is derived from the canonical Heckscher–Ohlin model which, under highly restrictive assumptions, shows that optimal resource allocation can be achieved by the liberalisation of all trade restrictions. According to this model, trade should be based on the comparative advantage of countries, which in turn is determined by the relative abundance of production factors. Over the past two decades, however, these conclusions and assumptions have been questioned by a huge body of theoretical models which address the complexities of international trade and show that deviations from free trade can often enhance growth and welfare (Krugman 1984). Despite this, the forward march of neoliberalism in international trade policy has continued unabated.

The neoliberal case for openness in trade policy emphasises positive effects on growth, productivity and poverty. Below, we examine the theoretical and empirical bases of these propositions.

TRADE AND GROWTH

Neoliberal economists use several theoretical arguments to support the predictions that openness boosts economic growth and that economies that are more open grow faster than those that are closed. Free trade is seen as leading to both static and dynamic gains, with the latter being more significant than the former. Static, 'once-and-for-all' gains from trade arise as resources shift from inefficient to efficient sectors following the dismantling of trade restrictions. It is acknowledged, however, that the magnitude of these static gains is small. The growth-enhancing effects of openness arise, therefore, essentially from the long-term dynamic gains. A variety of arguments relating to the long-term gains from free trade are evident in the literature. Many of them, however, hinge on fairly arbitrary assumptions and have been shown to be theoretically fragile (Rodrik 1995; Deraniyagala and Fine 2001).

Static welfare gains from trade have been enlarged by incorporating political economy issues, in particular rent seeking. It is argued that the resource costs of trade interventions are multiplied several fold by the existence of rent seeking. Freer trade regimes are seen to boost economic growth by reducing rents and increasing resources available for growth promotion. However, whilst some estimates show the magnitude of rent seeking costs under protection to be large, their accuracy has been questioned (Ocampo and Taylor 1998).

Increasing returns to scale are frequently cited as an important source of dynamic gains from trade liberalisation. The creation of a neutral trade regime is seen to encourage exporting and participation in world markets, allowing firms to produce higher output levels and benefit from scale economies. This in turn boosts overall economic growth rates. This argument, however, is based on the assumption that liberalisation will necessarily expand activities subject to increasing returns (Rodrik 1995). If scale economies are concentrated in protected sectors which contract after liberalisation, the dynamic gains from trade will not materialise.

Many of the theoretical arguments relating to openness and growth, therefore, are contingent on specific assumptions and conditions, indicating that the positive causal link between openness and growth may be the exception rather than the norm. Partly for this reason, much of the debate on openness and growth has been largely empirical.

The neoliberal resurgence in international trade in the 1980s was strongly influenced by the economic collapse of developing countries which, until then, had followed protectionist import-substitution policies. This collapse was interpreted as being directly caused by interventionist trade policy (Balassa 1988). However, there are several problems with this interpretation. Many developing countries experienced satisfactory rates of economic growth under protection until around the mid 1970s, with some sub-Saharan countries being among the fastest-growing developing countries. Productivity growth in some import-substitutionist regimes, especially in Latin America, was also robust. Whilst developing countries did experience a serious economic downturn after the mid 1970s, this is better explained by external shocks (in particular the 1973 oil price hike) and the inability to adjust macroeconomic policy to cope with these shocks. To attribute the growth collapse of the late 1970s to trade policy alone, therefore, involves confusing macroeconomic failures with trade-policy failure.

In the 1990s, the orthodox position on trade liberalisation claimed strong support from a few highly influential econometric studies which estimated the effects of trade policy and economic growth (Dollar and Kraay 2000). These studies claimed to show a significant, positive causal link between trade openness and economic growth. However, problems with econometrics and data have resulted in some damning critiques (Rodriguez and Rodrik 2001). Much of the work is plagued by measurement problems, with many of the measures of trade openness reflecting trade volume rather than trade-policy orientation. The direction of causality is also difficult to establish, given the strong likelihood of faster growth leading to increased trade. It is also difficult to isolate the effects of trade policy on growth, given the numerous other potential influences.

Contrary to the claims of the neoliberal camp, therefore, empirical support for the argument that free trade boosts economic growth remains inconclusive. The orthodox belief in the growth-enhancing potential of free trade, however, remains undiminished. As Winters et al. (2002, p. 10) note in their comprehensive review of empirical research on trade and growth, 'the attraction of simple generalisations has seduced much of the profession into taking their results seriously'.

TRADE AND PRODUCTIVITY

The neoliberal case for free trade has also focused on identifying the specific channels by which trade affects long-term economic growth. A central focus is on productivity growth. It is claimed that trade liberalisation will lead to faster productivity growth, particularly in manufacturing, but also in agriculture. Given that the static gains from liberalisation are acknowledged to be negligible, productivity growth is seen as the key mechanism by which liberalisation boosts growth. A closer examination of these claims, however, shows them to be theoretically and empirically inconclusive.

Long-term productivity gains are seen to ensue because protection discourages cost-cutting technological change by providing a captive market for domestic producers. In much of the orthodox literature, however, the precise mechanisms by which trade liberalisation promotes technological change and productivity are never spelt out, largely because orthodox theory is silent on the issue. Some proponents of liberalisation argue that increased levels of competition are sufficient to promote productivity-enhancing technological change across all sectors (Balassa 1988). Such simplistic propositions ignore alternative studies which have found that technological change is sometimes promoted by oligopolistic market structures (Deraniyagala and Fine 2001).

A substantial body of empirical research has examined the effects of trade policy on productivity at the industry and firm level (Rodrik 1995). Overall, the evidence this research provides remains inconclusive. While some researchers find a negative correlation between import substitution and productivity growth, accelerating rates of productivity have also been found in sectors with high and low levels of protection. Again, these empirical studies are marked by notable shortcomings. They vary in country coverage and definitions of trade regime, making any generalisability difficult. Many of them fail to adequately control for other influences on productivity growth and to establish the direction of causality. This does not, however, seem to diminish neoliberal claims about the positive effects of openness on productivity. Many analysts simply proceed by *assuming* the existence of a positive causal link.

TRADE AND POVERTY

In the 1990s, the neoliberal approach to trade strongly emphasised the claim that greater openness fosters poverty reduction. Trade and poverty are linked through economic growth, and faster economic growth following trade liberalisation is seen to be poverty-reducing. Although faster economic growth could worsen a country's income distribution, this is seen not to be the case for growth arising from freer trade. Thus, greater openness is seen not to result in a drastic worsening in income distribution, and this offsets the positive growth effects on poverty (Winters, McCulloh and McKay 2002). Again, however, the orthodox research on trade and poverty is marked by theoretical inconsistencies and empirical flaws evident in much of the neoliberal literature on international trade (see Chapter 15).

Some mechanisms by which openness translates into poverty reduction have been identified. Creating a neutral trade regime is seen to increase labour-intensive production in many developing countries as resources move out of capital-intensive import-substitutionist activities. This increases the demand for labour, especially unskilled labour. This, together with potential upward pressure on unskilled wages could lead to a reduction in the incidence of poverty. Whether the incidence of poverty falls as a result, however, would depend on whether incomes for unskilled workers rose above the poverty line. Further, there is the possibility that the most intensively used labour in export sectors may be relatively skilled by developing-country standards. If the relatively skilled are under-represented among the poor, a fall in poverty is unlikely.

Agricultural growth following trade liberalisation is also seen by orthodox trade economists as poverty-reducing (see Chapter 14). Increased agricultural output following liberalisation is expected to translate into a lower incidence of rural poverty. However, as noted earlier, the expected agricultural-supply response to improved price incentives may often not be forthcoming. Furthermore, even if a small group of farmers respond to price rises by expanding output, poor farmers may be left out of this process (if they are engaged in subsistence farming with little surplus) and the positive effect on rural poverty will be small. Trade-policy reform is also predicted to induce a switch from subsistence agriculture to cash crops, bringing increased incomes for the poor. There could, however, be other effects that counteract this. If cash-crop prices are subject to fluctuations, farmers may not be willing to bear the increased risk and uncertainty, and output of cash crops may not increase. The effects of liberalisation on poverty will also depend on whether the rural poor are largely net sellers or net buyers of agricultural produce, especially food. If the majority of the poor are net buyers of food, a rise in food prices could lead to increased poverty.

Trade openness is also argued to reduce poverty via its effects on corruption and rent seeking (see Chapter 2). The neoliberal assumption that rent seeking falls after liberalisation leads to the claim that resources for poverty reduction will be greater following reform. Apart from problems with the assumption of a fall in rent seeking, it is important to note that the resource and revenue implications of trade policy reform are often more complex than this. Openness could sometimes constrain poverty-reduction efforts if it reduced the ability of governments to increase revenue by taxing mobile factors such as capital. Trade liberalisation can also affect poverty indirectly via its impact on trade taxes. In the very early stages of liberalisation, revenue collected from trade taxes may in fact rise as a country moves from quantitative restrictions to fairly high-level tariffs. Subsequently, however, revenue from tariffs will fall as the average level of tariffs falls. This fall in revenues is seen as constraining government expenditure on poverty reduction. However, this link is not immutable, but must certainly be borne in mind when analysing the effects of openness on poverty.

NEOLIBERALISM AND POLITICAL PHILOSOPHY

The discussion in this chapter has indicated theoretical and empirical weaknesses in the neoliberal belief in the growth- and welfare-optimising potential of free trade. As we have noted, whilst a vast literature which details these various shortcomings now exists, this has not, however, led to a fundamental rethinking of the case for free trade by the neoliberal camp. In the revised orthodoxy of the 1990s, the commitment to free trade remains, with the constituent elements of trade policy reform being broadened in the post-WTO era.

Ultimately, therefore, the neoliberal support for openness appears to be based on political and philosophical grounds rather than on sound economics. Whilst economic theory does not prove that the free-market case is more efficient, the free market is still preferred over government interventionism on philosophical grounds. The neoliberal stance is captured aptly by Lal and Rajapathirana (1987, p. 209) who argue for the need to make a stand 'for markets versus mandarins'. Bhagwati (1980, p. 41) too notes that even though economic theory may be fragile in its support for free trade, 'common sense and wisdom should prevail in favour of free trade'.

CONCLUSION

This chapter has dealt with the limitations of the neoliberal case for free trade. Apart from the specific points dealt with here, the proposition that openness is universally beneficial suffers from another fundamental failure. This is the assumption that the claim that 'openness is good for growth and poverty' applies equally in varying institutional and historical contexts. Thus, despite some revisions in the late 1990s, the neoliberal approach pays little attention to institutional factors, which often mediate between trade policy and its outcomes. The implementation of trade liberalisation policies and their effects are highly contingent on historical and political factors specific to individual countries. The experience of trade liberalisation in developing countries over the past two decades shows that a uniform set of policy 'blueprints' often has divergent effects on key indicators such as growth and poverty. Whilst the promotion of trade liberalisation by the neoliberal consensus means that free or freer trade is now heavily favoured by the economics profession, it has done little to deepen our understanding of country-specific historical and political economy factors that make the outcome of any trade policy complex and hard to predict.

REFERENCES

Balassa, B. (1988) 'Interests of Developing Countries in the Uruguay Round', *World Economy* 11 (1), pp.39–54.

Bhagwati, J. (1980) 'Is Free Trade Passé after all?', *Welwirtschaftliches Archiv* 125, pp.17–44.

Deraniyagala, S. and Fine, B. (2001) 'New Trade Theory versus Old Trade Policy: A Continuing Enigma', *Cambridge Journal of Economics* 25 (6), pp.809–25.

Dollar, D. and Kraay, A. (2000) 'Growth is Good for the Poor', World Bank Development Research Group, working paper 2507.

Krugman, P. (1984) 'Import Protection as Export Promotion', in H. Kierkowski (ed.) *Monopolistic Competition and International Trade*. Oxford: Oxford University Press.

Lal, D. and Rajapathirana, S. (1987) 'Foreign Trade Regimes and Growth in Developing Countries', *World Bank Research Observer* 2, pp. 189–217.

Ocampo, J. and Taylor, L. (1998) 'Trade Liberalisation in Developing Countries: Modest Benefits, but Problems with Productivity Growth, Macro-Prices and Income Distribution', *Economics Journal* 108 (3), pp.1523–46.

Rodriguez, F. and Rodrik, D. (2001) 'Trade Policy and Economic Growth: A Skeptic's Guide to Cross-National Evidence', in B. Bernanke and K. Rogoff (eds) *NBER Macroeconomics Annual 2000.* Cambridge, Mass.: MIT Press.

Rodrik, D. (1995) 'Trade and Industrial Policy Reform', in J. Behrman and T.N. Srinivasan (eds) *Handbook of Development Economics*, vol. 3b, Amsterdam: North-Holland.

Winters, A., McCulloch, N. and McKay, A. (2002) *Trade Liberalisation and Poverty: The Empirical Evidence*, University of Nottingham, CREDIT Research Paper 02/22.

11
'A Haven of Familiar Monetary Practice': The Neoliberal Dream in International Money and Finance

Jan Toporowski

Cross-border credit and money capital transfers, and international money, in the sense of cross-border payments, have always played a key role in the world-view of economic liberalism. Frequently, international money and financial activity have been regarded as proving that, without any government or social direction, trade can reach all corners of the globe and foster capitalist business enterprise everywhere. Behind this view is a nostalgia for the era of the gold standard, approximately between 1870 and 1914, when world currencies were convertible into gold at a fixed rate. The breakdown of that system during the First World War was associated with suspensions of international payments and capital flows. Its return in 1925 was welcomed by Oliver Sprague, adviser to the US government and the Bank of England, in the following terms:

> This return to the haven of familiar monetary practice is significant of the widespread conviction that the gold standard is an essential factor in the maintenance of a reasonable measure of international stability, for which there is no practicable substitute. (League of Nations 1930, p. 53)

Financial instability had come to be associated with the absence of a gold standard for money and exchange rates. Such instability gave rise to, and continues to foster, the delusion that the international financial system can provide an automatic mechanism to deal with economic problems. As the National Bureau of Economic Research in New York reported in 1940:

> Before 1925 concentration upon the goal of a return to normal and upon the achievement of stable exchange rates, and after 1925 the splendours of a stable exchange rate blinded the eyes of bankers and of the world in general. The illusion that the economic maladjustments would be corrected by automatic forces was dominant in the world's financial thinking. (Brown 1940, p. 801)

International finance remains crucial to the neoliberal project of a capitalism in which any imbalances are spontaneously eliminated by market forces that make supply equal to demand. Any financial instability is blamed on imperfections in the national or international financial system that may be remedied without challenging the capitalist system. In our time, this is a view that has re-emerged following the dismantling of the Keynesian system of 'big government' and economic stabilisation policies (see Chapter 2). In the period of Keynesian direct and indirect government direction of the economy, apologists for laissez-faire capitalism argued that such Keynesian policies were undermining economic stability and capitalist enterprise. Today, governments subordinate their economic policies to promoting business and finance. (Over a century ago, Hobson condemned the use of 'the public purse . . . for private gain', and the use of 'public resources' as 'the pledge of private speculations' (1938, pp. 97 and 59).) The increased economic instability that followed the abandoning of Keynesian stabilisation policies requires both an explanation of that instability and some alternative measures of promoting stability. The system of international finance offers an obvious source of economic disturbances and a target for the reforming zeal of those apologists for capitalism who cling to the 'gold standard' belief that there is some set of international monetary and financial arrangements under which the problems of capitalism will automatically be resolved by market forces.

THE RISE OF INTERNATIONAL FINANCE

As the Second World War came to an end, the political leaders of the Western Allies sought a 'return to the haven of familiar monetary practice' at the intergovernmental economic conference that was held in Bretton Woods in the United States in 1944. But by then there was no possibility of any return to the gold standard. Central banks without gold reserves could not return to the gold standard, and over four-fifths of the gold outside the Soviet Union was in the United States. The result of the Bretton Woods deliberations was an indirect gold standard. Central banks and their governments were obliged to maintain fixed exchange rates against the US dollar, while the Federal Reserve Bank of New York was given the responsibility of keeping the US dollar convertible for gold at a rate of US$35 per fine ounce of gold. The International Monetary Fund (IMF) was set up to police the system of fixed exchange rates. Governments were not allowed to change the exchange rate of their currency without the IMF's approval. If a central bank was running out of gold or dollars with which to maintain their fixed exchange rate, then the IMF would lend dollars, under very strict conditions. The World Bank also was set up at Bretton Woods to finance the reconstruction of countries devastated by the war, and subsequently to finance the economic development of poorer countries.

From this period dates the hegemony of the US dollar in international finance. This was the currency for which all other currencies and assets could be bought, virtually anywhere in the world. Every other currency was good for payments in the country in which it was issued, but was less acceptable outside that country. However, the exchange rate stability was not sustainable. Through the 1940s and the 1950s, the United States had balance-of-payments deficits averaging over a billion dollars per year. These dollars rarely returned to the United States to buy US goods or financial assets: US interest rates were low, and the status of the dollar as a reserve currency meant that any bank abroad was willing to hold that currency. This gave the United States a unique privilege of 'seigniorage': its residents could pay for their excess imports with dollars conveniently printed for them by the Federal Reserve system. Virtually every other country had to keep its demand for imports under control, by deflationary demand management, in order not to run out of foreign currency to pay for imports. The intervention of the United States in Korea and Taiwan, followed by its costly war in Vietnam, added to the steady outflow of dollars.

The dollars held outside the United States were principally held in unofficial and unregulated dollar markets that emerged first in London and then in Singapore. Interest rates in these markets were considerably higher than the regulated ones in the United States. This made it even more attractive to deposit dollars in these 'Euromarkets', whose principal banks were in any case American. Borrowers also found it convenient to borrow from them, because they did not have to submit to central-bank regulations over foreign-currency borrowing. Such regulation was an important part of the way in which central banks kept to the exchange rates fixed at Bretton Woods. Governments, in particular, found that they could borrow from the Euromarkets with fewer questions asked than they could from the International Monetary Fund. The Euromarkets then spawned smaller markets in other 'Eurocurrencies' held 'offshore', or outside their country of issue, and a Eurocurrency bond market.

Some of the dollar outflow did return and was exchanged for gold, so that these decades were also marked by a steady outflow of gold reserves from the United States. By 1970, it was clear that the United States was having difficulty in maintaining dollar convertibility against gold at the rate fixed in Bretton Woods. In 1971, the US government suspended gold payments. In 1973, fixed exchange rates were abandoned (see Chapter 22).

PROBLEMS OF INTERNATIONAL FINANCE

After the breakdown of the Bretton Woods system in 1971, the main capitalist economies were plunged into inflationary recessions that were dubbed 'stagflation'. The prices of raw materials rose sharply, most notably that of crude oil, which quadrupled between 1973 and 1976. Developing countries suddenly experienced huge export surpluses (if they were lightly populated and had an expensive commodity like oil to export), or were plunged into trade deficits if they were oil importers. The enlarged export revenues, in particular of the oil-exporting countries, found their way into the Euromarkets. There, the principal borrowers were now those countries with unsustainable trade deficits. It could only be a matter of time before this 'recycling' of export surpluses, through the international banking system to countries with chronic trade deficits, broke down in a debt crisis.

In December 1982, the Mexican government, followed rapidly by those of Brazil, Argentina and Poland, declared that they were unable to meet their foreign debt obligations. (Domestic debt is always an easier matter, because governments can raise taxes or take credits from their central bank to repay domestic debt.) Left to market forces, the banks which lent to them would have become insolvent and collapsed. Once the debt had been 'eliminated' in this way, more prudent international borrowing from the surviving banks would eventually have resumed. However, while economic liberals applauded the enterprise of predominantly

American international banks during the 1970s in inflating international debt, the market-loving government of the US President, Ronald Reagan, shrank from allowing the market to have its way with those banks during the 1980s. Not for the first time, the failure of US banks during the depression of the 1930s was used to conjure up economic catastrophes that would result from 'systemic failure' if the American international banks were allowed to collapse.

The IMF, which had been marginalised during the 1970s by the collapse of fixed exchange rates and the ease with which governments could borrow from the Euromarkets, now came into its own again. Its new function was to rehabilitate the predominantly American international banking system by refinancing the debts of governments that had borrowed from it (Strange 1986). The price of that refinancing was a severely deflationary financial stabilisation package known as 'structural adjustment'. This was ostensibly voluntary, but governments applying for loans knew what would secure the approval of the IMF (see Chapter 12). An appeal to international banks to lend more, the Baker initiative of 1986, failed: most bankers were sufficiently worldly to realise that lending more money to governments that could not repay existing debt was imprudent, to say the least.

The Brady initiative, in 1989, was more successful. This involved exchanging foreign bank debt for bonds secured on US government bonds, with some reduction in the value of that debt. The involvement of the US Treasury in guaranteeing those Brady bonds was, depending on your point of view, indicative of the responsibility that the American government now took for the stability of the international financial system, or symptomatic of the way in which international finance had been taken over by US interests. Either way, it was not particularly neoliberal, with the US Treasury and the IMF organising the refinancing of US banks. Their commitment to this refinancing contrasts with the draconian purges recommended and imposed on foreign banks during the 1990s, in the wake of emerging market crises (Brenner 2002).

STABILISATION OF INTERNATIONAL FINANCE

The Brady initiative owed its success to the inflation of markets for long-term securities that was a notable feature of financial developments in Japan (until 1991) and in the United States and the United Kingdom during the 1980s and the 1990s. This made it easy and relatively inexpensive to sell long-term bonds into the capital markets of those countries in order to refinance banks and indebted governments. Such inflation of long-term securities markets had two consequences. First of all, the Bank for International Settlements, under the Basle Accord of 1989, was able to impose additional capital requirements, which banks were supposed to hold against their more risky foreign assets or loans. Banks with access to liquid capital markets were able relatively easily to raise the additional capital requirements.

The second effect of rising, i.e. liquid, capital markets in North America and the United Kingdom was that other governments sought to engineer such markets in their own countries. Such markets would offer governments in developing or newly industrialised countries the possibility of issuing debt domestically, which was easier to manage and repay because it was in local currency. Such financial development had already been envisaged under the 'structural adjustment' policies imposed on indebted governments during the 1980s. The theory behind 'structural adjustment' was that private enterprise would naturally flourish in the absence of government regulation. However, to expand private enterprise requires financial resources. This brought financial liberalisation, or 'financial deepening', as its advocates call it, to the forefront of the neoliberal agenda, as a way of mobilising domestic saving for private investment, and as a way of augmenting domestic saving with foreign savings. Financial liberalisation was promoted by encouraging money centre and stock market activities in developing and newly industrialised countries. Domestic money inflows were secured by directing pension contributions into these markets. Once the stock market was rising, foreign portfolio investment was attracted by the possibilities of speculative gains. This brought in foreign money capital, whose conversion into local currency helped to stabilise the country's exchange rate. Such markets in developing and newly-industrialised countries were called 'emerging markets', to denote their emergence from backwardness and government control ('financial repression') into the orbit of the modern, rational and enlightened market forces of international finance.

However, capital inflows into emerging markets could flow out even more quickly than they had come in. In particular, financial inflation, and any investment boom arising out of it, increased prodigiously the demand for imports into an emerging market country. Higher imports then increased further the amount of capital inflow that was needed to keep the exchange rate stable. If the exchange rate fell, then this would devalue the assets of foreign capital holders (principally investment funds based in North America and western Europe). Any threat of such a devaluation could cause capital to flee an emerging market. Such devaluations were in fact inevitable, and caused financial markets to crash in Mexico in 1995, in east Asia in 1997, in Russia in 1998, in Turkey in 2001 and in Argentina in 2002 (Stiglitz 2002).

As a general rule of thumb, each crisis, from the international debt crisis of 1982 to the Russian crisis of 1998, cost twice as much to refinance as the previous one, so that the 1995 Mexican crisis cost twice as much as the 1982 debt crisis to resolve; the 1997 east Asian crisis cost twice as much as the Mexican crisis to settle; and the Russian crisis cost twice as much as the east Asian crisis. This escalation in the expense of avoiding the collapse of international banks and investment funds has been largely borne by the International Monetary Fund and the people of emerging market countries. The IMF has had to lend money to governments of emerging-market countries, while the people in those countries have had to put up with the economic recession and degradation of public services that were the price of IMF assistance. By the mid 1990s it was clear that this situation was not sustainable, if only because the US government provides nearly 40 per cent of IMF resources, and was thus obliged to put more and more money into securing international financial stability.

To limit its financial commitments, the IMF moved at the end of the 1990s to a system of selective automatic assistance to governments. The IMF now reports on the financial stability of its member governments, and only those with 'robust' financial systems can expect support from the Fund. However, emerging-market governments are aware of the influence that American international banks have in Washington. Keeping such banks operating in an emerging market is therefore an insurance policy that secures support in Washington in the event that the emerging market experiences a crisis. In this way, the IMF was eventually and reluctantly induced to help Argentina in 2002.

CONCLUSION

Neoliberals believe that the unfettered pursuit of private gain can be kept in check and turned to the general social and economic benefit by naturally occurring market forces. This doctrine overlooks the political and social power that financial wealth bestows, a power that became apparent when this doctrine was applied to international finance. Far from being rational and transparent, as the advocates of financial liberalisation had wanted, the system remains corrupt and dependent on state support. Only the beneficiaries of the corruption have changed. Previously, petty bureaucrats in poor countries channelled scarce financial resources to their favourite projects. Now international bankers and fund managers, and their supporters in the US Government and its allies, channel finance to pro-American governments and companies they favour. At the same time stability has not been secured: selective assistance to countries with 'sound' financial systems simply means that the IMF will not help if a crisis arises, unless that crisis happens to be in a country that has friends in Washington.

Critics of international finance have made various proposals to stabilise the system and make it more appropriate to the purposes of economic and social development. The most common suggestion has been a return to the cross-border capital controls that existed during the 1940s and the 1950s. Such controls, in many cases, were not eliminated until the 1990s. However, international bank deposits and financial assets held abroad are now so large that it would be difficult to enforce such controls. Indeed, the main reason for getting rid of such regulations was precisely because they could not be enforced.

Among the most famous stabilisation measures suggested has been a Tobin tax, put forward by the distinguished American Keynesian James Tobin during the 1970s as a way of stabilising exchange rates. This would be a tax of between half and one per cent on every foreign exchange transaction. Recent proponents of this tax have suggested putting its proceeds to finance development projects in poor countries. This has genuinely popular support among activists who campaign for a more just international order. However, critics, such as the American post-Keynesian Paul Davidson, have argued that it would be ineffectual in view of the scale of the international financial problem. The Scottish economist John Grahl has argued that it would simply make it more difficult to develop financial markets outside the United States (Grahl and Lysandrou 2003). The Cambridge Keynesian Geoffrey Harcourt has advocated a tax on speculation. There is no doubt that the funds raised from such taxes could finance major social and economic improvements. But from the point of view of financial stabilisation, there is no evidence that such a tax would by itself eliminate speculation. Markets could become even more unstable if speculation is concentrated where the return is highest. This author has argued that central banks should regulate financial markets more effectively by buying and selling securities to balance speculative selling or buying (Toporowski 2003). But this would need a major change in the way in which central banks operate.

For the citizen of a developing country, experiencing poverty, underemployment and the collapse of the social fabric of her or his society and polity because her or his government is being turned into a debt collector for foreign banking and financial interests, it will be of little comfort to know that the system also degrades the economic, if not the social, fabric of the countries of its principal beneficiaries. The United States and the United Kingdom, whose financial systems have been most inflated by laissez-faire finance supported by compulsory subscriptions to funded pension schemes, have slow industrial growth and employment (see Chapters 22 and 23). Their poor investment record belies the conventional wisdom of financial neoliberals, that the best way to encourage real investment is to entrust even more money to an investment banker or international fund manager. However, as long as there are speculative gains to be made from the markets, there will be powerful interests opposing the international co-operation required to reform the system and make it more efficient.

REFERENCES

Brenner, R. (2002) *The Boom and the Bubble: The US in the World Economy*. London: Verso.

Brown, W.A. (1940) *The International Gold Standard Reinterpreted, 1914–1934*. New York: National Bureau of Economic Research.

Grahl, J. and Lysandrou, P. (2003) 'Sand in the Wheels or Spanner in the Works? The Tobin Tax and Global Finance', *Cambridge Journal of Economics* 27 (5), pp. 597–621.

Hobson, J.A. (1938) *Imperialism: A Study*. London: George Allen & Unwin (first published in 1902).

League of Nations (1930) *First Interim Report of the Gold Delegation of the Financial Committee*. Geneva: League of Nations.

Stiglitz, J.E. (2002) *Globalisation and Its Discontents*. London: Allen Lane.

Strange, S. (1986) *Casino Capitalism*. Oxford: Basil Blackwell.

Toporowski, J. (2003) 'The End of Finance and Financial Stabilisation', *Wirtschaft und Gesellschaft* 29 Jahrgang, Heft 4.

12

From Washington to Post-Washington Consensus: Neoliberal Agendas for Economic Development[1]

Alfredo Saad-Filho

During the last two decades, the debate over economic development policy has been dominated by the so-called 'Washington consensus'. This 'consensus' reflects the convergence of three institutions based in Washington, D.C., the World Bank, the International Monetary Fund (IMF) and the US Treasury Department, around neoclassical economic theory and neoliberal policy prescriptions for poor countries. The consensus has subsequently been expanded to include other institutions, for example the World Trade Organisation and the European Central Bank.

This chapter offers a political economy review of the theory and policy prescriptions associated with neoliberalism and the Washington consensus, and the relationship between them and the so-called 'post-Washington consensus'. The chapter concludes with some reflections on the problems of economic development in the era of neoliberalism.

NEOCLASSICAL ECONOMIC THEORY AND THE WASHINGTON CONSENSUS

Three aspects of modern neoclassical theory are especially important in explaining the policies associated with neoliberalism and the Washington consensus. At the microeconomic level, neoclassical theory presumes that the market is *efficient* and the state is *inefficient*. Therefore, the market rather than the state should address such economic problems of development as industrial growth, international competitivity and employment creation (see Chapter 3).

At the macroeconomic level, this approach presumes that the world economy is characterised by capital mobility and the relentless advance of 'globalisation' (see Chapter 7). Although these offer the possibility of rapid growth through the attraction of foreign productive and financial capital, this can be achieved only if domestic policies conform to the short-term interests of the (financial) markets – otherwise both foreign and domestic capital will be driven elsewhere. Finally, the most important economic policy tool is the interest rate. The presumption is that the 'correct' interest rates can deliver balance-of-payments equilibrium, low inflation, sustainable investment and consumption and, therefore, high growth rates in the long term.

In other words, neoliberalism implies that the main reason why poor countries remain poor is not because they lack machines, infrastructure or money (as used to be generally accepted by economists) but, rather, because of misconceived state intervention, corruption, inefficiency and misguided economic incentives. Neoliberals also claim that international trade and finance – rather than domestic consumption – should become the engines of development.

The neoliberal premises of the Washington consensus imply that certain development policies are 'naturally' desirable. First and foremost, the state should be 'rolled back' in order to focus on three functions only: defence against foreign aggression, provision of legal and economic infrastructure for the functioning of markets, and mediation between social groups in order to preserve and expand market relations (see Chapter 6). As 'free markets' spontaneously expand in the wake of the withdrawal of the state, relative prices will be determined by resource availability and consumer preferences, rather than politically. Free-market prices are important because they provide the 'correct' incentives for economic activity. Economic policies contributing to these outcomes include privatisation, deregulation and the extinction of state planning.

Fiscal and monetary policy discipline ought to be imposed, in order to eliminate the government budget deficit, control inflation and – once again – limit the scope for state economic intervention. This can be done through tax reforms, expenditure cuts, and the shift of government investment away from directly productive sectors (e.g. electricity provision, telecommunications) and towards the provision of public goods, especially health and education.

Neoliberalism also recommends the liberalisation of foreign trade and the devaluation of the exchange rate. Whereas the former compels domestic firms to become more efficient, due to the pressure of (presumably more competitive) foreign producers, the latter stimulates exports and promotes specialisation according to the country's comparative advantage. The capital account of the balance of payments should also be liberalised in order to facilitate foreign investment inflows, which will supplement domestic savings and investment capacity (liberalisation will facilitate capital outflows, but this presumably also enhances the attractiveness of the recipient country). Finally, it is important to liberalise the domestic financial system, in order to increase the availability of savings and the rate of return on investment.

Essential, too, is the 'flexibilisation' of the labour market, supposedly in order to increase employment and labour productivity. This includes the simplification of hiring-and-firing regulations, the decentralisation of labour relations, the curtailment of trade union rights, the elimination of collective agreements and protective regulation, and the reduction of social security benefits.

This combination of policies, regulations and incentives is designed to reduce the economic role of the state. In doing so, it transfers to the (financial) markets the ability to determine the pattern of international specialisation and the capacity to determine the economic priorities, both inter-temporally (levels of investment and consumption) and inter-sectorally (allocation of investment funds and determination of the composition of output and employment).

Countries suffering from severe balance-of-payments disequilibria, due, for example, to debt or currency crises, can borrow from the IMF and the World Bank only if they agree to follow a stabilisation and structural adjustment programme agreed with these institutions. 'Agreement' is of course a misnomer, because when the scarcity of foreign exchange becomes extreme, countries generally find that banks and other financial institutions will refuse to lend them money *unless* a neoliberal adjustment programme is in place (Weeks 1991). Around 100 poor countries have been compelled to agree to one or more such programmes in the last 20 years, leading to the cumulative imposition of the neoliberal policy menu around the world.

CRITIQUES OF THE WASHINGTON CONSENSUS

There is no question that the neoliberal policy reforms can deliver short-term macroeconomic stability and growth to many countries. This is not necessarily because they are appropriate. It is simply because most investors and financial institutions consider these reforms to be 'credible', which can bring rewards in the form of foreign capital flows, especially to middle-income countries, such as Argentina, Brazil, Mexico, South Africa, South Korea or Thailand. Given the right circumstances, especially an abundance of funds, with relatively unattractive opportunities in the rich countries, foreign capital can finance the growth of investment and consumption in these countries for several years. This avenue is not generally available to low-income countries, such as Bangladesh, Bolivia, Ethiopia, Paraguay, Swaziland or Tanzania, because they offer few attractive opportunities for foreign investors and have low capacity to absorb capital inflows. The consequences of neoliberalism in these countries tend to be more severe, and their prospects are bleaker than those of middle-income countries.

Critiques of neoliberal development policies can be divided into two broad areas: the theoretical and methodological shortcomings of neoliberalism, and the empirical problems of the Washington-consensus policies.

THEORETICAL AND METHODOLOGICAL PROBLEMS

Four issues are especially prominent. At the theoretical level, the neoliberal faith in markets contradicts even neoclassical theory. The (thoroughly neoclassical) second-best analysis of Lipsey and Lancaster shows that, if an economy departs from the perfectly competitive ideal on several counts – as all economies invariably do – the removal of one imperfection (e.g. privatisation of the state oil monopoly) may not make the economy more efficient or productive. Therefore, each policy reform ought to be justified in its own terms, rather than being rolled into an all-encompassing package.

Politically, in the rich countries neoliberalism seeks to cancel the 'Keynesian consensus' and roll back the welfare state, at least partially. In contrast, in the poor countries, Keynesianism and the welfare state have never existed, and although state intervention was often unwieldy and inefficient, it was indispensable for rapid growth and the promotion of social justice, among other areas. In these countries, Washington consensus policies reduce state capacity to address pressing social problems, including poverty, unemployment and the concentration of income and wealth.

It is also noticeable that, whereas neoliberals often calculate the costs of state intervention in order to press the case for market reforms, they systematically fail to consider the costs of the neoliberal policies. These include the loss of dynamic benefits resulting from permanently lower growth rates, the social and economic costs of high unemployment, foreign currency waste in (liberalised) imports of luxury consumption goods and capital flight, and the negative impact of the contraction of the industrial base which invariably follows the neoliberal reforms.

Finally, there is no shortage of examples of alternatives to neoliberalism. In particular, the rich countries did *not* become rich by following neoliberal policies (Chang 2002); periods of rapid growth in both rich and poor countries have *not* coincided with neoliberalism; and the policies associated with rapid growth in Latin America (1930–82), East Asia (1960–98) and China (1978 to the present), for example, flatly contradict the prescriptions of the Washington consensus on several counts.

IMPLEMENTATION PROBLEMS

Implementation problems can be grouped into five areas. First, Washington consensus policies systematically favour large domestic and foreign capital, especially financial capital, at the expense of smaller capitals and the workers. The ensuing transfer of resources to the rich, and the growth slowdown triggered by the neoliberal obsession with inflation, have led, in virtually every country, to higher unemployment, wage stagnation and concentration of income (see Milanovic 2002). Moreover, volatile capital flows to poor countries have frequently triggered severe financial crises (e.g. Mexico in 1994–95, East Asia in 1996–98, Russia in 1998, Brazil in 1999, Turkey and Argentina in 2001).

Second, economic deregulation reduces the degree of co-ordination of economic activity and state policy-making capacity, and precludes the use of industrial-policy instruments for the implementation of socially determined priorities – for example, it can be difficult to reduce production costs through the optimisation of the country's transport network if the ownership of the network is fragmented between competing firms. 'Market freedom' increases economic uncertainty and volatility, and facilitates the onset of crisis.

Third, the neoliberal reforms introduce mutually reinforcing policies that destroy jobs and traditional industries that are defined, often *ex post*, as being inefficient. The depressive impact of their elimination is rarely compensated by the rapid development of new industries, leading to structural unemployment, greater poverty and marginalisation, the disarticulation of existing production chains, and a more fragile balance of payments.

Fourth, the neoliberal macroeconomic strategy is heavily oriented towards 'business confidence'. This is unsatisfactory because confidence is both intangible and elusive, and it is subject to sudden and arbitrary changes; moreover, this strategy almost invariably overestimates the levels of investment that can be generated by the adherence to neoliberalism.

Finally, neoliberal policies are not self-correcting. However, their failure generally leads to the *extension* of IMF and World Bank intervention beyond economic policy-making, and into governance and the political process, with the excuse of ensuring implementation of Washington's favourite policies.

THE POST-WASHINGTON CONSENSUS

In the 1980s and 1990s, dissatisfaction with the Washington consensus spread across the poor countries, and it was articulated by critics of the mainstream in academia and in civil-society organisations (see Chapters 15, 19 and 27). Their dissatisfaction centred on the inability of the Washington consensus to explain the economic success of East Asian countries, the incapacity of neoliberal policies to deliver significant improvements in economic performance, and the unnecessarily harsh measures included in the adjustment programmes, which have highly negative consequences for the poor. Gradually and unevenly, even economists based at international financial organisations began to admit that the adjustment programmes were not working.

This shift away from the neoliberal orthodoxy became evident after the appointment of Joseph Stiglitz as chief economist of the World Bank, in 1997. Stiglitz is one of the main proponents of the 'new institutional economics' (NIE), and he used his new position to articulate what he called a 'post-Washington consensus'. Although he was ejected from the World Bank in 1999, Stiglitz's ideas have not been abandoned, and they remain influential around the world.

NIE shifts the analytical focus away from the neoclassical emphasis on competition and markets, and towards the implications of market failure, the institutional setting of economic activity, and the potential outcomes of differences or changes in institutions. This approach can provide a more nuanced understanding of economic development (Harriss et al. 1995). For example, development is no longer simply the process of increasing per capita GDP or consumption levels, as in neoclassical theory. It now includes changes in the distribution of property rights, work patterns, urbanisation, family structures, and so on, which clearly are significant aspects of development. It follows that, for NIE, poor countries often fail to grow because of misguided regulation of economic activity, ill-defined property rights and other institutional constraints. In this respect, new institutionalism has important advantages vis-à-vis neoliberalism. For example, it can offer positive guidelines for state intervention, including not only changes to economic policy, but also detailed recommendations for legal and judicial changes (primarily in order to protect property rights and secure the profitability of enterprise), the development of market-friendly civil society institutions, financial reforms beyond the privatisation of state-owned banks, anti-corruption programmes, democratic political reforms (not primarily because of concerns with freedom and human rights, but in order to dilute state power and reduce its capacity to influence economic outcomes), and so on (Pender 2001). This broader set of policy recommendations has been called 'enhanced conditionality'.

CRITIQUES OF THE POST-WASHINGTON CONSENSUS

The post-Washington consensus rightly acknowledges the fact that at the core of the development process lies a profound shift in social relations, for which an analysis limited to macroeconomic aggregates is both insufficient and potentially misleading. This conclusion vindicates some of the criticisms that political economists have raised against neoliberalism since the early 1980s.

However, in spite of these advantages the post-Washington consensus suffers from weaknesses similar to those of the Washington consensus.[2] In particular, they share the same methodological foundations, including reductionism, methodological individualism, utilitarianism and the dogmatic presumption that exchange is part of human nature rather than being an aspect of society (see Saad-Filho 2003). Consequently, for the post-Washington consensus the market is a 'natural' rather than a socially created institution, and although its optimality can be questioned under certain circumstances, the market itself cannot be challenged. Second, the Washington and post-Washington consensuses recommend very similar policies for poor countries. They are both highly conservative in fiscal and monetary policy, and support 'free' trade, privatisation, liberalisation and deregulation. The only significant difference between them concerns the speed, depth and method of reform, because new institutionalism accepts the potential usefulness of localised state intervention in order to correct specific market failures.

The heated exchanges between Stiglitz and the IMF can make the differences between the Washington and the post-Washington consensuses appear to be large. However, they do not correspond either to differences between the underlying economic theories, which are largely compatible, or between policy recommendations to poor countries, which are essentially indistinguishable. The two consensuses are, in effect, two branches of the neoliberal onslaught in development economics and policy.

CONCLUSION

It has been obvious for many years that the policy prescriptions of the Washington and the post-Washington consensuses are successful only exceptionally. However, there is an even deeper problem. For the critical issue is *not* the comparison between the growth rates achieved by economies with or without adjustment programmes, or the contrast between growth rates before and after such programmes, or whether policy reform should be imposed by the IMF or by followers of Stiglitz.

The main problem for the majority concerns the *type* of growth promoted by the two versions of neoliberalism. This growth pattern is undesirable, because it concentrates income and power, perpetuates deprivation, and prevents the realisation of human potential. The limitations and insufficiencies of neoliberalism make it essential for the poor majority, who have hardly benefited from economic development for an entire generation, to consider alternative policies for their countries. These policies should respond to the imperatives of equality, democracy and social justice, and foster economic growth, mass employment, social inclusion, the satisfaction of basic needs and the provision of welfare for the vast majority of the population. Experience shows that these objectives can be achieved only through the deployment of centrally co-ordinated industrial and investment policy.

In other words, the shortcomings, failures and inefficiencies of the economic systems of poor countries are not due to excessive state intervention per se. A strong democratic state, with clear objectives, internal cohesion, popular legitimacy and the capacity to control economically powerful fractions of the population and direct the use of their resources, can achieve democratic economic objectives much better than the market alone, however defined. It is possible to mobilise economic and social institutions towards these socially determined ends without any implication that the state will either command or control the entire economy or society, which would be undemocratic. Achievement of these objectives requires recognition of the strongly negative consequences of neoliberalism, popular mobilisation against them, clarity of objectives and relentless political determination by the vast majority.

NOTES

1. I am grateful to Ben Fine and Carlos Oya for allowing me to read some of their unpublished papers during the preparation of this manuscript.
2. See the excellent essays in Fine et al. (2001) and Standing (2000).

REFERENCES

Chang, H.J. (2002). *Kicking Away the Ladder: Development Strategy in Historical Perspective*. London: Anthem Press.

Fine, B., Lapavitsas, C. and Pincus, J. (eds) (2001) *Development Policy in the Twenty-First Century: Beyond the Post-Washington Consensus*. London: Routledge.

Fine, B. and Stoneman, C. (1996) 'Introduction: State and Development', *Journal of Southern African Studies* 22 (1), pp. 5–26.

Harriss, J., Hunter, J. and Lewis, C. (1995) *The New Institutional Economics and Third World Development*. London: Routledge.

Milanovic, B. (2002) 'True World Income Distribution, 1988 and 1993: First Calculation Based on Household Surveys Alone', *Economic Journal* 112, pp. 51–92.

Pender, J. (2001) 'From "Structural Adjustment" to "Comprehensive Development Framework": Conditionality Transformed?', *Third World Quarterly* 22 (3), pp. 397–411.

Saad-Filho, A. (2003) 'Introduction', in *Anti-Capitalism: A Marxist Introduction*. London: Pluto Press.

Standing, G. (2000) 'Brave New Words? A Critique of Stiglitz's World Bank Rethink', *Development and Change* 31, pp. 737–63.

Weeks, J. (1991) 'Losers Pay Reparations, or How the Third World Lost the Lending War', in *Debt Disaster? Banks, Governments, and Multilaterals Confront the Crisis*. Geonomics Institute for International Economic Advancement Series, pp. 41–63.

13
Foreign Aid, Neoliberalism and US Imperialism

Henry Veltmeyer and James Petras

Overseas Development Assistance (ODA) is widely viewed as a catalyst of economic development, providing a needed boost to developing economies to assist them in the process of industrial development and modernisation already traced out by the more advanced countries that make up the rich club of 'developed countries' at the centre of the system. But it is possible to look at foreign aid differently – as a means of advancing the geopolitical and strategic interests of the governments and organisations that provide this aid, designed to benefit not the recipient but rather the donor. In 1971, at the height (but impending crisis) of the Bretton Woods world economic order, this view was expressed in the notion of 'aid as imperialism'.

In the early 1970s, however, this world economic order was close to falling apart, as the 'golden age of capitalism' came to an end (see Chapters 1, 2 and 22). As a result, the entire 'system' had to be re-engineered – to create the conditions for renewed expansion and the accumulation of capital on a global scale. But it was not until the 1980s that a strategic solution to the crisis was found in the neoliberal model of capitalist development – the creation of a global economy based on the principles of free enterprise and the free market. This model would also be used by the US government as a means of restoring its hegemony over the world system.

The dynamics of these changes are well known. Less well known is the role of ODA in the process. The purpose of this chapter is to expose some critical elements of this role, particular as regards the neoliberal model of global capitalist development.

AID IN THE 1940s AND 1950s: COMBATING THE LURE OF COMMUNISM

According to Wolfgang Sachs (1992) and his associates, development was 'invented' in the late 1940s as a form of imperialism – to impose new relations of domination on peoples in diverse countries struggling to liberate themselves from the yoke of colonialism. The idea of 'development' itself is often traced back to the 'Four Point' programme of overseas development assistance (ODA) announced by President Truman on 10 January 1949. But in its multilateral form it goes back to projects funded by the International Bank of Reconstruction and Development (subsequently known as the World Bank) in Chile in 1948 and in Brazil and Mexico the year after. The World Bank is an institutional pillar of the Bretton

Woods system designed so as to resurrect a global form of capitalist development and a process of international trade.

In regard to ODA, the US government was the major donor by far, and the geopolitical and strategic foreign-policy considerations of the US government the most relevant in shaping the form that it would take. These considerations were extensively debated. From the beginning, there existed a policy debate as to the possible uses of 'foreign aid'. The central issue had to do with how the broader geopolitical strategic interests of the United States could best be served. In this connection, voices were raised to the effect that it would not be in the interest of the United States to promote economic development in the backward areas of the world and that efforts to contain the underdeveloped countries within the Western bloc would be 'unrealistic' and not fruitful for American interests. But the prevailing view was that ODA was a useful means of advancing the geopolitical interests of the United States (to prevent the spread of communism) without damaging its economic interests.

AID IN THE 1960s AND 1970s: REFORM OR REVOLUTION?

In the developing world, the emphasis of 'aid' was on building the administrative capacity of the state and providing the infrastructure for both public and private enterprise – 'nation-building' in the parlance of imperial policy. In Latin America, however, the main concern was to stave off pressures for revolutionary change – to prevent another Cuba. To this end USAID promoted state-led reforms and the public provision of credit and technical assistance to the rural poor.

A large part of ODA took a bilateral form, but increasingly USAID turned to non-governmental organisations (NGOs) as their executive arm, bypassing governments to channel funds more directly to the local communities. These NGOs ('private voluntary organisations' in the United States) not only provided a useful channel for ODA but various collateral 'services' or benefits to donors, including the strengthening of local organisations opting for development and the weakening of class-based organisations with an anti-systemic orientation. In this context, the NGOs were also used, almost incidentally – and somewhat 'innocently' from the perspective of many of their personnel – not only to avoid revolution and promote economic and social development, but to promote the virtues of democracy and capitalism – use of the electoral mechanism in politics, the market mechanism in economics and reform as the modality of change.

In effect, these NGOs served as executive agents of US imperialism, promoting values and behaviour functioning in the economic and political interests of the growing US empire. They resembled the missionaries in the old imperialism, in that they tended to spread the gospel – in this case the good word about reform and democracy, as well as information about the evil forces (communism, revolutionary change) that were lurking in the land.

The difference between the new missionaries and the missionaries of old – though perhaps there is no fundamental difference – is that more often than not the new missionaries were unaware of the broader implications of their interventions. NGOs were not ideologues, concerned to spread the gospel. They generally involved well-intentioned individuals concerned to make a small difference in the lives of people they touched with their assistance. Nevertheless, in their mediations between the donors and recipient organisations, they could not help but promote an alternative to the politics of revolutionary change – and it was to this end that USAID financed them.

USAID and the broader donor community used NGOs as partners in the shared development enterprise. In this they helped turn local communities away from revolution and to promote a reformist approach to change.

FOREIGN AID IN A SYSTEM IN TRANSITION: 1973–83

The immediate postwar period has been described as a 'golden age of capitalism', but this era came to an end in the early 1970s with the onset of an extended period of crisis and efforts to restructure the system in the search for a way out. One strategic response involved a direct assault by capital on labour. Other responses included the institution of a more flexible form of regulation – post-Fordism, a global restructuring of development finance – provided primarily in the form of 'official' ODA, which at the time dominated global North–South capital flows ('international transfer of resources' in official discourse); and a set of national policy 'reforms' (the 'structural adjustment programme') based on what has become known as the 'Washington consensus'.

As to financial capital, the dominant stream took the form of ODA, designed as a supplemental form of finance needed to stimulate economic growth. Until 1983, such official transfers of 'financial resources' were channelled into projects designed to establish the infrastructure for economic activity. However, after the onset of a region-wide debt crisis, 'official' transfers took on a different form – loans premised on policy reforms oriented towards the free market.

Until this point, the World Bank and other International Financial Institutions (IFIs) took the position that ODA would service development strategies 'owned' by the developing countries, which were expected to pursue their own paths. After 1983, however, with the leverage provided by the debt crisis, bank lending was predicated on reforms designed within what has been termed the 'Washington consensus'. In the wake of the global crisis, the commercial banks in the United States and Europe initiated a policy of commercial loans that led to an explosion of private capital and debt financing that would exceed the 'official' flows of capital (ODA) – and, for some years (in the late 1970s and then again in the early 1990s) it exceeded the flow of capital in the form of FDI associated with the MNCs. Table 13.1 provides a picture of these flows of capital, as well as their returns.

These data reflect several global trends including: the eclipse by private capital of ODA in the 1990s; a dramatic decline of commercial lending in the 1980s (with the debt crisis) and then again in the 1990s (after the financial crisis in Latin America and Asia); the growth of FDI as the dominant capital flow (the 'backbone of private sector external financial flows', as the IMF puts it) – used in the acquisition of privatised enterprises and mergers with other firms, leading to a global process of asset and income concentration.

Table 13.1 also points towards an enormous outflow of productive and financial resources from the developing countries to those at the centre – a veritable

Table 13.1   Long-term North–South capital flows, 1985–2001 (US$ billion)

	1985–89	1990–94	1995	1996	1997	1998	1999	2000	2001
Capital inflows									
ODA	200.0	274.6	55.3	31.2	43.0	54.5	46.1	37.9	36.2
Private	157.0	547.5	206.1	276.6	300.8	283.2	224.4	225.8	160.0
Total	357.0	822.5	261.4	307.8	343.8	337.7	270.5	263.7	196.2
Capital outflows									
FDI profits	66.0	96.5	26.5	30.0	31.8	35.2	40.3	45.4	55.3
Debt payments	354.0	356.5	100.8	106.6	112.9	118.7	121.9	126.7	122.2
Total	420.0	453.0	127.3	136.6	144.7	153.9	162.2	172.1	177.5

Source: IMF (2002); World Bank (2002); OECD (2000)

haemorrhage of their lifeblood. In this regard it is estimated that over the last decade in Latin America alone, outflows of capital in the form of various types of return on investments (profit repatriation, interest payments on debt and equity investments) were in excess of US$750 billion (ECLAC 2002).

These 'transfers' represent a huge drain of potential capital that could have been used to expand production in the developing countries. Even ODA in this connection has served as a mechanism of capital drain: in 2002 repayments by the developing countries to the World Bank exceeded total outlays of new 'financial resources'. According to ECLAC (2002) over US$69 billion in interest payments and profits were remitted from the region to the US head offices of the multinational corporations and banks in just one year. If we take account of the billions in royalty payments, shipping, insurance and other service fees, and the billions more illegally transferred by Latin American elites via US and European banks to overseas accounts, the total pillage for 2002 was closer to US$100 billion. And this is in just one year in one part of the US empire.

AID IN AN ERA OF GLOBALISATION: THE 1980s AND 1990s

With the debt crisis, bank loans dried up as the creditors lined up behind the World Bank and the IMF. Table 13.1 shows that in just five years (from 1985 to 1989) over US$350 billion in the form of debt payments were diverted from development projects and programmes in the developing countries (primarily Latin America) to the head offices of the commercial banks—a capital drain that led directly to a 'decade lost to development', both in Latin America and in sub-Saharan Africa. As of 1995, virtually no new loans have been extended to developing countries by the commercial banks, while another US$800 billion were 'lost to development' due to policy reforms insisted on by the World Bank as a conditionality of further 'aid' (see Chapter 11 and World Bank 1998).

The 1990s saw the global spread of a virus that affected first Mexico and then, in mid 1997, south-east Asia. Caused by the volatile and deregulated movement of hundreds of billions of dollars in capital in search of short-term profit, the 'Asian [financial] crisis' devastated economy after economy in the region, stilling any talk (and much writing) about the 'economic miracle' of rapid growth in one part of the world system.

The financial crisis resurrected the spectre of a more generalised economic crisis, even the collapse of the system. Under these conditions, the multinational commercial banks again pulled out, leaving a vacuum filled by FDI, leading to another half decade 'lost to development' (ECLAC 2002). Official aid flows in this context were minimal and largely 'unproductive' (spent rather than invested), as were the much larger FDI flows. The results of these 'developments' are not hard to find. They are exemplified in the experience of Argentina, hitherto the most developed economy in Latin America but now (and for the past five years) in the throes of a far-reaching crisis.

ALTERNATIVE DEVELOPMENT AND IMPERIALISM IN AN ERA OF GLOBALISATION: 1983–2003

ODA originated as a policy for meeting the strategic foreign policy requirements of the US state. In retrospect it can quite properly be described an imperial policy – in the service of the US state. Subsequently, with the agency of the NGOs, the development project was pressed into the service of the empire as a means of defusing pressures for revolutionary change within its client states. The history of the US state (political and military) intervention in Central America – one of the more successful arenas for the projection of US state power – testifies that more often than not development did not work. True, no other Cubas emerged in the region, but this was the result not so much of the operations of USAID as of the projection of military force and the extensive 'aid' provided to counter-insurgency forces in the region.

In the 1980s, an entirely new context was created for ODA by a new neoliberal project of globalisation based on structural adjustment programmes (SAPs) and market reforms (see Chapter 12). In this context, the development project was not abandoned but restructured – designed as an alternative, more participatory form of development based on the partnership of intergovernmental ODA organisations and non-governmental organisations, which would mediate between the donors and the grassroots in the execution of a new generation of development projects targeted at the problem of poverty. The actual flow of funds channelled through these NGOs, many of which were unwittingly converted into agents of the new imperialism – bearers of the gospel about free market capitalism and democracy – was actually very modest (less than 10 per cent of the total), but enough to serve the purpose of turning organisations in the popular sector away from direct action against the system and to persuade them to opt instead for a 'participatory' form of 'local development'. This development is predicated on the accumulation not of natural, physical and financial assets, but of 'social capital' – which does not require a political confrontation with the power structure, or substantive change.

FOREIGN AID AS A CATALYST OF REGRESSION

Until the 1980s ODA was the dominant form of 'international resource flows'. The rationale for ODA was an assumed incapacity of developing countries to accumulate sufficient capital to finance their development. The provision of supplementary finance was deemed to have a catalytic effect, generating conditions that would reduce poverty and stimulate economies to grow. However, over 50 years of experience has demonstrated that, in fact, aid is more likely to serve the interests of the donor country; and that ODA functions as do other forms of 'resource flows' – as a mechanism of surplus transfer, a catalyst not of development, but of regression.

The evidence is clear. After two decades of rapid growth within the Bretton Woods system, the development process stalled precisely in areas subject to structural adjustment and dependence on FDI, commercial bank lending – and ODA. Parts of the 'Third World' – to be precise, a group of newly industrialising countries (NICs) in east and south-east Asia – continued to experience high rates of economic growth, and with this growth a substantial improvement in social and economic conditions. However, these countries neither pursued a neoliberal model nor were subjected to SAPs. In Latin America and sub-Saharan Africa, policies of neoliberal reform and ODA were (and are) associated with a decided deterioration in social economic conditions – including a dramatic growth in the inequality in the distribution of wealth and income and a substantial increase in the number of people living and working in conditions of abject poverty.

By the end of the 1990s, an estimated three billion people, close to 44 per cent of the world's population, were identified as being unable to meet their basic needs, and an estimated 1.4 billion are forced to subsist on less than a dollar a day, under conditions of abject poverty (see Chapter 15). Some of this poverty is rooted in long-standing structures of social exclusion, but a large part either originates in, or is exacerbated by, the policy reforms attached to ODA. In this context, aid can indeed be viewed as a catalyst of underdevelopment and regression rather than of growth and development.

The historic record on this point could not be clearer. In the neoliberal era of globalisation and structural adjustment, this regression is the direct result of the policy conditionalities of ODA. In a brief on 'corporate globalisation and the poor', Russel Mokhiber and Robert Weissman (2003) report on a study by the Centre for Economic and Policy Research (CEPR) in which 72 per cent of 89 countries surveyed experienced a decline in per capita income of at least five percentage points between 1960–80, a period governed by a state-led developmentalist model, and 1980–2000, an era dominated by the 'new economic model' of free-market capitalism. The only developing countries that did well in the latter context were those that ignored the policy prescriptions of the IMF and the World Bank. The CEPR estimates that 18 countries would have doubled their per capita income if they had stayed on their earlier development path.

CONCLUSION

The dynamics of ODA can best be understood with reference to three strategic geopolitical and economic projects advanced in the post-Second World War period: *international development*, *globalisation* and *imperialism*. Under conditions generated by these projects, ODA is an instrument of US foreign economic policy and is thus a catalyst of regression. Of course, this regression is not the intended outcome of development. But it is the inevitable, if unintended, outcome of the conditionalities attached to ODA. The problem is that economic development – and the whole ODA enterprise – is predicated on the adoption of reforms designed to serve the interests of the donors rather than the recipients. The historic record shows that in this sense ODA, and the development project generally, has been eminently successful. Foreign aid, as Hayter pointed out over three decades ago, is a form of imperialism, nothing more or less.

REFERENCES

ECLAC (Economic Commission for Latin America and the Caribbean) (2002) *Statistical Yearbook for Latin America and the Caribbean*. Santiago: ECLAC.

Hayter, T. (1971) *Aid as Imperialism*. Harmondsmouth: Penguin.

IMF (International Monetary Fund) (2002) 'Recent Trends in the Transfer of Resources to Developing Countries', Global Development Finance, Country Tables, Washington, D.C.: IMF.

Krueger, A., Michalopoulos, C. and Ruttan, V. (1989) *Aid and Development*. Baltimore: Johns Hopkins University Press.

Mokhiber, R. and Weissman, R. (2003) 'Other Things you Might Do With $87 Billion', *Corp-Focus*, September 10 <lists.essential.org/pipermail/corp-focus/2003/000160.html>.

OECD (Organisation of Economic Co-operation and Development) (2000) *DAC Geographic Distribution of Flows*. Paris: OECD.

Veltmeyer, H. and Petras, J. (1997) *Economic Liberalism and Class Conflict in Latin America*. London: Macmillan.

Veltmeyer, H. and Petras, J. (2000) *The Dynamics of Social Change in Latin America*. London: Macmillan.

World Bank (1998) *Assessing Aid: What Works, What Doesn't, and Why*. New York: Oxford University Press.

World Bank (2002) *Global Economic Model*. Washington, D.C.: World Bank.

14
Sticks and Carrots for Farmers in Developing Countries: Agrarian Neoliberalism in Theory and Practice

Carlos Oya

This chapter explores the origins, rationale and implementation of neoliberal ideas in agriculture, with a greater focus on developing countries. This chapter argues that there are important biases stemming from unrealistic theoretical and empirical assumptions in the neoliberal agricultural framework. Furthermore, the impact of neoliberal agricultural policies has been extremely uneven and generally negative for the agricultural sectors of poor countries, exacerbating social differences and marginalizing the 'poor'. Finally, we will see that the application of 'agricultural neoliberalism' has been asymmetrical, insofar as only the least powerful developing countries have been compelled to abide by the rule of liberalised markets, while the most powerful world producers still maintain markedly interventionist policies behind a pro-free-market rhetoric.

THE ADVENT OF AGRARIAN NEOLIBERALISM AND ITS RATIONALE: THE THEORY

The dominance of neoliberal ideas – in the academic world and in particular circles of the development policy debates, notably the World Bank, the IMF, the regional development banks and, more subtly, in some UN institutions (FAO, IFAD) – began to gain momentum in the early 1980s, coinciding with a turn in the economic and political model predominant in the United States, the United Kingdom and some European countries (see Chapter 12). Moreover, the influence of the US government on key multilateral institutions and other OECD governments provided a basis for the emergence and diffusion of neoliberal ideas across the world.

The premises of neoliberalism are applied to agriculture: the state–market dichotomy, whereby the state and the market are regarded as 'distinct and mutually exclusive institutions'; the efficiency of the market mechanism as opposed to the inherent inefficiency of state institutions; the distorting effects of state intervention in terms of rent seeking, technological backwardness and resource misallocation.

These premises were clearly evident in some of the most widely cited works on state intervention in agriculture in Africa, e.g. the World Bank's 1981 Berg Report and the study by Bates (1981), which offered a basis for the pervasive application of neoliberal agricultural reforms from the early 1980s onwards. In Latin America, the neoliberal agenda for agriculture had already started in the 1970s, especially in countries such as Chile, where the dictatorial regime swiftly embraced neoliberal policy reforms (Kay 2002). The neoliberal policy stance in agriculture has its roots in mainstream neoclassical work, which is based on idealised agricultural house-hold models. In these theoretical abstractions, agricultural producers are assumed to be rational profit maximisers, treated as 'competitive firms' and as consumers at the same time. Farmers are supposed to make rational decisions on their abun-dant resource – labour – and to be responsive to price incentives and subject to constraints and shocks (weather, water, roads, pests).

The use of neoclassical household models and the reliance on their assumptions have led to a misleading concept of the 'average representative farmer' which ignores important historical differences in agrarian structures, differing techno-logical conditions and significant degrees of inequality and stratification in rural areas of poor and middle-income countries. Imagine the differences between the agrarian structures of former settler economies in Africa (Zimbabwe, South Africa, Kenya), Sahelian countries (Senegal, Mali, Niger), Nigeria, Côte d'Ivoire, large middle-income countries in Latin America (Brazil, Mexico, Colombia, Argentina) and transition countries in Africa (Ethiopia, Mozambique, Angola) and Asia (China, Vietnam, Lao PDR, Cambodia). The assumptions of a 'universal peasant farmer' or 'homogeneous peasantries' in these different contexts are sim-ply inconceivable. Treating peasant farmers as representative 'firms' that consti-tute a notional 'agricultural sector' in poor countries has therefore created the illusion of a homogeneous mass of atomised peasant farmers, who, in the absence of policy distortions, should behave like competitive firms in almost perfectly competitive markets.

From these theoretical underpinnings, we are left with a focus on the constraints faced by an ideal representative farmer and his or her responses to incentives. Constraints are treated separately, so one can focus on those which governments supposedly control. Not surprisingly, output prices, which are affected by state reg-ulation of markets, constitute one of the obsessions of typical neoliberal frame-works (Schiff and Valdés 1992). Thus, 'getting prices right' became the cornerstone of the neoliberal agenda for agriculture in developing countries (Sender and Smith 1984). Neoliberals expect that the removal of price distortions will unleash the pro-ductive potential of otherwise 'exploited' and 'heavily taxed' peasants. Their unduly 'pricist' focus and the dubious validity of partial-equilibrium analyses and indicators used to justify neoliberal arguments have been subject to much criticism from many angles. Essentially, theoretically and empirically, much of the work underpinning neoliberal reforms is flawed and misleading.

THE WASHINGTON CONSENSUS AND AGRICULTURE
IN DEVELOPING COUNTRIES: THE PRACTICE

In the creation of a 'consensus', the influence of the World Bank and the IMF, especially on poor African countries, has set and transformed policy debates and established the development agenda to which many governments and researchers have also been committed. Most analyses, especially those supported by the World Bank, have attempted to demonstrate the need for reform and the expected outcomes in terms of greater *allocative* efficiency, higher production and lower fiscal deficits. The starting point for the assessment of policies prior to neoliberal reforms included two basic elements for African countries (Sender and Smith 1984, p. 12): (1) the assumption that pre-reform policies were caused by 'mistakes' – associated with ignorance, poor state capacity or rent seeking – that could be corrected by a better-informed technocratic class supported by multilateral institutions; and (2) an exaggerated pessimism in the assessment of the agricultural performance in the 1960s and 1970s, to show that 'wrong' policies led to agricultural stagnation.

In broad terms, agricultural adjustment was conceived as a complement to macroeconomic adjustment to generate a positive supply response. The main policy targets implemented in the 1980s and 1990s were, first, the removal of subsidies on agricultural inputs and consumer food prices, i.e. the demise of 'cheap' food policies allegedly favouring a privileged class of urban consumers. Second, the elimination of the currency over-valuation, through mega-devaluations, in order to provide incentives to peasant export agriculture. Third, the elimination or drastic reform of parastatal marketing and processing agencies, to enable competitive markets and encourage private traders, allegedly favouring peasant farmers, and to reduce fiscal deficits associated with parastatal agencies. Fourth, the deregulation and liberalisation of agricultural prices (or alignment with world market prices), which would potentially increase producer prices and encourage a positive supply response. Finally, the replacement of subsidised agricultural credit with 'alternative' measures to establish 'sustainable' financial institutions, stabilise financial markets, and reduce bad debts and fiscal deficits.[1]

In this framework, the state was (supposedly) left with a set of vaguely defined core functions, e.g. to 'enable the market' and 'provide a favourable environment for private investment'. The formulations currently found in agricultural policy documents are rather vague and do not clearly state how specific interventions would promote new state roles: e.g. the provision of market and price information to farmers and traders; the promotion of private and co-operative activity; building market infrastructure; ensuring the proper use of weights and measures; control of the quality of exports; the establishment of a legal framework for deepening competitive marketing; the reduction of barriers to regional trade.

In practice, a neoliberal programme comprises a double, mutually inconsistent package of measures: one towards liberalisation and deregulation of markets, and the other towards the withdrawal of the state from direct support to farmers. The contradictory effects of these reforms on different classes of farmers are seldom emphasised by mainstream analyses, while great effort has been devoted to assessing the impact of neoliberal reforms on agriculture (see Gibbon et al. 1993 and Kherallah et al. 2002). There are important methodological limits in these evaluation exercises and serious technical problems in the econometric work based on poor data. Usually, although the agricultural policy package is universal, the actual measures of reform do vary from country to country. Thus, measuring the extent and sequencing of reform cannot be done properly if these differences, in the number and quality of proposed measures, are not controlled for.

After the publication of standard neoliberal works such as Schiff and Valdés (1992), the neoliberal agenda in agriculture seems to have slightly weakened with the emergence of the 'post-Washington consensus' (PWC), which claims to broaden the scope of development and agricultural policy in the 1990s, beyond 'getting prices right' slogans and macroeconomic adjustment and without an exclusive focus on the failure of governments and policy (see Chapter 3). In the PWC, a more balanced view of states and markets and their respective roles, the extent of market failures, the praise for institution building and 'good' governance have added a new flavour to World Bank thinking on agriculture. However, the arguments against state intervention in agriculture and the conventional Washington Consensus (WC) solutions to encourage markets are maintained; but greater emphasis is given to non-price factors, though without acknowledging the pernicious effects and contradictions of market liberalisation.

Apart from these methodological considerations, the narrowness of WC studies and neoliberal agricultural policies in developing countries has been extensively criticised. For instance:

SAP [structural adjustment] policies largely dismantled African Marketing Boards and parastatals that had serviced peasants' input requirements, enforced commodity standards, and provided single-channel marketing facilities and controlled prices. The private traders, who replaced them, varied in their performance through time and space, but mounting evidence points to the fact that they have not lived up to the hopes vested in them by International Financial Institutions. (Bryceson 1999, p. 7)

The neoliberal literature had persisted in its over-optimistic expectation of the rapid emergence of a growing 'private sector' in trade, services, finance, farming and the supply response of farmers. However, private traders have often restricted themselves to output or seed markets, leaving other input markets almost untouched, because of low profitability, high marketing costs and scarce working capital – realities often ignored by neoliberal analyses (Kherallah et al. 2002). Competition has not been as strong as expected and barriers to entry, even in output markets, have been significant. This, coupled with falling levels of public investment in agriculture, has usually resulted in growing under-capitalisation of farmers, greater indebtedness and falling productivity, forcing 'failed' farmers to look for alternative non-farm income sources (Bryceson 1999; Kay 2002; Oya 2001; Ponte 2002).

In general, the impact on prices has been uneven and has affected different classes of rural people differently: input prices invariably went up, leading to a less intensive use of yield-enhancing inputs, while export prices, increasingly aligned to world prices, followed international market conditions, which worsened in the 1980s and the late 1990s; imported food prices decreased or increased depending on the net effects of devaluation, but increased for domestically produced food after the removal of price controls (Kherallah et al. 2002); the removal of controls often exacerbated seasonal and regional price fluctuations, so price volatility generally increased, hitting producers located in remote regions and poorer farmers compelled to sell at lower prices after the harvest. By and large, these effects adversely affected the poorest under-capitalised farmers, who could not afford to buy more expensive inputs, landless workers, net food buyers in rural areas and poorer urban consumers, hit by food price increases and wider fluctuations, while richer farmers and local traders could reap the benefits of higher price levels and greater price variability (Gibbon et al. 1993; Kay 2002; Ponte 2002).

Land reform has been a cornerstone in the marriage between neoliberal and neo-populist ideas on agriculture, both embedded in the tradition favouring small peasant farming. Moreover, the influence of institutionalist approaches in emphasising the importance of appropriate institutional frameworks, notably the focus on secure private property rights and contract enforcement as a means of maximising agricultural investment and equality in the rural areas, has also been critical. Neoliberal authors have pursued the agenda of market-led land reform (willing seller, willing buyer), encompassed by the formalisation of private property rights and the development of land markets, expecting that this would almost simultaneously lead to efficiency and equity. There are important fallacies in this discourse too. First, the alleged superiority of small farms (in terms of crop yields per hectare) remains unproven for different technological levels, crops and agro-ecological regions (Dyer 2000). Second, the effect of land titling on access to credit, and therefore on private agricultural investment, has not been supported by any convincing evidence in the context of poor countries with underdeveloped rural financial markets (El-Ghonemy 2003, p. 237). Third, the few experiences of consistent market-led land reform, applied in contexts of increasing deregulation and diminishing state support, have shown a remarkable tendency towards land concentration, exclusion of the poorest and growing proletarianisation. In essence, market approaches to land reform are naive, apolitical and misleading (El-Ghonemy 2003; Kay 2002).

In sum, what seems to emerge from different assessments of the neoliberal experiment in developing countries, including middle-income countries, is that neoliberal policies have diverse effects on the rural population, with some people gaining and others losing. A stylised fact is that processes of social differentiation and growing inequality intensify during and after the implementation of neoliberal reforms. The usual winners are the few capitalist and rich farmers, living closer to urban areas, economically and politically capable of adjusting to new market conditions, i.e. the economically and politically 'viable' farmers; while the usual losers are the poorer peasant farmers, who, with little competitive potential, struggle to subsist, and those dependent on rural wages, whose working conditions have become more precarious (Bryceson 1999; Gibbon et al. 1993; Kay 2002; Oya 2001).

'ANTI-NEOLIBERALISM' IN PRACTICE IN ADVANCED CAPITALIST COUNTRIES: THE PARADOX

Despite the dominance of agricultural neoliberalism in academic and international policy spheres, the reality of the political economy of agriculture in advanced capitalist countries is very different. The agricultural markets of Europe, the

United States and Japan are characterised by their conspicuous protectionist measures, e.g. systematic export dumping (keeping prices below domestic production costs), artificial incentives to create mounting farm surpluses, and import restrictions on agricultural products (Berthelot 2001).[2] The fact that the EU and the United States have not changed their protectionist policies for agriculture has always been remarked on by the critics of structural adjustment and liberalisation in poor countries and only recently noted and more openly criticised by the World Bank (Schiff and Valdés 1998, pp. 26–30). Why should the champions of neoliberalism not apply the range of policies they attach to agricultural adjustment loans in their own home countries? Why should very 'efficient' and technologically advanced farmers from the EU and the United States not be exposed to the discipline of the international markets? The answer might lie in the traditional importance of the farm sector as an arena for political conflict, lobbying and mobilisation of electoral support at the local, regional and national level, both in the United States and in some of the influential EU member states. Urban constituencies in conjunction with farmers' associations and large agribusinesses exert great pressure on agricultural policy decisions under the aegis of an alleged defence of national or regional food security, quality and sovereignty (Berthelot 2001). The 'agricultural sector' somehow becomes culturally and politically constructed in a way that influences policy decisions beyond the dictates of technocratic efficiency considerations.

The reality is that most examples of successful agricultural development and transformation, even when uneven or discriminatory, have relied on some form of state support or coercive measures, either through cheap subsidised inputs, credit, income support, output price subsidies, price stabilisation schemes, or land reform (Byres 2003, pp. 69–73). In Africa, where agriculture is deemed to be weakly competitive, cases of success have hinged upon different forms of state intervention, whether in the marketing and distribution of inputs or in research and public infrastructure for irrigation. Capitalist farming has historically been dependent on various forms of direct and indirect state support, subsidisation of various forms and pressure from the state, both in settler economies with capitalist farms and in countries with different agrarian structures (Byres 2003).

At the same time, most examples of successful industrialisation have relied on substantial flows of food imports, often financed by external capital flows, in line with long-term structural changes (Sender and Smith 1984). Therefore, the idea that the neoliberal agenda can only be opposed by clinging to the romantic concepts of food sovereignty, food security or a pro-poor-farmer benevolent state is naive and politically short-sighted.

CONCLUSION

Agriculture is a risky activity, especially in developing countries, with unsophisticated technology and vulnerability to bad weather, pests and poor rural infrastructure. Because of the high risks associated with potential gains under these conditions, peasant farmers are conventionally perceived as risk-averse. Allowing market forces to operate under these *real* conditions, together with volatile prices and dumping, may condemn most peasant farmers and (quasi-)landless workers to a permanent state of vulnerability and uncertainty. Eventually, a large proportion of peasant farmers may stop farming altogether as working conditions for farm workers become increasingly precarious. Hence, the expansion of agricultural output, investment in technological improvements and adoption of new techniques *without* the direct support of the state, or some other legitimate agency, remain wishful thinking.

If improving 'market access' is automatically interpreted as liberalising agricultural markets and exposing farmers in the North and the South to the uncertainty and volatility of international markets, and to the decisions taken by gigantic retail agribusinesses controlling various layers of the commodity chain, opposition from both constituencies of agricultural producers, i.e. small farmers in the North and food and export farmers in the South, should be expected. In the end, we are left with forms of 'market access' and preferential arrangements made within a regulated framework that aims to protect the interests of particular constituencies in rich and poor countries. This is *real politics*. In turn, governments in developing countries should be given back the right to protect their farmers and apply *selective* policies (on domestic prices and imports) to increase the competitiveness of their agricultural sectors, while not penalising net food buyers, both in rural and urban areas. This shows the importance of protection and selective policies for viable farming and other forms of agricultural development. These should maximise the development potential of countries and permit a relative stability of earnings for farmers and their workers in both developed and developing countries. This is particularly important in the latter, which have disproportionally borne the burden of ill-designed neoliberal agricultural experiments.

NOTES

1. Apart from the promotion of NGO-led micro-finance programmes, the 'alternative' mechanisms for rural credit have invariably failed to appear, reinforcing the credit squeeze brought about by the reform of parastatal agencies.
2. The EU normally spends €40 billion a year in agricultural subsidies and income support to farmers, consuming a great proportion of the EU budget. EU reforms of the CAP will be timid and will target some of the largest farm enterprises, mainly in the United Kingdom (Berthelot 2001). In May 2002, President Bush announced a package of US$190 billion worth of farmers' subsidies for the next decade (BBC, 13 May 2002). All these recent developments signal little change in the protectionist stance of the EU member states and the United States, in spite of the free-trade rhetoric used in WTO negotiations.

REFERENCES

Bates, R. (1981) *Markets and States in Tropical Africa: The Political Basis of Agricultural Policies.* Berkeley: University of California Press.
Berthelot, J. (2001) 'The Reform of the European Union's Farm Policy', *Le Monde Diplomatique*, April.
Bryceson, D. (1999) 'Sub-Saharan Africa Betwixt and Between: Rural Livelihood Practices and Policies', ASC Working Paper 43/1999, Leiden: African Studies Centre.
Byres, T. (2003) 'Paths of Capitalist Agrarian Transition in the Past and in the Contemporary World', in V.K. Ramachandran and M. Swaminathan (eds) *Agrarian Studies: Essays on Agrarian Relations in Less-Developed Countries.* London: Zed Books.

Dyer, G. (2000) 'Output per Hectare and Size of Holding: A Critique of Berry and Cline on the Inverse Relationship', Working Paper 101, Department of Economics, SOAS, University of London.

El-Ghonemy, R. (2003) 'The Land Market Approach to Rural Development', in V.K. Ramachandran and M. Swaminathan (eds) *Agrarian Studies: Essays on Agrarian Relations in Less-Developed Countries*. London: Zed Books.

Gibbon P., Havnevik, K.J. and Hermele, K. (1993) *A Blighted Harvest: The World Bank and African Agriculture in the Eighties*. London: James Currey.

Kay, C. (2002) 'Chile's Neoliberal Agrarian Transformation and the Peasantry', *Journal of Agrarian Change* 2 (4), pp. 464–501.

Kherallah, M., Delgado, C., Gabre-Madhin, E., Minot, N. and Johnson, M. (2002) *Reforming Agricultural Markets in Africa*. Baltimore: Johns Hopkins University Press.

Oya, C. (2001) 'Large- and Middle-Scale Farmers in the Groundnut Sector in Senegal in the Context of Liberalisation and Structural Adjustment', *Journal of Agrarian Change* 1 (1), pp. 123–62.

Ponte, S. (2002) *Farmers and Traders in Tanzania*. James Currey: London.

Sender, J. and Smith, S. (1984) 'What is Right with the Berg Report and What's Left of its Critics?', IDS Discussion Paper 192, University of Sussex.

Schiff, M. and Valdés, A. (1992) *The Political Economy of Agricultural Pricing Policy*, vol. 4: *A Synthesis of the Economics in Developing Countries*. London: Johns Hopkins University Press.

Schiff, M. and Valdés, A. (1998) *Agriculture and the Macroeconomy*. Policy Research Working Paper no. 1967. Washington, D.C.: World Bank.

15
Poverty and Distribution: Back on the Neoliberal Agenda?

Deborah Johnston

Concern about poverty and distribution has united many academics, NGOs and policy makers in revulsion at the outcomes of neoliberalism. Neoliberals have responded by raising issues of poverty and distribution within their own policy paradigm. However, this chapter will argue that the reformed neoliberal approach is not a significant departure from previous arguments and that it will continue to obstruct the development of policies that will have a positive effect on the poorest.

POVERTY, DISTRIBUTION AND NEOLIBERAL POLICIES

Neoclassical economics proposes that the unimpeded operation of markets will optimally utilise all economic resources (physical and financial assets, as well as labour power). All individuals participating in the market will be enabled to earn the best return possible, with poor people conceptualised as holding few, or relatively unproductive, assets. Whilst textbook neoclassical economics does not directly concern itself with the initial allocation of assets, attempts to change an existing asset distribution through government policies (such as taxation, land reform, minimum wages, etc.) do matter. Such meddling is thought to distort market processes and lead to lower efficiency. As a result, neoclassical textbooks have warned readers of an equity–efficiency trade-off, with attempts to improve distribution undermining efficiency.

By suggesting that free markets lead to superior economic efficiency, the neoclassical framework provides a rationale for neoliberalism's imposition of market imperatives on the economy. Using the convenient concept of 'trickle down', neoliberals have concluded that the resulting increase in economic growth will benefit all. Thus, overall output growth will lead to an improvement in living standards for the population as a whole, because improved economic opportunities will 'trickle down' even to the poorest (see Chapters 3 and 22).

Neoliberals have contrasted this beneficial state of affairs with the outcome of Keynesian or state-planning approaches, which, it is argued, led to stagnant growth, spiralling inflation and balance-of-payments crises. Crucially, neoliberals have argued that measures to 'artificially' reduce poverty or compress income distributions have been as complicit as other government interventions in this poor economic performance. The equity–efficiency trade-off was resurrected from the pages of the economics textbook (see Chapter 2).

In OECD countries, neoliberals argued that attempts to redistribute income from the rich to the poor had blunted economic incentives. High marginal tax rates had apparently reduced economic incentives among all categories of income earner, while high welfare benefits meant that work 'no longer paid' for the poor.[1] Neoliberals argued that redistribution, coupled with the apparently distortionary effects of trade-union activity and labour-market regulation, had led to unnaturally high wages, high inflation and unemployment. Although the exact composition of neoliberal policies varied, they often involved policies to improve work incentives, such as cuts in both tax rates and the real value of benefits. Other policies were introduced to encourage investment and to make labour markets 'more flexible', such as reductions in trade-union power and 'lighter' government regulation. These policies were intended not only to stimulate growth and employment, but also to reduce apparent welfare dependency by providing incentives to work.[2]

Less developed countries had not had large welfare states, but neoliberals suggested that other poverty-reduction polices had distorted economic incentives. Many countries had subsidised food and other wage goods, while public sector administration was often geared towards the provision of employment. Neoliberals suggested that these, and other interventionist government policies, were responsible for the slow growth and balance-of-payments crises experienced by many poorer countries in the 1980s. Neoliberal policies, often sponsored by the World Bank and the IMF as a condition for the disbursement of grants or soft loans, were varied, but usually incorporated dramatic cutbacks in public-sector activity and employment, as well as the removal of price controls and other economic restrictions. Happily, neoclassical trade theory seemed to guarantee that such liberalism was to benefit the poor. Removing trade barriers in developing countries would increase demand for their abundant low-skilled labour, expanding unskilled employment and earnings (see Chapter 10 and World Bank 2000, p. 70). Better still, there were predictions that the combination of trade liberalisation and the dismantling of state intervention would stimulate the agricultural sector. As the rural poor were typecast as small-scale agricultural producers, this was yet another reason for a lack of concern about the impact of liberalisation on the poor (World Bank 2000, p. 67).

Finally, neoliberals argued that trade liberalisation would lead to a convergence in growth rates between countries. The neoclassical Swan–Solow growth model suggested that growth rates depend on the rate of technological change. If free-market policies led to greater economic integration and this led to a convergence in levels of technology, this would in turn lead to convergence in growth rates between different countries.

GROWING REVULSION TO POVERTY AND INEQUALITY

From the late 1970s onwards, a number of countries in both the North and the South implemented neoliberal polices. Growth responses were mixed. Those critical of neoliberalism blamed it for the poor growth performance of many countries in the 1980s and 1990s, while neoliberals blamed the insufficiency of reforms. Evidence about the impact of policy reform and liberalisation on the poor led to considerable concern among some NGOs, academics and policy makers. A range of publications sought to document the negative impact on the poor of various components of liberalisation policies. For example, in an influential academic publication linked to UNICEF, Cornia et al. (1987) discussed the human cost of liberalisation in less developed countries.

Cornia and others pointed to the detrimental impact on purchasing power of the poor arising from cuts in subsidies (especially for food) and rises in user charges for government services in the areas of health and education. In many countries, public-sector employment (and wages) had been drastically cut back, while private-sector employment had rarely expanded to offset this. Furthermore, private-sector employment was now often in low-wage or relatively unprotected employment, given the removal of legislation to protect wages and labour conditions. Employment opportunities did not seem to have grown in the way predicted by neoclassical trade theory and certainly had not kept pace with increases in the workforce. Furthermore, poor rural people had not seen an across-the-board creation of agricultural livelihoods. The multidimensional nature of this vulnerability was recognised by many academics and NGOs, extending beyond simple income poverty into broader concepts of disempowerment and insecurity (see Chapter 19 and Streeten 1994).

In OECD countries, similar concerns were raised, with a growing academic and activist concern about the erosion of benefit levels and the creation of low-wage employment. In the United States, there was concern about an economic 'underclass', while in the United Kingdom and France, this translated itself into a focus on 'social exclusion'. The concept of social exclusion brought a wider focus to the concept of poverty, taking into account the manner in which people may be 'shut out from society', but also shifting the focus to individual inadequacies (see Chapter 6 and Atkinson 1998).

During the 1980s and 1990s, although the data are often poor, there was a clear rise in income inequality in many countries, rich and poor alike (see Cornia 2003). Cornia (2003) argues that key factors have been changes in tax and benefit policies, as well as the demise of trade unions and deregulation of the labour market. Overall, the share of income accruing to capital appears to have grown at the expense of the share received by labour, and this has had the effect of boosting the income earned by the richest in comparison to that of the poorest. Cornia provides evidence of the rise in capital income for India, Turkey, Thailand, Venezuela and South Africa.

However, the object of concern was not just within-country distribution, but also the growing divergence between countries in terms of growth rates. A number of academics have come to the same conclusion as Pritchett (1997), that divergence is occurring 'big time'. Pritchett estimated that from 1870 to 1990 the ratio between the per capita incomes of the richest and the poorest countries increased by roughly a factor of five. Whilst there had been some income convergence between rich countries, growth rates had been diverse and volatile among poor countries. For example, between 1960 and 1990, the annual growth rates of less developed countries varied from −2.7 per cent to +6.9 per cent. Over the same period, 16 less-developed countries had negative growth, many others had stagnant growth and only 11 had growth rates high enough to catch up with rich countries. While the data are poor and the methodology subject to debate, most academics have concluded that the global income distribution has widened.

A RESPONSE: BACK ON THE AGENDA

These growing concerns about poverty and inequality have led to a number of new initiatives within neoliberal thought. One set of changes is concerned with improvements in poverty definition and monitoring. Several governments and agencies have adopted multidimensional definitions of poverty (e.g. World Bank 2000). Furthermore, the advent of the UN's Millennium Development Goals (MDGs)[3] has also required that the World Bank collect comprehensive data on poverty. However, the criticisms of the technique used by the Bank to compute the data are so damning as to suggest that little confidence can be placed in it (Reddy and Pogge 2003). Even taking the World Bank statistics at face value suggests that, while the share of those in poverty may be falling, once China is excluded, the absolute number of people in poverty has grown during the 1990s (World Bank 2003).

However, whatever the changes in the definition and monitoring of poverty, there is continued belief by neoliberals in the core role of liberalisation in poverty reduction. Although the IMF and the World Bank have recognised some criticisms of earlier structural-adjustment and stabilisation policies, the new lending facilities linked to Poverty Reduction Strategy Papers (PRSP) remain based on a neoliberal economic-policy recipe. Therefore, although the PRSP process is intended to refocus government and donor expenditure on priority areas for poverty reduction, it has been criticised as simply being old wine in new bottles (UNCTAD 2002).

In the same way, although the World Bank's 2000 World Development Report 'Attacking Poverty' sets out some new concerns about the role of equality, security and empowerment in poverty reduction, the overall focus continues to be on liberalisation. This is despite the fact that the World Bank has announced that inequality is back on the agenda (World Bank 2000), because for the Bank inequality is not a result of liberalisation. Instead, the Bank sees inequality as stemming from non-economic factors and it argues that inequality is detrimental to growth because it can cause social unrest, inappropriate government policy and, importantly, can restrict the ability of the poor to invest in education or production. This latter argument suggests that if poor people cannot access loans to finance 'lumpy' expenditure due to failures in the financial markets, then there will be less investment either in capital goods or in education. With capital market failures, inequality would then be related to slow growth and to continued poverty. The World Bank advises that there should be some redistribution of assets within a system of liberalised markets, although these assets are limited to land and education ('human capital').

While the Bank now discusses issues of empowerment and security, it sees these as being improved by economic growth and as secondary to a process of liberalisation. A strong faith remains, therefore, in the poverty-reducing power of growth following liberalisation.[4] This is built on statistical work by David Dollar and Aart Kraay in the Development Research Group of the World Bank (World Bank 2000, p. 66). Using a sample covering 137 countries over the period 1950–99, Dollar and Kraay investigated the relationship between changes in GDP per capita and changes in the income of the poorest quintile. They conclude that the data show a strong and consistent relationship between growth rates in average income and in the income of the bottom 20 per cent. Dollar and Kraay conclude that 'trickle down' does indeed occur and that growth spurred by liberalisation benefits the poor as much as it does the typical household.

The conclusion for the World Bank is that growth-enhancing, liberalising policies should be at the centre of any successful poverty-reduction strategy. There is a limited concession that in some countries poverty and inequality have worsened because of the time needed to respond to new incentives or where the costs of transition to the new environment are concentrated in one social group. In these cases, the Bank admits that there is some case for social policies to ease the burdens imposed by reform (World Bank 2000, p. 66), but overall the focus should be on making markets do more for poor people. This would include increasing access to micro-finance, land and education, as well as lightening and improving regulation.

Those applying neoliberal policies in OECD countries have come to similar conclusions. For example, in the United Kingdom, the focus on social exclusion is often narrowed in policy to a focus on labour-market exclusion, with the poor being seen as lacking access to appropriate skills.

A CHANGE IN AGENDA?

The reformed neoliberal approach narrows the discourse on poverty. It argues that with greater education and training, lighter regulation and some asset redistribution, poor people will participate more effectively in markets. How likely is it that this reformed agenda will lead to poverty reduction or greater equality?

The reformed neoliberal approach recognises the inadequacy of the old textbook equity–efficiency trade-off. However, the new equity–efficiency harmony is just as simplistic. It detracts from an understanding of the more complex political economy and seems designed to placate those who would like a more people-friendly development strategy. That issues of distribution are complex is illustrated by the relationship between inequality and growth. While Dollar and Kraay find a neutral overall average, this hides great diversity in the data (Ravallion 2001). The manner in which certain social groups may benefit or lose out during certain growth processes needs to be understood better. However, the reformed view on inequality seems unlikely to assist.

The reformed approach to poverty seems equally inadequate. An account that focuses on asset redistribution (limited to land and education but aided by some additional micro-credit) assumes that this will be sufficient for the poor to earn higher incomes in liberalised markets. The examples that follow suggest that there are reasons for concern. On the issue of land reform, Chapter 14 concludes that market approaches to land reform are naive, apolitical and misleading.

On education, the evidence also suggests that educational access may be necessary but not sufficient to reduce poverty, if employment or self-employment opportunities are missing. Bennell (2002) has argued that the benefits to education have been declining in sub-Saharan Africa due to the collapse in employment opportunities there. This ties in with Sender's (2003) argument that the neoliberal approach allows no discussion of economic policies, forms of state investment and intervention that might promote labour-intensive industry. In addition, the neoliberal discourse also eschews state intervention to support workers' rights and wages, such as government regulation or support to trade unions. This area of empowerment continues to be left off the neoliberal agenda. Sender's (2003, p. 419) conclusion is that 'appropriate sectoral policies and industrial strategies are unlikely to be developed if the most influential development economists insist that poverty can be reduced only when markets are deregulated and when states abandon their old-fashioned aspirations to formulate industrial policy'.

The conclusion is that continued belief in liberalisation within the reformed approach prevents the implementation of those policies that would most benefit the poor. Poverty and inequality are unlikely to improve. Prospects for a reduction in the global divergence discussed above look equally unpromising.

NOTES

1. J.K. Galbraith pointed to the absurdity of this argument, saying that it is based on the improbable case that the rich are not working because they have too little income, the poor because they have too much.
2. For example, commentators in the United Kingdom during the 1980s suggested that inequality was necessary in order to provide necessary economic incentives. This found a resonance in earlier approaches such as Kaldor's work in the 1950s which suggested that inequality might be good for growth if capitalists had a higher propensity to save than workers.
3. The MDGs are an agenda for reducing poverty and improving welfare agreed by world leaders in September 2000. In terms of poverty, the MDG target is to halve the proportion of people living on less than one dollar a day.
4. The emphasis given to liberalisation in poverty reduction proved controversial for the Bank as it led to the resignation of the lead author of the World Development Report on poverty. See Wade (2001) for a discussion.

REFERENCES

Atkinson, A.B. (1998) 'Social Exclusion, Poverty and Unemployment', in A.B. Atkinson and J. Hills (eds) *Exclusion, Employment and Opportunity*. Centre of Analysis of Social Exclusion, paper no 4. London School of Economics.

Bennell, P. (2002) 'Hitting the Target: Doubling Primary School Enrollments in Sub-Saharan Africa by 2015', *World Development* 30 (7), pp. 1179–94.

Cornia, G. (2003) 'Globalisation and the Distribution of Income Between and Within Countries', in H.-J. Chang (ed.) *Rethinking Development Economics*. London: Anthem Press.

Cornia, G., Jolly, R. and Stewart, F. (1987) *Adjustment with a Human Face: Protecting the Vulnerable and Promoting Growth*. Oxford: Oxford University Press.

Prichett, L. (1997) 'Divergence, Big Time', *Journal of Economic Perspectives* 11 (3), pp. 3–17.

M. Ravallion (2001) 'Growth, Inequality and Poverty: Looking Beyond Averages', *World Development* 29 (11), pp. 1803–15.

Reddy, S.G. and Pogge, T.W. (2003) 'How Not To Count The Poor', Discussion Paper, version 4.5, March 26, Columbia University.

Sender, J. (2003) 'Rural Poverty and Gender: Analytical Frameworks and Policy Proposals', in H.-J. Chang (ed.) *Rethinking Development Economics*. London: Anthem Press.

Streeten, P. (1994) 'Human Development: Means and Ends', *American Economic Review* 84 (2), pp. 232–7.

UNCTAD (2002) *Economic Development in Africa: From Adjustment to Poverty Reduction: What is New?* Geneva: UNCTAD.

Wade, R.H. (2001) 'Making the World Development Report 2000: Attacking Poverty', *World Development* 29 (8), pp. 1435–41.

World Bank (2000) *World Development Report 2000/2001: Attacking Poverty*. Washington, D.C.: World Bank.

World Bank (2003) *Global Economic Prospects*. Washington, D.C.: World Bank.

16

The Welfare State and Neoliberalism

Susanne MacGregor

The idea of a 'welfare state' was a key feature of Western politics in the twentieth century. One of the best definitions was given by Asa Briggs:

> A 'welfare state' is a state in which organised power is deliberately used (through politics and administration) in an effort to modify the play of market forces in at least three directions – first, by guaranteeing individuals and families a minimum income irrespective of the market value of their work or their property; second by narrowing the extent of 'social contingencies' (for example, sickness, old age or unemployment) which lead otherwise to individual and family crises; and third by ensuring that all citizens without distinction of status or class are offered the best standards available in relation to an agreed range of social services. (Briggs 1961, p. 288)

In political debate, the progressive voice argued for a move from the nightwatchman state to a social-service state and thence to a welfare state, which some saw as a step towards socialism. It was thought that to bring about a full welfare state, governments would need to emphasise education as a key social service, accept responsibility for ensuring full employment and pursue policies of economic growth and redistribution of income from rich to poor.

In no society did social policy achieve all of these unambiguously. In Scandinavia, policies and public opinion favoured a wider remit for social policy. The United States, with its residual welfare state, favoured a much narrower range. Most advanced democracies fell somewhere between these two points. And positions changed over time. At one stage, it was thought desirable to aim at increasing the coverage of state social policy. After the 1970s, and under the influence of neoliberal ideas, the pendulum swung in the opposite direction. Cutting government expenditure, leaving more to the individual and the market, became the dominant idea.

The battle between neoliberalism and socialism raged through the 1970s and 1980s. What was the outcome? It is often said that 'we are all capitalists now' and that the market has emerged victorious over the state. Third Way politics, promoted by Bill Clinton and Tony Blair, who saw the destruction and polarisation produced by rapid and excessive adoption of neoliberal policies, argued that markets are not enough. The ideal would be a kinder and gentler form of capitalism (see Chapters 5 and 21).

How much do the changes we observe today result from this battle of ideas and how much do they stem from other forces? By the end of the twentieth century, welfare states needed to change. They arose in periods of secure growth, male breadwinner family systems and stable labour markets. The late twentieth century saw a so-called crisis of the welfare state – both a fiscal and a legitimation crisis. This resulted from a complex mix of influences, ranging from globalisation to technological change: changes in families – increasing divorce and separation rates and greater numbers of lone-parent families; ageing populations; new patterns of migration; and changes in political ideology. Other key changes included the collapse of the Soviet Union, the weakening of socialist ideas, developments in the European Union, the reunification of Germany, the emergence of consumer capitalism, and the increasing employment of women. Alongside these also occurred a shift from manufacturing to services, a rise in unemployment, and lower rates of economic growth. Together these demanded a number of changes in social policies (see Chapter 24).

Taking the share of national income spent by government as a simple measure, there is little sign that governments have retreated. In general, in rich industrial countries, the share of government expenditure tends to be around 45 per cent (see Chapter 3). What is important is what government spends its money on, whether on defence or health, on social services or prisons. Governments can choose different ways to effect social control, either encouraging social integration through welfare-state policies or dealing with the problems of polarisation through coercive action.

Much research has tried to explain what is going on. A key problem with these studies lies in the type of evidence they use. Studies with data on social expenditure, social security or pensions tend to reach different conclusions from those looking at education, caring, health or housing. Since different countries have different social-policy profiles, that is, they choose a different balance between spending on the various social groups or sectors, they end up located in different categories, depending on which measures are selected.

What does seem clear is that, while the welfare state has survived better than expected in the face of neoliberal challenges, the ideal of a welfare state is unlikely to be pursued by middle- or low-income countries in future. Pressure from global institutions committed to the neoliberal agenda, such as the World Bank and the IMF, means that other models will shape their futures.

Neoliberal social policy emphasises the market; the doctrine that 'private' is superior to 'public' (seeing this as the way to enhanced quality and efficiency); and the ideas and values of individualism and freedom of choice. Social protectionist laws are viewed as indirect barriers to trade. The welfare state is thought to hamper economic growth, to encourage unemployment by undermining work incentives and setting poverty traps, and to be an unaffordable burden on the economy and a hindrance to international competitiveness (see Chapter 15).

Of course, welfare-state arrangements do not exhaust the ways of providing economic security. Some writers have proposed the term 'social protection by other means', a clumsy phrase, but one that is revealing. Singapore's hierarchical and authoritarian system is evidence that you do not have to have public funding to have public control. Traditionally, Australia offered economic protectionism through the use of subsidies, compulsory wage arbitration and immigration control, combined with the aim of maintaining high levels of employment. Japan offered full employment and job security through a combination of loyalty to the firm and loyalty by the firm. State socialist systems aimed at full employment for both men and women, based on the principles of the right and duty to work combined with consumer subsidies: the Soviet system was inefficient but met basic needs overall.

What emerged from this *fin de siècle* battle of ideas in the new conditions of post-industrial society? Reality is complex and muddy and different societies have adopted different solutions. But the new policy paradigm contains some recognisable features. There is a general move away from the full employment goal towards *activation policies* – such as the use of unemployment benefit to ensure compulsory training or redeployment, combined with support for low-paid work. For example, in the United States there is TANF (transitional aid to needy families) and in the United Kingdom, child tax credits. These reforms are helping to create a layer of low-paid workers on the margins of the labour market, dependent for their living standards on state benefits. A cultural shift accompanies these policies, with increased emphasis on personal responsibility (memorably encapsulated in the US Personal Responsibility and Work Opportunity Reconciliation Act 1996). Those included in the economy and society have to exercise responsibility to provide for themselves and their families. For the excluded, however, the policies are not so much neoliberal as neo-conservative or authoritarian, with more intervention by the state, more intrusive policies and surveillance.

THE IMPACT OF CHANGES IN WELFARE STATES

Are all developed countries converging to at least a mild version of neoliberalism? So far, there appears only limited evidence of convergence. Recent studies have reported that the European welfare state is more or less alive and well – in better shape than might be expected, given the arguments and the sensation of change experienced over a quarter of a century. Welfare spending continues to increase. Public opinion still supports welfare arrangements. However, for all governments, the ambition is to remain competitive, so all must pay attention to productivity and employment rates. All seem to aim increasingly to target benefits and expand the private sector.

The impact of change has varied across countries, with those embracing neoliberal policies seeing greater restructuring. The tendency to labour-market polarisation has been most marked in the United Kingdom, where we see the reappearance of low-paid, low-quality casual work. Inequality has increased most sharply in the liberal countries (the United States and the United Kingdom) and least in the continental European and Nordic groups. The Nordic welfare states have survived the 1990s, challenged and weakened but viable.

Where neoliberal policies were introduced most emphatically, as in the United Kingdom, key indicators show an increase in relative poverty and inequality. In 1979, in the United Kingdom, 5 million people were living in households whose income was less than half the average income. In 1991–92, 13.9 million people were living in such households – a rise from 9 to 25 per cent of the population. The real incomes of the bottom 10 per cent of the population fell by 17 per cent during the 1990s. The 'winners and losers' philosophy appeared vindicated, since the population as a whole saw a rise of 36 per cent on average, with a 62 per cent rise after housing costs for the wealthiest 10 per cent.

Huber and Stephens remark that

> the increase in inequality in the United Kingdom was the largest recorded in the LIS [Luxemburg Income Study] data and moved the United Kingdom to a position second only to the United States as the most inegalitarian country among the eighteen [countries compared]. (Huber and Stephens 2001, p. 325)

THE POLITICS OF CHANGE IN WELFARE STATES

The agenda for welfare-state restructuring cannot be reduced to one of straight-forward retrenchment: 'no self-fuelling process of a welfare state race to the bottom is in sight' (Leibfried and Obinger 2001, p. 1). Counterbalancing the intense pressures for austerity is the continuing popularity of welfare-state arrangements and the willingness and ability of some groups to oppose reversals.

Reviewing developments in nine countries (Sweden, Norway, Finland, Denmark, Austria, Germany, the Netherlands, Australia and New Zealand) and considering evidence from other studies of developed societies, Huber and Stephens found that

> the predominant pattern is of a slowdown of expansion and then a stagnation; and finally pervasive but generally modest or at least not system-transforming cuts in entitlements. Only in Britain and New Zealand can one see large reductions, true system shifts, in the systems of social protection. (Huber and Stephens 2001, p. 6)

These authors explain that this was because 'Britain and New Zealand were countries with constitutions that produced very high power concentration and made it possible for governments with minority support to push through unpopular changes' (p. 7). It is important to recall that in the United Kingdom there was much resistance – the 1980s was a decade of turmoil and protest, with resistance from local authorities, professional bodies, voters, social movements, trade unions, and One-Nation Tories. All were defeated because of strong centralised power, combined with determined leadership and divided opposition.

So overall, only in the United Kingdom and New Zealand was change rapid and dramatic. The United Kingdom moved from being a 'social democratic' to a 'liberal' type of social-policy regime in the space of a decade. Why was the same radical change not observed in continental Europe or in Scandinavia? How can differences in the values and policies of different societies be accounted for? Why is it that some are more compassionate and show social solidarity, while others are more selfish and individualistic? The answer lies with politics – the political system and the values of the electorate.

The majority of explanations in the social-policy literature rest on 'new institutionalism'. They argue that 'past commitments, the political weight of welfare constituencies and the inertia of institutional arrangements' are key influences (Leibfried and Obinger 2001, p. 4). Electoral politics plays a key role. Huber and Stephens (2001, p. 3) found that 'existing power relations, public opinion, policy configuration, and institutional arrangements limit what any sitting government can do but that governments do have a measure of political choice'; over time, decisions may move a social protection system onto a new path.

Key factors influencing the shape and direction of change are the partisan complexion of governments, the relative power of trade unions and employers, the system of interest mediation and the institutional legacy of a welfare state-regime. Accounts show that schemes that mainly redistribute horizontally and protect the middle classes are more likely to be resistant to cuts. (Horizontal redistribution is seen as a humane transfer of resources from the better off to the worse off, defined not in terms of income level but according to need; for example, from the healthy to the sick, from the middle-aged to the old and young, from the employed to the unemployed, from the single and childless to those with families. Such redistribution operates horizontally at every income level and does not require a test of means).

What about that all-purpose explanation: globalisation? 'Many of the pressures on the welfare state are wrongly attributed to globalisation; they are actually generated primarily within affluent democracies' (Pierson 2001, p. 4). So the conclusion is that institutions matter: the same global forces create different problems depending on the kind of welfare institutions they affect; 'domestic institutions remain crucial in mediating any effects emanating from the international economy' (ibid.). A key argument relates to 'veto points', clusters of power that can prevent or delay change. Equally important is the ability to accelerate change. Huber and Stephens (2001, p. 335) comment that 'all of the ideologically driven cuts were carried out by secular right-wing parties in societies with declining union movements and without significant Christian democratic presence'. Where more consensual politics exists, often founded on systems involving proportional representation, then recalibration (or adaptation to new circumstances and protection of key aspects of welfare systems) can be achieved by governments negotiating with key interests without adversarial clashes. An important factor is the place of trade unions in social policy institutions: in Finland and Sweden, for example, unions administer unemployment benefits.

These accounts also argue that 'politics matters': the 'failure to take voters seriously helps to explain why analysts systematically underestimated the welfare state's resilience over the past two decades' (Pierson 2001, p. 8). For example, in both Sweden and Finland, electorates rejected centre-right governments after experience of cutbacks and threats to reduce social expenditure further. Dissatisfaction with austerity saw the return of left-wing parties – which then resumed the cutbacks but managed the political consequences more astutely than their predecessors had done.

Overall, the picture is that change is most rapid in areas where support is weaker – and where key policies are linked more directly to the labour market, especially with regard to unemployment and social security. Where middle-class interests and professional intermediaries defend the services, as in health and education, then change is less rapid. Welfare-state policies are often popular and these generate networks of support. The nature of coalitions of interests in different parts of welfare states is important. And these alliances vary across societies. For example, Sweden included the interests of women in its arrangements. There, a strong alliance of women and trade unions supported the welfare state against attempts at retrenchment.

As to the future, one should note that in the early neoliberal accounts, social policy was viewed as being, for employers, nothing more than a financial burden. But it may also be a business opportunity – privatisation of human services is a key development and business opportunity now, in social care, health provision, pension provision, even in areas of education. This may influence the next stage of these developments.

Some other important changes, especially migration, are themselves the result of economic and political trends and are likely to continue to pose challenges. Migrants are often excluded from welfare entitlements. Welfare states depend on social solidarity. Social solidarity is greater where there exists a sense of common identity and awareness of shared risk. The individualising tendencies of contemporary advanced capitalist societies undermine both of these.

PROSPECTS AND CHOICES FOR THE FUTURE

Some argue that, in spite of little evidence of major change, more significant change is around the corner, especially because, rather belatedly, neoliberal ideas have gained more prominence in key countries such as Germany and France. Taylor-Gooby concludes that:

> while welfare policy has so far resisted pressures for retrenchment and radical reform with considerable success, shifts in policy-making, made possible by changes in institutional structure, the organisation of welfare and the modernisation of social democratic parties, imply that the European welfare state is set on a new trajectory. Current (and recent) experience is not a good guide to the future. (Taylor-Gooby 2001, p. 1)

This chapter has focused on the importance of ideas, institutions and interests in explaining what happens. At present, many forces are selling the story that 'there is no alternative'. Alternative scenarios have been delegitimised. Dominant discourses play down state-centred solutions. Urgently a new battle of ideas is needed to argue for progressive reform.

Deacon et al. (1997, p. 195) argue that the social-policy analyst's classical concern with social needs and social citizenship rights should become the quest for supra-national citizenship and for justice between states. There is a growing social movement for a longer-term vision of transnational citizenship. International

NGOs and social movements aim for a global welfare state founded on the principles of equity, equality and democracy, environmental protection, social rights and duties, shared contributions and the meeting of needs on a human or world-citizen basis rather than on ability to pay.

More immediately, and at the level of institutions, it makes sense to support those which have acted as bulwarks against radical neoliberalism, especially social democratic parties and trade unions. This links to ideas for the further development of a European public sphere. Related to this is the need to recover democratic socialist ideas and seize the initiative from those who have taken over and undermined labour movements and parties. Such action would link to the mobilisation of a wide range of interests, in which individuals are seen as caring human beings and sharing citizens rather than as self-interested consumers. The interests of the majority of humanity lie with a more compassionate and socially just society. In all this, the protection and promotion of the values and practices of democracy is crucial.

All this may sound far-fetched. Faced with the relentless noise from neoliberal interests and a world characterised by an astounding callousness, it is difficult not to feel pessimistic at times. A major challenge to progressive politics lies in apathy and cynicism. What is needed is a revived engagement with political action, to envision alternatives and to recapture the language of reform. In particular, there is a need to internationalise opposition and to strengthen cross-national and supranational alliances of trade unions, NGOs and other social movements (see Chapter 19).

REFERENCES

Briggs, A. (1961) 'The Welfare State in Historical Perspective', *European Journal of Sociology* 2 (2), pp. 221–58.
Deacon, B., Hulse, M. and Stubbs, P. (1997) *Global Social Policy: International Organisations and the Future of Welfare*. London: Sage.
Huber, E. and Stephens, J.D. (2001) *Development and Crisis of the Welfare State*. Chicago: University of Chicago Press.
Leibfried, S. and Obinger, H. (2001) 'Welfare State Futures: An Introduction', in S. Leibfried (ed.) *Welfare State Futures*. Cambridge: Cambridge University Press.
Pierson, P. (2001) 'Investigating the Welfare State at Century's End', in P. Pierson (ed.) *The New Politics of the Welfare State*. Oxford: Oxford University Press.
Taylor-Gooby, P. (2001) 'The Politics of Welfare in Europe', in P. Taylor-Gooby (ed.) *Welfare States under Pressure*. London: Sage.

17
Neoliberalism, the New Right and Sexual Politics

Lesley Hoggart

In the late 1970s, a variant of conservative politics that became known as the New Right burst onto the political scene throughout the Western world. Closely related to neoliberalism, the New Right contained a number of disparate conservative currents. It can be distinguished from postwar conservatism by its rejection of welfare capitalism (see Chapter 16 and Levitas ed. 1986). The New Right was active on a number of political fronts, some of which went beyond the concerns of neoliberalism. With most of the politics, however, there were clear connections. The neoliberals and the New Right attacked the 'dependency culture' generated by welfare policies and social-security expenditure. They sought to defend the 'traditional' nuclear family and criticised those who were outside that norm (such as lone mothers) and those who challenged that norm (such as feminists). They were generally concerned with what they saw as a moral decline associated with the 'permissiveness' of the previous two decades, and mounted an attack on the progressive social and political gains of the 1960s and early 1970s.

For the neoliberals and the New Right, moral decline was seen as one cause of economic decline. This chapter will focus upon Britain and the United States, where repressive moralistic politics and conservative family policies were posed most strongly and where Thatcherism and Reaganism were early beneficiaries of the rightward turn (Hall and Jacques, 1983). In turn, the New Right was given an enormous boost by the electoral victories of Ronald Reagan and Margaret Thatcher. Although variants of New Right politics grew in strength internationally throughout the 1980s, the movement in the United States and Britain remained at the forefront of attempts to reverse the liberalism of the 1960s and 1970s (see Chapters 22 and 23).

This chapter begins by discussing the relationship between neoliberalism and the New Right. It then moves on to discuss the politics of the New Right in two particular areas. First, New Right politics of the family will be analysed. Second, some of the campaigns on sexual politics, closely associated with the New Right, will be considered. The chapter ends with a brief consideration of the contradictory nature of the combination of economic liberalism with the call for state intervention in sexual politics.

NEOLIBERALISM AND THE NEW RIGHT

The New Right was centrally involved in the neoliberal challenge to Keynesianism, principally through its political attack on the postwar Keynesian welfare settlement. It criticised the inefficiency of the welfare state, which it connected to the loss of competitiveness of national economies. The accompanying attack on the culture of 'dependency' connected moral anxieties with the economic ideology of neoliberalism. Moral decline was seen as a cause of economic decline and welfare benefits were seen as stifling individual initiative and responsibility. Ideologies of collectivism and social responsibility gave way as the citizen became the consumer. The argument was that state planning and collective provision of welfare serve to deprive the citizen (now a consumer) of choice. The New Right sought to reassert a traditional moral and social order underpinned by values of individual self-interest, family and self-reliance (Williams 1999). It also maintained that the market and not the state was the best guardian of political stability and freedom (Lowe 1999).

Reaganism and Thatcherism were important parts of this conservative New Right, though the New Right was broader than either. One of Thatcher's claims was that, in its support of the welfare state, the postwar Conservative Party had made too many compromises with 'socialism'. Part of her mission was undoing this: 'Welfare benefits, distributed with little or no consideration of their effects on behaviour, encouraged illegitimacy, facilitated the breakdown of families, and replaced incentives favouring work and self-reliance with perverse encouragement for idleness and cheating' (Thatcher 1993, p. 8).

The deeper social issue at stake was the need to tame the working-class movement. Thatcher made speeches praising inequality, was determined to privatise the nationalised industries and, crucially, she set out to defeat the trade union movement. Her greatest triumph was the defeat of the 1984–85 miners' strike. These defeats paved the way for a more direct attack on the collectivist principles of the welfare state towards the end of the 1980s.

The only exception to the New Right's call for individualism and independence was the promotion of the nuclear family. Thatcher's declaration – 'We are the party of the family' – at the 1977 Conservative Party conference was to be repeated on many occasions over the next two decades. In 1982, Thatcher linked rising figures on illegitimacy, divorce and juvenile crime to 'the birth of the permissive society' (cited in Durham 1991, p. 131).

The New Right's support of the nuclear family was part of the 'backlash' against the 'permissive' politics of the 1960s. The backlash was connected to a number of campaigns that sought to restore traditional morality and reverse many of the progressive reforms of the 1960s and early 1970s. Underpinning all these campaigns was a conservative view of the family.

THE NEW RIGHT AND THE POLITICS OF THE FAMILY

The New Right were economic liberals but defenders of the traditional family, and also favoured strong government action and incentives to sustain the family. One obvious question is why did the family become so important in an ideology so strongly committed to individualism? The answer can be traced back to Hayek, who argued that the family was a unit of equal importance to the individual. Its purpose was to transmit traditional morality and qualities that foster success in the market (Pascall 1997).

One of the New Right's criticisms of the welfare state was that it had replaced the family as a provider of welfare (Glennerster 2000). Links were also claimed between the decline of the nuclear family and other 'social problems': fathers abandoned families, boys turned to crime and girls became teenage mothers. The assumed link between the breakdown in the family and crime was pressed by writers such as Charles Murray (1990).

In the United Kingdom, the defence of the form and values of the traditional family was strongly associated with the New Right and Thatcherism. In the 1980s the New Right think tank, the Institute of Economic Affairs, began to produce titles such as *Families without Fatherhood* and *The Family: Is It Just Another Lifestyle Choice?* (Pascall 1997). These publications sought to promote the family and were a direct challenge to those feminists who had attacked the institution and ideology of the nuclear family as a source of women's subordination.

Feminists protested that women's burden of domestic labour in the home generated inequalities and sexual segregation in employment. They challenged the sexual division of labour inside and outside the home. Many feminists realised that equality in the public sphere of work and politics is not possible without shared responsibilities in the 'private sphere' of housework and child-rearing, and without more flexible work practices designed to accommodate such responsibilities for men and women (Rowbotham 1989). Socialist feminists also called for collective, public provision of much that had been deemed 'private', especially childcare. Feminists therefore proposed that since the public and the private are intertwined, families should be seen not as private but as public and political.

By way of contrast, the New Right reasserted the importance of a strict sexual division of labour in which women should be responsible for nurture and in which there is a strict separation of the public and private spheres. In the United States they were provocatively anti-feminist: 'I think the women's movement really hurt women because it taught them to put the value on career instead of the family', declared Beverly LaHaye of Concerned Women for America (largest female New Right group in the United States; cited in Faludi 1991, p. 258). Likewise, Connie Marshner of the Heritage Foundation claimed: 'A woman's nature is, simply, other-oriented ... Women are ordained by their nature to spend themselves in meeting the needs of others' (cited in Faludi 1991, p. 241). The New Right's political call was for the state to withdraw and for the family to take on more responsibilities, particularly for young people.

In the United Kingdom, a number of measures were designed to encourage young people's dependency on their families. In 1988, Income Support was withdrawn for 16–18 year olds. This single measure was felt by many to be largely responsible for a massive surge in young people joining the ranks of the homeless. In 1986, benefits were reduced for 18–25 year olds, and in 1996 (when the Jobseeker's Allowance replaced Unemployment Benefit), the same group of young people faced a 20 per cent drop in benefit (Glennerster 2000, p. 196). Other conservative measures targeting the family included the Criminal Justice Act that introduced the idea of parental responsibility for a child's crimes. The introduction of student loans and the withdrawal of benefits from students undermined their economic independence. John Major, following in Thatcher's footsteps, led a renewed call for the return to traditional family values and a chorus of complaints about single parents abusing the social-security system.

In the United States and the United Kingdom, the New Right's attack on lone mothers brought together the neoliberal position on benefit dependency and the championing of the traditional family. Unmarried mothers, especially young unmarried mothers, were portrayed as irresponsible, manipulative 'scroungers', dependent on social security, who jumped the queue for social housing (Murray 1990). One of the measures taken by the Conservatives in response to this was to try and force fathers to pay maintenance. The Child Support Act (1991) established that all lone mothers on benefits must authorise the Child Support Agency to recover maintenance from an absent father. The final form of the legislation was ideologically driven: Thatcher decreed that every penny of the money received from the father should be taken out of the mother's benefits. Women saw no point in co-operating with the Agency and many men actively obstructed its work.

Meanwhile, extra-parliamentary campaigns concerned with family values and sexual morality gathered pace in the 1980s. Their aims included defending the family against the state, promoting sexual morality and attacking promiscuity. In the United Kingdom, a plethora of new pro-family organisations included the Conservative Family Campaign, Family Forum, Family Concern and the Campaign for Family and Nation (Somerville 2000). Other moral conservative groups, such as the Order of Christian Unity, the Nationwide Festival of Light and the Responsible Society, joined the campaigning activity. The National Viewers and Listeners' Association (VALA) launched by Mary Whitehouse in 1964 campaigned against 'obscenity'; and anti-abortion, 'pro-life' organisations, such as the Society for the Protection of the Unborn Child (SPUC) and LIFE, mounted a series of attacks on abortion provision. In the United States, religious and conservative groups came together in Jerry Falwell's Moral Majority.

It has been argued that not all these moral crusading organisations found favour with the conservative administrations (particularly in the United Kingdom), and that sexual politics were not prominent in the New Right's challenge to the postwar consensus (Durham 1991). Nevertheless, these campaigns shared a hostility to the perceived 'permissive' society, to socialism and to feminism, and were certainly all part of the conservative 'backlash'. Sexuality, morality and the family were viewed as part of the battle between the Left and the Right.

THE NEW RIGHT, MORAL CAMPAIGNERS AND SEXUAL POLITICS

Moral campaigners were active on many fronts. In the United Kingdom, progressive liberal reforms on divorce, contraception and family planning, homosexuality and abortion all came under heavy fire. In the United States, the Moral Majority picked up on issues such as abortion, pornography, feminism and homosexuality and promoted itself as a bible-believing coalition out to save the American family (Somerville 2000). The American New Right, first and foremost, promoted itself as anti-feminist (Faludi 1991).

Abortion was, and still is, undoubtedly the most important single issue for moral campaigners. The 1967 Abortion Act in the United Kingdom and the

Roe v. *Wade* and *Doe* v. *Bolton* 1973 Supreme Court decisions in the United States had liberalised the law on abortion. What followed was an attack on that liberalisation by anti-abortion organisations. The politics of abortion developed into a running battle based upon a competing rights dialogue: the right of women to exercise reproductive choice and the right to life of the unborn child. The pro-choice movement was ranged against the pro-life movement. The anti-abortionists claim that abortion is actually the murder of the innocent and view the foetus as a distinct entity somehow detached from and independent of a woman's body.

Abortion as a political issue, however, is much deeper that a single-issue campaign. It is also about women's position in society, the politics of the family and issues of sexuality. As feminists have made very clear, breaking the connection between sexual intercourse and having children is an essential part of women's aims for gender equality and bodily autonomy. For women to participate in society on an equal footing with men (setting aside other social inequalities) reproductive control is one necessary demand. It is connected to challenging the sexual division of labour in the home, to rethinking sexual relationships and, above all, to contesting a politics of motherhood which defines women as mothers (Luker 1984). As the National Abortion Campaign declared in 1977: 'the fight for abortion rights is an essential part of the fight for women's liberation and against all those forces who want to ensure women's sexuality remains forever tied to the reproductive function in the nuclear family'.[1] Likewise, for the anti-abortionists much wider issues are involved. They seek to assert the centrality of motherhood, a role that many feminists believe to constitute the essence of women's oppression. In the United States this was particularly clear, as the pro-life organisations collaborated with pressure groups opposed to the Equal Rights Amendment (ERA)[2] to the Constitution. These two forces together constituted a mass pro-family, anti-feminist movement.

Another significant sexual morality campaign in the United Kingdom, led by Victoria Gillick, challenged Department of Health and Social Security (DHSS) guidelines (May 1974) that stated that contraception should be available regardless of age. The Gillick campaign focused on the evil of permissiveness and the dangers of undermining parental authority, and sought to relate these to the theme of national decay. It attracted significant support and extensive press coverage. Eventually, in October 1985, the House of Lords decided in favour of the DHSS. In this case the attitude of the Conservative government was a bitter disappointment to the campaigners and indicated that there was no automatic support from those who actively pursued neoliberal economic policies for the sexual morality and pro-family campaigns.

Other high-profile sexual morality campaigns were also underpinned by conservative views on the family and sexual equality. These included campaigns in favour of an amendment to a UK law against the 'promotion' of homosexuality or the teaching of its 'acceptability' as 'a pretended family relationship' (Clause 28). The Conservative government of Margaret Thatcher enacted Section 28 of the Local Government Act (1988) and in so doing made a clear statement on the form of sexual relationship it approved of. Clause 28 was in fact one part of a general battle around sex education in which organisations like Family and Youth Concern argued that society would like to see the end of sex education altogether (Durham 1991, p. 110), and in which the DHSS was criticised for funding the Family Planning Association and other agencies concerned with sex education and contraception. Sex education was seen as a vehicle for an anti-family amoralism that encouraged intercourse and corrupted the young. Moral campaigners clearly viewed heterosexuality and family life as the norm and anything outside that framework as deviant. They were to respond to HIV and AIDS by categorising these illnesses as diseases of promiscuity and homosexuality and thus played an important role in facilitating the categorisation of AIDS as a 'gay plague' by section of the press.

CONCLUSION: NEOLIBERAL LIBERTARIANISM OR STATE INTERVENTION IN SEXUAL POLITICS?

This chapter has considered the politics of the New Right and discussed them in relation to some of the morality campaigns of the 1970s and 1980s. These politics can be summarised as anti-feminist and thoroughly reactionary. Above all, they sought to protect and promote the 'traditional' family. As Martin Durham (1991) has pointed out, the New Right (and even more so the morality campaigners) should not be viewed as identical with neoliberalism. There is an obvious contradiction between on the one hand, the individualism and libertarianism fundamental to neoliberalism and on the other, the call for state intervention to regulate sexuality within private lives. This was a contradiction that divided some neoliberal organisations. Supporters of the free-market pressure group the Freedom Association, for instance, were divided over whether calls for the Conservative government to lead the fight against immorality were inimical to individual freedom (Durham 1991). In addition, whilst Thatcherism and Reaganism undoubtedly made the most of 'traditional family values' some pro-family campaigners, such as Victoria Gillick and the pro-life movement in Britain, were bitterly disappointed by the low level of support they received from the Conservatives in government.

It is important to emphasise, however, that all these conservative forces belonged to the same political camp. The economic recession of the 1970s opened the door to neoliberal and New Right attacks on progressive social forces. Moreover, many ardent neoliberals were also committed to moral issues. Norman Tebbit, for example, consistently praised family life and sought to claim it for the Conservative Party as part of the defence against immoral permissiveness. In a widely publicised article in the *Daily Express* (15 November 1985) he claimed: 'we understand as does no other Party that the defence of freedom involves a defence of the values which make freedom possible without its degeneration into licence' (cited in Durham 1991, p. 132). There were significant overlaps between the moral-lobby activists and the political right. In the United States, the Moral Majority and other conservative groups played an active role campaigning against abortion, and in Britain, Conservative MPs were far more likely than Labour MPs to vote against abortion.

The New Right was concerned above all with defending the nuclear family. The moral crusading organisations attempted to make issues of sexual morality central to this debate. Pro-family, 'morality' politics moved centre-stage as part of the neoliberal political agenda in cases where a clear connection could be made between 'morality' issues and the New Right's economic and welfare policy. This was most obvious in the transatlantic attack on lone mothers as welfare scroungers.

NOTES

1. NAC leaflet for the 1977 National Union of Student's Conference (Contemporary Medical Archive Centre, Wellcome Institute for the History of Medicine).
2. The amendment proposed that equality of rights should not be denied on account of sex.

REFERENCES

Durham, M. (1991) *Sex and Politics: The Family and Morality in the Thatcher Years*. London: Macmillan.

Faludi, S. (1991) *Backlash: The Undeclared War against American Women*. New York: Crown Publishers.

Glennerster, H. (2000) *British Social Policy since 1945*, 2nd edn. Oxford: Blackwell.

Hall, S. and Jacques, M. (eds) *The Politics of Thatcherism*. London: Lawrence & Wishart.

Levitas, R. (ed.) (1986) *The Ideology of the New Right*. Cambridge: Polity Press.

Luker, K. (1984) *Abortion and the Politics of Motherhood*. Berkeley: University of California Press.

Lowe, R. (1999) *The Welfare State in Britain since 1945*, 2nd edn. London: Macmillan.

Murray, C. (1990) *The Emerging British Underclass*. London: Institute of Economic Affairs.

Pascall, G. (1997) *Social Policy: A New Feminist Analysis*. London: Routledge.

Rowbotham, S. (1989) *The Past is Before Us*. London: Pandora.

Somerville, J. (2000) *Feminism and the Family*. London: Macmillan.

Thatcher, M. (1993) *The Downing Street Years*. London: HarperCollins.

Williams, F. (1999) 'Good Enough Principles for Welfare', *Journal of Social Policy* 28 (4), pp. 667–87.

18

Neoliberal Agendas for Higher Education[1]

Les Levidow

Increasingly we see attempts to privatise education, especially in primary and secondary schools. In many cases, buildings and services are outsourced to private companies. Although officially justified as improving quality and efficiency, such changes aim to subordinate education to commercial values and vocational skills.

In universities, overt privatisation has mainly targeted non-educational aspects such as catering and security. For higher education overall, the main threat should be understood less as privatisation than as marketisation. This means changing people's relationships and values towards simulating those of the market, while operating the institution as if it were a business.

Recent tendencies have been called 'academic capitalism'. Although university staff are still largely state-funded, they are increasingly driven into entrepreneurial competition for external funds. Under such pressure, staff devise 'market or market-like efforts to secure external monies' (Slaughter and Leslie 1997).

Such efforts go beyond simply generating more income, as higher education has become a terrain for marketisation agendas. Since the 1990s, universities worldwide have been urged to adopt commercial models of knowledge, skills, curriculum, finance, accounting, and management organisation. Supposedly they must do so in order to warrant state funding and to protect themselves from competitive threats.

These pressures complement wider neoliberal strategies for reshaping society on the model of a marketplace. The original nineteenth-century liberalism idealised and naturalised 'the market' as the realm of freedom; its militants pursued this vision through land enclosures and 'free trade', while physically suppressing any barriers or resistance as unnatural 'interference' (see Chapter 5). By analogy, today's neoliberal project undoes past collective gains, privatises public goods, uses state expenditure to subsidise profits, weakens national regulations, removes trade barriers, and so intensifies global market competition. By fragmenting people into individual vendors and purchasers, neoliberalism imposes greater exploitation upon human and natural resources.

THE WORLD BANK'S 'REFORM AGENDA'

For several years the World Bank has been promoting a global 'reform agenda' on higher education. Its key features are privatisation, deregulation and marketisation. These principles were self-confidently proclaimed by a World Bank report:

> The reform agenda ... is oriented to the market rather than to public ownership or to governmental planning and regulation. Underlying the market orientation of tertiary education is the ascendance, almost worldwide, of market capitalism and the principles of neoliberal economics. (Johnstone et al. 1998)

The report identifies teachers and their traditional protections as the main obstacle to market-based efficiencies. In its future scenario, higher education would become less dependent upon teachers' skills. Students would become customers or clients. As the implicit aim, private investors would have greater opportunities to gain from state expenditure, while influencing the form and content of education. Business and university administrators would become the main partnership, redefining student–teacher relations.

The World Bank report soon becomes a political weapon for recasting academic freedom as a commitment to neoliberal futures. In subsequent proposals, university administrations have characterised academic freedom as a duty 'to uphold the balance' between 'the spiraling demand for higher education on the one hand, and the globalisation of economic, financial and technical change on the other'. At a 1998 Unesco conference, for example, this conflict was fudged by declaring that faculty members should enjoy 'academic freedom and autonomy conceived as a set of rights and duties, while being fully responsible and accountable to society' (quotes from CAUT 1998).

Presumably the university administrations meant 'accountable' to a neoliberal globalisation agenda, not to the forces resisting it. Indeed, academic accountability often means subordination to accountancy techniques. In response to these attacks, professional societies have defended academic freedom as a right of free expression.

Although the World Bank agenda has little support among educators, some key elements are being implemented. Through structural adjustment policies, conditionalities for debt relief force Southern countries to liberalise and downsize higher education (see Chapter 12). However, this chapter focuses on Northern countries, where the main impetus comes from internal forces.

NORTH AMERICA: COURSES AS INSTRUCTIONAL COMMODITIES

In North America, many universities have adopted entrepreneurial practices. They act not only as business partners, but also as businesses in themselves. They develop profit-making activities through university resources, faculty and student labour (Ovetz 1996).

Within an entrepreneurial agenda, universities have developed online educational technology, e.g. electronic forms of course materials. Of course, this medium could be used to enhance access to quality education, and to supplement face-to-face contact, as some European universities have been doing for a long time. In North America, however, the aims have been clearly different – namely, to commodify and standardise education.

Those aims have been resisted by students and teachers. For example, in 1997 UCLA established an 'Instructional Enhancement Initiative', which required internet web sites for all its arts and sciences courses. Its aims were linked with a for-profit business for online courses, in partnership with high-tech companies. Similar initiatives at York University led to a strike by staff, backed by the students. They raised the slogan 'the classroom versus the boardroom' (Noble 2003). Critics have held conferences to devise opposition strategies.

What problem was the new technology supposed to solve? After university rules were changed to permit profit-making activities, their research role was commodified. Substantial resources were shifted from teaching to research activities, which were expected to result in patents and royalties. With less staff time devoted to teaching, student–teacher ratios increased, thus increasing the burden on them both. This result of profit seeking was attributed to educational inefficiency.

From that standpoint, a logical solution is to increase efficiency by standardising course materials. Once lectures are submitted to administrators and posted on web pages, these materials can be merchandised to other universities. Better yet, the course-writing can be outsourced on contract to non-university staff. By transferring control to administrators, the technology can be designed to discipline, deskill and/or displace teachers' labour.

This approach changes the role of students, who become consumers of instructional commodities. Student–teacher relationships are reified as relationships between consumers and providers of things. This marginalises any learning partnership between them as people.

Students readily become objects of market research. In Canada, for example, universities have been given royalty-free licenses to Virtual U software in return for providing data on its use to the vendors. When students enrol in courses using this software, they are officially designated as 'experimental subjects', who grant permission for the vendor to receive all their 'computer-generated usage data' (Noble 2003). Such treatment contrasts with much distance education in Europe, which emphasises tutor support for students and critical evaluation of texts.

EUROPE: FLEXIBLE LEARNING

In Europe, public services and state expenditure have been targeted for neoliberal change by the European Round Table (ERT) of Industrialists since the 1980s (Balanyá et al. 2000). The ERT's agendas have been adopted by leading politicians and European Union officials. In particular, they have sought to change the form and content of education.

The ERT have regarded education and training as 'strategic investments vital for the future success of industry'. European business 'clearly requires an accelerated reform' of educational programmes. Unfortunately, however, 'industry has only a very weak influence over the programmes taught', and teachers 'have an insufficient understanding of the economic environment, business and the notion of profit'.

They further argued: 'As industrialists, we believe that educators themselves should be free to conduct the same kind of internal searches for efficiency without interference or undue pressures exerted on them.' European industry has responded to globalisation, but 'the world of education has been slow to respond', the ERT lamented. As a remedy, 'partnerships should be formed between schools and local business'.

More recently they have promoted Information and Communication Technology (ICT) as an essential learning tool – in schools today and for work tomorrow. As the key virtues cited, ICT opens up the world of knowledge, allows individual enquiry and powerfully motivates learning. Also important is the link with 'life-long learning', necessary for Europeans to remain employable amidst the changes brought by global competition.

ICT has a more specific role in the neoliberal business agenda, as critics have argued (Hatcher and Hirtt 1999). First, it facilitates the individualised and flexibilised learning which is required for the modern worker, who must become individually responsible for managing his/her own human capital in the workplace. Second, ICT diminishes the role of the teacher – a desirable change, e.g. because teachers have 'an insufficient understanding' of business needs, and because their present role hinders 'internal searches for efficiency', as the ERT complained.

Along the lines of the ERT agenda, EU member states have undertaken to promote 'flexible labour markets', so that the EU can 'remain globally competitive'. Accordingly, the 1997 EU Council recommended 'a restrictive restructuring of public expenditures ... to encourage investment in human capital, research and development, innovation and the infrastructure essential to competitiveness'. It encouraged 'training and life-long learning' in order to improve 'the employability of workers'.

Since then, official documents have promoted 'citizen education' for future workers to participate better in labour markets. They have foreseen and even welcomed 'the decline in the role of the teacher, which is also demonstrated by the development of new sources of learning, notably by the role of ICT and of human resources other than teachers' (CEC 1998). Through such language, the empowerment of vendors and business partners is represented as greater freedom for students. A student–teacher learning relationship is potentially replaced by a consumer–producer relationship.

An overall neoliberal agenda was taken forward at the 2000 Lisbon summit, which set the EU goal to become the 'most competitive and dynamic knowledge-based society in the world'. This was soon elaborated to require 'the adaptation of education and training to offer tailored learning opportunities to individual citizens at all stages of their lives'. Such life-long learning has a long history of progressive features, e.g. by enhancing citizens' capacities as social actors, yet in recent years it has been appropriated for neoliberal agendas with a humanistic façade.

In policy documents of the OECD and the European Commission, life-long learning becomes an instrument for enhancing individual, regional and national competitiveness. Individual responsibility for learning becomes transformed into a duty to flexibly reskill oneself, according to ever changing imperatives of employability, as a means towards social inclusion. Although still advocating 'active citizenship', this is readily reduced to the role of producers and consumers

(Borg and Mayo 2003). Ensuing conflicts over the content and aims of life-long learning should be understood as a struggle against a neoliberal agenda.

THE UNITED KINGDOM: THE UNIVERSITY AS A BORDERLESS BUSINESS

As the vanguard of the neoliberal project in Europe, the United Kingdom epitomises pressure towards marketising higher education. The government has pressed for a substantial increase in student numbers, while providing little increase in funds. Under pressure from the Research Assessment Exercise, many university departments have shifted resources from teaching to research, while seeking more research funds from industry. For both those reasons, there have been less resources for student–teacher contact, and thus greater pressure to standardise curricula and assessment criteria. Similar pressures come from formal assessment exercises, which require teachers to produce explicit 'learning aims and outcomes'.

Students have become more subject to accountancy versions of educational values. In the late 1990s the government abolished maintenance grants for most students and introduced tuition fees. As these changes led students into greater debt than before, they felt under pressure to choose academic programmes which would lead to more highly paid jobs, rather than arts or humanities programmes, for example.

Student protests have opposed tuition fees, while linking this burden to more general dependence upon private finance: 'In providing this funding, business is assuming more direct and indirect control of our education system ... Students should not be forced to choose on the basis of what [courses] businesses are prepared to make available', argues the Campaign for Free Education.

In some ways, the problem is even worse: namely, that universities themselves are increasingly acting like businesses. Their marketisation agendas link two neoliberal meanings of flexibility. First, student–customers (or their business sponsors) seek learning for flexible adaptation to labour-market needs. Second, global competitors flexibly design and sell courses according to consumer demand, so universities must anticipate and counter such competition. Such language can operate as a self-fulfilling prophecy by helping to create market relations.

In a similar vein, the United Kingdom's university executives have aimed to abolish borders between the university and business, as well as those between domestic and international 'markets' for educational goods. They have promoted internet-based delivery as a key means to become a 'borderless business' (Universities UK 2000). Going further than the ERT diagnosis, they regard the university as already a business, albeit a deficient one which must be fixed by applying corporate principles.

As a central weapon to create markets, several institutions formed a consortium to establish an e-university. UNIVERSITAS 21 started its portfolio of e-learning with an online MBA programme in May 2003, from its headquarters in Singapore. According to the press launch, it marked 'a paradigm shift from the bricks-and-mortar education formula to address an estimated US$111 billion global demand for higher education'.

Driving this agenda is a broader commercialisation of public services, with universities being assigned a special role. They are expected to extend competition at several levels – e.g. in enhancing students' skills for the labour market, in comparing staff to each other (e.g. through performance-related pay) and in allocating research funds to strengthen the 'competitive, knowledge-based society'. Partnership is extended for subordinating research to the needs of private funders. Thus UK universities are prepared to export 'educational services' worldwide, especially to take advantage of liberalisation (Nunn 2002).

A similar market logic underlies the proposal that each university should be entitled to set 'top-up fees' for tuition. This policy has been advocated as a means to increase the subsidy of lower-income students, yet it would entrench class divisions. Differential tuition fees would reinforce a cost–benefit mentality, in which students instrumentally calculate their future financial gain from a specific educational programme, as a basis for incurring great debt while a student. Indeed, such a change in educational ethos would complement the overall commercialisation agenda.

CONCLUSION: WHAT GLOBAL COUNTER-STRATEGIES?

Neoliberal agendas can be broadly described as marketisation of higher education, i.e. restructuring its form and content according to market models. While only some forms of marketisation turn education into a commodity, they all impose accountancy criteria for valuing education and its human products. The 'investment' metaphor readily becomes literal: universities and their staff may be held accountable for delivering the dividends in measurable terms.

To counter the neoliberal agenda, imaginative efforts will be needed. First, links among various types of marketisation must be demonstrated. Marketisation measures can take subtle forms – e.g. ideological language, funding priorities, public–private partnerships, tuition fees, cost–benefit analysis, performance indicators, curriculum changes, new technology, students as consumers of pre-packaged goods, etc. Critics need to demonstrate how all these aspects are linked, how they change the content of academic work and learning, and how they arise from efforts to discipline labour for capital, as part of a global agenda.

Second, resistance across constituencies and places must be linked. Neoliberal strategies are turning us all into fragments of a business plan, e.g. competitors, partners, customers, etc. In response, we need an international network for several purposes: to link all targets of the neoliberal attack worldwide, to circulate analyses of anti-marketisation struggles, to enhance solidarity efforts, and to turn ourselves into collective subjects of resistance and learning for different futures. Such networks need to span all relevant constituencies (teachers, students, NGOs), as well as the geographical regions which are supposedly competing with each other.

Third, information and communication technology (ICT) must be de-reified. ICTs can be designed in ways which either facilitate a marketisation agenda, e.g. by reifying student–teacher relations – or else hinder marketisation, e.g. by enhancing critical debate among students and with teachers. In that vein, we need to distinguish between various potential designs for ICT, in order to de-reify them as social relations. Although the internet is widely used for distributing critical analyses, we need to ensure that these analyses are included and used imaginatively in accredited courses.

Finally, alternatives must be developed. It is inadequate simply to oppose marketisation or to counterpose whatever existed beforehand. Resistance would be strengthened by developing alternative pedagogies which enhance critical citizenship, cultural enrichment and social enjoyment through learning. These efforts could also stimulate debate over how to define our collective problems and aspirations, beyond making our labour more readily exploitable. In such ways, academic freedom can be linked with public debate over potential and desirable futures.

NOTE

1. This chapter is partly based on 'Marketising Higher Education: Neoliberal Strategies and Counter-Strategies', available online at <http://attac.org.uk/attac/html/view-document.vm?documentID = .'38> or at <http://www.commoner.org.uk/03levidow.pdf>.

REFERENCES

Balanyá, B., Doherty, A., Hoedeman, O., Ma'anit, A. and Wesselius, E. (2000) *Europe Inc.: Regional and Global Restructuring and the Rise of Corporate Power.* London: Pluto Press (see Corporate European Observatory, <http://www.corporateeurope.org>).

Borg, C. and Mayo, P. (2003) *The EU Memorandum on Lifelong Learning: Diluted Old Wine in New Bottles?* Unpublished manuscript available from peter.mayo@um.edu.mt

CAUT (Canadian Association of University Teachers) (1998) 'Unesco Declaration Puts Academic Freedom at Risk', <http://www.caut.ca/English/CAUTframe.html>.

CEC (Commission of the European Communities) (1998) 'Education and Active Citizenship in the European Union', <http://europa.eu.int/comm/education/citizen/citiz-en.html>.

Hatcher, R. and Hirtt, N. (1999) 'The Business Agenda Behind Labour's Education Policy', in *Business, Business, Business: New Labour's Education Policy.* London: Tufnell Press, <http://www.tpress.free-online.co.uk/hillpubs.html>; see also <http://users.skynet.be/aped>.

Johnstone, D.B., Arora, A. and Experton, W. (1998) *The Financing and Management of Higher Education: A Status Report on Worldwide Reforms.* Washington, D.C.: World Bank, Departmental Working Paper, <http://www-wds.worldbank.org>.

Noble, D. (2003) *Digital Diploma Mills: The Automation of Higher Education.* New York: Monthly Review Press.

Nunn, A. (2002) 'GATS, Higher Education and "Knowledge-Based Restructuring" in the UK', *Education and Social Justice* 4(1), pp. 32–43.

Ovetz, R. (1996) 'Turning Resistance into Rebellion: Student Struggles and the Global Entrepreneurialisation of the Universities', *Capital and Class* 58, pp. 113–52.

Slaughter, S. and Leslie, L.L. (1997) *Academic Capitalism: Politics, Policies and the Entrepreneurial University.* Baltimore, Md.: Johns Hopkins University Press.

Universities UK (2000) *The Business of Higher Education: UK Perspectives,* <http://www.universitiesuk.ac.uk.>.

19

Neoliberalism and Civil Society: Project and Possibilities

Subir Sinha

Neoliberalism, the grand political project of our time, ostensibly aims to roll back the state and redistribute its functions to the market, but it also has a politics with respect to civil society. The revival of 'civil society' has occurred at the same time as the neoliberal ascendance, and it has been integral to the discourses and apparatus through which neoliberalism proliferates and makes itself legitimate. A critique of neoliberalism thus requires an analysis of the location of civil society within this project, and also of the complex, dynamic and transnational processes through which other forms of 'civil society', opposed to neoliberalism, are taking shape.

Neoliberal ideas and practices are dispersed in varying degrees of concentration across a vast intellectual, political and policy terrain, including international organisations, states, transnational corporations, academic approaches and development interventions (see Chapters 5–7). Because it has key influence in shaping global and national agendas of rule, and since it poses itself, and is accepted in many circles, as not having an alternative, it claims to be hegemonic. This claim is challenged through two questions. How does the neoliberal project seek to organise a new politics of civil society? How successful is it in controlling the process of remaking civil society? This chapter explores these issues with reference to developing countries.

NEOLIBERALISM AND THE CONSTITUTION OF WORLD ORDER

Two different trends have influenced neoliberalism as an intellectual position. The Freiburg approach, arguing that 'the state', 'economy' and 'markets' were not natural facts but constructs, rejected the notion that capital had an independent 'logic' or innate tendencies to crisis, or that there were any necessary conflicts between state, market and society. It saw economic competition as the highest expression of liberalism and advocated state regulation of society and political and legal – institutional changes to foster competition. Chicago neoliberals rejected the Freiburg school's assumption of three relatively autonomous domains of state, market and society. Instead, they argued that the singular rationality of utility maximisation pervades all behaviour and institutions: 'the entirety of human action ... is characterised by the allocation of scant resources for competing gains' (Lemke 2001, p. 197). Such rationality attempts to make all forms of actions and 'non-economic areas' intelligible in these terms. It becomes the principle both for understanding and for reorganising state and society. Unlike classical liberalism, *Homo economicus* is not a limit on state action, but a 'behaviorally manipulable being' (p. 200). Neoliberal constructs and policies aim to create rational individuals.

How do these theoretical constructs become politically powerful? Overbeek and van der Pijl (1993) argue that a project becomes hegemonic when its key concepts can be used to analyse a variety of situations, when they can be used to create policy in a variety of domains, and when they can generate generalisable institutional forms. The liberal internationalism of the late nineteenth and early twentieth centuries aimed to create an interstate system to work for 'the general interest' of 'all humankind'. Under the illiberal phase of state monopolism of the inter-war years, national trusts and cartels, a national 'society' and labour movements were key forms of organisation, pursuing a narrow agenda of 'national interest'. Corporate liberalism of the postwar decades synthesised Fordism, with state control and 'normative interventions' into private life to regulate labour. Its key institutional forms were the multinational corporation, some form of social democracy, the bureaucratisation of everyday life, and a 'national interest' policy framework located within the 'bloc' politics of the cold war.

Neoliberalism, the 'new normalcy' of the last two decades, was constructed as a project to deal with a 'crisis of normality' of corporate liberalism, brought about by labour militancy, new social conflicts, the effects of the Vietnam war and general model exhaustion. Neoliberal politics have drawn on a combination of elements: individualism, choice, market society, laissez faire, minimal government intervention in the economy, strong government in non-economic domains, social authoritarianism, disciplined society, hierarchy and subordination, and a cult of the nation (Overbeek and van der Pijl 1993, p. 15). This combination forms the 'politics of support' for ruling agendas in countries undergoing neoliberal reforms.

While these distinctions between forms and periods are useful in comprehending the intellectual and political histories of neoliberalism in advanced capitalist countries, they do not have easy correlates in developing-country contexts. Corporatism, more widespread in Latin America than in Africa and Asia in the postwar period, was more populist and socially authoritarian than welfarist and social democratic as in Europe. The multinational and entrepreneurial forms central to corporate liberalism in Western capitalism were viewed with suspicion in many developing countries. Nationalisation, the threat of nationalisation, extensive public sectors and caps on equity and profit repatriation were key political modes of regulating them. Society was articulated with the state through caste, regional, ethnic-group and political-party configurations, differently from OECD corporatist tripartite arrangements. Additionally, the presence of the communist bloc as a source of development ideas and assistance limited the scope of exporting the corporate liberal model.

This changed with the neoliberal ascendancy. The collapse of communism, the allegedly dismal record of development regimes, structural adjustment programmes, the emergence of new political formations, and shifts within the social sciences, especially economics, created conditions to create and generalise a new model. The new orthodoxy coalesced as the development regime labelled the (post-) Washington consensus. The IMF and the World Bank played key roles in spreading it across the developing world; they also deeply influenced the development-intervention policies of bilateral agencies (see Chapters 3 and 12). At its core, the new theoretical construct is based on assumption of rational – that is utility-maximising – behaviour and the goal of capital sovereignty, the notion that capital should be either unregulated or self-regulated. These precepts are now used both to analyse state and society and to transform them. Nation-states today adopt differing versions of neoliberalism, depending on their power in relation to international institutions, the domestic constellation of political power and interests, the spread of consumer culture (and thus the logic of consumerism) and compatibility with other elements of national agendas of rule.

NEOLIBERALISM, CIVIL SOCIETY AND DEVELOPMENT

This section explores the location of civil society within the neoliberal project, briefly reviewing the analytical categories deployed to reframe questions and inform interventions, and the effects of such methodological and policy innovations in developing countries.

Neoliberal explanations of the failure of development proceed from a critique of the state, which also opens up the space for civil society. They are not concerned with 'the state' but with 'government', and its failure to adequately provide public goods, understood as a result of the rent-seeking behaviour of governmental agents, the problem of aggregation and transaction costs inherent in bureaucracies, and the stultifying effects on markets of state regulation and public sectors. They wish to reform the state through the good-governance agenda, including decentralisation, participation, accountability and transparency. In developing countries, where markets have not sufficiently developed, they have argued for the distribution of government's social functions to 'civil society'. Neoliberal international development agencies identify 'civil society' with NGOs, and attempt to define their form and function by disbursing large flows of development funds and by incorporating these in making and implementing policy.

The role given to NGOs in the neoliberal project has had effects. Its ongoing identification of functions to be taken away from the state influenced the creation of new sectors of NGO activity, including empowerment, gender, sustainable development, capacity building, institutional design, participation, evaluation and so on. While NGOs had been associated with these activities before, they now approached them increasingly within neoliberal frames of analysis. As NGOs began to work more closely with the state and international agencies, the claim that they were 'closer to the people' became more difficult to sustain. Contract work funded by international development assistance created incentives for demobilising some NGOs into private, for-profit development consultancies which provide professional expertise without commitment. This dispersed the new development orthodoxy across civil society, including the use of new institutional approaches to development, and rational-actor models of the behaviour of states and of the beneficiaries of NGO action.

From the early 1990s, neoliberals expanded their notion of civil society to include the concept of 'social capital'. Referring to trust, norms, reciprocity and social networks, they advanced social capital as crucial for solving collective problems, and for creating civil society, democracy and development. Fukuyama (1999), a key neoliberal intellectual, ties this concept to the generalisation of market rationality. For him, co-operation is necessary to achieve selfish ends, but it is difficult to mobilise because of a lack of trust. He turns to iterated prisoner's dilemma games – repeated interactions between rational actors – to explain the creation of trust. Free markets are the perfect setting for interactions that produce social capital, which for him is the key ingredient in creating civil society, democracy and good governance.

Neoliberal advocacy of good governance, which redefines the state and its role, creates an added space for civil society. The ideal state now is decentralised and participatory. It streamlines its bureaucracy, undertakes new public management reforms, and becomes more accountable and transparent. It concentrates on core functions, and opens out increasing space for private (including international) capital and NGOs, in carrying out its production, reproduction and redistribution functions. As well, NGOs are given a role in training, monitoring and evaluating new institutions of governance.

Apart from these modes of institutionalising the forms and roles of civil society, neoliberalism aims also to limit forms of oppositional civil society. For example, it attempts to depoliticise labour by conceptualising it as 'human capital', considering it to be not an independent factor in the production of goods, but a special type of capital, a combination of physical–genetic attributes and skills acquired as a result of 'investment'. As a result, 'labourers are ... autonomous entrepreneurs with full responsibility for their own investment decisions ... They are the entrepreneurs of themselves' (Lemke 2001, p. 199). Collective labour politics becomes redundant as labourers become agents who negotiate individually. Neoliberalism demobilises labour by declaring unions illegitimate and through flexible labour relations comprising individuated performance objectives, evaluation, salaries and bonuses, responsibilities, and so on (Bourdieu 1998).

Similarly, neoliberals reconceptualise 'the environment' and 'resource use' to pre-empt political opposition to their project. To understand these, they draw on 'property rights' and 'new institutionalist' approaches. They argue that the right to benefits from private property should be matched by full responsibility for costs imposed on others in the enjoyment of these rights, thus removing problems of externalities such as pollution. Rational actors, who are vigilant regarding their rights and those of others, with proper information and institutions for monitoring and sanctioning resource use, also prevent resource depletion. One way to institutionalise these precepts is through the World Business Council for Sustainable Development, which seeks to retain 'the environment' as a domain of the 'sovereignty of capital' and also deploys rational-actor models to curb overuse and pollution. Another is the principle of 'pollution permits', based on individual utility maximisation, to be generalised globally via the Kyoto protocol. In rural settings, neoliberals have created new institutions in which 'user groups' comprising rational individuals can internalise cost–benefit analysis in their resource use.

COUNTER-MOVEMENTS TO NEOLIBERALISM

So has neoliberalism succeeded in creating a supportive civil society? With respect to NGOs, though it has provided new logic and operating principles, it has not been able to completely internalise them within its project. NGOs have developed internationally over the past 150 years, and retain autonomy. International NGOs such as Oxfam work with neoliberal agencies such as the World Bank, but oppose core aspects of neoliberalism. Others, such as Bretton Woods Watch, monitor neoliberal multilateral institutions. NGOs such as War on Want or Third World Network provide support to social movements that oppose neoliberalism.

Neoliberals grant a role to civil society in holding the state accountable for growth and service provision. But forms of civil society offer an alternative politics of accountability. The Right to Information Movement in India demands information to make government accountable not only for good governance, but as an element of citizenship rights. Accountability has spilled over from governance to cover general relations between states and citizens. In Porto Alegre, participatory budgets are tied overall to a politics supportive of the Worker's Party and its demand for a new national project; and in Kerala, decentralisation is tied to the rejuvenation of left-wing party politics. NGOs and social movements extend the politics of accountability to neoliberal formations, such as the World Bank, and transnational corporations, and to neoliberal attempts to expand the domain of capital sovereignty.

Though neoliberals recognise and warn against illiberal and exclusivist forms of social capital, their formulation still neglects the limits imposed by social class and inherited status, which remain key determinants of social power in all societies. 'Iterated prisoner dilemma' interactions, in this view, produce social capital, taking place between abstract and equal individuals. Neoliberal policy interventions are structured around depoliticised collectivities such as 'stakeholders' and 'user groups' as key agents of producing social capital. But such ideal types do not describe the situated and stable power of groups: landlords, men, bureaucrats, capitalists, dominant castes, ethnicities, etc. The neoliberal notion of social capital, by not recognising the power of these collectivities, limits the success of its policy interventions. National and regional histories of voluntary association and social movements, often waged against entrenched relations of power, provide further complexity. These alternative 'reserves of social capital' (Bourdieu 1998), created by past histories of solidarity and the collective articulation of interests, are what the neoliberal 'programme of the methodical destruction of collectivities' has to contend with.

In neoliberal times, formalised labour, especially in the public sector, is less secure. 'Illegal' workers without rights or protection are widely employed, and the 'strict discipline/low wage conditions' of sweatshops and the 'informal sector' proliferate. But neoliberalism's individuating tendency faces countermovements. Because neoliberalism threatens labour unions, and because it attacks the public sector as a whole, labour politics aims to reconstitute a regulatory and redistributive state, the opposite of the neoliberal ideal (Bourdieu 1998). Neoliberalism directly affects production processes, constituting them as a key site for anti-neoliberal politics (Gill 2000). New labour organisations challenge capital sovereignty (van der Pijl 1993), and do so in new ways, linking internationally along specific corporations (Coca-Cola, Enron), by sector (fisheries, farms) and by gender. They ally with transnational farmers' movements, radical democrats, consumer groups, university students, and political parties. Older union formations have adapted to new conditions and have generated new forms of politics, and independent unions have taken shape around 'liberalisation' and privatisation. Recently, faced with the collapse of the state and the economy, Argentinian workers sustained for a time a novel solidarity economy autonomous both of the state and of capital: workers' collectives took over production of food items and distributed them through stores that had also been taken over by workers' collectives. The success of the neoliberal aim to spread rational individualism of human capital and to subordinate labour under capital sovereignty thus remains in question.

Recent environmental politics differ substantially from both the neoliberal logic of property rights and the precept of capital sovereignty. Movements of global fish workers oppose factory fishing funded by transnational capital and taking advantage of deregulation and liberalisation, contrasting it with their low-intensity methods that allow for greater regeneration of marine species. Their global union questions the sovereignty of capital and demands labour rights and protection and regeneration of resource stocks. Uncontained within the property-rights logic, the environment is multiply articulated in oppositional agendas. Movements of 'indigenous people' link biodiversity and cultural diversity. Feminists link gender with resource access and rights. Oppressed minorities in the United States link environmental issues to historical patterns of racism. The challenge to GM crops links issues of consumer rights, food safety, farmer rights and corporate power. The multiply articulated 'environment' thus provides a site for a range of eclectic coalitions.

CONCLUSION

Neoliberalism heralds the desirability and inevitability of capitalist development, promising a way out of the previous 'crisis of development'. During its ascendancy, some countries in eastern Europe and Asia have seen unprecedented levels of growth, though not necessarily because they have followed neoliberal policies. But in Latin America and some other eastern European and Asian countries, neoliberalism has been notoriously crisis-prone. While some social groups in some countries have benefited, the chronic instability and growing inequality of the neoliberal period has limited its success: it has been dominant but not hegemonic. As neoliberalism has been scrutinised and opposed, its votaries have declared oppositional forms of social capital and civil society illegitimate, as seen in the heavy police repression unleashed on anti-globalisation protestors from Seattle to Genoa, as neoliberals retreat to ever more fortified and remote locations for their annual meetings. The coercive nature of these new state–capital configurations can be seen in the Iraq war and the rapid privatisation of its economy. In Miami, police forces invoked 'war on terror' laws to attack demonstrators protesting the Free Trade Area of the Americas. Other forms of association now declared illegitimate include Islamist networks as well as the revolutionary left. States have arrogated sweeping new coercive powers to deal with their opponents, but have also succumbed to political pressures to adopt populist protectionist policies. Such state assertion with respect to markets and civil society indicates that the neoliberal project to redistribute state power to markets and social actors is under transformation.

REFERENCES

Bourdieu, P. (1998) 'The Essence of Neoliberalism', *Le Monde Diplomatique*, December.

Fukuyama, F. (1999) 'Social Capital and Civil Society', paper presented at the IMF Conference on second-generation reforms, Washington D.C.

Gill, S. (2000) 'Towards a Postmodern Prince? The Battle in Seattle as a Moment in the New Politics of Globalisation', *Millenium* 29 (1), pp.131–40.

Jenkins, R. (2002) 'Mistaking "Governance" for "Politics": Foreign Aid, Democracy and the Construction of Civil Society', in S. Kaviraj and S. Khilnani (eds) *Civil Society: History and Possibilities*. Cambridge: Cambridge University Press.

Lemke, T. (2001) 'The Birth of Bio-Politics: Michel Foucault's Lecture at the Collège de France on Neoliberal Governmentality', *Economy and Society* 30 (2), pp.190–207.

Overbeek, H. and Pijl, K. van der (1993) 'Restructuring Capital and Restructuring Hegemony: Neoliberalism and the Unmaking of the Post-War Order', in H. Overbeek (ed.) *Restructuring Hegemony in the Global Political Economy: The Rise of Transnational Neoliberalism in the Nineties*. London: Routledge.

Pijl, K. van der (1993) 'The Sovereignty of Capital Impaired: Social Forces and Codes of Conduct for Multinational Corporations', in H. Overbeek (ed.) *Restructuring Hegemony in the Global Political Economy: The Rise of Transnational Neoliberalism in the Nineties*. London: Routledge.

20
Neoliberalism and Democracy: Market Power versus Democratic Power

Arthur MacEwan

Once upon a time, the rich had little trouble in justifying their economic privileges and their control over the levers of political power. The concept of divine right, buttressed by all sorts of nonsense about noble blood, provided the rationale for their riches and their rule. While armed force supplied the ultimate protection for power and privilege, an ideology that encouraged acquiescence of the populace was also an essential basis for stable elite rule.

Things are not so simple for today's elite. With the rise of democratic ideals, the propertied classes have increasingly faced the problem of a challenge from below. There is a certain irony in this challenge, in that today's elite – a capitalist elite – rose to power in Europe and the United States partly by demanding that the old elite – the monarchs and the nobility – cede a share of political control; and the ideology through which these demands were articulated was democracy.

The problem, if not the irony, was well recognised by those who were engaged in reshaping the political systems and ideologies of the early capitalist states. The English political philosopher John Locke, who is often credited with providing ideological underpinnings of modern democracy, dealt with the problem by implicitly limiting who would participate in the democratic process. When Locke said in his *Second Treatise on Government* (1690) that 'the people shall judge' whether or not the political authorities act correctly, his definition of 'people' included only (white) men of property.

In the United States, during debates over the adoption of the Constitution at the end of the eighteenth century, the problem was confronted directly by James Madison, the principal author of the Constitution, in his famous *Federalist No. 10* (1787). Madison was concerned with the possibility that, with a democratic system of government, factions would develop and 'whether amounting to a majority or minority of the whole [would act adversely] to the rights of other citizens … ' And ' … the most common and durable source of factions has been the various and unequal distribution of property. Those who hold and those who are without property have ever formed distinct interests in society.' His concern was clear: how to maintain liberty and popular government while guarding against a 'rage for paper money, for an abolition of debts, for an equal division of property, or for any other improper or wicked project … ' Madison's solution, embodied in the US Constitution, was a republican, or representative, form of democracy rather than 'pure democracy,' and, in particular, a sufficiently large republic so that, first, the populace would be well removed from direct involvement in the affairs of government and, second, they would be divided into numerous factions which could not effectively coalesce to threaten the privileges of property (see Chapters 5 and 6).

Madison's prescription of 'divide and rule' and of distancing the populace from power has continued to play a role in US politics, and similar political structures have served the same functions in other nations. Yet during more modern times, the challenges to economic privilege and elite authority have grown and undermined the Madisonian prescription. In large part, the change has been a result of the success of capitalism, as accumulation has tended to eliminate artisans, small farmers and small businesses, has generated a homogenisation of the life conditions of working people, and has yielded 'the growing numerical and potential electoral preponderance of the working class' (Bowles and Gintis 1986, p. 55). Under these circumstances, the fundamental principle of democracy – *one person, one vote* – is an increasing threat to the position of the propertied classes.

There are of course many ways by which modern capitalists respond to this threat. For example, money has become increasingly important in elections, and money provides influence over and direct access to elected representatives. Also, wealth is a basis from which to affect ideology, through the media, the schools and other venues. Moreover, the state's armed power is often used to repress groups that threaten the status quo. Yet it is the domination of society by the market – the realm which is ruled by *one dollar, one vote* – that most effectively limits democracy and supports the continuance of capitalist authority.

SOCIETY AND MARKETS

Markets are very useful institutions, providing the mechanism by which people interact with one another to fulfil their material needs. As Karl Polanyi pointed out, however, the *domination* or

> control of the economic system by the market is of overwhelming consequence to the whole organisation of society: it means no less than the running of soci-ety as an adjunct to the market. Instead of economy being embedded in social relations, social relations are embedded in the economic system. (Polanyi 1944, p. 57)

Historically, markets have in fact been embedded in social relations – limited by social customs, constrained by social demands for fairness, and, at least in part, directed towards social goals. While a transformation towards greater domination by markets has been under way for decades (Polanyi's 'great transformation'), it has not proceeded without constraint. Welfare states have been a modern attempt to place social controls on markets, and countries in east Asia achieved rapid economic growth in recent years by managing markets to achieve social goals. In these cases there have been tensions between market outcomes and social relations, but these experiences have demonstrated that markets need not operate outside of social relations nor fully dominate social relations.

Neoliberalism is the current ideology and policy programme that would further transform societies towards economic life characterised by market domination. Calling for a minimal role for the state and a maximal role for markets in organising economic life, neoliberalism provides an agenda for, to use Polanyi's formulation, 'running society as an adjunct to the market.' By removing as much activity as possible from the political realm and by erecting high barriers between the economic and political realms – in the name of protecting private property – the neoliberal programme makes democracy in the political realm of limited relevance to economic affairs. Democracy in the sense of universal suffrage and the associated rights of political involvement can exist, but the realm of political authority, the realm where suffrage operates, does not cover the central material aspects of people's lives.

The insulation of economic affairs from political authority does not, however, mean that the state is weak. On the contrary, neoliberalism requires a strong state that can ensure the primacy of private property, preserve the dominance of markets over social control, and thus limit the operation of democratic power. Also, neoliberalism often requires a strong state, sometimes a dictatorial state, for its implementation (see below).

PRIVATISATION

More clearly than any other plank in the neoliberal platform, the privatisation of state enterprises in recent decades has removed activity from the political realm and transferred it to the realm of the market. Privatisations raise issues of democracy especially sharply when they involve enterprises where public and private interests are likely to dictate very different sorts of decisions. For example, in the case of public utilities, the populace has interests in limiting fees to assure that distribution is in accord with the provision of basic needs and the development of certain industries or regions. A private operator of public utilities, however, has one interest – profits – that is likely to come into conflict with any programme that would limit fees.

A good illustration of conflict surrounding public utilities is provided by experience in Cochabamba, Bolivia, where privatisation of the water supply led to a major, popular political protest during 2000 (Finnegan 2002). The protest focused on both specific grievances – a large increase in water rates – and the relatively abstract view that access to water, like access to oxygen, was a basic human right. Yet the fundamental issue in the Cochabamba struggle – which stands out because it resulted in reversal of the privatisation – was how this vital economic activity would be controlled, whether by the political process or by profit-driven market decisions. A 'political process' does not necessarily mean a democratic process (see below), but once an activity is removed from the political realm a democratic process becomes impossible.

Steps toward the privatisation of education also underscore the conflict between politically-determined and market-determined decisions. In Chile, where policies imposed under the Pinochet dictatorship led many advocates of neoliberalism to present the country as a showcase for their agenda, by the late 1990s over

40 per cent of primary school students attended private schools. Many governments, under pressure from the International Monetary Fund (IMF) and the World Bank to cut government funding, have imposed fees for public schooling, a de facto privatisation. In the United States, neoliberalism has taken a variety of forms in education; perhaps the most important of these has been the operation of formally public school systems by private, for-profit companies.

Contrary to these recent changes, societies have long designed school systems to meet a broad set of social needs – including the creation of social equality, social cohesion, and common values and language. When schooling is privatised and education becomes a commodity, these broader social needs are submerged beneath the need of the private school operators to make a profit and the decisions of individuals who are buying an education to meet their particular needs. As it becomes a commodity, the nature of the education 'product' gets transformed (Leys 2001, ch. 4). Democratic control over what goes on in the schools is harshly curtailed, if not eliminated entirely.

Not all privatisation is the same, of course. The privatisation of manufacturing facilities, for example, in some countries may be a reasonable step, depending on the particular circumstances. When the production and distribution of a good or service has limited impacts on people not directly involved in the market transactions of the enterprise, it may be appropriate (in a capitalist society) for that enterprise to be in the private sector. In such cases, there is unlikely to be a divergence between public and private decisions.[1] Also, even when activity such as water supply or education takes place in the private sector, it is not necessarily beyond the reach of public regulation.

NEOLIBERAL GLOBALISATION AND DEREGULATION

Public regulation, however, like public ownership, is a prime target of neoliberalism. One of the defining features of the present phase of globalisation, distinguishing it from previous surges of international economic connections, is the emphasis that the architects of globalisation place upon deregulation. In fact, when neoliberals advocate deregulation, in practice they are advocating a different kind of regulation. Instead of regulation whereby government limits the operation of markets, neoliberalism imposes regulation that assures the separation of markets from social control.

Yet the central ideological and rhetorical thrust of neoliberalism has become one of opposing almost all forms of state regulation of economic activity. The IMF, the World Bank, the World Trade Organisation and the US government all preach the gospel of deregulation of international commerce. They also pressure national governments to reduce labour market 'distortions' (e.g., minimum wage laws) and oppose association between trade agreements and environmental regulation or labour rights.

Such deregulation is rationalised with the argument that it yields economic efficiency, i.e. maximum market-measured output on the basis of existing resources. This rationale for deregulation, however, excludes consideration of social goals other than maximisation of market-measured output. Without regulation, the basic-needs goals or the regional-development goals of public utilities, for example, are not valued. Or, for another example, when a private firm moves from a relatively high-wage community to a low-wage site of production, there may be considerable social disruption and distress; but, without regulation, the firm will not consider these social impacts. Likewise, profit maximisation often comes into conflict with environmental preservation, and environmental preservation cannot be attained without regulation. The balancing of different goals of economic activity can only be accomplished by a political process, but, insofar as the relevant activities have been deregulated, that political process cannot occur and balancing cannot take place.

The efficiency rationale for deregulation is also misleading, because it assumes away the time dimension of economic activity. Private firms do not simply maximise profits; they maximise profits over time. The particular way they weigh the gains and costs in different periods will vary according to many factors – for example, inflation will lead firms to give little weight to gains in the future relative to immediate gains. The populace in general, however, may or may not share private firms' view of the time dimension of economic activity. One purpose of economic regulation is to force firms to operate in a manner consistent with the longer-run interests of society. Environmental considerations provide an obvious and important example. Also, with international commerce, short-run inefficiencies imposed by protectionist regulation may be necessary to generate long-run efficiency through technological change; this is the classic 'infant industries' argument for protectionism. Such larger social interests can only be promoted through a political process regulating private activity.

Each step that reduces social control over markets confers a power on firms that allows them to undermine the imposition of new regulation. When the political process yields – or threatens to yield – actions contrary to the interests of private firms, then, to the extent that those firms are free (unregulated) to respond in ways that serve to maintain their own profits, they can undermine those actions. New taxes on firms or new labour protections or new environmental regulations can, for example, lead firms to reduce production and employment or perhaps relocate to another site. Such a response can result simply from the unregulated effort of each firm to maximise its profits, and it is a response that can halt the imposition of the new regulations. The unregulated market, then, confers a political power on firms, the power to override the democratic process.

NEOLIBERALISM VERSUS DEMOCRACY

While neoliberalism pulls society away from democracy, its proponents often defend it as an instrument for the promotion of democracy. When the political process in a country is not democratic and political regulation of the market is used to create and protect the wealth and privileges of an elite, then deregulation – neoliberalism – can be readily associated with democracy. Historically, as noted earlier, democracy (however limited) and the market advanced together against the regulation of societies dominated by monarchs and nobility. During the current era, in many parts of the world, highly corrupt dictatorial regimes have used economic regulation to preserve their positions of power and wealth. Examples range from Indonesia during the Suharto reign, to the Soviet bloc governments, to Haiti in the years of the Duvalier regimes. Under these circumstances, economic freedom (neoliberalism) and democracy can become the joint rallying cries of the opposition. This identification of neoliberalism with democracy has been a prime reason why it has been able to gain, at times, some popular support.

To be sure, the implementation of the neoliberal programme has relied primarily on power, either military or financial. Chile, where that programme came out of the barrel of a gun, provides a telling example. Elsewhere, especially in Latin America and sub-Saharan Africa, neoliberalism has generally been imposed by repressive regimes, though they often operate formally as democracies. Also, external pressure has been an important factor, as the IMF and the World Bank, backed by the US government, have used their financial strength to lead national governments toward market-dominated economic organisation. Under these circumstances, where economic programmes are imposed by repressive regimes pressured and guided by the international lending agencies, it is not difficult to understand the widespread opposition that has often arisen. The 'anti-globalisation movement', along with its many national components, has been the most visible form of this opposition. Nonetheless, while political and financial power are essential bases for the implementation of neoliberal programmes, neoliberals have also tended to prevail because they have been able to present the choice for society as that between traditional (i.e. undemocratic, often corrupt) state control of economic activity and the market.

Efforts to counter neoliberalism with democracy therefore depend on *both* an assertion of effective power and the articulation of an alternative view of the choice, one that posits a *democratic* political process as an alternative to both traditional state control and the market. The problem is one of finding ways for society to use markets rather than being dominated by markets. Much of the experience of modern European welfare states, with all their limitations, provides some useful guidance. Also, in many low-income countries where democratic processes exist, popular movements have been able to establish social-welfare legislation protecting workers from the vicissitudes of the market. On the regional level, India's southern state of Kerala is an especially important case in which democratic political processes have constrained the market (see Chapter 19).

The problem, however, is not one that should be attacked only at the level of national and regional governments. Popular movements can work at the local level to resist privatisation *and* to establish democratic control of public institutions. Schools are an especially important example in which popular engagement not only serves a larger political purpose but is also likely to improve conditions for students. Similarly, popular engagement with health clinics provides an avenue for democratic action; as with schools, experience in Kerala suggests that such engagement has positive local impacts. The struggle in Cochabamba offers another example in which local action provides resistance to neoliberal programmes and the potential for the establishment of democratic control. Also, agricultural co-operatives offer an avenue for the local creation of structures that constrain and use the market rather than accepting market domination; international efforts to respond to disastrous market conditions in the coffee trade are moving in this direction. The challenge in all of these situations is to turn resistance to domination of society by the market into practical democratic operation of the institutions.

Still, national and international action is an essential component in resistance to the neoliberal agenda and for establishment of democracy. Agricultural co-operatives in low-income countries cannot thrive without improved infrastructure, agricultural extension services and a fair international trading system. Local control of public utilities cannot operate when the national government goes around them to provide contracts to multinational firms, as in Cochabamba. Locally controlled schools and health clinics cannot succeed without state financing. Traditional political struggle at the national and international level is a necessary part of the effort to counter neoliberalism. That larger political struggle is most effective when it is based on parallel local efforts. Both are necessary components of a democratic movement.

NOTE

1. Regardless of the activity being moved from the public to the private sector, privatisation has often been a highly corrupt process, as, for example in Mexico and the former Soviet Union. This is an important issue. But then public enterprises too can be rife with corruption. Also, privatisation is often a means to eliminate unions. Privatisations to break unions have nothing to do with efficiency or cost-cutting, the usual rationales for the action, but are simply ways to redistribute costs – i.e. onto the workers.

REFERENCES

Bowles, S. and Gintis, H. (1986) *Democracy and Capitalism: Property, Community, and the Contradictions of Modern Social Thought*. New York. Basic Books.

Finnegan, W. (2002) 'Letter from Bolivia: Leasing the Rain', *The New Yorker*, April 8.

Leys, C. (2001) *Market-Driven Politics: Neoliberal Democracy and the Public Interest*. London: Verso.

Polanyi, K. (1944) *The Great Transformation: The Political and Economic Origins of Our Time*. Boston: Beacon Press.

21
Neoliberalism and the Third Way

Philip Arestis and Malcolm Sawyer

This chapter is concerned with the nature of the economic analysis (and particularly macroeconomic analysis) that underpins the ideas of what has been termed the 'Third Way'. The notion of the 'Third Way' discussed here was born in the mid 1990s, and closely associated with the election of a 'New Labour' government in the United Kingdom in 1997, the election of the Schröder-led Social Democratic government in Germany and the 'new Democratic' project of Clinton in the USA[1].The term 'Third Way' is now used less frequently, and terms such as 'modernisers' (Giddens 2003), 'modernising centre-left' (Rutelli 2003) and 'progressive governance' (the title given to a conference organised in London in July 2003, attended by a range of leaders and former leaders of centre-left parties such as Blair, Schröder and Clinton).

The Third Way is viewed as being between the free market ideology of the Right and social democracy. Tony Blair, for example, stated that 'New Labour is neither old left nor new right ... Instead we offer a new way ahead, that leads from the centre but is profoundly radical in the change it promises' (Blair 1997, p. 1). In a similar vein, Giddens (1998) locates the Third Way by reference to two other ways, those of 'classical social democracy' and 'neoliberalism'. He also contrasts the 'modernising left' with the 'traditional left' when he writes that 'the future, in other words, lies with the modernising left, not with those who would wish to cling to more traditional leftist beliefs' (Giddens 2003, p. 38).

The Third Way has been described as 'neoliberalism with a human face' (see Chapters 2 and 23). It shares with neoliberalism the acceptance of the dominance of the market in economic life and the extension of the market into all areas of human activity. The market and the pursuit of profits is viewed as the best (or perhaps only) way of organising the economy. But the Third Way does acknowledge a role for government in the correction of 'market failure': as discussed below, the Third Way accepts that monopoly positions arise which should be constrained by regulation or anti-trust policies, and that government should be involved in the provision of goods and services such as education and health. But within the government provision of, for example, education, there should be some mimicking of the market through, for example, competition between schools, for funding and for pupils.

Although there has been some notable contributions on the Third Way (e.g. Giddens 1998, 2000), there has been rather little specifically on the economic analysis underpinning it, though speeches and other pieces by Blair (1997, for example) and Brown (2000, for example) provide some material[2]

In the section entitled 'The Essentials of the Third Way', we sketch out what we see as the analysis of a market economy, which underpins the ideas of the Third Way. It is our view that the economics of New Labour and of the Third Way is embedded in 'new Keynesianism', and this is highlighted. In the section that follows, entitled 'Neoliberalism and the Old Social Democracy', an attempt is made to draw out the distinction between neoliberalism and old social democracy.

THE ESSENTIALS OF THE THIRD WAY

We argue that the economic analysis of the Third Way can be viewed as 'new Keynesian', through its emphasis on the supply-side-determined equilibrium level of unemployment (the 'natural rate' or the non-accelerating inflation rate of unemployment, the NAIRU; see Chapter 2); its neglect of aggregate or effective demand and of fiscal policy; the elevation of monetary policy; and the concern over the 'credibility' of economic policies (Brown 2000, for example).[3] Further, the microeconomic neoclassical notion of 'market failure' can be interpreted to support significant government intervention when 'market failures' are viewed as widespread. 'Market failure' is viewed as arising from the existence of externalities, from the 'public good' nature of some goods, and from monopoly.

We postulate that the economics of the Third Way can be understood as being based on the eight elements listed below, which we would argue justify the description of a new Keynesian variety (see also Giddens 2000). These eight elements are:

First, the market economy is viewed as essentially stable, and macroeconomic policy (particularly discretionary fiscal policy) may well destabilise the market economy. Markets, and particularly the financial markets, make well-informed judgements on the sustainability of economic policies, especially so in the current environment of open, globalised, capital and financial markets.

Second, monetary policy can be used to meet the objective of low rates of inflation (which are viewed as always desirable, since low, and stable, rates of inflation are conducive to healthy growth rates). However, monetary policy should not be operated by politicians but by experts (whether banks, economists or others) in the form of an 'independent' central bank. Politicians would be tempted to use monetary policy for short-term gain (lower unemployment) at the expense of long-term loss (higher inflation). An 'independent' central bank would also have greater credibility in the financial markets and be seen to have a stronger commitment to low inflation than do politicians. The only credible policy is the one that leaves the authority no freedom to react to developments in the future; even if aggregate demand policies matter in the short run in this model, a policy of non-intervention is preferable.

Third, the level of economic activity fluctuates around the NAIRU, and the NAIRU is a supply-side phenomenon closely related to the workings of the labour market. The source of domestic inflation (relative to the expected rate of inflation) is seen to arise from unemployment falling below the NAIRU, and inflation is postulated to accelerate if unemployment is held below the NAIRU. However, in the long run there is no trade-off between inflation and unemployment, and the economy has to operate (on average) at the NAIRU if accelerating inflation is to be avoided. In this long run, inflation is viewed as a monetary phenomenon, in that the pace of inflation is aligned with the rate of increase of the stock of money. Monetary policy is, thus, in the hands of central bankers. Control of the money supply is not an issue, essentially because of the instability of the demand for money, which makes the impact of changes in the money supply a highly uncertain channel of influence.

The focus of economic policy then becomes attempts to shift the NAIRU, usually by making the labour market 'more flexible'. For example,

> There are more than 20 million unemployed people in the EU countries, a high proportion of them located in Germany, France and Italy – all societies that have largely unreformed labour markets. Liberalisation of labour markets is not the only policy orientation needed to tackle high levels of unemployment, but it is a key one. (Giddens 2003, p. 38)

In a similar vein,

> We must continue along the path of labour market reform. We must increase flexibility and mobility: but they must be combined with new, modern forms of security – those that focus on active labour market policies, and in particular retraining and lifelong learning: this philosophy is well captured by the notion of 'flexicurity'. (Rutelli 2003, p. 33)

Fourth, the essence of Say's Law holds, namely that the level of effective demand does not play an independent role in the (long-run) determination of the level of economic activity, and adjusts to underpin the supply-side-determined level of economic activity, which itself corresponds to the NAIRU (see Chapter 3). Shocks to the level of demand can be met by variations in the rate of interest to ensure that inflation does not develop (if unemployment falls below the NAIRU). Fiscal policy has a passive role to play, in that the budget-deficit position varies over the business cycle in the well-known manner. The budget (at least on current account) can and should be balanced over the course of the business cycle.

Fifth, the market system involves 'market failure', in the neoclassical sense of the term. Markets do not reach an optimum outcome, because of the presence of externalities, public and quasi-public goods (that is goods which are non-rivalrous in use and non-excludable) and monopoly situations. The policy conclusion is straightforward, namely that government seeks to correct externalities through appropriate taxation, subsidy and regulation and makes provision for 'public goods', either itself or through paying the private sector to provide the goods; and competition policy can be used to reduce or restrain monopoly positions. This idea is, of course, not unique to the Third Way, and has been a central element in conventional welfare economics.

> Being pro-market requires that we guarantee that the market itself functions correctly. I believe in a liberal regulation of the economy, in competition, in

consumer protection, in environmentally sustainable development. On a global scale, modernisers need to support public policies, private incentives, and the removal of protectionist barriers. (Rutelli 2003, p. 34)

Sixth, long-run growth in income per head depends on investment decisions, with human capital seen as particularly important. Since the public sector is a heavy provider of education, and education adds to human capital, the public sector is again seen to play a significant role in growth. 'Endogenous growth theory' also postulates that there are overall increasing returns to scale; but that includes some factors of production that are not privately owned.[4] Knowledge and information, for example, add to productive potential but are not generally privately owned. These 'public goods' (in the technical sense of being non-excludable and non-rivalrous) will generally be underprovided by the private sector, and the public sector has a role to play in providing them, or encouraging their provision. In effect, endogenous growth theory again points to the role of the state in terms of the correction of market failure, and specifically in this context the provision or subsidy of 'public goods', with research and development, education and training being the major examples.

Seventh, in the economics of the Third Way there is concern over inequality of outcome rather than inequality of possibilities (or of opportunities) (see, for example, Giddens 1998). Inequality of outcomes (e.g. in terms of income) could be seen to be addressed through a progressive tax system and a redistributive social security system. Inequality of possibilities (opportunities) can be addressed through education and training (initial endowments), through 'employability' policies (for inclusion in the labour market and employment), and through seeking to change the rewards offered by the market. With the exception of the national minimum wage, it could be said that there has been little attempt to modify the rewards thrown up by the market. As Giddens (1998, p. 101) notes, a 'winner-takes-all' element in parts of the labour market means large inequalities. But also Giddens perceives that 'incentives are necessary to encourage those of talent to progress and that equality of opportunity typically creates higher rather than lower inequalities of outcome' (2000, p. 86). It could be argued, though, that inequality of opportunity acts for many as a barrier to fulfilling their potential. Those disadvantaged do not forego education because of a lack of incentives in terms of higher pay for the more educated, but because of a range of barriers to their doing so. Greater opportunity would be expected to increase the supply of the well trained, etc., and to reduce the pay of the well trained relative to the pay of the untrained. A stress on reducing inequality of opportunity leads to policies designed to change the distribution of abilities to compete and to make education more egalitarian; but these policies accept that competition will generate inequalities of income, wealth and outcomes.

Finally, eighth, globalisation, in the form of increased international trade, a larger role for foreign direct investment by transnational corporations and an enhanced scale of movements across the exchanges, is embraced by the Third Way. The Third Way generally perceives globalisation as having virtually eliminated the possibilities of industrial policy (other than competition policy) and of macroeconomic policy. The mobility of industrial and financial capital is seen to preclude independent national economic policies in these regards. However, the nation-state still has a role to play, though there are trends towards moving government away from the nation-state, sometimes in a downward decentralised direction (e.g. to regions within a country) and sometimes in an upward direction (e.g. to the European Union). But the role of government is seen to shift towards creating a favourable environment for transnational investment, whether in the form of low taxation on profits, subsidies to inward investment or the creation of a highly skilled work force. The effects of globalisation on policy perspectives is orchestrated in terms of a shift from the industrial policy and Keynesian demand measures favoured by 'old' social democracy, but also from regulation to the deregulation and market liberalisation emphasised by neoliberals. 'The aim of macroeconomic policy is to keep inflation low, limit government borrowing, and use active supply-side measures to foster growth and high levels of employment' (Giddens 2000, p. 73). Blair and Schröder argue in a similar fashion: 'In a world of ever more rapid globalisation and scientific changes we need to create the conditions in which existing businesses can prosper and adapt, and new businesses can be set up and grow' (1999, p. 163). Hombach reinforces the point when he suggests that '[i]t is not only the forces of globalisation that demand the modernisation of our institutions and political programmes, but, to no less an extent, changes in patterns of employment, in values and in demographic and social structures' (2000, p. 31).

> Modernising leftists can, or should, have a clear idea of the kind of society they are seeking to create. It is one whose economy is competitive in the global marketplace, but which remains cohesive, inclusive and egalitarian. Bringing into being such a society means running with the tide of the great social changes of our era – not just the emergence of the knowledge economy, but the impact of globalisation and of rising individualism. (Giddens 2003, p. 38)

NEOLIBERALISM AND THE OLD SOCIAL DEMOCRACY

The question arises as to how the Third Way differs in its policy approach from the 'old' social democracy. An answer may be attempted once it is recognised that like the 'new' social democratic economic policies (see, for example, Arestis and Sawyer 2001b), the 'old' social democrat economic policies did not fit into a single mould, and of course varied over time and across countries. Specifically, for example, the policies of the 'New Labour' government in the United Kingdom have not coincided with those of the SPD government in Germany: for example, the former could be said to have placed more emphasis on 'labour market flexibility' than the latter. At the cost of gross oversimplification (and no doubt other costs as well), we would suggest that the following played significant roles in the 'old' social democrat' policies (at least so far as the United Kingdom is concerned). There was an acceptance of some key aspects of Keynesianism, particularly that budget deficits can be used to support aggregate demand, and fiscal policy was given an active role. Each postwar Labour government, and other 'old' social democratic governments, made some extension of public ownership. The perceptions of the 'failures' of the economy were broader than 'market failure'. These failures have ranged over lack of exploitation of economies of scale, poor management, under investment, etc. Unemployment was addressed through regional and industrial policies rather than labour-market policies. There was generally a use and development of some form of corporatism, for example, through a tripartite approach to industrial policy, the operation of incomes policy etc.

It is clear that the third way and the New Labour government operate along quite different lines from the 'old social democracy'. Macroeconomic policy is of the 'new Keynesian' type, with an emphasis on control of inflation rather than the reduction of unemployment and a perceived need to acquire credibility in the financial markets. Monetary policy, with an 'independent central bank', is solely concerned with inflation. Fiscal policy is relegated in importance. We have described microeconomic policy as concerned with the correction of 'market failures': this can also be seen as a policy that accepts the beneficial operation of markets, albeit one that can be improved by appropriate government action. Regulation of privatised utilities replaces public ownership. Instead of nationalisation, the New Labour government confirms the privatisation of the preceding Thatcher government and proceeds with a 'creeping' privatisation in the guise of the Private Finance Initiative. The Third Way does appear to seek to equip individuals to compete in the market, e.g. through training and education. Ultimately, we agree with Tsakalotos that these features suggest 'an explicit rejection of many of the economic, political and philosophical ideas of social democracy, let alone democratic socialist ideas' (2001, p. 43).

NOTES

1. There have been other cases of a Third Way. For example, the Swedish social democracy of the post-war period, the Yugoslav self-management, are two cases, which have all been described as the Third Way. Clearly, they were very different from the Third Way discussed here.
2. The collection of essays in Arestis and Sawyer (2001a) is a critical appraisal of Third Way policies pursued in a range of countries (and the European Union).
3. Although this approach is labelled as 'new Keynesian', it does not incorporate the basic insight of Keynes that the level of economic activity is determined by the level of effective demand. For an introduction to new Keynesian economics see, for example, Hargreaves Heap (1992).
4. For an overview of endogenous growth theory see Barro and Sala-i-Martin (1995).

REFERENCES

Arestis, P. and Sawyer, M. (eds) (2001a) *The Economics of the Third Way: Experience from Around the World*. Cheltenham: Edward Elgar.

Arestis, P. and Sawyer, M. (2001b) 'Economics of the British New Labour: an assessment', in P. Arestis and M. Sawyer (eds) *The Economics of the Third Way: Experience from Around the World*. Cheltenham: Edward Elgar.

Barro, R.J. and Sala-i-Martin, X. (1995) *Economic Growth*. New York: McGraw-Hill.

Blair, T. (1997). 'Introduction', in *New Labour: Because Britain Deserves Better*. London: Labour Party.

Blair, T. and Schröder, G. (1999) 'Europe: The Third Way/Die Neue Mitte', in B. Hombach, *The Politics of the New Centre*, Oxford: Polity Press, 2000.

Brown, G. (2000) 'Conditions for Growth and Stability', lecture delivered at the Royal Economic Society Annual Conference, University of St Andrews, 13 July.

Forder, J. (2000) 'The Theory of Credibility: Confusions, Limitations, and Dangers', *International Papers in Political Economy* 7 (2), pp. 3–40.

Giddens, A. (1998) *The Third Way: The Renewal of Social Democracy*. Oxford: Polity Press.

Giddens, A. (2000) *The Third Way and its Critics*. Oxford: Polity Press.

Giddens, A. (2003) 'The Challenge of Renewal', *Progressive Politics* 1 (1), pp. 36–9.

Hargreaves Heap, S. (1992) *The New Keynesian Macroeconomics*. Aldershot: Edward Elgar Publishers.

Hombach, B. (2000) *The Politics of the New Centre*. Oxford: Polity Press.

Rutelli, F. (2003) 'Beyond Division', *Progressive Politics* 1 (1), pp. 27–35.

Tsakalotos, E. (2001) 'European Employment Policies: A New Social Democratic Model for Europe?', in P. Arestis and M. Sawyer (eds) *The Economics of the Third Way: Experience from Around the World*. Cheltenham: Edward Elgar.

PART III
Neoliberal Experiences

22

The Birth of Neoliberalism in the United States: A Reorganisation of Capitalism

Al Campbell

Preliminary considerations of neoliberalism thrust four questions to the fore: what? why? how? and where? What is neoliberalism? What distinguishes it from the form of capitalism that preceded it? Why did capital impose this reorganisation of capitalism? This question is particularly important to address in that capital's central concern, its rate of profit, has generally performed worse in the 1980s and 1990s than it did under the previous Keynesian-compromise organisation of the 1950s and 1960s. How was this reorganisation achieved, what changes in policies, practices and institutions constituted the change? And finally, where is neoliberalism going?

This chapter will address the third question, how this reorganisation of capitalism was achieved, in the case of the United States. It will focus on changes in policies, practices and institutions on the one hand, and the effects on the working class on the other. It will be necessary to comment briefly on the first two questions, 'what?' and 'why?', as background for the discussion here on 'how?'.

Four brief comments are important for indicating aspects of the frame that will be used here to consider neoliberalism. First, neoliberalism is not (a) globalisation, (b) the internationalisation of production as some inevitable result of technological changes, particularly in telecommunications and transportation, nor (c) the inevitable result of intensified international competition. Neoliberalism is an organisation of capitalism. There are important international aspects of the neoliberal organisation of capitalism, just as there were important international aspects of every previous organisation of capitalism. These international aspects, however, like its domestic aspects, can be properly understood only in terms of the goal and purpose of capitalism itself.

Second, as will be apparent in the presentation in this chapter, the birth of neoliberalism in the United States was a process that extended over many years. It is only within that framework that the beginning of neoliberalism can be dated to 1979, for reasons discussed below. The point to stress here is all the qualifications that go with this 'birth date' that come immediately from seeing this as only one step in a process (see Chapters 1, 2 and 7).

Third and fourth, this chapter argues that two 'stylised facts', accepted by a number of Marxists and other radicals, are often misinterpreted: that neoliberalism represents the return to hegemony of finance capital; and that the essence of the Keynesian-compromise organisation of capitalism was a capital–labour truce. While these can be useful shorthand ways to refer to certain relations, it is argued here that they are often understood in ways that are contrary to the realities they refer to. Both of these issues are important in explaining the approach taken by this chapter, neoliberalism as a reorganisation of capitalism.

WHAT IS NEOLIBERALISM AND WHY DID CAPITALISM ADOPT IT?

What is neoliberalism? There is a danger in the stylised fact that 'neoliberalism represents a return to hegemony of finance capital'. This shorthand expression suggests to many people that finance capital imposed itself, its will and its programme, on non-financial capital. The transfer of profits from non-financial capital to financial capital in the United States indeed did increase dramatically under neoliberalism. This consideration poses the question: given that finance capital was roughly 15 per cent of total capital in the United States before neoliberalism (and grew to roughly 25 per cent under neoliberalism), how could this minority impose its will on the majority of capital? Why did non-financial capital, the majority of capital, allow this increased transfer at its expense to a minority of capital? It is important to recognise that most finance capital never accepted the Keynesian compromise and always advocated an immediate return to economic liberalism. However, it is also important to accept, as opposed to the 'return to hegemony' thesis, that it is essential to understand why productive capital subscribed to Keynesian ideas after the Second World War and then came to abandon nearly all of them by the 1970s and 1980s. This approach makes clear that the issue is not whether financial capital has power over non financial capital, which by in large it does not, but rather why the main part of capital, productive capital, switched to accept the ideas that the smaller financial capital had always advocated, but which were (partially) rejected under the Keynesian compromise.

Similarly, a number of people hold that a capital–labour truce that allowed a meaningful amount of the expanding national wealth to really 'trickle down' to labour was the essence of the Keynesian compromise (e.g. Bowles et al. 1983, 1990), and hence that the essence of neoliberalism was the abandonment of this truce. The historical record, however, just does not support a story of capital–labour peace, though it needs to be interpreted very carefully. On the one hand, class conflict continued throughout the post-Second World War period and was an important causal component of labour's gains in compensation: they were not a 'gift' by a Fordist capitalism consciously and willingly raising wages in what it perceived as its own interests. On the other hand, there was a 'social understanding', a social accord, a generally (not universally) accepted social norm, as to what the continuing class conflict between capital and labour would be fought over, and what was for the present (though this continually changed over time) not under contention. One part of neoliberalism was an end to this social understanding or accord.

Neoliberalism is a reorganisation of capitalism. After the Second World War, capital decided that a particular set of restrictions on the behaviour of individual capitals would be beneficial to the goal that capital has always had, accumulation. There were two reasons for this decision. One was fear. While US capital never experienced a serious fear of the overthrow of capitalism at home, reading its discussions from 1945 to 1955 make clear the deep fear it had of an extension of

Soviet-type economic relations in Europe, and the importance this played in generating support for some of the measures discussed here, for example capital controls. But it would be a serious overstatement to claim that the policies, practices and institutions that defined Keynesian-compromise capitalism flowed exclusively from a fear by capital of the overthrow of its system. Equally important, capital adopted Keynesian ideas because it believed that the various restrictions and regulations would be beneficial to the process of capital accumulation at that historical moment, particularly in comparison with the poor record of accumulation presented by its recent experience without those restrictions during the Great Depression. Neoliberalism consisted of the negation of a number of those restrictions and regulations.

It must be stressed that neoliberalism is not about 'letting markets operate freely', or about removing government regulation of markets in general. Markets never operate freely. The assertion they do so is part of neoliberal ideology. Both markets themselves and the environments they operate in are always created by government regulations, and cannot exist without them (see Chapter 6).

Why did capitalism adopt neoliberalism? Broadly, there was a structural crisis of capitalism. That is, the policies, practices and institutions that had been serving well capitalism's goal of capital accumulation ceased to do so. More narrowly, one can say that capitalism abandoned the Keynesian compromise in the face of a falling rate of profit, under the belief that neoliberalism could improve its profit and accumulation performance.

With these very brief statements of 'what' and 'why' to establish the frame used in this work to consider neoliberalism, the discussion now turns to the main topic of this chapter, 'how' this reorganisation was achieved: what changes in policies, practices and institutions constituted neoliberalism?

Keynesian-compromise capitalism was born as a reaction to the greatest crisis of the international capitalist system to date, the Great Depression of the 1930s. It consisted of three broad new types of policies, practices and institutions. The first consisted of specific restrictions on certain behaviours of some capitals, above all finance capitals – both domestic and international behaviours. The second consisted of macroeconomic intervention policies to stimulate the economy, both monetary and fiscal. The third consisted of certain labour and welfare policies. The negation of those policies, the birth of neoliberalism, was a process that spanned many decades.

THE ELIMINATION OF INTERNATIONAL CAPITAL CONTROLS AND THE 'RE-EMERGENCE OF GLOBAL FINANCE'

The existence of capital controls on international capital activity was nearly universal throughout the capitalist world after the Second World War, in the advanced capitalist countries as well as in the Third World. The outstanding exception was the United States, which had very few restrictions on international capital movements other than for a short period in the 1960s (see Chapters 3 and 11).

The starting point for understanding this advocacy by capital, which immediately after the Second World War was overwhelmingly US capital, in favour of international capital controls was, as always, its interest in creating the optimal conditions at a given moment for accumulation. The moment, and the consciousness of capital at that moment, was strongly influenced by the recently experienced Great Depression. Broad sections of productive capital came to hold that financial liberalism was antithetical to the stable environment needed for production and growth, which were necessary for optimal accumulation. In regard to international capital movements, speculative international capital was held to have contributed to balance-of-payments crises and price instability that had undermined international trading, which in turn was one important component of the Great Depression and the profit losses for productive capital.

Banking and financial capital (and of course some representatives of productive capital) never accepted either the broad rejection of liberalism and what in the 1990s became known as 'market fundamentalism', nor the specific rejection involved in capital controls. In schematic terms, while productive capital requires conditions appropriate for production (and sale) of commodities, financial capital desires an environment where it is permitted to do whatever it chooses in the pursuit of its own profits. As a logical possibility, it might be that the actions of financial capital harm the environment for productive capital to produce and sell and thereby make profits. That is in fact exactly what productive capital came to believe as a result of the Great Depression. Financial capital, to the contrary, largely continued to adhere to the liberal line, that unregulated markets always work best, including financial markets.

The beginning of the widespread elimination of the near universal capital controls, which as one would expect did not occur all at once, was the first major campaign of the birth of neoliberalism. By 1958, European countries felt they had accumulated enough international reserves, primarily dollars, for them to restore currency convertibility. New York banking circles were pleased, and were now able to take on significantly more of the role of lender to the world, a role which they had fought for since 1945. Productive capital also backed this change at the time. Their concern had always been creating conditions suitable for trade. Speculative capital will always attack any currency not backed by sufficient reserves and thereby cause a disruption of trade, as in fact happened during the ill-conceived attempt promoted by the New York banks to move Europe immediately to full convertibility in 1945–47. As discussed thoroughly at Bretton Woods, capital controls require currency controls to be fully effective, since otherwise capital will avoid the controls under the guise of current account transactions. But currency control is itself detrimental to trade. Hence productive capital was happy to see these restrictions removed as soon as the countries had the reserves necessary to prevent disruptive speculative currency attacks. Long-term capital controls were not removed.

At the same time, Britain was experiencing problems in its sterling balances, and in 1957 imposed restrictions on financing trade outside the sterling area by British banks. As a response, the banks began to extend dollar credit against the dollar deposits they had from foreign customers (what we would today call a 'financial innovation'). When the restrictions were lifted in 1959, the banks decided to continue with what had turned out to be a profitable business. The British government, which was promoting the rebuilding of London as an international financial centre, allowed the Euromarket to be physically located in London, but to be exempt from most British financial restrictions and regulations. The Eurodollar market was born. In 1963 Britain allowed it to expand to the issuance of bonds.

The Euromarket was very much a compromise. While the elimination of exchange controls in 1958 was a big step in eliminating capital controls (and weakening remaining ones), it was far from ending them. The Euromarket provided a largely unregulated arena for international capital transactions as desired by financial capital (and hence supported by the US Treasury and the Federal Reserve), but at the same time it left capital controls in place in Europe as desired by the Keynesian concern for the ability to regulate one's domestic economy (frequently referred to as 'policy autonomy').

Increased lending by the US banks on top of the already existing balance-of-payments deficit generated a balance-of-payments problem, if not quite a crisis. With foreign holdings of US dollars continuing to climb, the first run on the dollar occurred in October 1960. The United States was unwilling to drive up its interest rate to attract international capital. It applied as much pressure as possible on foreign governments and even private citizens to hold dollar assets, and the expansion of the Eurodollar market helped significantly in this respect. But with US balance of payments continuing to stay negative year after year, the US turned to implementing various capital controls, starting in 1963. This of course increased greatly the importance of the Euromarket to US financial capital. It moved into the market massively in the 1960s, and this unregulated market came for a time to replace New York as the centre for international capital transactions.

With large amounts of capital now relatively unregulated, pressure on the dollar kept increasing. But the United States refused to correct its balance-of-payments problem, gold continued to drain from the United States, and eventually the Bretton Woods exchange rate system crashed. After the United States ended its backing of the dollar with gold in August 1971, two years of negotiations followed on how the international exchange system should be reconstructed. Europe and Japan argued for adjusting the exchange rates to realistic levels and then re-establishing fixed exchange rates, backed by significantly strengthened capital controls based on international co-operation. But the United States rejected this approach in favour of the neoliberal approach: remove all capital controls, and let exchange rates float. Faced with a currency crisis in February 1973, the United States announced it would end all capital controls by December 1974, and in fact eliminated them by January 1974.

The main cause for this major shift was the diminished relative economic power of US productive capital, which manifested itself in the continual balance-of-payments deficits. Faced with this, the United States decided to use its continued dominance of world financial markets to support its deficits at a sustainable level. Two other factors contributed to this change. First, because of the tremendous expansion of US-owned productive capacity overseas over the course of the 1960s, productive capital came to strongly oppose all international capital controls, both domestic and foreign, for its own operational reasons. President Johnson implemented the first capital controls on direct foreign investment in 1968 to try to alleviate the ongoing balance-of-payments problem, and business interests responded by lobbying Nixon during the election campaign for the removal of capital controls. Second, after 1973 OPEC suddenly had a huge amount of capital that it wanted to invest. Europe, Japan and the Arab countries all favoured channelling significant amounts of this through the IMF to alleviate deficits around the world induced by the oil-price hike. The United States blocked such efforts in the name of free financial markets, knowing that left the capital only one place it could be absorbed: US financial markets (including Eurodollars), thereby underwriting the US ability to continue running its deficits.

THE REDUCTION OF RESTRICTIONS ON DOMESTIC FINANCE CAPITAL

There are four fundamental types of regulation governments put on finance capital: fraud, disclosure of information, protection of investors' assets and competition. Only the last of these regulations has come under attack by neoliberalism. Since a negligible amount of business borrowing was done in the commercial paper market at the beginning of the Keynesian-compromise period, for reasons of space the discussion will focus here on bank regulation.

There were four main regulations limiting competition: 'Regulation Q', the separation of financial and non-financial firms (no universal banking), the separation of commercial banking from investment banking, and branching restrictions. All except one (and that one was chipped away at) were to fall to neoliberalism.

Regulation Q restrictions placed ceilings on the amount of interest banks could offer on deposits. The purpose was to promote production and growth by keeping the interest rate low at which productive capital could borrow. Finance capital of course, to the contrary, was interested in getting as high returns on its loaned capital as possible, that is, as high as the market for loans would support. Through the 1950s and early 1960s market interest rates were generally comparable to the Regulation Q limits, so there was no large incentive to eliminate them. Following the credit crunch of 1966, but more generally as nominal market interest rates rose, that changed.

Two fundamental ways were created to circumvent Regulation Q. The first was simply to loan the money directly to the borrowing corporations. Commercial paper was only 2 per cent of short-term business financing in 1960, but it was up to 7 per cent by 1970 and 10 per cent by 1980. The second way was for banking and non-banking financial institutions to develop a plethora of financial instruments that operated like the instruments restricted by Regulation Q, but which were unrestricted because they were technically different. As one example, investment companies developed money-market mutual funds, which appeared to customers equivalent to savings accounts, but actually involved the company pooling small investments to buy large commercial paper and treasury bills. By the end of the 1970s, these funds amounted to nearly US$200 billion, about 15 per cent of the assets of all commercial banks at the time. By 1980, it was clear that Regulation Q was ineffective at keeping down interest rates. The 1980 Depository Institutions Deregulation and Monetary Control Act mandated a complete phase-out of interest-rate ceilings by 1986.

The separation of commercial from investment banking was similarly intended to limit the power of financial capital, and thereby its ability to raise interest rates at the expense of productive capital. The regulations on what each could and could not do were extensive and detailed, but two key provisions were that investment banks could not take deposits of any kind, and commercial banks could not under-write corporate securities (or even hold any other than regulator-approved corporate securities as part of their assets). Over the 1980s and 1990s, these restrictions were largely eliminated.

Both Regulation Q and the separation of commercial from investment banking were parts of the Banking Act of 1933 (commonly called the Glass–Steagall Act), the foundation act for the whole restriction of domestic finance during the Keynesian compromise. The Gramm–Leach–Bliley Financial Services Modernisation Act of 1999 repealed most of what was left of the Glass–Steagall Act, and certified the existence of the neoliberal domestic financial order that was by then already very largely in place.

One Glass–Steagall restriction that has not yet been eliminated is the prohibition against a single company doing both banking and commerce, 'universal banking'. Over time, that too has been chipped away at. The automobile companies have been allowed to operate major credit services for purchasing automobiles, and General Electric Capital has become a major financial institution. By and large, however, the restrictions against universal banking are still intact.

The 1927 McFadden Act proscription against interstate bank branching was intended to assure that credit would be available to small-scale local productive capital, which it was feared would not be the case with large national banks with local branches. On the one hand, these restrictions were partially 'innovated around' throughout the Keynesian compromise period. On the other hand, the innovations never overcame the basic restriction on the prerogative of the major sections of financial capital to pursue their profit interests in whatever way they considered optimal. In 1994, the Riegal–Neal Interstate Banking and Branching Efficiency Act provided a three-year phase-in of the almost complete elimination of branching restrictions.

NEOLIBERAL FISCAL AND MONETARY POLICIES.

As discussed at the beginning of this chapter, neoliberalism sees the key to optimal accumulation of capital as establishing a 'free-market' regime and protecting the value of money. The simple neoliberal theory of fiscal policy follows from this. Government spending should only be on those things markets cannot do (and neoliberals consider that list to be very short), and taxes should be levied to pay for those activities. There is no role for fiscal policy concerning the performance of the macro-economy (in particular, to provide increased growth or employment as proposed in Keynesian thought).

In practice, fiscal policy during the post-1979 neoliberal era in the United States has often been very non-neoliberal. This is not because of the massive military spending increases under Reagan and Bush Jr. On the one hand, those were partially offset by cuts in government-provided services, but on the other hand, even if it isn't offset, military spending is something only the government can do, and so any levels thought to be necessary are compatible with neoliberal thought. The fiscal policies have been non-neoliberal because the spending has not been covered by taxes: the government has run large domestic deficits. This in general is inconsistent with the neoliberal goal of protecting the value of money. Under Reagan, inflation was avoided by the large inflow of foreign capital that financed his deficit. It is far from certain that this same result will obtain for the large Bush Jr. deficits.

Under Keynesian thought, the prime role of monetary policy is to promote production and growth by maintaining a relatively low real interest rate. Real interest rates were typically between 1 and 2 per cent in the 1950s and 1960s, and negative for much of the 1970s. With the onset of neoliberalism, they jumped to nearly 4 per cent, and higher in the 1980s.

Three things came together in the late 1970s that led to the final consolidation of neoliberalism, and monetary policy was the instrument used to enact the new policy. First, economy-wide profits continued to fall. Second, inflation took off again. The business community and the Carter administration blamed these on labour compensation, which continued to rise at about 2 per cent a year in real terms after the 1973–74 recession, even though productivity growth had dropped to almost nothing. They could as well have blamed the inflation on the falling dollar, to be discussed next, but they did not. Third, with continued balance-of-payments deficits, as discussed above, plus a newly increased domestic inflation, the value of the dollar continued to fall. Despite ongoing efforts throughout the 1970s to support the dollar, Saudi Arabia now began to sell its dollar reserves, and in addition threatened an oil-price increase if the United States did not act to stop the fall. Most important, a massive flight from the dollar began in the now huge and essentially unrestricted private capital markets. The dollar faced going into free fall.

At the end of 1978, the Carter administration made a sharp policy change. Its central concern during its first two years with growth and a reduction in unemployment was replaced by fighting inflation. Both fiscal and monetary polices were changed to become restrictive. Interest rates rose, but there were minimal impacts on the rise in labour costs, inflation, or the value of the dollar. Stronger measures were needed, but those would necessarily cause a significant recession, and Carter was not willing to do that.

In August 1979, Carter decided to send a message, in particular to international money markets, by appointing a known 'hard money' man to head the Federal Reserve, Paul Volcker. On 6 October, the Fed announced a draconian tightening of the money supply. Interest rates jumped dramatically, and as planned the economy went into recession in 1980. But only part of the goals were achieved. Confidence in the dollar was restored, and its fall ended. But inflation was not checked, and it actually rose to 13.5 per cent in 1980. Real labour costs did begin to fall, but it was more from the continued accelerating inflation than from reductions in nominal compensation increases: nominal unit labour costs had gone up by 8.9 per cent in 1978, and they went up by more than 10 per cent in 1980.

More of the same tight money policy finally broke the inflation. After a brief upturn in the economy, interest rates went to new heights, and the economy went into a 'second dip'. The 1981–82 recession was the worst since the Great Depression, with output dropping by 2.2 per cent in 1982 and unemployment reaching 9.7 per cent. Inflation dropped from 13.5 per cent in 1980 to 3.2 per cent in 1983.

With inflation down to almost zero by July 1982, the Fed loosened its monetary policy. Inflation went up almost four points in a short time, but then stabilised, and has not meaningfully gone above that level during the two decades since then.

With maintaining low inflation requiring little action in the 1980s and 1990s, the main action issue for the Fed, again in line with its concern to facilitate capital accumulation, was rapidly resolving developing financial crises, generally by playing the role of lender of last resort in one fashion or another. This was a lesson learned from its failure to do so in the Great Depression. It had already played this role in the 1966 credit crunch and the 1970 Penn Central and 1974 Franklin National Bank financial crises. The Fed continued its successful conduct of this role in the period of neoliberal consolidation in the 1982 Penn Square Bank and the Mexican default crises and especially in the potentially extremely disruptive 1987 stock market crash.

NEOLIBERAL LABOUR AND WELFARE POLICIES

Two different incorrect ideas about the nature of the Keynesian-compromise labour policies must be dismissed before one can understand neoliberalism's labour policies. The more radical is a version of the 'Fordism' thesis in which capital recognises it faces a permanent 'realisation problem' (insufficient demand) and consciously moves to increase labour's compensation to (temporarily and partially) overcome this problem. The less radical version is that some sort of capital–labour truce was a central aspect of the Keynesian compromise.

What was true was that immediately after the Second World War there was a broad fear that the drop in government demand with the sharp reduction in military spending would return the economy to the pre-war depression. This view was dominant in the government planning agencies, had important support among academics, and was reflected in Truman's call for wage increases in a 30 October 1945 radio programme. But the Great Strike Wave of 1945–46 showed that business as a whole neither subscribed to the idea that it was in its interest to raise wages, nor even that there was a capital–labour truce. Similarly, in 1947 Congress passed the strongest anti-labour act of the twentieth century, the Taft–Hartley Act (interestingly, over Truman's veto), itself a witness that there was no truce, and a bill that assured a reduction of labour's share of production compared to what it would have been able to win without that act (see Chapter 2).

In Keynesian thought, production, sales and growth are central to profits. With demand for US products assured by the post-Second World War situation, 'stability' of production was considered central to profits. Output lost through strikes, or even less acute labour conflicts, meant profits lost. The late 1940s and 1950s saw the introduction of multiyear contracts and the fight by capital to lengthen them. When the 1957 slowdown came, so that strikes became temporarily less costly, capital used that to increase its confrontation with unions, over wages, mechanisation, and intensification of work (often euphemistically called 'conditions of work', 'labour productivity' or 'manpower utilisation'), but they fought over these issues at some level throughout the whole period. When exceptionally high profits were generated in the mid to late 1960s, they were not automatically shared with labour. Rather, significantly increased strike action was needed for some of the profits to 'trickle down'. Throughout the whole period, capital fought tenaciously to prevent the unions from spreading geographically or increasing numerically. It slowly drove down the union percentage of the workforce from its high of 35 per cent in 1945 to 33 per cent in 1955, 31 per cent in 1960, 27 per cent in 1970 and 23 per cent in 1980. Neither claims of Fordism nor of a capital–labour truce correspond to the reality of the Keynesian-compromise labour relations. There was, rather, a capital–labour accord, that (generally) consisted of two basic aspects: there was no effort to break the unions outright in places where they were established (even after major defeats, such as the strike against GE in 1959), and labour was entitled to some part of productivity gains.

The fundamental change under neoliberal thought was the concept of the key to profits and the accumulation of capital. Instead of production, sales and growth, with its implied stability, neoliberal thought sees the key to enterprise profits as cutting costs. That could be by mechanising or improved management, but it also includes lowering labour's compensation or intensifying labour. Beginning with the 1970s, capital, backed by government policies, especially after the consolidation of neoliberalism, introduced a plethora of policies and practices aimed at reducing the growth of, or even absolutely reducing, workers' real wages and benefits.

There were at least six concrete attacks on labour launched by capital in the 1970s and 1980s that together determined the shape of the new capital–labour relations and the end of the old accord. First, capital greatly increased its overseas production and purchase of foreign-produced productive inputs. On the one hand this contributed to increased domestic unemployment and hence downward pressure on wages and benefits, but even more important was its value as a threat against demands for wage increases or unionisation. Second, capital introduced wage freezes and outright wage cuts. These were almost nonexistent before 1980, and then they appeared full-bodied, like Athena from the head of Zeus, with the 1981–82 recession. In 1982, 44 per cent of unionised workers bargaining for new contracts took wage cuts or a wage freeze for at least the first year of the contract; in 1980 there had been no such contracts. Third, Cost of Living Adjustment (COLA) clauses were rapidly eliminated from most contracts at the beginning of the neoliberal era. In 1985 alone, 40 per cent of workers renewing contracts who had COLAs lost them: 50 per cent of new contracts had COLAs in 1983, 40 per cent in 1984 and 30 per cent in 1985. Fourth, two-tiered wage structures appeared that gave much lower wages to new employees doing exactly the same work as established workers. In the best of cases, such as the auto workers, these workers reached parity in a year; this was not too different from the lower wages during the probationary period that already existed in most contracts. In the worst cases, workers started at almost half wages and it took ten years or more to reach parity. While government is discussed below, Reagan gave a strong endorsement to this practice by instituting a two-tier wage system in the US Postal Service. Fifth, full time workers were replaced by 'temps' (or 'contingent workers'), generally with particularly large savings for capital on health, pension and other benefits. Sixth, 'union avoidance' took on new dimensions. It has already been mentioned above that capital fought the spread of unions throughout the whole Keynesian-compromise period. The only change in that respect is that capital's fight against new unions became more intense (as measured by money and effort spent fighting them, violations of labour law, etc.). The new dimension was extensive union busting. Again, Reagan sanctioned this in his first year in office with his famous elimination of PATCO. While sometimes they simply broke a union, much more often they eliminated unions by closing a plant and opening a new non-union one (overseas or in the United States), or occasionally through bankruptcy (with assets then sold to another company who operated them as non-union).

The government supported this attack on labour in at least five ways:

1. By its tight money policies it slowed growth compared to what it had been under Keynesian-compromise capitalism, thereby weakening the ability of labour to fight back against capital's assault.
2. It allowed the minimum wage to drop in real value.
3. It reinterpreted labour law in ways much more favourable to capital. Reagan appointed anti-labour figures to the National Labour Relations Board (NLRB), and in a series of rulings over the 1980s they sharply reduced labour's ability to organise new unions, bargain effectively with employers, or strike.
4. As a signal, it directly engaged in two practices that private capital was developing, union busting and the two-tiered wage system, as noted above.
5. It weakened the welfare safety net. It did a number of things in this regard. It reduced unemployment insurance benefits, beginning under Carter and deepening under Reagan. It reduced trade adjustment assistance, beginning under Reagan. The 309,000 Public Service Employment jobs that existed when Reagan took office were eliminated in his first year. It reduced Aid to Families with Dependent Children (AFDC). Under Carter, the real value of benefits dropped. Under Reagan, they continued to drop, and in addition changes in eligibility caused about half a million families to be removed from the programme.

CONCLUSION

Neoliberalism is a particular organisation of capitalism. Its birth consisted of a reorganisation of the previous organisation of capitalism. Under the Keynesian compromise, both private capital and its collective agent, the government, focused on ensuring that the conditions existed for minimally interrupted production, sales and growth as the key to optimising capital accumulation. That organisation of capitalism, which had worked well for two decades in the specific conditions of rebuilding Europe and Japan, went into a crisis in the late 1960s and the 1970s. A falling rate of profit was a key manifestation of the crisis of accumulation. Neoliberalism shifted the policies of private capital and government that were considered to be optimal for capital accumulation, given the concrete conditions that had come to exist by the 1970s and 1980s. Protecting the value of existing capital and, most important to this organisation, sharply intensifying the drive to reduce labour's compensation and labour's share of output, are the key components to neoliberalism's strategy for optimal capital accumulation under current conditions.

REFERENCES

Armstrong, P., Glyn, A. and Harrison, J. (1991) *Capitalism Since 1945*. Oxford: Basil Blackwell.

Block, F., Cloward, R., Ehrenreich, B. and Piven, F.F. (1987) *The Mean Season: The Attack on the Welfare State*. New York: Pantheon.

Bowles, S., Gordon, D. and Weisskopf, T. (1983) *Beyond the Waste Land*. Garden City, N.Y.: Anchor Press/Doubleday.

Bowles, S., Gordon, D. and Weisskopf, T. (1990) *After the Waste Land*. Armonk, N.Y.: M.E. Sharpe.

Duménil, G. and Lévy, D. (2004) *Capital Resurgent*. Boston: Harvard University Press.

Duncan, R. (2003) *The Dollar Crisis*. Singapore: John Wiley & Sons (Asia).

Harrison, B. and Bluestone, B. (1988) *The Great U-Turn: Corporate Restructuring and the Polarizing of America*. New York: Basic Books.

Helleiner, E. (1994) *States and the Reemergence of Global Finance: From Bretton Woods to the Nineties*. Ithaca, N.Y.: Cornell University Press.

Kochan, T., Katz, H. and McKersie, R. (1994) *The Transformation of American Industrial Relations*. Ithaca, N.Y.: ILR Press.

Meeropol, M. (1998) *Surrender: How the Clinton Administration Completed the Reagan Revolution*. Ann Arbor: University of Michigan Press.

Rosenberg, S. (2003) *American Economic Development Since 1945*. London: Palgrave.

Wolfson, M. (1994) *Financial Crises: Understanding the Postwar US Experience*, 2nd edn, Armonk, N.Y.: M.E. Sharpe.

23
The Neoliberal Experience of the United Kingdom

Philip Arestis and Malcolm Sawyer

The election of the Conservative government under Margaret Thatcher in May 1979, replacing the 1974–79 Labour government, can be viewed as a major shift in British politics and economic policy. The extent of the change and how far it can be precisely dated has long been a matter of debate, and policies such as control of money supply and the monetarist approach to inflation (and indeed some privatisation) can be seen as having been partially adopted by the previous government. Further, the dramatic rise in inequality in the United Kingdom, which characterised the Thatcher government (see below for the relevant figures), may be seen as having started a few years earlier as the general trend in the United Kingdom in the direction of diminishing inequality was reversed. The replacement of Thatcher by John Major as prime minister in 1990, and the election of a Labour government in 1997, have led to minor shifts in policy and in the rhetoric of policy (particularly with regard to the European Union). But the general neoliberal thrust has continued throughout (see Chapter 21). This chapter covers the following issues: privatisation, industrial policy, inequality and macroeconomic policy.

PRIVATISATION

The belief in the superiority of the market to the state and of private property to public and social ownership, the major components of neoliberalism, is exemplified by the programme of privatisation. Over the past two decades, privatisation has taken two major forms: the sale of publicly owned assets, and the more creeping form under the heading of the private finance initiative (hereafter PFI, and itself part of public private partnerships, PPP). The first has seen the sale of most of the major utilities (starting with telecommunications in 1984, then gas, electricity, water and railways). This privatisation programme represents a sharp break with previous policies (though there had been a small number of previous privatisations, such as the denationalisation of steel in the early 1950s and the sale of companies such as Thomas Cook by the Heath government in the early 1970s). The major programme of nationalisation in the postwar period was undertaken by the Labour governments of 1945–51. During that period, industries such as coalmining, railways, part of road haulage (later denationalised), gas, electricity and the Bank of England were nationalised. Nationalisation in the 1960s and 1970s was concentrated on industries in long-term decline (such as steel, shipbuilding and aerospace). Individual firms such as British Leyland and part of Rolls-Royce came into public ownership more by accident than design, as a response by the government to the threat of the extinction through bankruptcy of those firms.

There were many factors pushing towards privatisation, and privatisation as a policy served a range of purposes. The factors included the reduction of government involvement in industry; improvement of efficiency in both the privatised companies and what remained of the public sector; reduction of the public sector borrowing requirement (PSBR) through the receipts of the sale of public assets; weakening the power of trade unions in public-sector wage bargaining; widening share ownership through promotion of share sales in small amounts; the encouragement of employee share ownership and the gaining of political advantages (especially through the initial financial gains accruing to those who bought shares in privatised companies, resulting from the deliberate underpricing of the shares put on sale).

Each of the privatised public utilities was subject to regulation by a newly created regulatory agency with controls over their pricing and other policies. The privatisation programme shifted all of the major utilities, with the exception of the postal service, from the public to the private sector, and included the sale of a wide range of companies, such as Britoil, Jaguar Cars and National Freight. Proceeds from the sale of public assets fluctuated from year to year, but they reached £5 billion or more from the mid 1980s to the mid 1990s. Employment in public corporations fell from 1,867,000 in 1981 to 599,000 in 1991 and further to 379,000 in 2002 (*Economic Trends*, September 2003).

The privatisation of utilities has been small in the past decade, mainly for the reason that there is little left to sell. The Post Office remains the only major public utility, though that is under some threat. The Labour government since 1997 has made no attempt to reverse privatisation (whereas in election manifestos of 1987 and 1992 it had promised to do so), and has continued with small privatisations, such as the partial privatisation of National Air Traffic Services (NATS), in which the government retains a 49 per cent ownership with a golden share. Opportunities to reverse the privatisations have been scorned: the failure of Railtrack (operating, as its name suggests, tracks, stations and signalling) did not lead to nationalisation, but to an alternative form of private ownership with the formation of Network Rail, a company limited by guarantee with no shareholders, but with members from the rail industry and public authorities, as well as individuals, who do not receive dividends or share capital, the profits being reinvested into the rail infrastructure.

The form of privatisation which has flourished under the post-1997 Labour government has been the private finance initiative (PFI). It has also always been the case that the private sector has provided goods and services to the public sector. The type of goods and services which have been provided by the private sector and the type which have been produced 'in-house' by the public sector have, of course, varied over time and differed between countries. But a widespread feature in the past 20 years or so has been the shift away from the 'in-house' provision of goods and services (and particularly the latter) by the public sector and towards the contracting out of services to be provided by the private sector. These services contribute to the provision of services by the government to the public, but the services themselves are supplied by the private sector rather than by public sector employees.

The introduction and development of the PFI has led to changes in the form of financing for public sector investment and the degree of contracting out of services to private-sector provision. In terms of the private ownership of assets utilised by the public sector and in the private-sector provision of public services, the PFI represents further privatisation. The general feature of the PFI is that a private company undertakes a capital investment project (e.g. the construction of a school), which it finances itself. The capital project is leased to the public sector (often for 25 or 30 years) and the private company typically supplies services, related to the capital project, to the public sector. These services may range from maintenance of the capital project to provision of cleaning services for the construction concerned.

PFI involves further private provision of services to the public sector, which would otherwise have been provided by the employees of the public sector. This is a form of creeping privatisation, whereby public services are provided by the private sector. It also involves the private ownership of capital facilities such as schools and hospitals, which also would formerly have been owned by the public sector. Dubious claims have been made that PFI generates higher levels of investment, lower costs and the transfer of risk. As shown elsewhere (Sawyer 2003) these claims cannot be substantiated and have shown the higher effective cost of finance (to the public sector) that is involved in the PFI (as compared with the alternatives). The PFI means the government has entered into future commitments on the leasing payments for the assets paid by the PFI, with consequences for future public expenditure.

INDUSTRIAL POLICY

The central element of the neoliberal approach is the promotion (and almost the worship) of the private market over other modes of economic organisation. It requires the removal of what are perceived as barriers and obstacles to the operation of the market, notably the removal of regulations that limit entry into a market or industry. The neoliberal approach has been to shy away from government intervention in industry (whether of the form of restructuring industry, use of forms of indicative planning, etc.) and to promote the market and competition. In policy terms, this has shown up in the retreat from the industrial policies pursued (in varying degrees) both by Conservative and (more vigorously) by Labour governments in the postwar period up to 1979. These policies ranged over the use of indicative planning (e.g. under the National Plan of the 1960s) in conjunction with the corporatist 'social partners' approach (e.g. National Economic Development Office), the restructuring of industries (as with the textile industry in the 1950s, the promotion of mergers and of large-scale production under the Industrial Reorganisation Corporation and the nationalisation of the steel and shipbuilding industries) and the National Enterprise Board of the late 1970s. In contrast, industrial policy in the neoliberal era has shifted far away from interventionist policies, and such industrial policy as there is can be summed up as development of competition policy and the promotion of foreign direct investment (FDI).

There is, though, a paradox here: if the market works so well through the process of competition why is there a need for competition policy? The models of competition (e.g. perfect competition) on which the arguments for competition are based do not contain any hint that competition is not self-sustaining. The idea that the process of competition leads to centralisation and concentration is firmly rooted in the Marxian, not the neoclassical or Austrian concepts of competition! Yet the basis of competition policy (monopoly and mergers policy) is that firms act to create monopoly positions, limit entry by other firms, merge and acquire to enhance market dominance, etc.

Competition policy has been in place in the United Kingdom in some form since 1948 (with extensions to restrictive practices in 1956, mergers in 1965, and the creation of the Office of Fair Trading in 1973), and there was little change under the Conservative government between 1979 and 1997. The incoming Labour government placed rather more emphasis on competition policy, and many significant changes in the working of competition policy in the United Kingdom were made in the Competition Act of 1998, including the creation of the Competition Commission (CC) which took over the previous role of the Monopoly and Mergers Commission (MMC), with revised and enhanced functions and powers. This Competition Act made significant changes, which shifted UK policy closer to that of the European Union. The Competition Act 1998 brought in two sets of prohibitions relating to agreements (whether written or not) that prevent, restrict or distort competition, and to conduct by firms that amounts to an abuse of a dominant market position. The Enterprise Act 2002 amended the framework for the control of UK mergers and acquisitions. The two most significant changes were that in general, mergers are to be assessed just against a competition test, rather than against the wider public-interest test which formerly applied; and that decisions on merger control will, in general, be taken by the Office of Fair Trading and the Competition Commission, rather than, as previously, by the Secretary of State for Trade and Industry. The government's own view on this was made clear when it said:

> At home, DTI [Department of Trade and Industry] has already modernised the UK competitive framework through the Competition and Enterprise Acts. The challenge ahead is to make it work effectively by lifting unnecessary regulations, eliminating cartels and allowing fair markets to prevail. And by reducing barriers to entry we will encourage new business start-ups, which are an important source of innovation. (DTI 2003a, p. 21)

It can be questioned how far the operation of competition policy impacts on firms' behaviour and performance: for example, the proportion of proposed mergers and acquisitions which are examined and then overturned is rather small (around 3 per cent). The number of investigations carried out by the competition authorities each year is also rather small and rarely results in major modifications to industrial structure and the degree of market power. However, the changes in competition policy are at least indicative of changes in the stance of government. The balance of industrial policy has clearly swung away (almost entirely) from intervention and towards the promotion of competition. Further, besides the alignment of UK policy with European policy, the changes introduced a series of prohibitions on certain types of behaviour. The shift in the criteria for judging mergers under the Enterprise Act 2002 is also significant. Previously the effects of mergers (and indeed monopoly positions) were judged against the criterion of the public interest. Although 'public interest' was not precisely defined, it was often interpreted in terms of assessing mergers and monopoly positions in terms of impact on employment, regional distribution of industrial activity, etc. This has now been subsumed under the criterion of competition: in effect the public interest has become identified with competition.

The United Kingdom has long been a large receiver of FDI (mostly from the USA) and the source of much investment in other countries. At many times, the concern expressed over FDI has involved the scale of the outward flow of investment, and the degree to which that detracted from investment (and employment) at home. It remains the case that the United Kingdom is generally a net 'exporter' of FDI. At the end of 2002, the stock of inward investment stood at US$638.5 billion and the outward stock at US$1,033 billion.[1] However, the policy concerns over the past two decades have firmly swung in the direction of the promotion of inward FDI, rather than any attempt to limit outward investment. The general view of FDI is well summarised by DTI (2003b):

> International trade and investment is central to the prosperity of the UK. Businesses which trade internationally tend to be more productive and competitive than those which do not. They grow more quickly. They spend more on innovation. They are more capital intensive and their productivity is higher. That is why the work done by British Trade International is crucial. Through its networks and partners within the UK and its staff at FCO posts overseas, British Trade International helps thousands of companies each year to take their place in the global market, creating wealth and jobs: and the foreign direct investment which it brings to the UK not only creates jobs but brings about the transfer of technology, skills and best practice to help make the UK more competitive.

Furthermore, the key target of Invest UK's Public Service Agreement is 'to maintain the UK's position as the number one location in the EU for foreign direct investment'. This is measured by trends in the UK stock of FDI, as recorded in the United Nations Conference on Trade and Development (UNCTAD) world investment report league table of inward stock of foreign investment.[2] It is also worth quoting the information sheet of UK Trade and Investment:

> The flexible approach to skills, training and employment that characterises UK businesses and workers is reinforced by a well-regulated labour market that offers: highly competitive staffing costs, with one of the lowest social security costs in Europe … a truly international and multicultural workforce … wage

costs that are highly competitive ... social costs on wage bills that are amongst
the lowest in Western Europe ... Businesses in the UK have long benefited
from one of the lowest corporate tax rates, making it one of the most competitive and attractive business locations ... The UK has a highly flexible labour
market, which enables foreign investors to use a great deal of flexibility in their
employment and management of staff ... In the UK, employees are used to
working hard for their employers. In 2001 the average hours usually worked
per week by full-time employees were 45.1 hours for males and 40.7 hours for
females. The EU average was 40.9 hours and 38.8 hours for males and females
respectively ... UK law does not oblige employers to provide a written
employment contract.[3]

The enhanced use of competition policy does not itself represent a major change
from pre-1979 policies, though the sole emphasis on competition rather than public interest is a tell-tale sign of a change in outlook. Similarly, the policies towards
FDI are not a sharp change, in that FDI into the United Kingdom has never been
discouraged. But these policies have been given much more prominence as previous forms of industrial intervention and of regional policy have been discarded.

MACROECONOMIC POLICY

At the risk of considerable oversimplification, in the era before 1979 macroeconomic policy had been primarily fiscal policy, though monetary policy was of
increasing importance during the 1970s; not to forget, of course, incomes policies,
especially what was then known, in the 'old' Labour government of the 1970s, as
the social contract. The objectives of macroeconomic policy were often recited (at
least in the text books) as being full (or a high level of) employment, low inflation, growth and a sustainable balance-of-payments position. Some commitment
by government to full employment could be traced back to the White Paper of
1944 (Ministry of Reconstruction, 1944). It became clear, as unemployment
mounted during the 1970s and into the 1980s that any pretence of seeking to
secure full employment had been dropped, and the Keynesian notion that fiscal
policy could generate sufficient demand to reach full employment had also been
jettisoned. The thrust of this approach was questioned, however, in the 1970s, in
view of the inflationary pressures throughout that decade, leading to the demise of
fiscal policy and to the upgrading of monetary policy and the institutionalisation
of independent central banks. The end of the Keynesian demand-management era
is often linked with the speech of Labour prime minister James Callaghan to the
Labour Party conference in October 1976, when he argued that:

We used to think that you could spend your way out of a recession, and
increase employment by cutting taxes and boosting government spending.
I tell you in all candour that that option no longer exists, and that in so far as it
ever did exist, it only worked ... by injecting a bigger dose of inflation into the
system.

The general approach is well illustrated by a White Paper (Department of Employment 1985) in which it was argued that

> the one thing clearly not responsible for unemployment is lack of demand. Demand has grown by about 8 per cent in each of the last two years, giving ample scope for higher output and more jobs. The problem has been that too much of the growth has been dissipated in higher prices and in higher pay for those with jobs, effectively at the expense of those without. (Department of Employment 1985, p. 12)

It was instead argued that

> unemployment reflects our economy's failure to adjust to the circumstances and opportunities of today; to the changing pattern of consumer demand; to new competition from abroad; to innovation and technological development; and to world economic pressures. The countries that have met this challenge successfully are those with efficient, competitive, innovative and responsible labour and goods markets. Improving the working of the labour market is particularly important. Jobs will be created to the extent that people are prepared to work at wages that employers can afford ... The biggest single cause of our high unemployment is the failure of our job market, the weak link in our economy ... [though] to think of workers as part of a market is not to devalue them; it is to recognise that the realities of economic life are not waived just because the factors are people, not things. (pp. 1, 13)

The adoption of the Medium Term Financial Strategy in 1980 signalled a belief in the power of monetary policy (indeed of the money supply) to control inflation, which became the key objective of macroeconomic policy, and the gearing of fiscal policy to the achievement of monetary targets (under the mistaken belief that there was a close relationship between budget deficits and growth of stock of money). Monetarism promised a relatively easy way of reducing inflation: reduce the growth of the money stock (see Chapters 2 and 3). Some economists argued that it would be fairly painless: people would quickly adjust their inflationary expectations in light of the declared intention for growth of the money stock to come down, and any unemployment would be temporary, as the economy soon bounced back to the 'natural rate of unemployment'. Further, reductions in unemployment benefits and in marginal tax rates and removal of trade union 'privileges' would lower the 'natural rate of unemployment'. Monetarism soon proved to be a 'false prophet': controlling the money supply failed, unemployment rose sharply and inflation remained high. But the rise of monetary policy and the shift of objectives to inflation and away from full employment remained. Indeed it continues to this day under New Labour: what we have elsewhere labelled 'new monetarism' (Arestis and Sawyer 1998). Monetary policy has shifted away from aiming for a money supply target to the use of a central-bank-determined interest rate: this 'repo' rate is now set by an 'independent' central bank (with operational independence having been set as the first act of the incoming Labour government, in May 1997). An 'independent' central bank represents a triumph of the use of 'experts' (bankers and economists) over politicians in arriving at key economic decisions, and the pursuit of low inflation as the major macroeconomic objective.

INEQUALITY

It is undeniable that inequality has dramatically increased in the United Kingdom since the late 1970s, with most (but not all) of that increase arising during the Thatcher era (1979 to 1990).[4] Amongst households, the share of income received by the top 10 per cent increased from 20.4 per cent in 1979 to 26.0 per cent in 1990 and to 27.8 per cent in 2002, whilst the share of the bottom decile decreased from 4.2 in 1979 to 2.9 in 1990 and 2.7 per cent in 2002.[5] For individual earnings, amongst men the ratio of the 10th percentile to the 90th percentile rose from 2.38 in 1979 to 3.08 in 1989 and 3.51 in 2002, and the corresponding figures for women were 2.29, 2.86 and 3.15. The share of wages in national income was over 68 per cent in 1980, but fell to under 65 per cent in 1990 and then to 61 per cent in 1996, though it has been rising year by year since then. Perhaps the only indicator of inequality which did not increase was the ratio of women's earnings to men's earnings, with women's average hourly pay as a percentage of men's average pay rising from around 70 per cent to 82 per cent in 2002.

The neoliberal agenda of the Thatcher years and after was a major contributor to these increases in inequality, in a variety of ways. The promotion of the market and of the use of incentives and rewards gave legitimacy to rising inequality. Whatever outcomes were generated by the market were viewed as right and proper, and those with enhanced market power gained at the expense of those without. The rhetoric of incentives pushed up the earnings of the highly paid, and reduced the income tax to be paid (see Chapter 15). The Thatcher government particularly made substantial changes in the social security system, which, for example, replaced the link between pensions and earnings with a link between pensions and prices, with the inevitable result that the basic state pension declined relative to earnings. The shifts in the tax system from direct to indirect taxation and, especially, the reduction particularly of high marginal income tax rates also made a significant contribution. The attacks on trade union power and the diminution of the role of collective bargaining were further contributory factors.

The rise in inequality was particularly pronounced during the Thatcher years and has largely levelled off, but it has left the United Kingdom as one of the most unequal countries in the OECD area, having previously been amongst the less unequal. The incoming Labour government has taken some steps to address inequality, notably the setting of a national minimum wage, some restoration of the link of pensions with earnings and the setting of targets for the reduction of child poverty. One of the targets set was for a reduction of the number of children in poverty by one quarter over the period 1998–99 and 2004–05: the assessment of the Institute of Fiscal Studies in March 2004 was that the government was on course to meet that target (Brewer 2004). But whether the incoming Labour government has managed to reduce inequality as much as it had been expected is a moot point.

CONCLUSIONS

This chapter has sketched the shifts in economic policy since the replacement of 'old' Labour by the Thatcher government initially, followed by the Major government and more recently by the New Labour government led by Tony Blair. Since May 1979, all governments have pursued neoliberal policies. The chapter has also covered issues such as privatisation, macroeconomic policy, industrial policy and inequality. It was shown that there is a clear departure from the economic policies pursued by the 'old' Labour government(s), which have been replaced ever since May 1979.

NOTES

1. Figures taken from UNCTAD (2003). Inward investment was US$130 billion in 2000, US$62 billion in 2001 and US$24.9 billion in 2002: there was a worldwide decline in FDI in these years, but more pronounced in the United Kingdom. The corresponding figures for outward investment were US$249.8 billion, US$68.0 billion and US$17.5 billion in 2000, 2001 and 2002 respectively.
2. See DTI (2003b), especially the introduction, 'Promoting and Safeguarding UK Trade and Investment'.
3. See <www.uktradeinvest.gov.uk> (accessed in March 2004).
4. For details, see Goodman et al. (1997), Gottschalk and Smeeding (1997) and Sawyer (2004).
5. Based on income before housing costs, and derived from information on the Institute of Fiscal Studies web site.

REFERENCES

Arestis, P. and Sawyer, M.C. (1998) 'New Labour, New Monetarism', *Soundings: A Journal of Politics and Culture* 9, pp.24–41.

Brewer, M. (2004) 'Will the Government Hit its Child Poverty Target in 2004–05?', *The Institute for Fiscal Studies*, Briefing Note No. 47.

Department of Employment (1985) *Employment: The Challenge for the Nation*, Cmnd. 9474. London: HMSO.

DTI (Department of Trade and Industry) (2003a) *The Strategy*. London: HMSO.

DTI (Department of Trade and Industry) (2003b) *International Trade and Investment*. London: HMSO.

Goodman, A. Johnson, P. and Webb, S. (1997) *Inequality in the UK*. Oxford: Oxford University Press.

Gottschalk, P. and Smeeding, T. (1997) 'Cross-National Comparisons of Earnings and Income Inequality', *Journal of Economic Literature* 35 (2), pp.633–87.

Ministry of Reconstruction (1944) *Employment Policy after the War.* London: HMSO.

Sawyer, M.C. (2003) 'The Private Finance Initiative : A Critical Assessment', in D. Coffey and C. Thornley (eds) *Industrial and Labour Market Policy and Performance*. London: Routledge.

Sawyer, M.C. (2004) 'Income Distribution and Redistribution', in M. Sawyer (ed.) *The UK Economy*. Oxford: Oxford University Press.

UNCTAD (2003), *World Investment Report*, Annex. Geneva: UNCTAD.

24

European Integration as a Vehicle of Neoliberal Hegemony

John Milios

Twenty-five years of neoliberal policies in Europe have influenced every aspect of social life. Starting from the late 1970s in most European countries, the privatisation of the welfare state, the downsizing of government, the emergence of new forms of social exclusion, the increasing unemployment and the polarisation of wages,[1] and the 'free-market' delivery systems for health, education, and welfare are changes which affect not only the economy but also the politics of European societies.

According to the conventional wisdom of official thinking, what is involved is a transition period until there is an upturn in investments corresponding to a rise in business profits, whereupon a new virtuous circle of development will get underway, with rising incomes. Yet, despite a clear recovery in profit levels and decreasing public deficits and inflation rates, neither investments nor economic growth rates are near the levels required for recovery in employment and living standards anywhere in Europe. On the contrary, the economic situation of broad social strata is deteriorating. In the name of private interest and the flawless workings of the market, social considerations take second place (Pelagidis et al. 2001).

As no alternative has been created to this way of managing public affairs in Europe, neoliberal economic strategies of 'deflation' are continuously 'rejuvenated', despite falling prices and fiscal stabilisation. Within this framework, misfits and the marginalized are perceived as a 'burden.' Even the so-called progressive socialist parties regard the cost of solidarity as unacceptably high.

This chapter focuses on the way that the ruling social, economic and political forces in Europe have channelled the process of European integration into an apparatus ensuring and reproducing the hegemony of neoliberal policies and ideas in European countries. A concluding section explores what ensures the sustained hegemony of neoliberalism, and the prerequisites for a change.

DIFFERENT GOVERNMENTS, SAME POLICY

In the 1980s or early 1990s, conservative parties obtained the support of the middle classes in many European countries and won elections on the strength of a clear 'liberal' political slogan: 'Let market forces act freely; fight all forms of bureaucratic, corporatist or monopolistic distortions of the market mechanism and the high growth rates of the past will be achieved again'. This conception was then concretised in a restrictive economic programme aimed at curtailing wages and social spending, deregulating markets – including the labour market – and privatising public enterprises.

However, as the promised economic prosperity failed to materialise, liberal ideologies met with diminishing public acceptance. Most conservative parties, after a period in office – lengthy in the case of Britain and Italy, shorter in, for example, France or Greece – lost elections in the middle or late 1990s to centre-left parties.

Despite this shift in government power, though, economic and social policies did not change much in Europe. Exactly the same conservative policy was followed, sometimes slightly leavened by measures of social protection for certain marginalised sectors of the population. What actually took place was a retreat of the political and ideological visions of the (ruling) left and of social-democratic intellectuals, who now confine themselves to the continuous reiteration of the simple thesis that *full* deregulation can never exist and that therefore centre-left governments are more effective than conservative ones.[2]

Centre-left governments persist in not prioritising the reduction of unemployment or the promotion of growth by public spending. Instead, they prioritise price stabilisation, the reduction of public deficits, the promotion of 'labour-market flexibility' and the privatisation of public enterprises. So they appear as 'moderate' exponents of conservative policy, 'neoliberalism with a human face' as it were (see Chapters 2 and 21). These policies boosted the profit share in most European countries during the last two decades. Official statistics give the following data for the increase in the profit share between 1981 and 2003 (*European Economy*, Statistical Annex, Spring 2003, pp. 94–5): Italy: from 23.3 per cent to 32.3 per cent; Germany: from 26.9 per cent to 33.6 per cent; France: from 20.6 per cent to 30.7 per cent; Spain: from 25.4 per cent, to 34.5 per cent, and the United Kingdom: from 25.6 per cent to 26.5 per cent.

This persistence of neoliberal policies and ideas has been achieved through policies officially aiming at the promotion of economic, monetary and political unity among EU member states. These states seem actually to have declared that the process of European integration has as a prerequisite the implementation and maintenance of neoliberal strategies. In this way, they declare that, in order to promote European unification, these strategies must remain untouched by any critique and cannot be subjected to any substantial revision or change. By identifying it with European unification, the leading political and economic forces in Europe present neoliberalism as a taboo that cannot be violated.

There were three major agreements among EU states aiming at legitimising neoliberalism as the means of European unification par excellence: the 1992 Maastricht Treaty on European Union, the 1996–97 Stability and Growth Pact (SGP) and, most recently (2003–04), the [draft] European Constitution elaborated by the European Convention.

THE 'MAASTRICHT CRITERIA' AND THE 'STABILITY PACT'

In February 1992, the Treaty on European Union, signed in Maastricht, formulated certain economic 'convergence criteria', which were supposedly the precondition that would enable them to proceed to the third and final stage of a

Monetary Union (MU) and to launch the single currency: low inflation and interest rates, exchange rate stability, and, above all, public deficits and government debt no higher than 3 per cent and 60 per cent of gross domestic product respectively (Council 1993).

The restrictive 'deflationist' policy adopted by EU countries before the introduction of the common currency (the 'Maastricht criteria') was perpetuated after the circulation of the euro on the basis of the so-called SGP, signed in Dublin in December 1996. This 'pact' reasserts that budgetary restrictions should remain the keystone of economic policy, as government budget deficits shall not exceed a fixed upper limit of 3 per cent of GDP. Countries failing to restrict public deficits to the 3 per cent of GDP limit would have to face punitive measures, such as fines, up to 1.5 per cent of GDP. The SGP constitutes, therefore, an important instrument for implementing neoliberal policies of reducing the role of the state in the economy and of fiscal restructuring in favour of capitalist enterprises and higher income groups, in the post-euro era (European Economists 2003).

These neoliberal policies are being constantly reassessed in the Commission's Broad Economic Policy Guidelines (BEPG), where, for example, we read that 'wage developments should remain moderate' (European Commission 2003, p. 5), and that 'monetary policy, budgetary policy and wage growth' should always be 'compatible with price stability and the need to enhance confidence among business and consumers in the short run' (p. 16). Price stability is always supplemented by tax reduction, further liberalisation of financial markets, deregulation of labour markets and 'reform' of the pension system so as to shift it from public pay-as-you-go schemes to privately funded capital-market schemes (see Chapter 16).

However, these neoliberal policies proved to be very ineffective in the conjuncture of economic stagnation, which has hit the world capitalist economy since the turn of the century. Most European economies, following the restrictive course of the Commission's guidelines, were suddenly in danger of getting caught in a deflationary spiral. The declarations made at the Lisbon summit in March 2000 – the EU economy should become 'the most competitive economy of the world' within a decade, with an average growth rate of 3 per cent during the current decade – have been dramatically refuted: the GDP growth rate in the Eurozone declined from the average annual level of 2.1 per cent in the decade 1991–2000 to 0.4 per cent in 2003 (estimates of the European Commission), while growth rate of investment (Gross Domestic Capital Formation) declined from 2.0 per cent in 1991–2000 to −2.6 per cent in 2002 (*European Economy*, Statistical Annex, Autumn 2003, p. 87).

Despite cuts in the systems of unemployment benefits and social welfare, the 3 per cent of GDP limit for public deficits has proved a difficult target to meet in a conjuncture of weak growth and stagnation, coupled with tax reductions for corporate profits, capital gains and higher incomes. In November 2002, EU finance ministers voted to discipline Portugal for missing deficit targets. However, at the same time the German finance minister warned the Commission that his country was also unlikely to comply with the SGP deficit target for 2002. In fact, the German public deficit surged from 1.4 per cent of GDP in the year 2000 to

2.8 per cent in 2001, 3.6 per cent in 2002 and 4.2 per cent in 2003, while it is expected to remain above the 3 per cent of GDP limit until the year 2006. The situation developed in a similar pattern also in France, the second largest economy in the EU, as the country's public deficit ran over the 3 per cent limit and reached 4.2 per cent of GDP in 2003. As the two major EU economies involuntarily violated the SGP rules, the Commission declared, in March 2003, that the Iraq war provided an exception to EU deficit rules. However, after the protests by some of the smaller EU countries, claiming that 'sound' (read neoliberal) policies will lose their public credibility if not followed by all countries, the Commission began a sanctions process against the two countries, which could have led to fines of as much as 0.5 per cent of each country's GDP. However, this process was eventually abandoned by EU finance ministers, meeting in November 2003 in Brussels, who rejected the Commission's recommendations that France and Germany should immediately undertake deeper cuts in spending to comply with the SGP rules, or otherwise face sanctions. The European Central Bank immediately criticised this decision of the Council of Finance Ministers, claiming that it 'risks undermining the credibility of the institutional framework and the confidence in sound public finances' of the EU countries (Rhoads and Mitchener 2003).

The SGP has not been renounced; it was simply broken as a consequence of stagnation, aggravated by restrictive neoliberal policies. By abstaining from punitive measures against France and Germany, European countries reasserted their national authority over their own budgets. However, they still insist on following the neoliberal course, despite the fact that it was proved to aggravate stagnation and thus to be a major obstacle to more employment and growth.

EU ENLARGEMENT AND THE 'DRAFT CONSTITUTION'

In May 2004, ten new member states entered the EU; these include Cyprus, Malta and eight central and eastern European countries (Czech Republic, Estonia, Hungary, Latvia, Lithuania, Poland, Slovakia and Slovenia). To be accepted into the EU, these countries have followed the restrictive policies connected with the Maastricht criteria and the SGP, despite the fact that some of them face major macroeconomic imbalances and a high unemployment rate (e.g. 19 per cent in the Slovak Republic and 20 per cent in Poland). The accession of two more countries (Bulgaria and Romania) is planned for 2007 or 2008.

To solidify the enlarged Union of 25 (and soon 27) member states, the ruling political forces in the EU have formed a 'Convention' which elaborated the draft of a 'Constitution for Europe', recently approved by the EU member states (European Convention 2003).[3] The Constitution aims at 'finalising' the institutional framework of the EU for the decades to come, so that the 'deepening' of the process of European (economic, political and social) unification may be facilitated. However, it is not difficult to understand that the 'Constitution' actually aims at making neoliberalism 'irreversible' in the enlarged EU. The 'Constitution' ascribes the character of 'constitutional order' to two major pillars of neoliberalism. First, deregulated markets. Article I-3 says that 'The Union's objectives: a single market where competition is free and undistorted'. Second, the priority of state security and 'military capacity' over human and social rights. Article I-40 says:

> The common security and defence policy ... shall provide the Union with an operational capacity drawing on assets civil and military. The Union may use them on missions outside the Union for peace-keeping, conflict prevention and strengthening international security in accordance with the principles of the United Nations Charter.[4]

More specifically with regard to economic and social policies, after some 'progressive' formulations concerning the economic and social 'objectives' of the EU in part I of the Constitution, which seemingly reproduce the general attitude of the 1948 UN Universal Declaration of Human Rights,[5] disinflation, the main motto behind all neoliberal policies, is acclaimed as a major 'constitutional' end: 'The primary objective of the European System of Central Banks shall be to maintain price stability' (Article I-29).

If one takes into account that in EU-15 the inflation rate (CPI) fell from 10.6 per cent on average in the 1970s to 6.5 per cent in the 1980s and to 2.1 per cent in 2000, to remain practically constant ever since, one can only reach the following conclusion: by choosing to further suppress inflation, European governments declare that they insist on the same neoliberal restrictive policies that have troubled the majority of the working people up to date, and that other goals, such as promoting growth, fighting unemployment, improving the welfare state, etc. are set aside for the whole historical period of 'consolidation' of the enlarged Union.

THE POSSIBILITY OF CHALLENGING NEOLIBERAL HEGEMONY

Neoliberalism is neither a 'correct' policy for economic reform and development, nor an 'erroneous' policy of certain governments, which could be amended through reasonable argumentation and discussion. It is a class policy, aiming at reshuffling the relation of forces between capital and labour on all social levels to the benefit of capital; it is a class offensive of capital against labour.

So far the capitalist offensive against labour has been resoundingly successful. It has succeeded in reducing labour's share in the net product: in the EU-15, it fell from an average of 73.9 per cent in the period 1971–80 to an estimated average of 68.3 per cent for the period 2001–05 (*European Economy*, Statistical Annex, Spring 2003, p. 94). In other words it has changed the relation of forces in favour of capital. Indeed, as a result a specific type of social consensus has been created, based on the acceptance by the labouring class of capitalist ideas and objectives. Isn't it consensus when trade unions accept that a key issue in social dialogue is how to increase profitability, or how to secure the national or European economy's competitive position in the global economy? It is consensus: consensus between the 'winners' and the 'defeated'.

By the same token, the post-Second World War welfare state can be seen as the product of class polarisation in the context of a balance of forces which no longer exists. In this context, policies of redistribution favouring wages, stimulation of demand among the popular strata and strengthening of social citizenship did not represent authentic democratic and social progress in general, but merely an alternative means for securing the rule of capital in a period which was relatively unfavourable for itself. It is clear then, that such policies, i.e. an anti-neoliberal agenda, cannot be implemented unless a radical shift in the present balance of forces between capital and labour takes place.

However, in order to establish a new distribution of the social balance of forces, the working classes must once again elaborate their own autonomous class objectives, independently of the capitalist imperative of labour discipline and profit maximisation. For this to be possible, labour must recreate its anti-capitalist strategy of social transformation. This is the great challenge that the 'movements against capitalist globalisation', rapidly growing in practically every part of the globe during the last years, are actually facing (Saad-Filho 2003).

Furthermore, the previous section has shown that the ruling social and political forces in Europe have managed to legitimise neoliberal policies as the means par excellence for 'economic convergence' and 'European unification'. Neoliberal economic and social policies in Europe have been shaped in the form of 'common European policies', 'convergence criteria' and a common European 'constitutional' framework.

The process of European unification is thus being transformed into an ideological and political weapon of the European capitalist classes, in their conflict with the labouring classes: it is used as a vehicle for neoliberalism, as it has been identified with the formulation and implementation of economic and social policies of austerity, privatisation, market deregulation and suppression of rights. This conclusion does not lead, though, to 'anti-European' theses but it rather emphasises once more the importance of the formulation of an alternative strategy all over Europe that would promote the interests of the European labouring classes. Demands for a complete rewriting of the EU's anti-democratic and deflationary institutional structure and political agenda are motivated not by anti-Europeanism but by anti-neoliberalism and anti-capitalism: social reform, democratisation and the shaping of a strategy of radical change aimed at overthrowing capitalism and displacing it with an egalitarian and humane social order – i.e. communism.

NOTES

1. The increasing polarisation in wages, represented by the increasing ratio between the upper and the bottom ten per cent of the distribution of wages, has been apparent in all European countries since the mid 1970s. The same phenomenon appears also in the United States and in Japan. Since this ratio was decreasing during the first three decades after the Second World War, Harrisson and Bluestone (1988) defined it as 'the Great U-Turn'. For more recent data on wage inequality and polarisation, see Borjas (2000, ch. 8).

2. '[M]arkets will never replace governments in making strategic choices, organizing solidarity over a given territory and still more in institutionalizing markets ... The state remains the most powerful institution to *channel and tame the power of markets*' (Boyer 1996, pp. 110, 108, emphasis added).

3. The draft Constitution had been adopted by all member states, with the exception of the clauses registering the weighting of votes in the European Council and the Council of Ministers. In

December 2003, the Council of European leaders failed to conclude on a final version of the Constitution, as Spain and newcomer Poland insisted on keeping the voting system crafted in 2000, which gave each of these countries almost as many votes as Germany, which has a much larger population than either. Germany and France insisted on reforming this voting system. A compromise was finally reached in June 2004.

4. In the same article it is further stated (as a constitutional clause!) that 'a European Armaments, Research and Military Capabilities Agency shall be established to identify operational requirements, to promote measures to satisfy those requirements, to contribute to identifying and, where appropriate, implementing any measure needed to strengthen the industrial and technological base of the defence sector, to participate in defining a European capabilities and armaments policy, and to assist the Council of Ministers in evaluating the improvement of military capabilities'.

5. e.g. Article I-3: 'The Union shall work for a Europe of sustainable development based on balanced economic growth, a social market economy, highly competitive and aiming at full employment and social progress, and with a high level of protection and improvement of the quality of the environment.' However, even at that general level, the European draft Constitution falls clearly behind the 1948 *Declaration* in relation to most social and human rights. With regard, for example, to the 'right to engage in work', we read in the draft Constitution: 'Everyone has the right to engage in work and to pursue a freely chosen or accepted occupation' (Article II-15) and '*Every worker has the right to protection against unjustified dismissal*, in accordance with Union law and national laws and practices' (Article II-30, emphasis added). For comparison, we quote the respective article of the 1948 *Universal Declaration of Human Rights: 'Everyone has the right* to work, to free choice of employment, to just and favourable conditions of work and *to protection against unemployment*' (Article 23, emphasis added).

REFERENCES

Borjas, G. (2000) *Labor Economics*. New York: McGraw-Hill/Irwin.

Boyer, R. (1996) 'State and Market: A New Engagement for the Twenty-First Century?', in R. Boyer and D. Drache (eds) *States against Markets: The Limits of Globalization*. London: Routledge.

Council (Council of the European Communities / Commission of the European Communities) (1993) *Treaty on European Union*. Brussels and Luxembourg: ECSC-EEC-EAEC, 1992.

European Commission (2003) *Commission Recommendation on the Broad Guidelines of the Economic Policies of the Member States and the Community (for the 2003–2005 period)*. Brussels, 8 April.

European Convention (2003) *Draft Treaty Establishing a Constitution for Europe*. Brussels, 20 June.

European Economists (European Economists for an Alternative Economic Policy in Europe – Euromemorandum Group) (2003) *Full Employment, Welfare and a Strong Public Sector – Democratic Challenges in a Wider Union*, <www.memo-europe.uni-bremen.de>.

Harrisson, B. and Bluestone, B. (1988) *The Great U-Turn: Corporate Restructuring and the Polarizing of America*. New York: Basic Books.

Saad-Filho, A. (ed.) (2003) *Anti-Capitalism: A Marxist Introduction*. London: Pluto Press.

Pelagidis T., Katseli, L. and Milios, J. (eds) (2001) *Welfare State and Democracy in Crisis: Reforming the European Model*. Aldershot: Ashgate.

Rhoads, C. and Mitchener B. (2003) 'Germany and France Dodge Effort to Rein In Spending; ECB Warns of Consequences', *Wall Street Journal*, 25 November.

25

Neoliberalism: The Eastern European Frontier

Jan Toporowski

Neoliberalism emerged as government policy in eastern Europe as a result of the financial crisis of the Communist state, which created a dependence on financial inflows from Western financial institutions. After a period of economic and financial crisis, economies stabilised and even resumed a growth path, but with high unemployment and rising social and economic inequalities. The post-Communist countries then divided into those that are being drawn into a specific western European kind of neoliberalism, as candidate members of the European Union, and those that gravitate between western Europe and the business-oligarchy model of post-Putin Russia.

In his classic book *The Great Transformation*, Karl Polanyi described economic liberalism as the rolling back of the influence of social and political institutions in order to allow spontaneous market forces to operate freely. As long as the markets were well co-ordinated, then the system appeared to operate effectively, as the classical economic liberals, Adam Smith and John Stuart Mill, believed it would. But Polanyi pointed out that the appearance of 'spontaneous order', which so attracted right-wing ideologues such as Friedrich von Hayek or Karl Popper, depended on a very fragile international financial system. When that broke down, after the First World War, the institutions to hold societies together were not there to prevent a descent into barbarism and war (see Chapters 3, 5 and 6).

In eastern Europe, under Communism, the integrating factor that prevented that descent was the state. This does not mean that Communist rule did not have barbaric episodes. However, by the 1970s the system was sufficiently stable to ensure that political outrages such as the Ukrainian famine, the political purges of the 1930s and the 1950s, the shooting of workers in Berlin in 1953, in Hungary in 1956 and in Poland in 1956 and 1970, anti-Semitic campaigns in 1968 and the late 1970s, the invasion of Czechoslovakia in 1968, were episodic occurrences. In the 1970s and 1980s, what came to be known as 'Brezhnevism' ensured a degree of economic integration among the countries in the Soviet sphere of influence, and redistributed income around those countries and their regions, to secure minimal standards of living for their populations. The economic integration consisted of the Soviet state and allied states co-ordinating larger common investment projects, and trade between those countries through the Council for Mutual Economic Assistance (CMEA or Comecon). The minimal standards of living tended to be higher in border regions (for example, in East Germany, the Baltic States and Armenia) where nationalist traditions or envy of more advanced neighbours (in West Germany, Scandinavia, or Turkey) needed to be kept in rein.

THE FALL OF COMMUNISM

The system was brought down by a combination of circumstances. US militarists have tended to emphasise the part played by the arms race initiated by the US president during the 1980s, Ronald Reagan. This supposedly forced the Soviet Union to devote such resources to military hardware and infrastructure, especially in Afghanistan, where the Soviet army was defending a friendly regime against Islamic fundamentalists and Afghan nationalists, that it brought down Communism. However, another factor was the emergence in the Communist countries of an educated middle class who compared their standards of consumption unfavourably with the middle classes of western Europe and North America. The new middle class was therefore less willing to settle for 'goulash socialism': the minimal standards of personal consumption that the political system guaranteed to everyone. When this dissatisfaction with relatively low living standards spread to the workers, in whose name Communist Parties ruled, the fate of the Communist regimes was sealed.

Internationally, the most serious economic difficulty was created by a dramatic rise in the indebtedness to Western capitalist banks of those countries which tried to buy technological progress during the 1970s and 1980s. In an effort to improve the standard of their industrial products, countries such as Poland and Hungary borrowed heavily to buy advanced equipment and technology. Like many countries in the developing world, the prospectus on which the debt was drawn largely depended on increasing exports to the capitalist West. As the West plunged into recession after the oil price shock of 1974, and interest rates rose dramatically at the end of the 1970s, Hungary and Poland were forced to join the queue of developing countries seeking rescheduling of their debt at the end of 1982. In fact they got better terms in their rescheduling because the Soviet Union was obliged to assist, at least in some degree.

The system came to an end when the last Soviet president, Mikhail Gorbachev, introduced a restructuring and transparency ('perestroika' and 'glasnost') that not only revealed corruption. His Soviet government also obliged allied governments to take responsibility for their own foreign debts. The alternative source of assistance was the International Monetary Fund. Initially this tried to maintain a fiction that its assistance was purely technical and unrelated to the political make-up of the borrowing government. But with the Communist system at the end of the 1980s running out of ideas to renew its political and economic momentum, and running out of foreign currency to service external debts, it became apparent who could get the best deal out of the IMF. Thus neoliberalism in eastern Europe was born.

The first stage of post-Communism in eastern Europe consisted of the removal of barriers to foreign trade, and the imposition of fiscal austerity in order to secure the IMF support needed to alleviate the post-Communist governments' desperate shortage of Western currency. This forced governments to withdraw the financial safety net that effectively guaranteed state industries in the region. Consumer demand, long held back by the absence of consumer goods, or their poor quality, was redirected to consumer goods imported from the West. Consumption goods industries were faced with a collapse in their markets, while investment goods industries lost the markets that were guaranteed by state investment and CMEA co-ordination of investment. However, the guaranteed incomes and welfare payments that were such a notable feature of Communism remained in place, because their removal would have been too unpopular for the new democratically elected governments to contemplate. The result was a catastrophic fall in industrial production and hyperinflation. Statistics from this period are very unreliable, because of the rapid structural changes that occurred. Some industries collapsed altogether: one has only to think of the East German Trabant cars, which went out of production because no one wanted to buy them after better Western models became available.

The other major change was a rapid widening of income differentials. Fortunes were made virtually overnight through supplying foreign consumer goods into the market, or taking over ownership of state economic assets through 'insider' agreements and reselling them, or securing outside finance for their management. This last, known as 'wildcat privatisation', resulted in what later came to be known as the 'mafia capitalism' that prevails in the former Soviet Union. At the other extreme, many more individuals and families were plunged into poverty as state and local enterprises ran out of money to pay wages. With the fall in industrial production and the removal of the elaborate system of industrial cross-subsidies that kept the Communist industrial system operating, unemployment rose. Frequently this reached as much as half of the labour force in provincial towns and villages situated away from the new trade and where the state no longer supported industry.

EASTERN EUROPEAN NEOLIBERALISM

It was at the start of the 1990s, that neoliberalism became a policy alternative in eastern Europe. Taking their inspiration from the economists at the University of Chicago, a number of politicians and economists argued that providing rights of ownership, enforcing contracts, and removing the state from economic activity would 'normalise' the economy and generate an economic recovery. Curiously, they always were only a minority of economists and politicians, but their allegiance to Chicago neoliberalism and the US economic model implied the support of the United States government and the Washington institutions, the IMF and the World Bank. The very simplicity of their recipe for emulating the economic success of the United States – ownership rights, privatisation, low taxes, but government budgets balanced in a very un-American way for low inflation – gave them the support of much of the new business elite. However, behind this was a kind of à la carte capitalism, suggesting that the rest of the world offered a free political choice between the whole range of political and economic institutions in existence and implying that a new start could be made and the legacy of history thrown off. This kind of 'voluntarism', or action based on a belief that all that was needed to create a new system was a political decision, has deep roots in eastern Europe. Since the eighteenth century, a revolutionary utopian tradition had emerged in reaction to the backward authoritarianism of eastern Europe. This utopian tradition urged the establishment of Western institutions in order to bring eastern Europe into the modern (i.e. the Western capitalist) world.

The abrupt leap towards capitalism that characterised the policies of, for example, the Polish finance minister in the early 1990s, Leszek Balcerowicz, and the Hungarian prime minister at that time, Miklós Németh, resulted, initially at least, in a sharp contraction of economic activity and even higher inflation. The neoliberals had expected a 'spontaneous order' of dynamic and entrepreneurial capitalism to emerge. At the crucial interface between the national economies and their foreign trading partners, a degree of normalisation set in once foreign exchange crises had been overcome with local currency depreciations, which impoverished local residents until excess demand for foreign imports was eliminated, and with foreign capital imports. However, in the rest of the economy, outside the main business centres, economic activity regressed to subsistence production and barter. This has been especially apparent in the former Soviet Union.

Crucial to the establishment of the neoliberal order was a stable financial system. Stock markets were quickly introduced in the main capitals of the region, only to succumb to rapid speculative bubbles and busts, along with the pyramid-banking schemes that emerged in Romania and Albania. More formal banking networks were developed. But the rapid expansion of credit payments among households and firms masked bank balance sheets weighed down with debts to state enterprises that could not be serviced or recovered. Smaller banks failed. Larger ones had to be renationalised, for example in the Czech Republic, to prevent wider financial crises.

Privatisation was only a limited success. Smaller retail service outlets, whose capital was of relatively low value, were either already private or were also quickly sold. The more profitable, or potentially profitable, state companies in manufacturing, took rather more time to sell. When finally transferred to the private sector, it was usually at a minimal price, to Western companies that could afford to re-equip plants that had suffered from years of underinvestment. Heavier extractive undertakings, in the oil and coal industries of Russia and the central Asian republics for example, were transferred, in effect if not quite legally, to managers often with opaque connections with Western transnational companies. This left governments in the region owning the heavy engineering plants that were the pride of Communist industrialisation. Many of these had not had new equipment put into them since the 1970s. Government budgets, already weighed down by the high social costs of transition to capitalism, had no money to spare for further investment in the remaining state industries. The result was the continuing decline of these industries. Since their plants had initially been located in areas of high surplus labour, this decline has exacerbated unemployment in regions already badly affected by the transition to capitalism. In spite of an overall increase in the population, employment in eastern Europe remains below the peak reached in 1980 (see Chapter 20).

Neoliberalism failed in eastern Europe because the imposition of what the Hungarian economist János Kornai called a 'hard budget' constraint on business and industry overlooked the safety valve which gives Western capitalist businesses their flexibility and dynamism, namely those businesses' accumulated liquid reserves. These are accumulated from money held back by companies for depreciation, and from their retained profits. Such reserves allow Western companies to get by if they experience losses in some activities, and to borrow and spend more freely, because cash or near cash reserves are available to repay borrowing or to pay for new activities. The new businesses of eastern Europe came into a harsh capitalist world without financial reserves (they had no need for them under the Communist system of industrial cross-subsidy). This affected their creditworthiness and increased their dependence upon potentially corrupt connections with governments, multilateral lenders and Western companies. Companies that are permanently short of liquidity do not invest much in plant and equipment, and usually try to get by with speculative activities: buying assets cheaply and selling them more expensively. Yet investment, or real capital accumulation, is the key to sustainable capitalist growth.

AFTER NEOLIBERALISM

In eastern Europe, the first wave of neoliberalism came to an end in the mid 1990s, and was effectively buried following the Asian crisis of 1996 and the Russian financial crisis of 1998. These revealed the weakness of any capitalism that was not based on strong financial institutions. In any case, by then governments in the region had entered into negotiations with the European Commission and western European governments, with a view to bringing a number of eastern European countries into the European Union. Local politics and regional sentiment largely dictated that the Baltic states (Latvia, Estonia and Lithuania), Poland, Hungary, Slovakia, Slovenia and the Czech Republic would join in 2004, with Bulgaria and Romania coming in afterwards. The politics and economics of western Europe are anything but neoliberal, even in those countries, such as Spain and Britain, whose governments most loudly proclaim the neoliberal creed. Western Europe has a strong statist tradition, and populations whose deep attachment to welfare-state provision is difficult to overlook in democratic states. Some of the new institutions of the European Union have been infected by neoliberal ideas, for example the ban on state subsidies to companies, and the 1992 Stability and Growth Pact limiting fiscal deficits among members of the European Monetary Union and new members of the European Union. Nevertheless, western Europe has provided some elements of an alternative model of a modern economy to the neoliberalism peddled from Chicago and Washington. Key elements of this alternative model are the institutions of social solidarity underpinned by a state that alleviates the deep inequalities generated by capitalism through redistributive taxation and transfer payments, and the provision of better quality public services than the state provides in the United States. Most importantly for the cash-strapped governments of eastern Europe, whose tax base has been whittled away by falling incomes from employment, irregular business practices and international 'tax competition' to attract capital imports, entry into the European Union offers regional aid from Brussels to poorer countries. This has made the establishment of commercial and legal institutions on the western European model (under the guise of the so-called 'acquis communautaire' which new member countries must have before entry) the priority for eastern European governments, rather than the minimal state in the Chicago model (see Chapter 24).

However, entry into the European Union brings with it the obligation eventually to join the European Monetary Union, bringing down government borrowing and fiscal deficits. This has made Eastern Europe a testing ground for the neoliberal ideas underlying the Monetary Union: it is apparent that the founding members of the Monetary Union, in particular France, Germany and Italy, have been able to evade the restrictions on their governments' fiscal policy imposed by the Monetary Union. The new eastern European members will not be allowed such laxity.

The opening up of new economic and political possibilities in the European Union has therefore split the former Communist bloc in eastern Europe into two segments. Those countries in central Europe and the Balkans with the prospect of becoming members of the EU see their economic and political future in western-European-style capitalism moderated by strong welfare-state provisions, and facilitated by regional aid from Brussels. Those countries left without such an immediate prospect have regressed into weak democracies (for example Russia, or the Ukraine) or the corrupt dictatorships notable in the new central Asian republics, or Byelorussia. Their economies have regressed too, with an apparent breakdown of commodity production in particular localities. The export of raw materials and import of luxury goods for the nouveaux riches maintains foreign-trade activity in the capitals and around the areas of extractive activity. But the rest of their domestic economy has fragmented into subsistence production and barter, with local informal money (using company or government IOUs) emerging, for example, after the 1998 financial crisis in Russia.

In this latter part of eastern Europe, neoliberalism increasingly appears inadequate beside the very apparent need in those countries to establish strong democratic states. Democratic institutions are necessary even under neoliberalism, if only to allow corruption to be exposed and to enforce property rights and contracts in accordance with law rather than through physical or financial coercion. Without such legal and political institutions, backed up by stable financial systems, the 'spontaneous order' which is the Mecca of neoliberalism cannot emerge.

In those parts of eastern Europe entering the European Union, where property rights have been secured after a fashion, and financial systems stabilised, neoliberalism has been reduced to addressing the present depressed phase of the business cycle in central Europe. Here its spokespersons have echoed governments in Britain and Spain, and officials of the European Central Bank, who blame the economic depression in central Europe on the 'inflexibility' of its labour markets, high taxes and the fiscal indiscipline of its governments. However, it is in the nature of capitalism that business investment, rather than fiscal policy or labour accommodation to employers' demands, is the key to economic growth. If business investment does not recover, then fiscal austerity and 'flexible' (i.e. low-wage) labour markets will only make the situation worse by depressing demand in the economy. If business investment rises, then no amount of labour inflexibility, taxation or government spending will prevent resulting economic boom.

REFERENCES

Andor, L. (2000) *Hungary on the Road to the European Union*. Westport, Conn.: Praeger.

Brus, W. and Laski, K. (1989) *From Marx to the Market: Socialism in Search of an Economic System*. Oxford: Clarendon Press.

Kregel, J., Matzner, E. and Perczyński, M. (eds) (1994) *After the Market Shock: Central and East-European Economies in Transition*. Brookfield, VT: Dartmouth.

Kowalik, T. (1991) 'The Polish Postscript, 1989' in M. Mendell and D. Salée (eds) *The Legacy of Karl Polanyi: Market, State and Society at the End of the Twentieth Century*. London: Macmillan.

Kowalik, T. (1994) 'Reply to M. Glasman' *New Left Review* 296, pp.133–44.

Milanovic, B. (1995) *Poverty, Inequality and Social Policy in Transition Economies*. World Bank Policy Research Working Paper 1530. Washington, DC: World Bank.

Polanyi, K. (2001) *The Great Transformation. The Political and Economic Origins of Our Times*. Boston: Beacon Press.

26

The Political Economy of Neoliberalism in Latin America

*Alfredo Saad-Filho**

This chapter examines the transition from import-substituting industrialisation (ISI) to neoliberalism in Latin America and briefly assesses the performance of neoliberal policies in this region, with special reference to the largest countries in the area: Argentina, Brazil and Mexico.

Four features of this region provide the background to this study. First, Latin America has always been characterised by social exclusion and profound inequalities of income, wealth and privilege. Second, strong oligarchies have generally ruled the region during the last five centuries, although this has often required the accommodation of shifts in their internal composition. Third, Latin American states were created in order to uphold the principles of social exclusion, oligarchic rule and ruthless exploitation of the majority, including the native population, slaves, poor immigrants and, more recently, peasants and formal and informal wage workers. These states tend to respond vigorously when inequality and privilege are challenged from below; in contrast, they generally react ambiguously and only weakly when the rules of the game are challenged by sections of the elite. Fourth, Latin American states have always intervened heavily in order to promote and regulate economic activity, including the enforcement of property rights, infrastructure provision, finance, export priorities and labour supply. They have also played an essential role in social engineering, usually as part of their promotion of selected economic activities. However, conflicts and divisions among the elite have often limited the efficacy of these policies and led to the adoption of inconsistent economic strategies.

This chapter reviews two examples of policy incoherence, ISI and neoliberalism. Their inconsistencies can be analysed at two levels: the 'internal' micro- and macro-economic limitations preventing these policies from achieving their stated aims, and the 'external' limits imposed by their exacerbation of the existing social conflicts.

ISI AND ITS LIMITS

ISI was the emblematic economic policy in Latin America between 1930 and 1980. ISI is an economic strategy based on the sequenced expansion of manufacturing industry, with the objective of replacing imports. The internalisation of manufacturing typically begins with the production of non-durable consumer goods (processed foods, beverages, tobacco products, cotton textiles, and so on).

It later deepens to include durable consumer goods (especially household appliances and automobile assembly), simple chemical and pharmaceutical products (e.g. oil refining and certain pharmaceutical products) and non-metallic minerals (especially cement). In the large countries, ISI can reach a further stage, including the production of steel, capital goods (such as industrial machinery and electric motors) and even technologically complex goods (electronic equipment, shipbuilding and aircraft design and assembly).

This economic strategy was associated with a specific type of property relations – a type of 'social division of labour'. Generally, the production of non-durable and capital goods was undertaken by domestic capital, while durable consumer goods were produced by transnational companies (TNCs). Infrastructure and basic goods (steel, electricity, telecommunications, water and sanitation, oil extraction and refining, air, road, rail and port links, and so on) were normally provided by state-owned enterprises (SOEs). Finally, state-owned banks played an important role in the provision of credit, especially for industrial development and economic diversification.

ISI was undeniably successful on several grounds. For example, between 1933 and 1980 the average annual economic growth rates in Brazil and Mexico were, respectively, 6.3 and 6.4 per cent. This outstanding performance is indistinguishable from that of the east Asian 'miracle' cases of South Korea and Taiwan.[1]

In spite of these important achievements, Latin American ISI was also severely limited, for five main reasons. First, its inability to overcome the *scarcity of foreign exchange*, leading to persistent balance-of-payments difficulties, which were one of the main causes of economic volatility during ISI. Second, the *fragility and inefficiency of the domestic financial system*, which failed to provide long-term finance for industrial development. Consequently, manufacturing investment was funded primarily by FDI, foreign loans, state-owned banks, state subsidies and firms' own resources. This combination of sources of finance would eventually prove to be unsustainable (see below). Third, *fiscal fragility*, because of the yawning gap between the budgetary demands of the activist industrial policies required by ISI, and the tax revenues available. This gap was due largely to social divisions and elite resistance against taxation (put crudely, the poor were unable to contribute enough, and the rich were unwilling to do so). The inability of Latin American states to fulfil their industrial policy roles while balancing their books led to persistent fiscal deficits, inflation, and the accumulation of sizeable debts by central and local governments. Fourth, *inflation*. Under ISI inflation was, on the one hand, a product of distributional conflicts, in which social groups fought for shares of the national income through higher prices, taxes and wage demands. On the other hand, it was a consequence of the limitations of the accumulation strategy, especially the persistent financial difficulties of governments and private firms. Specifically, insufficient taxation compelled governments to finance their expenditures through deficit spending, while financial fragility induced firms to fund their investment through price hikes and retained earnings. Finally, *lack of policy co-ordination*. Latin American states could rarely exercise the degree of co-ordination of economic activity required by their developmental objectives. They were constrained by conflicts within the elite and between the elite and the majority of the population, they were frustrated by their countries' dependence on foreign capital and technology, and states gradually became entangled in bitter conflicts between poorly co-ordinated economic sectors. Most states were eventually overwhelmed by the demographic, social, cultural and political changes wrought by ISI.

Latin American economies have shown increasing signs of stress since the mid 1960s, but the fragility of ISI was fully exposed only by the 1982 international debt crisis. The crisis showed that the combination of interventionist industrial policies, short-termist and speculative financial systems, weak tax systems and bubbling social discord was unsustainable. Economic symptoms of these tensions included financial crises, capital flight, economic stagnation and hyperinflation. In most countries they were accompanied by severe political instability.

THE NEOLIBERAL TRANSITION

The Latin American crisis of the early 1980s was part and parcel of the worldwide shift towards neoliberalism. The crisis was unleashed by the international economic slowdown that accompanied the disintegration of the Bretton Woods System; it was postponed by the accumulation of foreign debt facilitated by the new international financial architecture, and it erupted when the United States imposed punitively high interest rates on borrowers around the world, as part of its own neoliberal transition.

The effects of the debt crisis were devastating (see Chapter 11). In 1972, the total foreign debt of Latin America was US$31.3 billion, and it exceeded 33 per cent of GDP only in Nicaragua, Peru and Bolivia. In the late 1980s, the debt reached US$430 billion, and it exceeded 33 per cent of GDP in every single country in the region (Nicaragua's debt peaked at 1200 per cent of GDP in 1988). The growth of the debt stock and higher international interest rates made interest payments explode. They increased from 1 per cent of GDP in most countries in 1972 to, on average, 5.4 per cent of GDP in 1983 (up to 20 per cent in Costa Rica). The Latin American foreign debt reached US$750 billion at the turn of the millennium, and interest payments still exceed 2.5 per cent of GDP almost everywhere. Argentina, Bolivia, Chile, Costa Rica and Nicaragua have been penalised especially harshly.

Economic growth stalled, wages plummeted and inflation skyrocketed in the wake of the crisis (see below). It became easy to accept that ISI had collapsed, and equally easy to argue that it should be replaced by neoliberalism. This was the viewpoint promoted by the US government, the IMF, the World Bank and important sections of the Latin American elite. Their economic and ideological pressure, and the ferocity of the crisis, eventually created a new elite consensus in the region. The Latin American elites convinced themselves that the 'national development strategies' centred on ISI should be abandoned, and that economic dynamism could be restored – while preserving the existing patterns of social and economic exclusion – only by embracing neoliberalism and 'globalisation'.[2] This claim is doubly misleading. On the one hand, ISI was socially unfair, intrinsically limited and structurally fragile, but the crisis of the 1980s was not primarily due to its shortcomings; it was imposed from the *outside*. On the other hand, neoliberalism has been unable *either* to address most failings of ISI, *or* to match the growth performance of the previous period (see below).

It is a peculiarity of Latin American neoliberalism that the transition was frequently justified obliquely, by reference to the imperatives of inflation control. Neoliberal policies were, correspondingly, often disguised as 'technical' anti-inflationary measures. This conflation was facilitated by the specific form of the collapse of Latin American ISI, in which fiscal, financial and industrial crises often surfaced through runaway inflation. For example, annual inflation rates reached 14,000 per cent in Nicaragua (1988), 12,000 per cent in Bolivia (1985), 7,000 per cent in Peru (1990), 3,000 per cent in Argentina (1989) and 2,500 per cent in Brazil (1994). The urgent need for inflation stabilisation blurred the extent and the long-term consequences of the neoliberal transition. Having been unable to win the battle of ideas, and suffering from a persistent legitimacy deficit, the neoliberal elite consensus found it necessary to conceal its agenda in order to impose its policy preferences more easily.

Throughout Latin America, financial, trade and capital account liberalisation, the wholesale privatisation or closure of state-owned productive and financial firms, and profound fiscal and labour market reforms along neoliberal lines were imposed, allegedly because they were essential for short-term macroeconomic stability (i.e. inflation control) and long-term economic growth. At the same time, the institutions that had provided industrial policy co-ordination under ISI were systematically dismantled, and regulations constraining foreign investment were abandoned. The clearest examples of the instrumentalisation of inflation control in order to facilitate the transition to neoliberalism were the Argentine convertibility programme (1991) and the Brazilian *real* plan (1994). These anti-inflation strategies were premised upon the shift from ISI to a neoliberal system of accumulation (see below).[3]

THE IMPACT OF NEOLIBERALISM

Five policies played key roles in inflation control as well as in the neoliberal transition in Latin America. First, *import liberalisation*. ISI requires strong import restrictions in order to give local firms (including TNCs operating in the country) control of the domestic market. However, firms protected from foreign competition tend to have greater market power. They enjoy more freedom to raise prices, and more flexibility to accommodate wage demands, which increases the economy's vulnerability to inflation. Trade liberalisation helps to control inflation because foreign competition limits the prices that domestic firms can charge – otherwise their markets will be lost to imports. It also limits the workers' wage demands, since pay increases could make local firms uncompetitive. At a further remove, neoliberals claim that trade liberalisation forces local firms to compete against 'best practice' foreign producers, which should help to increase productivity across the economy. Finally, unsuccessful local producers will close down, and their capital and labour will presumably be deployed more productively elsewhere.

Second, *exchange-rate overvaluation* (i.e. an inordinate and sustained increase in the value of the local currency). Overvaluation artificially reduces the local currency price of imports, enhancing the impact of trade liberalisation on inflation and competitivity. The combination of import liberalisation and exchange-rate overvaluation is highly effective against inflation, and it can be very popular with consumers because imported consumer goods become, simultaneously, available *and* affordable. However, they can have a devastating impact on the balance of payments and on local industry and employment. For example, Argentine imports shot up from US$6.8 billion to US$19.3 billion between 1990 and 1992, Brazilian imports increased from US$28.0 billion to US$63.3 billion between 1992 and 1995, and Mexican imports rose from US$24.1 billion to US$51.9 billion between 1987 and 1990. In all cases, inflation tumbled *precisely* during this interval.

Cheap imports badly harmed local industry. In Argentina, Brazil and Mexico, the proportion of manufacturing value added to GDP reached, respectively, 31 per cent (1989), 35 per cent (1982) and 26 per cent (1987). By 2001, this ratio had declined to 17, 21 and 19 per cent. Industrial sector employment also fell, especially in Argentina, where it declined from 33 to 25 per cent of the labour force between 1991 and 1996. In Brazil, more than one million industrial jobs were lost between 1989 and 1997. During the neoliberal era, open unemployment across Latin America increased, *on average*, from 5.8 per cent to nearly 10 per cent of the workforce – but this excludes underemployment and informal employment, which may reach half of the labour force. Finally, average real wages fell by 16 per cent in Argentina, 8 per cent in Brazil and 4 per cent in Mexico between 1994 and 2001.

Third, *domestic financial liberalisation*. It was expected that the deregulation of the financial sector would help to increase savings and the availability of funds for investment. In fact, quite the opposite happened, and both savings and investment rates declined. In Argentina, savings fell from 22 to 17 per cent of GDP in ten years after 1989. In Brazil, they fell eight points, to only 20 per cent of GDP, between 1985 and 2001. In Mexico, they declined from 30 per cent of GDP in the early 1980s to only 18 per cent in 2001. Investment fell by one-third in Argentina, to less than 20 per cent of GDP, between the mid 1980s and the late 1990s. In Brazil, it declined from 25 to 20 per cent of GDP between 1989 and 2001, and in Mexico investment fell from 26 to 20 per cent of GDP between 1981 and 2001.

Fourth, *fiscal reforms* (tax increases and expenditure cuts), in order to address the government budget deficits that plagued Latin America and induced high inflation in the previous period. These reforms were largely successful, and budget balance was achieved in most countries. However, the cost of servicing the public debt increased sharply because of the much higher level of the domestic interest rates, which has been squeezing non-financial expenditures from the government budget, especially in Argentina, Bolivia, Brazil, Colombia and Costa Rica.

Finally, *liberalisation of the capital account of the balance of payments* (relaxing the rules governing movements of capital in and out of the country). This measure was supposedly essential to attract foreign savings and modern technology. But there was much more to it. The combination between trade liberalisation, currency overvaluation, high domestic interest rates and capital account liberalisation was a fail-safe strategy to reduce inflation and lock in the neoliberal reforms *simultaneously*. Cheap imports were allowed in, while high interest rates, foreign loans, mass privatisations and TNC takeovers of domestic firms brought the foreign capital that paid for them. Inflation tumbled while consumers indulged in flashy automobiles, computers and DVDs, and happily splashed out on artificially cheap foreign holidays. In Argentina and Brazil, consumer goods imports increased from US$242 million and US$606 million, respectively, to US$5.0 billion and US$8.2 billion between 1985 and 1998. During the same period, their foreign travel deficit increased from US$671 million to US$4.2 billion, and from US$441 million to US$5.7 billion. Euphoria reigned supreme. Neoliberalism bribed those that could not be convinced, and it seemed that it could do no wrong.

This happy state of affairs could not last. The reforms failed to resolve the shortcomings of ISI, explained in the first section, and they created new economic problems. They failed to relieve the foreign-exchange constraint, and increased countries' dependence on volatile foreign capital inflows. The financial reforms reduced the availability of savings and did nothing to improve the allocation of investment funds. Fiscal fragility resurfaced almost immediately, because of the weight of interest payments on the government budget. Finally, economic co-ordination suffered, because of the dismantling of specialist state institutions, the hollowing out of the industrial chains built during ISI and the reduction of the local content of manufacturing production. Wages and profits declined because of competing imports, the rising share of interest in the national income, and the difficulty of developing new competitive industries. Structural unemployment mounted. In sum, the neoliberal reforms destabilised the balance of payments and the productive system of most Latin American countries: neoliberalism discarded import substitution and promoted, instead, 'production substitution' financed by foreign capital.

Between 1990 and 2001, Latin America absorbed US$1.0 trillion in foreign financial resources (net debt flows, FDI, bonds and equity capital). However, capital outflows (debt service, interest payments and profit remittances) also rose, reducing the net inflows to only US$108.3 billion.[4] These inflows were insufficient to compensate the contraction of government investment and the decline of the savings rate. Investment fell, and growth petered out. Between 1981 and 2000, Argentina's average annual economic growth rate was only 1.6 per cent, Brazil's 2.1 per cent and Mexico's 2.7 per cent (cf. the much higher rates under ISI, above). Even considering only the 1990s, long after the debt crisis, the comparison bodes ill for neoliberalism. Argentina grew 4.5 per cent per annum, Brazil 2.7 per cent and Mexico 3.9 per cent. These economies were also rocked by severe crises: Mexico and Argentina in 1995, Brazil in 1999 and Argentina between 1998 and 2002.

The recent Argentine economic collapse brought to a close the 'triumphalist' phase of Latin American neoliberalism. As the reforms failed economically, mass resistance against neoliberalism has increased. New social movements in Argentina, Bolivia, Brazil, Ecuador, Mexico, Peru, Venezuela and elsewhere have challenged the neoliberal hegemony, and articulated popular demands for a democratic economic alternative.

CONCLUSION

The neoliberal reforms in Latin America often triggered a virtuous circle of macroeconomic stability and consumption-led growth financed by foreign capital. This state of affairs can become highly popular, especially among those who feel protected by their wealth and privilege from the ravages of unemployment, debt and economic insecurity.

In spite of these potential successes, neoliberalism is severely limited. If the required capital inflows fail to arrive, as they did in the mid 1990s and in 2000, countries must scramble to attract short-term funds by raising interest rates and cutting state expenditures in the name of 'credibility'. The economy is squeezed from two sides at the same time, and it eventually collapses, as it did in Argentina, Brazil and Mexico.

Neoliberalism is fragile not only because of its own intrinsic limitations, but also because the reforms have failed to address the most important shortcomings of ISI. Although high inflation has been eliminated, balance of payments is still vulnerable to shifts in international financial flows. Latin America's foreign debt has increased sharply, while savings and investment have fallen. Domestic financial systems remain unable or unwilling to channel savings to support economic growth, and fiscal deficits persist, in spite of drastic reforms to taxation and expenditure. These deficits are no longer due to poorly funded developmental initiatives, but to the high cost of servicing the domestic public debt – however, using the state budget to transfer resources from taxpayers to rentiers is entirely regressive in distributive terms. Finally, the state is less capable of addressing the problems of industrial co-ordination and growth than at any time since 1929. The combination of the unresolved weaknesses of ISI and the flaws of neoliberalism has entrenched economic stagnation and reduced the scope for the implementation of distributive economic and social policies in Latin America.

Rising popular resistance against neoliberalism shows that policy alternatives are urgently needed (see Chapters 19 and 20). This challenge is not limited to the election of governments programmatically committed to the search for an alternative economic model. After several elusive victories, it must be admitted that attempts to 'vote away' the neoliberal reforms are bound to fail. For these reforms are not limited to ideology or policy choice. They have acquired a material basis in the transformations that they have wrought on the economic fabric of Latin America. The tripartite division of labour between domestic, foreign and state-owned capital has been dismantled. Most SOEs were privatised, and foreign and domestic capital have established alliances at the level of firms across most market segments. Strategically important production chains established at high cost under ISI have been undone, Latin American finance has become closely bound up with the global circulation of capital, and the state has been transformed into the armed wing of the neoliberal elite consensus.

The construction of a new economic, social and political model will be costly and time-consuming. It can best be achieved at a regional level, or even globally, in the context of preferential links with middle-income economies in Asia and Africa. And it will never happen unless mass mobilisations are sufficiently strong and decisive not only to demand change *from* governments, or even changes *of* government, but also to entrench popular organisations *inside the state*, while preserving their political integrity, mass roots and accountability to the vast majority of the population. The construction of this new wave of popular movements is the most important challenge for the Latin American left during the next decade.

NOTES

*   I am grateful to the British Academy for funding the research that formed the basis of this chapter.

1. Between 1954 and 2000, South Korea grew 5.2 per cent per annum (6.6 per cent between 1963 and 1996), while Taiwan grew 6.1 per cent per annum between 1952 and 1998 (6.8 per cent between 1953 and 1997). See also Weeks (2000). The data sources used in this paper are Cepal (2003) and World Bank (2003a, 2003b).

2. There were two 'waves' of neoliberal reform in Latin America. The first wave was triggered by the Pinochet coup in Chile, in 1973, and it was embraced by the military dictatorships of Argentina and Uruguay. These experiences ended ignominiously in the early 1980s after severe de-industrialisation, enormous capital flight, the accumulation of vast foreign debts and profound economic crises (see Díaz-Alejandro, 1985). The second wave is analysed below.

3. These programmes are critically assessed by Iñigo Carrera (2005) and Saad-Filho and Mollo (2002).

4. This was insufficient to compensate the outflows during the debt crisis. Between 1980 and 2002, Latin America *transferred abroad* US$70 billion.

REFERENCES

Abreu, Bevilacqua and Pinho (2000) 'Import Substitution and Growth in Brazil, 1890s–1970s', in E. Cárdenas, J.A. Ocampo and R. Thorp (eds) *An Economic History of Twentieth-Century Latin America*, vol. 3. London: Palgrave.

Cepal (2003) *Statistical Yearbook of Latin America*. Santiago: Cepal.

Díaz-Alejandro, C. (1985) 'Good-Bye Financial Repression, Hello Financial Crash', *Journal of Development Economics* 19, pp. 1–24.

Iñigo Carrera, J. (2005) 'The Reproduction of Capital Accumulation through Political Crisis in Argentina', *Historical Materialism*, forthcoming.

Saad-Filho, A. and Mollo, M.L.R. (2002) 'Inflation and Stabilisation in Brazil: A Political Economy Analysis', *Review of Radical Political Economics* 34 (2), pp. 109–35.

Weeks, J. (2000) 'Latin America and the "High Performing Asian Economies": Growth and Debt', *Journal of International Development* 12, pp. 625–54.

World Bank (2003a) *World Development Indicators* (CD-ROM). Washington, D.C.: World Bank

World Bank (2003b) *Global Development Finance* (CD-ROM). Washington, D.C.: World Bank.

27
Neoliberalism in Sub-Saharan Africa: From Structural Adjustment to NEPAD

Patrick Bond

Distorted forms of capital accumulation and class formation associated with neoliberalism continue to amplify Africa's crisis of combined and uneven development. A new, supposedly home-grown strategy, the New Partnership for Africa's Development (NEPAD), corresponds to neoliberalism and relies upon compliant African politicians. There is little prospect that other mild-mannered global-scale initiatives being promoted by 'post-Washington consensus' reformers – for example, lower US and European Union agricultural subsidies, a little more debt relief, or slightly better access to brand-name anti-retroviral medicines to fight AIDS – will change matters, aside from increasing African elite acquiescence in the structures of power that keep the continent impoverished. New strategies and tactics, summed up in the terms 'deglobalisation' and 'decommodification', will be necessary for Africa to break from systemic underdevelopment. The continent's leading popular movements are taking steps in these directions.

Interlocking intellectual traditions of African political economy and radical political science have long attributed the continent's post-colonial crises to both external (imperialist) features and internal dynamics of class formation. Amongst the contributors are great organic intellectuals whose work was suffused with political urgency, including Ake, Amin, Biko, Cabral, Fanon, First, Kadalie, Lumumba, Machel, Mamdani, Mkandawire, Nabudere, Nkrumah, Nyerere, Odinga, Onimode, Rodney, Sankara and Shivji (see Arrighi 2002 and Saul and Leys 1999 for updated analyses).

There are many ways to demonstrate the two main points of this review: that neoliberalism as the most recent stage of global capitalism does not offer the scope for Africa to develop, and hence that reform strategies aimed at increasing integration will be counterproductive. Consider the main trends in these primary economic categories: financial accounts (including debt, portfolio finance, aid and capital flight), trade and investment.

Africa's *debt crisis* worsened during the era of globalisation. From 1980 to 2000, sub-Saharan Africa's total foreign debt rose from US$60 billion to US$206 billion, and the ratio of debt to GDP rose from 23 per cent to 66 per cent. Hence, Africa now repays more than it receives. In 1980, loan inflows of US$9.6 billion were comfortably higher than the debt repayment outflow of US$3.2 billion. But by 2000, only US$3.2 billion flowed in while US$9.8 billion was repaid, leaving a net financial flows deficit of US$6.2 billion.

African access to *portfolio capital* flows has mainly taken the form of 'hot money' (speculative positions by private-sector investors) in and out of the Johannesburg Stock Exchange (as well as those of Harare, Nairobi, Gaborone and a few others on occasion). In 1995, for example, foreign purchases and sales were responsible for half the share-trading in Johannesburg. But these flows have had devastating effects upon South Africa's currency, with crashes of over 30 per cent over a period of weeks during runs in early 1996, mid-1998 and late 2001. In Zimbabwe, the November 1997 outflow of hot money crashed the currency by 74 per cent in just four hours of trading.

Meanwhile, *donor aid* to Africa dropped 40 per cent in real terms during the 1990s, in the wake of the West's cold war victory (see Chapter 13). Most such aid is siphoned off beforehand by bureaucracies and home-country corporations, or is used for ideological purposes instead of for meeting genuine popular needs. The then director of the Harare-based African Network on Debt and Development, Opa Kapijimpanga, remarked:

> The donor creditor countries must keep all their aid and against it write off all the debt owed by poor African countries ... The bottom line would be elimination of both aid and debt because they reinforce the power relations that are contributing to the imbalances in the world. (Kapijimpanga 2001)

An important source of financial-account outflows from Africa that must be reversed is *capital flight*. James Boyce and Léonce Ndikumana argue that a core group of sub-Saharan African countries whose foreign debt was US$178 billion had suffered a quarter century of capital flight by elites that totalled more than US$285 billion (including imputed interest earnings): 'Taking capital flight as a measure of private external assets, and calculating net external assets as private external assets minus public external debts, sub-Saharan Africa thus appears to be a net creditor vis-à-vis the rest of the world' (Boyce and Ndikumana 2000).

Africa's underdevelopment through unbalanced *trade* is also a major problem. The continent's share of world trade declined over the past quarter-century, but the volume of exports increased. 'Marginalisation' of Africa occurred, therefore, not because of insufficient integration, but because other areas of the world – especially east Asia – moved to the export of manufactured goods, while Africa rapidly deindustrialised, thanks to excessive deregulation associated with structural adjustment. In the process, rapid trade-related integration caused social inequality, as World Bank economist Branko Milanovic (2003) concedes. The 'terms of trade' between Africa and the rest of the world deteriorated steadily, thanks in part to the artificially low prices of crops subsidised by G8 countries. The UN Conference on Trade and Development argues that if the terms of trade had instead been constant since 1980, Africa would have had twice the share of global trade than it actually did in the year 2000; per capita GDP would have been 50 per cent higher; and annual GDP increases would have been 1.4 per cent higher.

Foreign direct investment in sub-Saharan Africa fell from 25 per cent of the world's total at its peak during the 1970s to less than 5 per cent by the late 1990s, and those small amounts were devoted mainly to extracting minerals and oil, usually from extremely corrupt regimes in Nigeria and Angola, with transnational corporate bribery playing a major role. The only other substantive foreign investment flows were to South Africa, for the partial privatisation of telecommunications and for the expansion of automotive-sector branch-plant activity within global assembly lines. This was abundantly offset by South Africa's own outflows of foreign direct investment, in the forms of delisting and relocation of the largest corporations' financial headquarters to London, not to mention the repatriation of profits and payments of patent and royalty fees to transnational corporations. Moreover, official statistics ignore the long-standing problem of transfer pricing, whereby foreign investors underpay taxes in Africa by misinvoicing inputs drawn from abroad.

STRUCTURAL ADJUSTMENT AND DEBT

Neoliberalism was initially codified in Africa in the World Bank's 1981 *Berg Report* (written by consultant Elliot Berg). Very few countries resisted, and the effects were quite consistent. Budget cuts depressed economies' effective demand, leading to declining growth (see Chapters 11 and 12). Often, the alleged 'crowding out' of productive investment by government spending was not actually the reason for lack of investment, so the budget cuts were not compensated for by private sector growth. Privatisation often did not distinguish which state enterprises may have been strategic in nature, was too often accompanied by corruption and often suffered from foreign takeover of domestic industry; it gave scant regard to maintaining local employment or production levels (the incentive was sometimes simply gaining access to markets).

There is convincing documentation that the most vulnerable – women and children, the elderly and disabled people – are the primary victims, as they are expected to survive with less social subsidy, with more pressure on the fabric of the family during economic crisis, and with damage done by HIV/AIDS closely correlated to the tearing of safety nets by structural adjustment policies (Tskikata and Kerr 2002). Moreover, there were no attempts by World Bank and the IMF economists to determine how state agencies could supply services that enhanced 'public goods' (and merit goods).

Notwithstanding their failures, the Bank and the IMF demanded even more latitude to design the nature of reformed neoliberalism during the late 1990s, in areas such as debt relief, structural adjustment and institutional governance. Their success is witnessed by the fact that neoliberalism remains the dominant policy paradigm in Africa, notwithstanding systemic failure. The Highly Indebted Poor Countries Initiative (HIPC, initiated in 1996) was accompanied by a mere renaming of the structural adjustment philosophy in 1999 as Poverty Reduction Strategy Papers (PRSPs). These have proved inadequate in Africa, and are regularly condemned by civil society groups (see Chapters 15 and 19).

One reason for this is the maldistribution of power within the multilateral agencies, including the US veto (with just over 15 per cent of the institutions' ownership). There is just one African member on the 24-member board of the Bretton

Woods Institutions. But internal reform proposals to raise developing-country voting power from 39 per cent to 44 per cent and add one new African director were rebuffed by the United States in mid-2003. The same month, Ethiopian president Miles Zenawi poignantly implored an Economic Commission on Africa meeting, 'While we will not be at the high table of the IMF, we should be at least in the room where decisions are made.'

NEPAD TO NEOLIBERALISM'S RESCUE?

Because of such problems, as reflected in consistent 'IMF Riots' by angry survivors across Africa, neoliberalism began suffering a legitimacy crisis during the late 1990s. A home-grown variant was required. South Africa's president Thabo Mbeki introduced the core outline of what would be the 67-page document, NEPAD, in early 2001 at a telling site: the Davos World Economic Forum. By November 2001, NEPAD was formally released, in Abuja, Nigeria.[1] During 2002 the plan was endorsed by African rulers, the G8 summit in Canada, the World Summit on Sustainable Development and the United Nations heads-of-state summit (Bond 2002, 2004).

In areas of economic reform, such as financial flows and foreign investment, NEPAD offers only the *status quo*. Instead of promoting debt cancellation, the NEPAD strategy is to 'support existing poverty reduction initiatives at the multi-lateral level' including HIPC and PRSPs. In mid 2003, *Institutional Investor* magazine quoted the US government's chief Africa bureaucrat, Walter Kansteiner: 'NEPAD is philosophically spot-on.'

What, in contrast, was African civil society's input? In late 2001 and early 2002, virtually every major African civil-society organisation, network and progressive personality attacked NEPAD's process, form and content (Bond 2002). Until April 2002, no trade-union, civil-society, church, women's, youth, political-party, parliamentary, or other potentially democratic, progressive forces in Africa were consulted by the politicians or technocrats about NEPAD. Tough critiques emerged in mid 2002 from intellectuals (e.g. Adesina 2002), especially those associated with the Council for Development and Social Research in Africa (CODESRIA) (cited in Bond 2002). First, the neoliberal economic-policy frame-work lies at the heart of the plan, which repeats the structural-adjustment-policy packages of the preceding two decades and overlooks the disastrous effects of those policies. Second, in spite of its proclaimed recognition of the central role of the African people to the plan, the African people have not played any part in the conception, design and formulation of NEPAD. Third, notwithstanding its stated concerns for social and gender equity, it adopts the social and economic measures that have contributed to the marginalisation of women. Fourth, in spite of claims of African origins, its main targets are foreign donors, particularly in the G8. In addition, its vision of democracy is defined by the need for creating a functional market. It also underemphasises the external conditions fundamental to Africa's developmental crisis, and thereby fails to promote any meaningful measure to manage and restrict the effects of this environment on Africa development efforts. On the contrary, the engagement that it seeks with institutions and processes such as the World Bank, the IMF, the WTO, the United States Africa Growth and Opportunity Act and the Cotonou Agreement will further lock Africa's economies disadvantageously into this environment. Finally, the means for mobilisation of resources will further the disintegration of African economies that we have witnessed at the hands of structural adjustment and WTO rules.

CONCLUSION: AFRICAN RESISTANCE

It is because of such experiences that CODESRIA intellectuals, Jubilee activists and allied groups within the Africa Social Forum have become as radical as any activists across the world, when it comes to strategies addressing international economic relationships (see Bond and Ngwane 2004, Ngwane 2003 and Zeilig 2002). For example, not only do they try to kick the Bank and the IMF out of their countries and persuade their finance ministers to default on the illegitimate foreign debt; they are also intent, strategically, on abolition of the Bretton Woods Institutions and have developed at least one potentially devastating tactic: the World Bank Bonds Boycott.[2] US-based solidarity organisations such as Centre for Economic Justice and Global Exchange worked with Jubilee South Africa and Brazil's Movement of the Landless, amongst others, to ask of their Northern allies: is it ethical for socially conscious people to invest in the World Bank by buying its bonds (responsible for 80 per cent of the institution's resources), hence drawing out dividends which represent the fruits of enormous suffering?

As another example of what is being termed 'deglobalisation', the African Trade Network and the Gender and Trade Network in Africa put intense pressure on the continent's delegates to reject the World Trade Organisation's 2003 Cancun proposals. This proved successful when the Africa–Caribbean–Pacific group led the walkout that ended the Cancun meeting. A 'G20' group of middle-income agricultural exporters emerged to promote more rapid trade deregulation and Pretoria's role in the group amplified South Africa's differences with other African Countries (Bond 2004). The United States and the EU offered no concessions on matters of great importance to Africa (such as the decimation of west African cotton exports due to subsidies, or the halting of grain dumping), and instead rigidly insisted on moving the corporate agenda forward with other so-called 'Singapore' issues. Bilateral or regional trade deals – such as with the European Union and the US Africa Growth and Opportunity Act – may also be resisted from both civil society and African countries which are manifestly losing out.

On a more localised level, inspiring anti-neoliberal struggles for what might be termed 'decommodification' are underway in Africa, especially South Africa. There, independent left movements have partially succeeded in translating demands for basic needs into genuine human rights: free anti-retroviral medicines to fight AIDS and other health services; free lifeline water (at least 50 litres/person/day); free lifeline electricity (at least one kilowatt hour/person/day); thoroughgoing land reform; prohibition on services disconnections and evictions; free education; and even a 'Basic Income Grant', as advocated by churches and trade unions. Because the commodification of everything is still underway in South Africa, this is the sort of potentially unifying agenda that can serve as the programmatic basis for a wide-scale movement for dramatic social change.

Foremost amongst the problems that must be addressed, simultaneously, is the rescaling of many political–economic responsibilities. These are now handled by embryonic world-state institutions overly influenced by the aggressive, neoliberal US administrations. The decommodification principle is an enormous threat to their interests, whether in the forms of borrowed intellectual property (such as AIDS medicines), African agricultural systems protected against genetic modification, nationalised industries and utilities, or less pliant and desperate labour markets. To make any progress, deglobalisation from the most destructive circuits of global capital will also be necessary. Those circuits – finance, direct investment and commerce – rely most upon the three multilateral agencies, and hence a strategy and tactics are urgently required to close the World Bank, the IMF and the WTO.

Beyond that, the challenge for Africa's progressive forces, as ever, is to establish the difference between 'reformist reforms' and more radical strategies. Some struggles have more obvious possibilities to advance a 'non-reformist' agenda, such as for generous social policies stressing decommodification, and for capital controls and inward-oriented industrial strategies allowing democratic control of finance and ultimately of production itself. These sorts of non-neoliberal reforms would strengthen the democratic movements, directly empower the producers and perhaps, over time, open the door to the contestation of capitalism, of which neoliberalism is only a contemporary symptom.

NOTES

1. *New Partnership for Africa's Development*, 23 October 2001 <http://www.nepad.org>.
2. By 2003, institutions which have either sold World Bank bonds under pressure or committed never to buy them again in future include the world's largest pension fund (TIAA-CREF); major religious orders (the Conference of Major Superiors of Men, Pax Christi USA, the Unitarian Universalist General Assembly and dozens of others); the most important social responsibility funds (Calvert Group, Global Greengrants Fund, Ben and Jerry's Foundation and Trillium Assets Management); the University of New Mexico endowment fund; US cities (including San Francisco, Milwaukee, Boulder and Cambridge); and major trade union pension/investment funds (e.g. Teamsters, Postal Workers, Service Employees International, American Federation of Government Employees, Longshoremen, Communication Workers of America, United Electrical Workers). See <http://www.worldbankboycott.org>.

REFERENCES

Adesina, J. (2002) 'Development and the Challenge of Poverty: NEPAD, Post-Washington Consensus and Beyond', paper prepared for the Council on Development and Social Research in Africa, Senegal, <http://www.codesria.org/Links/conferences/Nepad/Adesina.pdf>.

Arrighi, G. (2002) 'The African Crisis: World Systemic and Regional Aspects', *New Left Review* 15, pp.5–36.

Bond, P. (ed.) (2002) *Fanon's Warning: A Civil Society Reader on the New Partnership for Africa's Development*. Trenton, N.J.: Africa World Press and Cape Town: Alternative Information and Development Centre.

Bond, P. (2004) *Talk Left, Walk Right: South Africa's Frustrated Global Reforms*. Pietermaritzburg: University of Natal Press and London: Merlin Press.

Bond, P. and Ngwane, T. (2004) 'African Anti-Capitalism', in R.Neumann and E.Burcham (eds) *Anti Capitalism: A Field Guide to the Global Justice Movement*. New York: Norton Press.

Boyce, J. and Ndikumana, L. (2000) 'Is Africa a Net Creditor? New Estimates of Capital Flight from Severely Indebted Sub-Saharan African Countries, 1970–1996', occasional paper, University of Massachusetts (Amherst), Political Economy Research Institute.

Kapijimpanga, O. (2001) 'An Aid/Debt Trade-Off: The Best Option', in G.Ostravik (ed.) *The Reality of Aid: Reality Check 2001*. Oslo: Norwegian Peoples Aid, <http://www.devinit.org/jpdfs/jok.pdf>.

Milanovic, B. (2003) 'Can We Discern the Effect of Globalisation on Income Distribution? Evidence from Household Budget Surveys', World Bank Policy Research Working Paper 2876, April.

Ngwane, T. (2003) 'Interview: Sparks in Soweto', *New Left Review* 22, pp.36–56.

Saul, J. and Leys, C. (1999) 'Sub-Saharan Africa in Global Capitalism', *Monthly Review* 51 (3), <http://www.monthlyreview.org/799saul.htm>.

Tskikata, D. and Kerr, J. (eds) (2002) *Demanding Dignity: Women Confronting Economic Reforms in Africa*. Ottawa: The North-South Institute and Accra: Third World Network-Africa.

Zeilig, L. (ed.) (2002) *Class Struggle and Resistance in Africa*. Cheltenham: New Clarion.

28

Neoliberalism and South Asia: The Case of a Narrowing Discourse

Matthew McCartney

Liberalisation first emerged in south Asia in response to the perceived failure of various radical economic reform efforts in the 1970s. Such was the hold of neoliberal thinking by the 1980s over economic discourse that the 'success' of radicalism was disparaged according to neoliberal criteria and liberalisation implicitly accepted as the only viable alternative. It is argued here that neoliberal discourse is based on an assumption that any growth in a free market must by definition be efficient. Policy reform then need only be concerned with implementing liberalisation and analysis need only measure the degree of implementation. This chapter argues that this narrowing of the discourse of reform is fundamentally unsound, that the concept of sustainability of reform is severely emasculated and that the presence of very real alternatives evident from a closer analysis of the development of south Asia are as a result ignored.

FROM RADICALISM TO NEOLIBERALISM IN SOUTH ASIA

After independence, India pursued a policy of self-sufficiency in trade, investment and technology. It was widely argued by the nationalist movement that free trade had been the means by which India had been exploited by colonial Britain. Ironically, the same argument underpinned the movement for independence of Bangladesh from Pakistan in 1970–71. During the early 1970s the Bangladeshi government moved rapidly to expropriate assets owned by Pakistani nationals and in so doing created a large interventionist state. In Pakistan, radicalism emerged later. Growth in the 1950s and 1960s was based on a close relationship between large-scale private enterprise, trade protection and state subsidies. The perception that inequality had widened rapidly proved a fruitful rallying point for the socialist rhetoric of Zulfikar Ali Bhutto. During his administration (1971–77), extensive nationalisation was heralded as the remedy needed to break the link between private industry and banking that underpinned exclusionary growth.

Liberalisation emerged as a remedy to the perceived failings of these development models. Though adopted for motives other than maximising growth, such as self-sufficiency, balanced regional growth and technological independence, such was the dominance of neoliberal thinking that by the 1980s 'success' was measured from a very narrow neoliberal perspective – for example the volume of foreign investment, rather than the technological capability of domestic industry.

In each case there was little consideration of alternatives, and the emphasis was on reducing government intervention, not reforming or improving it.

In India, liberalisation initially implied a gradual dilution of efforts to achieve self-sufficiency. Attempts to plan the economy, lead the process of development through state investment and restrict the space for private monopolies gave way to a growing though grudging role for the private sector. In Pakistan, after the coup of General Zia in 1977, the change was a more subtle adjustment comprising selective denationalisation and incentives for the private sector. The main change was the abandonment of radical rhetoric, and official support for the private sector. Bangladesh went furthest. As the chaotic state had never penetrated domestic industry and agriculture with the same rigour as in India and Pakistan during the post-Independence period of radicalism under Mujibur Rahman (1971–75), retreat was relatively easier and more quickly comprehensive. Foreign trade has been steadily increasing as a share of GDP since 1975. There was earlier and more widespread acceptance of privatisation of banks, insurance companies and large-scale industry. Pakistan followed this route later and India has yet barely begun.

Neoliberal reforms gained added impetus in the 1990s. A debt crisis in India, which had gradually emerged during the 1980s, fed by large budget and trade deficits, erupted in 1991 as oil prices rocketed during the first Gulf War and remittance income from expatriate workers in the Gulf region dried up. The IMF gave lending, in exchange for neoliberal economic reforms. That reforms have been sustained for a decade after the immediate crisis eased does need explaining. This persistence owes much to the influential body of non-resident Indian economists long converted to neoliberalism. Also important are the growth of a domestic business constituency with a predilection for foreign technology and international collaborations, rather than the red tape and abysmal infrastructure offered by a failing state and, finally, a growing internationalised middle class with similarly global consumption aspirations.

In contrast, the end of the Soviet–Afghan war in 1989, and the associated end of US military and economic assistance, threw into stark light the dependent nature of the Pakistani economy. Historically unable to mobilise savings or tax revenues[1] Pakistan has been dependent on foreign capital to finance domestic investment. Such dependence gave the IMF great leverage to dominate economic policy making for the next decade.

The most dramatic reforms were with regard to integration with the world economy. There was significant liberalisation in terms of import tariffs, quotas and licensing requirements and foreign investment. The narrow focus of reform can be traced back to particular features of the neoliberal discourse, which systematically and by assumption exclude alternatives and even meaningful debate (see Chapters 3 and 12).

EFFICIENT GROWTH (BY ASSUMPTION)

In neoliberal discourse, individuals are rational and exchange is voluntary. Under perfect competition, consumption will be distributed efficiently across time periods and firms will make optimal use of available savings for investment. The growth path will reflect preferences of individual agents, hence by assumption must be efficient, and there is no role for government intervention (see Chapter 5).

Neoliberal economic reform is based on this assumption of efficient growth. Stabilisation ensures that growth will be sustainable by reducing inflation, government budget deficits and any trade imbalance. Subsequently the reform process (synonymous with liberalisation) is simply an accelerator. There is no question of steering the economy, simply of speeding up ('deepening' is the typical metaphor) or slowing down the process of transition to a free market.

LIBERALISATION: MEANS AND ENDS

This assumption of efficient growth has *narrowed the discourse* of neoliberal theorists. The bulk of mainstream analysis of south Asia focuses nearly exclusively on the depth, pace and implementation of liberalisation. Much of the intellectual artillery for the neoclassical counter-revolution in economics was derived from close study of the experiences of countries that had pursued strategies of import substitution in the postwar period.[2] Industry was found to be high cost, capital intensive and to generate little employment. Far from achieving self-sufficient industrialisation, such countries continued to depend on imports of capital goods and inputs. The counterpart of industrialisation was a general discrimination against agriculture. This type of analysis provided important antecedents for the shift to strategies of outward orientation, often as intrinsic parts of structural adjustment programmes, from the 1980s onwards.

However, the widespread adoption of the neoliberal agenda has not seen a complementary pattern of analysis. The success of 'reform' is not typically measured in terms of employment, inequality and growth. Rather:

> The problem was that many of these policies became ends in themselves, rather than means to more equitable and sustainable growth. In doing so these policies were pushed too far, too fast, and to the exclusion of other policies that were needed. (Stiglitz 2002, p. 53)

A good example of the neoclassical evaluation of liberalisation in India is provided by Ahluwalia[3] (2002) and Bajpai[4] (2002). Ahluwalia (2002, p. 69) claims that: 'we consider the cumulative outcome of ten years of gradualism to assess whether the reforms have created an environment that can support 8 per cent GDP growth, which is the government's target'.

Ahluwalia in practice simply engages in the two-fold analysis typical of neoliberal economists. Firstly, considering whether growth is sustainable in a purely financial sense, examining trends in the fiscal deficit, current-account deficit and foreign-exchange reserves. Secondly, measuring how far liberalisation has been implemented, tariff reductions, the degree of integration with the world economy (as indicated by the share of imports plus exports in GDP), and the level of foreign direct investment, the removal of price controls and economic deregulation.[5]

Bajpai follows the same track. He compiles a review of liberal policy reforms – devaluation, current account convertibility, trade liberalisation, encouraging FDI inflows, opening capital markets to portfolio investment, permitting domestic companies access to foreign capital markets. Bajpai does not even make passing reference to the impact of these 'reforms' in any other context than the changes arising from India's integration into the world economy. He notes that over the course of the 1990s, the weighted average tariff fell from 90 per cent to less than 30 per cent, foreign investment increased from 0.1 to 1 per cent of GDP and the share of trade increased from 18 to 30 per cent of GDP.

The underlying assumptions of voluntary exchange and rational optimising individuals mean that it must by definition be the case that the level of growth reflects individual preferences and hence maximises welfare in a free market. The successful outcome of reform and the degree of implementation of liberalisation are arbitrarily collapsed by the a priori assumption that they mean the same thing.[6]

SUSTAINABILITY

The concept of sustainability is a severely emasculated one in neoliberal discourse. The first aspect is that of political sustainability, whether liberalisation has been 'locked in'. Important in this regard are commitments to regional trade associations based on free-trade arrangements,[7] central bank independence and of course IMF/WB lending conditionality. The concept extends further only to encompass a narrow financial conception (fiscal and trade deficits). There is no consideration that different growth paths may have different implications for long-term development.

Sachs et al. (2000) argue that more neoliberal economic reforms could help raise the volume of FDI towards US$10 billion per annum and thus enable India to emulate other Asian economies that have been more successful at attracting FDI. The most pressing difference they ignore is in the nature rather than the volume of FDI in India. For example most FDI into China takes the form of export-oriented, greenfield investment. By the 1990s, most export growth originated from part or wholly owned foreign enterprises (see Chandra 1999). By contrast, in India most FDI was directed at selling to the domestic market. Joint ventures in India have only been temporary, foreign investors soon buying out their local partners. Coca-Cola purchased the domestic Parle brand in order to access its local distribution network and Pepsi similarly purchased the Duke brand. FDI has not led a dynamic process of export-led growth and technological upgrading. India's export structure remains dominated by low-technology products concentrated in slow growing markets: 'Trade liberalisation will, when fully implemented, help realise existing competitive advantages, and induce activities near best practice levels to upgrade and enter international markets. But it is unlikely to dynamise export growth by itself' (Lall 1999, p. 1784).

ALTERNATIVES

The assumption that reform is synonymous with 'liberalisation', and that concern can be limited to the degree of implementation, ignores the real presence of *alternatives:* neoclassical economics, by assumption, does not admit the possibility of an alternative. A closer look at south Asia reveals how the narrowing discourse of neoliberalisation has prevented a full analysis of the reform process and the scope for beneficial government intervention.

Growth in Bangladesh has been sustained by the growth of textile exports. The industry made its initial appearance at the end of the 1970s and constituted nearly 30 per cent of total exports by 1986–87. By the 1990s, it employed 1.5 million people, 90 per cent of them women. This success has been used to justify extending and deepening the neoliberal reforms. However there must be some question over the sustainability of this leading sector. Bangladesh is not affected by textile quotas in developed countries (especially the multi-fibre agreement, MFA) so has filled an empty niche among developing countries. With the proposed abolition of quotas from 2005, Bangladesh will face renewed competition from other large countries, notably China. It is an open question whether the industry will successfully upgrade its production capabilities and skills, or rather intensify working conditions and squeeze wages to remain competitive. There is a potential role for government intervention to influence the process and push the sector towards the more desirable and progressive dynamic path of competition. There are realistic doubts about whether the state has the requisite capacity, and whether it would be distracted by the exclusive emphasis of the neoliberal discourse on deepening liberalisation.

India has implemented neoliberal reforms on a gradual but consistent basis. Ahluwalia (2002) attributes this to the slow workings of a heterogeneous and chaotic bureaucracy. Even where neoliberalism does not officially apply, like the heavily regulated labour market, in practise regulation is avoided through extensive and growing subcontracting to the unregulated informal sector. For example, the much heralded software sector saw exports rise from perhaps US$100 million to nearly US$8 billion during the 1990s. However, this sector has little impact on the aggregate economy. In many cases, expensive training merely equips migrants for better-paid jobs overseas. Evans (1995) has argued that the existing pattern of exporting lines of computer code and importing expensive branded software and hardware is uncomfortably reminiscent of selling (cheap) cotton to buy (expensive) cloth that characterised the much derided colonial pattern of trade in the nineteenth century.

Pakistan is severely constrained in terms of formulating and implementing policy. The IMF remains dominant in agenda setting. Other external factors are important; for example, the conflict over Kashmir underpins a domestic political economy of defence that seeks to retain military parity with India. The burden of defence expenditure combined with the interest on accumulated foreign and domestic debt crowds out developmental expenditure. Resource-mobilisation efforts have been undermined by the liberalising commitment to reduce import tariffs. High budget deficits combined with financial liberalisation have pushed up real interest rates and undermined private-sector investment. Such deep-seated contradictions reveal that liberalisation has not been framed with a realistic appreciation of underlying political-economy constraints on policy implementation. A pertinent example is the failure, despite frequent promises to the IMF, to improve resource (tax) mobilisation and close the budget deficit.

Rodrik (2000) argues that integration with the world economy cannot substitute for a development strategy. Development is increasingly viewed as synonymous with global integration and trade and investment being used as yardsticks for evaluating government policy. In actual fact, 'integration' may crowd out alternatives (see Chapters 5 and 10). Rodrik suggests that globalisation should be evaluated in terms of the needs of development, not vice versa.

It is clear that although there exists a near consensus on the positive relationship between openness and growth, 'there is a dirty little secret in international trade analysis. The measurable costs of protectionist policies – the reductions in real income that can be attributed to tariffs and import quotas – are not all that large' (Krugman 1995, p. 31).

And there is another fact that is often forgotten. Liberalisation and integration are not concerned solely with the removal of controls and the unwinding of government intervention. Free lunches there may be sometimes, but there is no such thing as a free market. There are in fact demanding institutional requirements. Rodrik notes that to comply with the full panoply of WTO obligations (customs, sanitary and phyto-sanitary regulations, intellectual property rights, etc.) would cost the typical LDC US$150 million. The small gains from trade noted by Krugman are undoubtedly offset by the potentially enormous gains from an alternative – such as basic education for girls (see Sen 1999). South Asia is distinctive as a region with very poor levels of social development, with the striking exception of Sri Lanka. In 2000, literacy rates in Bangladesh and Pakistan were both little over 40 per cent. The region is also marked, more than any other region, by striking disparities between gender outcomes. In 1999, only 28 per cent of females were enrolled in school at any level – among the lowest levels in the world despite the region's having a per capita income near middle-income status.

CONCLUSION

The a priori assumptions of neoclassical economics have led to a shrinking discourse. A discourse that merely measures political and financial sustainability and the degree of implementation, it is not concerned with the broader definitions of the sustainability of growth and the real presence of alternatives.

NOTES

1. In 1989–90, savings in India reached 22 per cent of GDP, and in Pakistan only 13 per cent.
2. For the case of India, see Bhagwati and Desai (1970) and Bhagwati and Srinivasan (1975).
3. Finance minister of the 1991–96 Congress government, which launched the first generation of liberalising reforms.
4. One of the famously influential American-based non-resident Indian economists who have done so much to promote the agenda of liberalisation in India over the 1990s.
5. There is concern only in passing with infrastructure and education, but this does not detract from the primary thrust, which is concerned with sustainability and the implementation of liberalisation.
6. There is therefore no need to examine the impact of liberalisation on such things as the productivity and level of investment, the degree of social cohesion, political and social stability, the level of spending on research and development, or the diversification of exports into more dynamic industrial sectors.
7. The exemplar is the case of the accession of Mexico to the NAFTA in the early 1990s.

REFERENCES

Ahluwalia, M.S. (2002) 'Economic Reforms in India Since 1991: Has Gradualism Worked?', *Journal of Economic Perspectives* 16 (3), pp. 67–88.

Bajpai, N. (2002) 'A Decade of Economic Reforms in India: The Unfinished Agenda', Harvard Centre for International Development, Working Paper No.89.

Bhagwati, J. and Desai, P. (1970) *India: Planning for Industrialisation, Industrialisation and Trade Policies Since 1951*. Oxford: Oxford University Press.

Bhagwati, J. and Srinivasan, T.N. (1975) *Foreign Trade Regimes and Economic Development: India*. Columbia: Columbia University Press.

Chandra, N.K. (1999) 'FDI and Domestic Economy: Neoliberalism in China', *Economic and Political Weekly*, 6 November.

Drèze, J. and Gazdar, H. (1996) 'Uttar Pradesh: The Burden of Inertia', in J.Drèze and A.Sen (eds) *Indian Development: Selected Regional Perspectives*. Oxford: Oxford University Press.

Evans, P. (1995) *Embedded Autonomy: States and Industrial Transformation*. Princeton: Princeton University Press.

Krugman, P. (1995) 'Dutch Tulips and Emerging Markets', *Foreign Affairs*, July/August.

Kumar, N. (2000) 'Economic Reforms and Their Macro-Economic Impact', *Economic and Political Weekly*, 4 March.

Lall, S. (1999) 'India's Manufactured Exports: Comparative Structure and Prospects', *World Development* 27 (10), pp. 1769–86.

Rodrik, D. (2000) 'Can Integration into the World Economy Substitute for a Development Strategy?', World Bank EBGDE European Conference, 26–28 June.

Sachs, J.D., Bajpai, N., Blaxhill, M.F. and Maira, A. (2000) 'Foreign Direct Investment in India: How Can $10 Billion of Annual Inflows be Realised?', Centre for International Development at Harvard University and Boston Consulting Group, 11 January.

Sen, A. (1999) *Development as Freedom*. Oxford: Oxford University Press.

Stiglitz, J.E. (2002) *Globalisation and its Discontents*. London: Penguin.

29

Assessing Neoliberalism in Japan

Makoto Itoh

More than two decades have passed since the basic stance of Japanese economic policies turned to neoliberalism. Neoliberalism in Japan initially took the form of administrative reform. Prime Minister Suzuki inaugurated a special commission in 1981 with the aim of achieving a balanced national budget to address the deepening fiscal crisis of the state. To achieve this objective, administrative reforms to reduce the size and role of the government were recommended. They included the reduction in the number of civil servants, privatisation of state-owned enterprises, and deregulation in a wide range of fields, all of which were thereafter continuously pursued.

The leading ideology underpinning the reforms was that free and competitive market principles provide the most efficient and rational economic order. Under such neoliberal policies, capitalist firms, especially big business, found it easier to trade, finance, invest, and 'rationalise' wage costs through use of cheaper irregular workers. The transnationalisation of Japanese industrial enterprises was also facilitated, with US and European transnationals also increasing their sales and investment in Japan. In many aspects, the Japanese socio-economic order was remodelled in the shape of the American model. In Japanese business circles, this was regarded as necessary to maintain international business opportunities, particularly in the United States.

However, the economic life of the workers and other vulnerable people has deteriorated and become more unstable. The power of Japanese trade unions declined as their organisation rate among employed workers fell from 35.4 per cent in 1970 to 19.6 per cent in 2003. Their strength was greatly reduced by the heavy blow to public-sector trade unions dealt by privatisation. When three state-owned enterprises – Japan National Railways (JNR), Nippon Telegraph and Telephone Public Corporation (NTT), and Japan Tobacco and Salt Public Corporation – were privatised in 1985, the aim of the policy was said to be to reduce the burden of their deficit on the state budget, to create a fund for the state by selling shares of privatised enterprises and to promote the competitive vitality of the market economy. However, an important practical effect of this privatisation policy was to weaken the militant wing of trade unions. For example, in the process of privatising JNR to create six JR (Japan Railways) corporations, ruthless 'rationalisation' took place and the number of workers was reduced from a peak of about 400,000 in 1982 to half that number by 1987. The number of JNR/JR trade union members declined sharply from 200,000 to 40,000 during that period, aided by selective firing of trade union activists and members, and discrimination against remaining union members. By 1996, 39 local labour-relations commissions had recommended rescue orders concerning 131 cases involving more than 14,000 workers. The ILO has also become concerned about the cases. Nevertheless, JR corporations would not comply with these recommendations, and they were supported by the government and the courts.

The General Council of Trade Unions in Japan (Sohyo) had been a strong national left-wing labour movement in the period following the Second World War, based largely on JNR and other public-sector unions. The heavy blow inflicted on these unions by privatisation was also destructive for Sohyo. The Japanese labour movement did not effectively unite in opposition to this neoliberal attack in the form of privatisation. One reason was probably the long-standing split between Sohyo and Domei (the Japanese Confederation of Labour), with the latter being based mainly upon the private sector. Domei was more closely aligned with the political centre, and tended to co-operate with business. The result was that the main current of the Japanese trade union movement shifted to Domei. In 1989, Sohyo was dissolved and merged with Domei to form a new national organisation of trade unions, Rengo (the Confederation of All Japan Trade Unions).

The dissolution of Sohyo and the withering of the left wing of the Japanese labour movement delivered a shock to the Japanese Socialist Party (JSP), added to by the collapse of the Soviet Union. This is one of the reasons why JSP changed its stance from socialist to social democratic 'realist'. When it temporarily joined a coalition government with the conservative Liberal Democratic Party (LDP) in 1994, it further diluted its pacifist and socialist policies. In 1996, JSP changed its name to the Social Democratic Party of Japan (SDPJ). Though JSP used to hold about one-third of all parliamentary seats, it lost seats throughout the 1990s and these losses were accelerated by the change in the constituency system into the single-seat electoral district system. At the general election for the lower House of Representatives in November 2003, SDPJ only won six out of 480 seats, and the Japanese Communist Party (JCP), which had marginally gained votes from JSP/SDPJ in the 1990s, also suffered a loss of eleven seats to get just nine. The Democratic Party of Japan obtained 177 seats and emerging as one of two big political parties, effectively replacing the former JSP in popularity. Consequently, there has clearly been an increasingly conservative tendency in Japanese politics as well as ideology, which facilitated the imposition of neoliberal policies.

The fiscal crisis of Japanese capitalism, and the costs of restructuring the state financially, were increasingly shifted to the shoulders of the workers and the socially unprotected strata of the population. Real wages have stagnated, despite increasing productivity, and 'rationalisation' to reduce wage costs became easier in most workplaces. A consumer tax of 3 per cent was introduced in 1989, and then raised to 5 per cent in 1997. Individual private contributions for medical services were also raised from 10 per cent to 20 per cent in 1997, and 30 per cent in 2003. In contrast, the corporate tax rate was reduced gradually from 42 per cent to 30 per cent, and the highest marginal income tax rate was reduced from 75 per cent to 37 per cent, together with a substantial reduction of the inheritance tax rate, favouring the wealthy groups of the population.

There was a general relaxation of protective labour laws in 1998. The employ-ment agency business was liberalised, and the range of jobs open to such business was expanded. Overtime work was made utilisable without regulation, and the time limit of one year on part-time employment was abolished, so as to enable companies to employ female part-time workers for long periods of time. It is clear that these neoliberal labour policies enhanced the freedom of capitalist firms to use cheaper workers flexibly in a competitive labour market.

A DIALECTICAL TURN AND A VICIOUS CIRCLE

What happened to the Japanese economy under neoliberal policies? The Japanese economy attracted global attention for its strength until the end of the 1980s. It recovered from the damage inflicted by the first and second oil shocks, and main-tained a growth performance stronger than most other advanced economies (3.9 per cent on average in 1974–90), although the Japanese growth rate dur-ing this period became less than half of the rates achieved during the preceding quarter-century. The Japanese style of business management, including life-long employment, a wage system based on seniority and company-based trade unions, had effectively mobilised the workers' loyalty and strengthened firms' competitive power in world markets, despite the continuous wide appreciation of the yen (from 360 yen per dollar until 1971 to 110 yen per dollar in June 2004) since the breakdown of the Bretton Woods system. The result was an increasing Japanese trade surplus. In 1987, national per capita income in Japan surpassed that in the USA, and gave a strong impression of Japan as 'number one' in the world.

Unexpectedly, however, the Japanese economy dramatically deteriorated in what is now called the 'lost decade' of the 1990s. The growth rate declined to less than 1 per cent per annum on average, and it was negative in some years. The 'lost decade' has extended also into the new century. The dramatic deterioration of the Japanese economy has occurred dialectically as a result of the successful restruc-turing of Japanese capitalism in the 1980s. On the basis of co-operative workers and trade unions, large Japanese firms have continuously intensified their com-petitive power by introducing increasingly sophisticated information technologies and automation systems at the workplace, assisted by the use of cheaper part-timers and other irregular workers. In my view, Japanese neoliberalism is not just a reaction to the failure of Keynesianism, but it also has a material basis in the development of capitalism to revive competitive labour and other markets through information technology.

Most large Japanese firms were able to clear their previous bank debts in the 1980s, and they tended to accumulate surpluses in the form of reserves of idle money capital without corresponding real investment. They have also increased direct finance both in the domestic and foreign capital markets to obtain money capital by issuing shares, convertible bonds and other securities. In contrast, Japanese banks have traditionally depended on the relatively high household savings rate in the country (more than 20 per cent in the 1980s) and they contin-ued to lend to large firms until the 1970s. As banks lost such safe traditional borrowers, they found themselves being forced to explore new business areas by lending to medium and small firms or to real estate agencies and construction companies, as well as providing housing finance.

Soon after the Plaza Accord in 1985 (see Chapter 9), which aimed at revaluing the yen against the US dollar in order to moderate the trade frictions with the United States, the rate of interest was reduced in Japan, and this strongly stimulated domestic demand. The accumulated idle money capital of large Japanese firms was rapidly mobilised into both foreign investment and domestic speculative investment. The appreciation of the yen created incentives for Japanese manufacturing firms to scale up their foreign direct investment (FDI), especially in east and south-east Asia. Japanese big business also increased its foreign portfolio investment by purchasing foreign shares and bonds. At the same time, the idle money capital of big businesses, Japanese banks and other financial institutions was poured into real-estate speculation in Japan, and into the Tokyo stock exchange. Between 1986 and the end of the decade, this led to a huge speculative bubble in both Japanese real estate and capital markets. It led to a domestic economic boom, apparently showing the success of the newly introduced neoliberal economic policies. However, the speculative bubble collapsed at the beginning of the 1990s, leading to a total loss in asset values of 1000 trillion yen by the middle of the decade, or 2.4 times the country's GDP. This was a huge loss, even compared with the United States' capital loss of 1.9 times GDP during the Great Crisis after 1929.

This gigantic meltdown of asset values created a severe problem of bad loans for the Japanese banks and other financial corporations, and negative equity for households. Moreover, in 1987 the Bank of International Settlement (BIS) made an agreement that banks engaged in international business should generally keep the ratio of own capital against total assets above 8 per cent after 1992. This agreement reflected the growing concern among Western bankers about the rapid international expansion of the Japanese banks. When it was made, Japanese banks believed that this regulation would be achievable as long as 45 per cent of the latent capital gains through the rising price of shares (i.e. the difference between the current share prices and their purchase price) were counted as part of own capital. However, in practice it proved to be difficult to comply with this regulation, as the latent capital gains of the banks disappeared or even became negative as a result of the collapse of the Tokyo stock market.

In order to stimulate domestic demand and mitigate the banks' financial difficulties, the Bank of Japan has gradually reduced the official interest rate from 6 per cent in 1990 to 0.1 per cent in September 2001. However, it has been difficult for the banks to use these easy credit conditions and expand their loans, given that their own capital has shrunk almost continuously due to, among other things, the deteriorating prices of shares and real-estate. Instead, the banks found themselves having to reduce their loans to meet BIS regulations. With the main business customers of Japanese banks now being medium and small businesses, as well as real-estate agencies and construction companies, the continuous difficulties faced by the banks and the resulting restriction of bank credit depressed these businesses further. Thus, the number of annual business failures has been high: around 14,000 between 1992 and 1995 and up to 19,000 in 2000.

Since more than two-thirds of Japanese workers are employed by medium and small enterprises, these business failures were among the most important causes of the rising unemployment in the country. In addition, the absolute number of employees in Japanese manufacturing began to decline after 1992, as Japanese firms accelerated their transnationalisation through FDI. The unemployment rate in Japan consequently increased from about 2 per cent in 1990 to 5.7 per cent in 2002. Considering that the definition of unemployment in Japan is extremely narrow, it is generally believed that the official statistics should be doubled to make them comparable with data in Western countries. In that case, the unemployment rate in Japan would be comparable with the depressed European economies.

Rising unemployment, bonus and overtime payment cuts and the use of cheaper part-time workers have led to a significant reduction in household income. Unsurprisingly, domestic consumption demand has been depressed since the beginning of the 1990s. Investment demand has also stagnated, given the existence of idle capacity. Thus, the bad loans of the Japanese banks have not been cleared up and, instead, they have fed the deflationary spiral of the economy. The result has been a vicious circle, with banks facing difficulties due to their bad loans and shrinking capital base, medium and small firms running into difficulties due to the credit crunch, and the resulting deterioration in workers' employment and income leading to depressed consumer demand and deflating real estate and share prices.

CONFUSED ECONOMIC POLICIES

The present Japanese government, led by Prime Minister Koizumi, came into power in May 2001. Koizumi's basic stance is neoliberal and ostensibly focuses on the removal of government intervention and bureaucracy in order to support the sound workings of the 'market'. For example, the privatisation of the post office system has been declared as being 'necessary' for Japan. The cabinet also promised to restrict the amount of annual issues of new state bonds to 30 trillion yen from the fiscal year 2002, and to solve the problem of bad bank loans within two to three years.

However, these policies are founded on an unsatisfactory analysis of the vicious circle in the Japanese economy. The link between the speculative bubble and neoliberal privatisation, deregulation of financial markets and labour market restructuring, has been neglected. The neoliberal reform has tended to re-form Japanese society into a more company-centred order with widening economic inequalities of income and wealth. The gradual hollowing out of Japan's manufacturing base, due to increasing competitive pressure from surrounding countries following the appreciation of the yen, and the depressed consumer demand, due to declining household incomes, have been of little concern to the government. However, as long as the Japanese public are fearful for the future in the spiralling economic depression of current-day Japan, it will be difficult to induce households to turn their accumulated financial assets (amounting to 1,400 trillion yen) into actual spending.

The neoliberal policies adopted since the 1980s have not only been unsuccessful, but also inconsistent. In order to reduce the fiscal deficit, the government has tended to increase the burden on the general public by introducing and raising consumer taxes. By emphasising 'individual responsibility', it has cut public support for medical services and education. The focus on pensions policy is also likely to shift towards greater 'personal responsibility', with a move towards private insurance or securities investment. The emergency economic policies introduced to mitigate the difficulties of construction companies and the fall in land prices, such as public investment in the construction of roads and public buildings, were primarily intended to assist capitalist firms and banks. The total public expenditure for economic recovery between 1992 and 2000 amounted to 120 trillion yen, not including the injection of public funds into the banks, which has amounted to about 30 trillion yen since 1998. In the meantime, the corporate and marginal income-tax rates were largely reduced. Thus, the performance of the tax revenues has been poor. As a result, in spite of the neoliberal policy target to reduce the fiscal deficit, the value of outstanding government bonds increased from 70.5 trillion yen in 1980 to 389 trillion yen in 2001, and it will amount to 489 trillion yen by the end of 2004. The aggregate public debt (including local government debt) reached 666 trillion yen (134 per cent of GDP) at the end of 2001, and it is still growing; it will probably reach 719 trillion yen (147 per cent of GDP) in 2004.

Paradoxically, the neoliberal Japanese governments have in practice been operating a Keynesian-like fiscal deficit policy (see Chapter 3). This Keynesian-like reflationary policy has been implemented under the name of an emergency economic policy, in order to shore up political support for the government parties. However, the effect of these policies is not straightforward. On the one hand, the collapse of Japan's speculative bubble has not led to an acute economic crisis, and unemployment has increased only gradually because of the strong fiscal stimulus, lax monetary policies and the injection of public money into banks. A global Great Crisis originating from Japan has hitherto been avoided. On the other hand, Japanese deflation has been prolonged, and massive public spending does not seem to have been very effective in raising effective demand.

In contrast with conventional Keynesian doctrine, the content of public spending *does* matter. In the current context of the Japanese economy, the composition of public expenditure has been inadequate to address the basic fear of working people about their economic future. The financial burden of raising children and obtaining education, medical services and care for elderly parents has not been addressed by public spending, and this burden has increased due to the deepening fiscal crisis of the state and its imposition of neoliberal social policies. One of its consequences is that the average birth rate of Japanese women has declined sharply, from above two at the beginning of the seventies to 1.29 in 2003, leading to a rapidly ageing society. A further increase in the consumption taxes and in charges for pensions and medical insurance is on the political agenda for the near future. Thus the fiscal crisis of the state is both the result and a cause of the widening inequality among the Japanese people, and it affects negatively the economic welfare and security of the workers and vulnerable people. Under such circumstances, depressed consumer demand is hard to revive, forming a vicious circle with the deepening fiscal crisis of the state.

Prime Minister Koizumi is, unsurprisingly, failing to keep his promise to restrict the new issue of state bonds to 30 trillion yen and to solve the problem of bad bank loans within two to three years. Despite his re-election as leader of the LDP in September 2003, his economic policies have begun to be opposed even within LDP and business circles. The tragedy of Japan, however, is the absence of a strong opposition party representing the interests of the workers, and able to provide a critique of, and an alternative to, neoliberal policies. The JCP, SDPJ and other left-wing political parties and groups are even weaker and remain divided. More than ever, international co-operation with the European left is both desirable and necessary if there is to be a better future for Japanese workers.

REFERENCES

(Titles in square brackets are in Japanese and translated here.)
Itoh, M. (1990) *The World Economic Crisis and Japanese Capitalism*. London: Macmillan.
Itoh, M. (2000) *The Japanese Economy Reconsidered*. Houndmills: Palgrave.
Miyazaki, G. (1992) [*Complex Depression*] Tokyo: Chuo-koron-sha.
Tachibanaki, T. (1998) [*Japanese Economic Inequality*] Tokyo: Iwanami-shoten.
Takumi, M. (1998) [*The Depression of a 'Great Crisis Type'*] Tokyo: Kodan-sha.

30
Neoliberal Restructuring of Capital Relations in East and South-East Asia

Dae-oup Chang

The main aim of this chapter is to show neoliberalism in east and south-east Asia as a restructuring process of the national and regional social relations between capital and labour. To do so, it explores the process by which the countries of east and south-east Asia (SEA) have been integrated into neoliberal-driven globalisation. It will be shown that, even if the shortcomings of neoliberal social policies were clearly revealed through the Asian economic crisis in 1997–98, there have been increasing attempts by the state and capital to revitalise capitalist competitiveness at the expense of the working class, who are gradually beginning to fight back for their rights.

THE BEGINNING OF INTEGRATION OF SOUTH-EAST ASIA INTO THE NEOLIBERAL GLOBAL ORDER

Capitalist development is marked by overproduction and growing competitive pressure on individual capitals. The basic reason for these problems lies in the fact that production for social needs is subordinated to the fundamental goal of profit making. In market competition, enterprises which manage to keep prices competitive without degrading quality win positions that are superior to those of other firms producing similar products. Even if it is obvious that only a few firms can reach these superior positions and run successful businesses, it is the expectation of winning the competition and dominating the market that attracts individual capitals to keep trying. In the meantime, however, more and more unprofitable productive forces are created, causing the problem of over-accumulation (see Chapter 4). The development of neoliberal-driven globalisation reflects the attempts of capital to overcome the problems of accumulation. This development involves a few primary policy methods. First, the unlimited *liberalisation* of access to commodity and financial markets; second, the full integration of human needs into the profit-making process, i.e. ever increasing *privatisation* of public utilities; and, finally, full *deregulation* of labour.

Developing countries in east Asia and SEA show no exception from this global trend. Since the 1980s, these countries have witnessed gradual integration into neoliberal-driven globalisation, while abandoning the nationalist – protectionist import-substitution development strategy. From the 1980s, developed countries increasingly pressured less developed ones to open financial markets to foreign investors. This changed the way in which the developing countries financed their development. Development plans backed by official loans and government-guaranteed bank loans became increasingly unrealisable. Expansion of transnational corporations (TNCs) into Asian developing countries also increased pressure on tariff barriers and other trade regulations. On top of this, their lack of financial resources, increasing pressure on their balance of payments, and their desire to pursue rapid capitalist development led them finally to liberalise the regulation of capital flow.

Thailand's economic development underwent a transition from the mid 1980s. Earlier development was based on the production and export of agricultural products and the promotion of import-substituting industries. Manufacturers enjoyed a protected domestic market and a stable financial supply from domestic banks that were individually tied to manufacturers and absorbed most domestic savings. It was not until the recession in the mid 1980s, due to the declining price of agricultural goods, high-value currency and balance-of-payments problems, that Thailand reoriented its strategy. Rather than pursuing industrialisation based on industrial production for local demands, Thailand began to promote export sectors, such as electronics and garments, which could boost the national economy primarily by earning foreign currency. This transition to export-oriented industrialisation (EOI) was done, following the first generation of Newly Industrialising Countries (NICs) in Asia, such as Korea and Taiwan, by implementing currency devaluation and offering tax exemptions and tariff cuts to export industries. However, in comparison to the first generation, export sectors in SEA were largely financed by local and particularly foreign private investment, rather than the official loans that marked the EOI of the first generation; this reflected a new environment of global investment flow. The Thai government introduced policies favouring foreign direct investment (FDI) in export sectors, allowing land ownership of foreign companies and offering full tax exemption and rebates. In addition, the liberalisation of interest rates and foreign exchange transaction in the early 1990s promoted foreign investment. With various financial resources, in addition to the commercial banks, open to emerging businesses, the traditional financial capitalists gradually lost their dominance and Thailand witnessed the full-blown development of domestic capitalists as well as foreign capital pouring into the country (Hewison 2001).

Other south-east Asian countries experienced similar transitions. Indonesia's early development began to take shape with the emergence of the New Order introduced by Soeharto's authoritarian regime, which had been firmly established through violent attacks on the Indonesian Communist Party (PKI) in 1965. The state itself became the biggest investor in strategic industries such as petrochemical, oil refining and steel. Capitalist development took the form of an immediate alliance between the state and domestic capitalists. The state allocated resources, and gave incentives and strong protection from competition with foreign capital in the domestic market directly to businesses run by the Soeharto family and other powerful families supporting the regimes. The national economy, exports in particular, was driven almost entirely by natural resources, particularly oil. From the early 1980s, deteriorating oil prices therefore undermined Indonesia's growth and led to the shift to EOI. The mid 1980s witnessed a massive devaluation of the

Indonesian rupia, reached a peak of 45 per cent at the end of 1986. Large-scale deregulation in trade and investment as well as export-promotion policies followed, liberalising foreign investment in export sectors and offering unrestricted duty-free access to imports to major exporters. However, the significant shift did not undermine the dominance of the existing ruling class. Rather, the resources concentrated in the hands of the state apparatus transferred smoothly to pro-Soeharto conglomerates, which took the opportunities provided by soaring foreign capital and the privatisation of state-owned enterprises (SOEs).

Malaysia's capitalist development was shaped by the New Economic Policy (NEP) from the early 1970s. NEP came out of the political resolution in 1969 of inter-ethnic violence, which had dramatically manifested increased poverty and inequality between the classes. The NEP was marked by strong state economic intervention, particularly by engineering an economic balance between ethnic Malay and Chinese and other foreign capitals. The plans aimed at promoting Malayan participation in the economy by utilising positive discrimination, including a 30 per cent quota allocated to participation in Malayan equity and employment (Khoo 2001, p. 185). In the meantime, the state purchased firms owned by foreign capital and thereby increased Malayan domination over the national economy. In addition, the state played an important role in guaranteeing the supply of a cheap workforce, by suppressing political and industrial conflicts on the basis of the Official Secrets Act and the Internal Securities Act. The state also mediated foreign capital with cheap Malay migrant workers by setting up Export Processing Zones (EPZs), which enjoyed full or partial exemption from regulations, tax and duty, backed by the Industrial Relations Act, which protected employers' interests with a five-year freeze on collective bargaining. The Malaysian economy faced serious challenges from the mid 1980s, due to the steep deterioration in the prices of major export commodities, including oil, tin, rubber, cocoa, and palm oil (Gomez and Jomo 1997, p. 77). The immediate response of the state was large-scale privatisation of SOEs, later formalised in the Master Plan for Privatisation in 1991. On the other hand, introduction of the Investment Promotion Act promoted foreign investment by offering foreign capital tax holidays and renewable pioneer status for export-oriented investment.

RESTRUCTURING CAPITAL RELATIONS IN THE FACE OF THE FREE FLOW OF GLOBAL CAPITAL

The ten-year period after the shift toward EOI and liberalisation certainly produced remarkable economic development. As export manufacturing emerged as the backbone of development, domestic capital in SEA expanded significantly. In Thailand, manufacturing employed 13.4 per cent of the labour force in 1995, in comparison to 7.1 per cent in 1981. Gross Domestic Product (GDP) per capita more than tripled between 1985 and 1995, reaching US$2,800 in 1995. In Indonesia the contribution of manufacturing to GDP overtook that of agriculture in 1990. GDP per capita increased from about US$500 in 1985 to over US$1,000 in 1995. Experiencing the fastest industrialisation in the region, Malaysia's manufacturing sector represented about 26 per cent of total employment in 1995, in

Table 30.1   FDI inflow to south-east Asian developing countries (US$ million)

	1980	1985	1990	1995	1997
Indonesia	180	310	1,092	4,346	4,677
Malaysia	934	695	2,611	5,816	6,324
Thailand	189	164	2,562	2,068	3,626
Philippines	−106	12	550	1,459	1,249
Asia	396	5,110	24,251	75,217	105,828

Source: UNCTAD database

comparison with 15 per cent in 1985. GDP per capita went beyond US$4,000 in 1995, double that of 1985.

Fast industrialisation integrated a large proportion of the population into capitalist social relations, and was accompanied by massive rural – urban migration, which supplied extremely cheap labour to local capital and TNCs seeking profitable business. During this period, Asian developing countries, such as Thailand, Malaysia, Indonesia and subsequently China and other least developed countries like Cambodia, relied on FDI as the main financial resource. Consequently, FDI in Asian developing countries increased from US$396 million in 1980 to US$102 billion in 2001 (UNCTAD 2002) (see Table 30.1). The investment flow into these nations accounted for a mere 0.7 per cent of global FDI in 1980. In 1996, it accounted for 24.1 per cent of the total FDI inflow, indicating Asia as a main destination of TNCs.

To attract FDI, the host countries of the investment increased the relaxation of labour standards and exemptions from labour law. The most important logic supporting these actions has been '*investors' confidence*': national economies will be in deep trouble if they undermine investors' confidence. Indeed, it was the low social cost of exploitation that boosted the confidence. Industrialisation developed on the basis of the unity between liberalised capital from developed countries and deregulated labour in the South, which integrated these developing countries into a particular global commodity or value chain. This value chain consisted of so-called high-value-added processes of production, such as R&D and the production of core and high-tech components, in the capital-exporting countries and so-called low-value-added (or labour-intensive) processes, such as assembling and final processing, in the capital-importing countries. As a result, while FDI increased faster than ever before, large numbers of the working population from the 1980s were left with no legal and union protection, testifying to *the anti-labour* nature of this development. This can be found in EPZs, where TNCs enjoy the freedom to ignore labour rights. Including different forms of EPZs, such as China's 'open areas and cities' and 'economic and technological development areas', the number of EPZs in Asia is well over 1,000 (Chang 2003). The fact that corporations are free to move to alternative EPZs elsewhere became the biggest barrier against organising labour.

This particular form of development in SEA is related to the changing social configuration of capital accumulations in the first generation NICs in Asia. Since the mid-1980s, favourable conditions in export-oriented labour-intensive industries, such as garments and shoemaking, began to move away from Taiwan and Korea. While Taiwan was witnessing an increase in workers' challenges that politicised the issue of the implementation of labour law and an erosion of the absolute domination of the anti-communist ruling party (KMT, Kuomintang), Korea's capitalist development also faced an explosion of the organised labour movement. Externally, growing protectionist pressure from the United States slowed export growth, while pressure to liberalise commodity and financial markets grew. Together, these motivated capital relocation. Following Japan, whose export competitiveness was largely undermined by appreciation of the yen against the US dollar, the first generation NICs started moving manufacturing sectors into SEA and later China. Foreign investment from Asian countries, not to mention that from Japan, as the main exporter of capital in Asia, grew from US$11.4 billion in 1990 to US$52.1 billion in 1996. A significant part of Asian direct capital investment went into Asia itself. Asian-originated firms in the labour-intensive sector, playing a mediating role between commercial capital from the West and workers in SEA, aimed at taking advantage of cheap labour in the region. The consequence was a race-to-the-bottom of labour standards and wages. TNCs benefit also from their enhanced power to restructure labour relations in their home countries merely by threatening to relocate capital. Introducing flexible labour is justified by the need to invest at home.

ASIAN ECONOMIC CRISIS AND AFTER

As far as capital accumulation was concerned, it seemed that liberalisation and suppressive labour control worked, during the boom between the late 1980s and the mid 1990s. However, it was revealed through the Asian economic crisis that this development could not be a model for resolving inherent contradictions in capitalist development. Thailand, where the Asian crisis began with massive capital flight, was a good example. Although FDI-driven development had led Thailand's export-oriented industrialisation, it could not overcome repeated deficits in the trade balance with investor countries, particularly Japan, whose massive investment was welcome by the government and local capital looking for joint ventures. This reflected the nature of the value chain, within which Thailand could boost export sectors only by importing most key parts, as well as the means of production (factories, machinery, tools, etc.), from the investor countries (Burkett and Hart-Landsberg 2000, pp. 170–1). This problem was particularly clear in the case of Japanese car manufacturers and electronics assemblers, and widened the trade imbalance. Thailand had to count on FDI to offset a shortage of foreign currency. Worse still, decent wages and rights were denied to workers and the living standard of the working class remained low. Millions of migrant workers from neighbouring countries, particularly Burma, were abused to keep wages down. In the end, intense competition for FDI and the concentration of FDI in China led Thailand to attract risky money, mainly portfolio investment in the equity and money markets, the collapse of which created economic turmoil in 1998. FDI-driven economic development enlarged Thailand's GDP, which is however in the hands of just a few domestic and foreign investors. Indonesia and

Malaysia experienced almost the same difficulties, resulting in massive dismantling of capital and growing unemployment during the crisis.

Korea's experience in the late 1990s showed the challenge that lay ahead of the first generation of NICs. Facing intensified competition with south-east Asian economies as well as that of China, Korea's response was to enhance the flexibility of labour by individualising labour relations on the basis of new personnel management and deteriorating employment stability on the one hand, and aggressive relocation of labour-intensive industries and introduction of effective means of production on the other. However, internally Korean capital could not overcome organised labour despite repeated attempts to overcome the recession at the expense of the working class, while accelerated liberalisation made it possible for non-competitive capital to survive on the basis of highly risky short-term loans. The consequence was a complete break down of capital accumulation during the Asian crisis.

Although the Asian crisis clearly showed the inherent limits of regional development based on neoliberal-driven globalisation, the state and capital in Asian developing countries have accelerated the implementation of neoliberal policies. In Thailand, Indonesia and Korea, full-scale structural adjustment plans were introduced in return for the IMF's and other international bail-out programmes. Those reforms consisted of stabilisation policies on the one hand, including tightening government expenditure and keeping higher interest rates; and structural adjustment policies on the other, including the immediate closing down of troubled financial institutions, a full commitment to liberalisation of financial flows, accelerated privatisation and enhanced flexibility of labour. The Malaysian government, although not accepting all the IMF recommendations, also introduced similar measures, including reducing federal government expenditure and tightening corporate credit. The immediate impact of stabilisation policies on economies was disastrous, particularly in the countries following the IMF's strict guidelines. Given that Asian corporations have relied on external debts for investment and the short-term circulation of capital, further collapses of firms, particularly small and medium-size firms, whose ability to survive under the financial pressure was weaker than larger firms, was not at all a surprise but, rather, was regarded as a 'necessary' remedy. In the face of growing difficulties in short-term roll-overs and snowballed foreign debt, due to huge devaluation, about two-thirds of Indonesian firms were estimated to go into bankruptcy during the crisis, while a total of 22,828 Korean firms went into bankruptcy during the year of 1998. Firms that survived still had to downsize investment and production. As a consequence, all economies affected by the crisis recorded serious negative growth of GDP in 1998: −13.1 per cent in Indonesia; −10.5 per cent in Thailand; −7.4 per cent in Malaysia, and −6.7 per cent in Korea. It was not until the massive liquidation of capital and financial institutions that the tight monetary policies were relaxed.

In the meantime, liberalisation of capital flow was pushed further, allowing foreign capital full ownership of local firms and relaxing the regulation of foreign banking operations. The most dramatic reform was found in Korea, which sustained relatively stricter regulation of foreign investment, scrapping restrictions on

FDI, the purchase of real estate, and mergers and acquisitions by foreign investors. Protection of state-owned companies was also relaxed, allowing foreign and domestic private capital to take over the business. Now TNCs can purchase firms operating in the areas that were formerly regarded as 'public sector', including state-owned public utilities such as electricity, gas, water suppliers, public transportation and telecommunication. The Indonesian government announced its plan to privatise many of the country's 160 SOEs in 1998. Accordingly, the biggest state-owned bank, PT Bank Madri Tbk, was privatised, following the privatisation of the second largest telecommunication company, PT Indonesia Satellite Corp Tbk, which was purchased by Singapore's ST Telemedia. As Thailand's economic crisis opened a great opportunity for foreign capital to buy troubled local firms, hundreds of firms have been sold to TNCs. The Thai government also put major financial institutions, and infrastructure- and natural-resource-related firms on the sale list. In Korea, the government targeted the public sector for harsh restructuring, beginning with downsizing of the government. The central government reduced the number of its employees by about 16 per cent (26,000) by the end of 2001. Twenty public institutions out of the 109 SOEs were privatised in 1998. Privatisation of large-scale SOEs, such as Korea Telecom, followed and the Korean Electric Power Corporation, the Korea National Railroad, and the Korea Gas Corporation were in the final stages of privatisation in 2003. Selling off extremely large SOEs directly affected workers in the firms. Management often reorganises existing labour forces en masse to make the company more attractive to buyers. It is common for the new owners to restructure employment, including mass lay-offs. In Korea, as a consequence of this restructuring process, 41,700 SOE workers had lost their jobs by 2000.

Obviously, the end result of the thoroughgoing neoliberal reforms has been the restructuring of the social relations between labour and capital in those countries. Millions of people who were kicked out of the labour market due to the structural adjustment had to suffer from the lack of a social safety net. Worse still, neoliberal-driven reforms have been focused on imposing a great degree of insecurity on labour, which enjoys neither the institutional rights of workers nor fully developed social safety nets. The reintegration of the once unemployed population into the job market was made possible not through the creation of new jobs with formal contracts and guaranteed labour rights, but through the region-wide informalisation of labour caused by increasingly diversified forms of informal employment, such as short-term contracted, dispatched, in-house subcontracted, and home-based workers. Often not regarded as workers, millions of workers in these forms of employment are not protected by law.

CONCLUSION

FDI-driven EOI at the expense of the working class was the key form of restructuring of social relations in this region since the 1980s. In spite of all the human cost that the restructuring caused, the Asian crisis eventually revealed that neither regional nor national development in east Asia can be a sustainable model of development. However, far from being reconsidered, the neoliberal restructuring of this region has been accelerated through the crisis, putting the vast majority of the population into misery. However, a widening gap between the poor and rich in the region is also consolidating attempts of workers to organise themselves in various forms. The future of this second round of neoliberal-driven restructuring is still open as workers' resistance against further restructuring constantly emerges in the region.

REFERENCES

Burkett, P. and Hart-Landsberg, M. (2000) *Development, Crisis and Class Struggle: Learning From Japan and East Asia*. New York: St Martin's Press.

Chang, D.O. (2003) 'Foreign Direct Investment and Union Busting in Asia', *Asian Labour Update* 48, pp. 1–8.

Hewison, K. (2001) 'Thailand's Capitalism: Development through Boom and Bust', in G. Rodan, K. Hewison and R. Robison (eds) *The Political Economy of South-East Asia: Conflicts, Crises and Change* Oxford: Oxford University Press.

Gomez, E.T. and Jomo K.S. (1997) *Malaysia's Political Economy: Politics, Patronage and Profits*. Cambridge: Cambridge University Press.

Khoo, B.T. (2001), 'The State and the Market in Malaysian Political Economy', in G. Rodan, K. Hewison and R. Robison (eds) *The Political Economy of South-East Asia: Conflicts, Crises and Change*. Oxford: Oxford University Press.

UNCTAD (2002) *World Investment Report: Transnational Corporations and Export Competitiveness*. New York: United Nations.

Contributors

Philip Arestis is professor of economics at the Levy Economics Institute, New York, and director of research at the Centre for Economic and Public Policy, University of Cambridge. In his recent research, Professor Arestis has addressed, among other topics, the current state of the US economy, financial issues in economic growth and development, inflation targeting, the 1520–1640 'Great Inflation', the financial crises in south-east Asia and issues that relate to the European Monetary Union. His work has appeared in many journals, including the *Cambridge Journal of Economics, Eastern Economic Journal, Economic Inquiry, Economic Journal, International Review of Applied Economics, Journal of Money, Credit and Banking, Journal of Post-Keynesian Economics, Manchester School* and *Scottish Journal of Political Economy*.

Patrick Bond is a professor at the University of the Witwatersrand in Johannesburg and a visiting professor at York University, Toronto. He has worked closely with social, labour and environmental movements in South Africa, Zimbabwe and internationally, including the World Bank Bonds Boycott <http://www.worldbankboycott.org>. Recent books include *Against Global Apartheid* (London: Zed Books, 2003), *Zimbabwe's Plunge* (London: Merlin Press, 2003, with Masimba Manyanya), *Unsustainable South Africa* (London: Merlin Press, 2002) and *Fanon's Warning* (ed., Trenton, N.J.: Africa World Press, 2002).

Terence J. Byres is emeritus professor of political economy at the University of London. Joint editor of *Journal of Agrarian Change* and former joint editor of *Journal of Peasant Studies*, he has written extensively on India, and more generally on the agrarian question. He is the author of *Capitalism from Above and Capitalism from Below: An Essay on Comparative Political Economy* (London: Macmillan, 1996), and the editor of *The State, Development Planning and Liberalisation in India* (Oxford: Oxford University Press, 1998); and *Redistributive Land Reform Today* (Oxford: Blackwell, forthcoming).

Al Campbell is professor of economics at the University of Utah. His research interests include the behaviour of contemporary capitalism, theoretical socialist alternatives and the Cuban economy.

Dae-oup Chang is a research co-ordinator at the Asia Monitor Resource Centre, based in Hong Kong, and is currently running a research and campaign project regarding Asian transnational corporations. He earned his Ph.D. on the Marxist critique of the theories and practices of the developmental state, at the Department of Sociology, University of Warwick. He has written on Korean labour relations and economic crisis, as well as other labour-related issues in Asia.

Simon Clarke is professor of sociology at the University of Warwick. He has written extensively on Marx and Marxist theory and, more recently, on the transition to capitalism in Russia, working closely with Russian and international trade union and labour organisations. He has written many books, including *Marx, Marginalism and Modern Sociology* (London: Macmillan, 1982 and 1991); *Keynesianism, Monetarism and the Crisis of the State* (Cheltenham: Edward Elgar, 1988); and *Marx's Theory of Crisis* (London: Macmillan, 1994).

Alejandro Colás teaches international relations at Birkbeck College, University of London. He is author of *International Civil Society: Social Movements in World Politics* (Oxford: Polity Press, 2002) and is on the editorial board of the journal *Historical Materialism*.

Sonali Deranyiagala is a lecturer in economics at the School of Oriental and African Studies, University of London. Her research interests include trade and industrial policy in developing countries, macroeconomic policy and poverty, and the dynamics of manufacturing firms in developing countries.

Gérard Duménil is an economist and research director at the Centre National de la Recherche Scientifique (MODEM, University of Paris X–Nanterre). He is the author of *Le Concept de Loi Economique dans 'Le Capital'* (Paris: Maspero, 1978), *Marx et Keynes Face à la Crise* (Paris: Econômica, 1977) and, with Dominique Lévy, *The Economics of the Profit Rate* (Aldershot: Edward Elgar Publishing, 1993) and three volumes published by PUF: *La Dynamique du Capital: Un Siècle d'Economie Américaine* (1996); *Au-delà du Capitalisme* (1998); and *Crise et Sortie de Crise: Ordres et Désordres Néolibéraux* (2000, English version: *Capital Resurgent: Roots of the Neoliberal Revolution*, Cambridge, Mass.: Harvard University Press, 2004). His most recent book, also in collaboration with Dominique Lévy, is *Analyse Marxiste du Capitalisme* (Paris: La Découverte, 2003).

Lesley Hoggart is a senior research fellow at the Policy Studies Institute in London. She is currently working on evaluation projects in the field of lone parents and employment. Her research interests include the politics of reproductive choice; young women and sexual decision-making; and young people, well-being and risk. Recent publications include *Feminist Campaigns for Birth Control and Abortion Rights in Britain* (Lampeter: Edwin Mellen Press, 2003).

Makoto Itoh is professor of economics at Kokugakuin University, Tokyo. He is also emeritus professor of the University of Tokyo, and has taught at eight other universities abroad, including in the United Kingdom and the USA. His books include *The Japanese Economy Reconsidered* (London: Palgrave, 2000); *Political Economy of Money and Finance* (London: Macmillan, 1999, with C. Lapavitsas); *Political Economy for Socialism* (London: Macmillan, 1995); and *The World Economic Crisis and Japanese Capitalism* (London: Macmillan, 1990).

Deborah Johnston is a lecturer in development economics at the School of Oriental and African Studies, University of London. She has worked on labour markets and poverty, and has undertaken consultancy work in the United Kingdom, Russia and a number of African countries. Most recently, she has co-authored a paper entitled: 'Searching for a Weapon of Mass Production in Rural Africa: Unconvincing Arguments for Land Reform', *Journal of Agrarian Change* (2004).

Costas Lapavitsas is senior lecturer in economics at the School of Oriental and African Studies, University of London. His research interests include money and finance, history of economic thought and the Japanese economy. His latest book is *Social Foundations of Markets, Money and Credit* (London: Routledge, 2003).

Les Levidow is a research fellow at the Open University, where since 1989 he has been studying the safety regulation and innovation of agricultural biotechnology. This research encompasses the European Union and the USA and their trade conflicts. He also has been managing editor of *Science as Culture* since its inception in 1987, and of its predecessor, the *Radical Science Journal*. He is co-editor of several books, including *Science, Technology and the Labour Process; Anti-Racist Science Teaching; and Cyborg Worlds: The Military Information Society* (London: Free Association Books, 1983, 1987, 1989).

Dominique Lévy is an economist and research director at the Centre National de la Recherche Scientifique (CEPREMAP, Paris). He is the author, with Gérard Duménil, of *The Economics of the Profit Rate* (Aldershot: Edward Elgar Publishing, 1993) and three volumes published by PUF: *La Dynamique du Capital: Un Siècle d'Economie Américaine* (1996); *Au-delà du Capitalisme* (1998); and *Crise et Sortie de Crise: Ordres et Désordres Néolibéraux* (2000, English version: *Capital Resurgent: Roots of the Neoliberal Revolution*, Cambridge, Mass.: Harvard University Press, 2004). His most recent book, also in collaboration with Gérard Duménil, is *Analyse Marxiste du Capitalisme* (Paris: La Découverte, 2003).

Arthur MacEwan teaches economics at the University of Massachusetts Boston. His most recent book is *Neoliberalism or Democracy? Economic Strategy, Markets, and Alternatives for the Twenty-First Century* (London: Zed Books, 1999). He was a founder of the magazine *Dollars & Sense*, for which he continues to write regularly.

Susanne MacGregor is professor of social policy in the Department of Public Health and Policy at the London School of Hygiene and Tropical Medicine, University of London. She has researched and written on issues relating to poverty and social exclusion, drugs misuse, and urban and community problems and policy. She is co-organiser of an ESRC seminar series on European Cross National Research and Policy <http://www.xnat.org.uk>.

Matthew McCartney is a lecturer in economics with reference to south Asia at the School of Oriental and African Studies, University of London. He has worked as an ODI fellow in the Ministry of Finance in Zambia, and has published widely on south Asian economic development. His research interests include the political economy of development in south Asia and the role of the state in late industrialisation.

John Milios is associate professor of political economy and the history of economic thought at the National Technical University of Athens. He is director of the quarterly journal of economic and political theory *Thesseis* and a member of the Board of Scientific Advisors of the annual journal *Beiträge zur Marx-Engels-Forschung: Neue Folge*. He has published more than 150 papers in referred journals (in Greek, English, German, French, Spanish, Italian and Turkish) and ten books, the most recent of which is *Karl Marx and the Classics: An Essay on Value, Crises and the Capitalist Mode of Production* (Aldershot: Ashgate, 2002, with D. Dimoulis and G. Economakis). He is also co-editor of *Welfare State and Democracy in Crisis: Reforming the European Model* (Aldershot: Ashgate, 2001). His research interests include value theory, the internationalisation of capital and theories of imperialism.

Ronaldo Munck is professor of political sociology and director of the Globalisation and Social Exclusion Unit <www.gseu.org.uk> at the University of Liverpool. Most recently he has published *Marx@2000* (London: Zed Books, 2000) and *Globalisation and Labour: The New 'Great Transformation'* (London: Zed Books, 2002). His forthcoming book, *Globalisation and Social Exclusion: A Transformationalist Perspective*, launches a series he is editing for Kumarian Press <www.kpbooks.com> entitled 'Transforming Globalisation'. He is currently researching aspects of the counter-globalisation movement from a labour movement perspective.

Carlos Oya is a lecturer in political economy of development at the School of Oriental and African Studies, University of London, where he completed his Ph.D. on agrarian political economy and liberalisation in Senegal. He worked in the government of Mozambique for nearly four years and recently carried out field research on rural labour markets and poverty in Mozambique. He has also undertaken consultancy work on rural poverty and PRSPs in Mali, Mauritania and Angola.

Thomas Palley is chief economist of the US–China Economic and Security Review Commission, established by the US Congress with a mandate to monitor and report upon national and economic security dimensions of US–China relations. He is the author of *Plenty of Nothing: The Downsizing of the American Dream and the Case for Structural Keynesianism* (Princeton: Princeton University Press, 1998) and *Post-Keynesian Economics: Debt, Distribution, and the Macro-Economy* (London: Macmillan, 1996). Recent articles include 'The Economic Case for Labor Standards: A Layman's Guide', *Richmond Journal of Global Law*

& Business (2001); and 'Asset Price Bubbles and the Case for Asset-Based Reserve Requirements', *Challenge* (2003).

James Petras is professor emeritus at Binghamton University, New York, and adjunct professor at St Mary's University, Halifax, Canada. He is the author or editor of 64 books and over 450 professional articles. His most recent book is *The New Development Politics: Empire Building and Social Movements* (Aldershot: Ashgate, 2003).

Hugo Radice teaches at the School of Politics and International Studies, University of Leeds. He helped to found the Conference of Socialist Economists in 1970. His recent work centres on globalisation and on capitalist restoration in eastern Europe, and he is currently writing a book on the political economy of global capitalism.

Alfredo Saad-Filho is senior lecturer in political economy of development at the School of Oriental and African Studies, University of London. He is the author of *The Value of Marx: Political Economy for Contemporary Capitalism* (London: Routledge, 2002), and *Marx's Capital* (4th edn., London: Pluto Press, 2004, with Ben Fine), and the editor of *Anti-Capitalism: A Marxist Introduction* (London: Pluto Press, 2003).

Malcolm Sawyer is professor of economics at the University of Leeds. He is managing editor of *International Review of Applied Economics*, managing co-editor of *International Papers in Political Economy* and joint editor of *Journal of Income Distribution*. He is the editor of the series *New Directions in Modern Economics* published by Edward Elgar, and an elected member of the Council of the Royal Economic Society. He is the author of eleven books; the two most recent are *The Euro: Evolution and Prospects* (Gloucester: Edward Elgar, 2001, with P. Arestis and A. Brown); and *Re-examining Monetary and Fiscal Policy for the Twenty-First Century* (Gloucester: Edward Elgar, forthcoming, with P. Arestis). He has edited 18 books including *The UK Economy* (16th edn., Oxford: Oxford University Press, forthcoming) and *Economics of the Third Way* (Gloucester: Edward Elgar, 2001, with P. Arestis). He has published nearly 150 articles and chapters, and recent papers include 'The NAIRU, Aggregate Demand and Investment' in *Metroeconomica* and 'Kalecki on Money and Finance' in *The European Journal of the History of Economic Thought*.

Anwar Shaikh is professor of economics at the Graduate Faculty of Political and Social Science of the New School University, New York. He is also a senior scholar and member of the Macro Modeling Team at the Levy Economics Institute of Bard College. He is the author of two books, the most recent being *Measuring the Wealth of Nations: The Political Economy of National Accounts* (Cambridge: Cambridge University Press, 1994, with E.A. Tonak). His recent articles include 'Nonlinear Dynamics and Pseudo-Production Functions' (forthcoming in *the Eastern Economics Journal*); 'Who Pays for the "Welfare" in the Welfare State?

A Multi-Country Study' (*Social Research*, 2003); 'Labor Market Dynamics within Rival Macroeconomic Frameworks' (in *Growth, Distribution and Effective Demand*, Gary Mongiovi (ed.), Armonk, N.Y.: M.E. Sharpe, 2004); and 'An important inconsistency at the heart of the standard macroeconomic model' (*Journal of Post Keynesian Economics*, 2002, with W. Godley). In addition, he has written on international trade, finance theory, political economy, US macroeconomic policy, growth theory, inflation theory and crisis theory. He is also an associate editor of the *Cambridge Journal of Economics*.

Subir Sinha is a lecturer in the Department of Development Studies at the School of Oriental and African Studies, University of London. His current interests are in the interplay between rule and resistance in development processes, on the history of Indian rural development, contemporary social movements of global solidarity, and international development regimes. He has published on Indian environmentalism, rural social movements, and on the constitution of ruling development agendas.

Jan Toporowski is Leverhulme Fellow and a research associate at the Centre for Development Policy and Research, School of Oriental and African Studies, University of London, and senior member, Wolfson College, University of Cambridge. After studying economics at Birkbeck College and at the University of Birmingham, he worked in fund management and international banking. Among his books is *The End of Finance: The Theory of Capital Market Inflation, Financial Derivatives and Pension Fund Capitalism* (London: Routledge 2000). He is currently working on an intellectual biography of the Polish economist Michał Kalecki.

Henry Veltmeyer is a professor of international development studies at St Mary's University, Halifax, Canada and Universidad Autónoma de Zacatecas, Mexico. He has recently co-authored with James Petras *Globalisation Unmasked: Imperialism in the Twenty-First Century* (London: Zed Books, 2001) and *System in Crisis: The Dynamics of Free Market Capitalism* (London: Zed Books, 2003).

Index